Think Like a Curator

AMERICAN ASSOCIATION for STATE and LOCAL HISTORY

AMERICAN ASSOCIATION FOR STATE AND LOCAL HISTORY
BOOK SERIES

Series Editor
Rebekah Beaulieu, Taft Museum of Art

Managing Editor
Aja Bain, AASLH

Editorial Board

Jessica Dorman, The Historic New Orleans Collection; Harry Klinkhamer, Venice Museum & Archives; Anne Lindsay, California State University–Sacramento; Steven Lubar, Brown University; Laura A. Macaluso, York County History Center; Ann McCleary, University of West Georgia; Debra Reid, The Henry Ford; Laura Roberts, Roberts Consulting; Zachary Stocks, Oregon Black Pioneers; Jamie Simek, Eiteljorg Museum; William Stoutamire, University of Nebraska–Kearney; William S. Walker, Cooperstown Graduate Program SUNY Oneonta

ABOUT THE SERIES

The American Association for State and Local History Book Series addresses issues critical to the field of state and local history through interpretive, intellectual, scholarly, and educational texts. To submit a proposal or manuscript to the series, please request proposal guidelines from AASLH headquarters: AASLH Editorial Board, 2021 21st Ave. South, Suite 320, Nashville, Tennessee 37212. Telephone: (615) 320-3203. Website: www.aaslh.org.

ABOUT THE ORGANIZATION

The American Association for State and Local History (AASLH) is a national history membership association headquartered in Nashville, Tennessee, that provides leadership and support for its members who preserve and interpret state and local history in order to make the past more meaningful to all people. AASLH members are leaders in preserving, researching, and interpreting traces of the American past to connect the people, thoughts, and events of yesterday with the creative memories and abiding concerns of people, communities, and our nation today. In addition to sponsorship of this book series, AASLH publishes *History News* magazine, a newsletter, technical leaflets and reports, and other materials; confers prizes and awards in recognition of outstanding achievement in the field; supports a broad education program and other activities designed to help members work more effectively; and advocates on behalf of the discipline of history. To join AASLH, go to www.aaslh.org or contact Membership Services, AASLH, 2021 21st Ave. South, Suite 320, Nashville, TN 37212.

Think Like a Curator

A Guide to Curatorial Practice in History Organizations

Donna R. Braden

ROWMAN & LITTLEFIELD
Lanham • Boulder • New York • London

Rowman & Littlefield
Bloomsbury Publishing Inc, 1385 Broadway, New York, NY 10018, USA
Bloomsbury Publishing Plc, 50 Bedford Square, London, WC1B 3DP, UK
Bloomsbury Publishing Ireland, 29 Earlsfort Terrace, Dublin 2, D02 AY28, Ireland
www.rowman.com

Copyright © 2025 by The Rowman & Littlefield Publishing Group, Inc.

All rights reserved. No part of this publication may be: i) reproduced or transmitted in any form, electronic or mechanical, including photocopying, recording or by means of any information storage or retrieval system without prior permission in writing from the publishers; or ii) used or reproduced in any way for the training, development or operation of artificial intelligence (AI) technologies, including generative AI technologies. The rights holders expressly reserve this publication from the text and data mining exception as per Article 4(3) of the Digital Single Market Directive (EU) 2019/790.

British Library Cataloguing in Publication Information Available

Library of Congress Cataloging-in-Publication Data Available

ISBN: 978-1-5381-8280-2 (cloth)
ISBN: 978-1-5381-8281-9 (paperback)
ISBN: 978-1-5381-8282-6 (electronic)

For product safety related questions contact productsafety@bloomsbury.com.

∞™ The paper used in this publication meets the minimum requirements of American National Standard for Information Sciences—Permanence of Paper for Printed Library Materials, ANSI/NISO Z39.48-1992.

Contents

Preface	vii
Acknowledgments	xvii
Chapter 1: The History Museum Curator	1
Chapter 2: Making Sense of Objects	21
Chapter 3: Shaping and Developing Collections	41
Chapter 4: Thinking Historically	65
Chapter 5: Curating Exhibitions, Large and Small	94
Chapter 6: Interpreting Historic House Museums	126
Chapter 7: Sharing Knowledge with the Public	155
Chapter 8: Leading from the Middle	181
Notes	201
Bibliography	245
Index	271
About the Author	279

Preface

I never set out to be a museum curator. I never even thought I wanted to be one. When I was growing up, my impression of curators was that they were old and, more often than not, they were men.

But I loved objects and what they said about people and cultures. I loved exploring old places—ghost towns, neglected buildings, small-town Main Streets—and soaking up the traces they left behind of the people who had once lived there. I amassed collections related to my various passions—postcards, comic books, and newspaper articles about my favorite singing groups—then endlessly organized and inventoried those materials. I was also a researcher at heart. Once I got interested in a new topic, I would delve deeper and deeper, leaving no stone unturned. Finally, I loved writing—the process of transforming ideas into something coherent, powerful, and lasting.

So, I guess you could say that my becoming a curator was almost decided for me. But it certainly wasn't something I planned from the beginning. Admittedly, everyone's journey to curatorial practice is different and unique. There is no one singular or correct pathway. With that in mind, what follows is the path of my own journey.

As an undergraduate at Ohio State University, I was intrigued by and decided to major in anthropology—the systematic study of humanity across time, societies, and cultures.[1] This led me to spend a semester during my sophomore year at the Universidad de las Américas in Mexico, studying Mexican culture, anthropology, and archaeology (see figure P.1).[2] The best part of this program was that classes were held only four days a week, leaving plenty of time to travel.

While other students headed to the Pacific-coast beaches of Acapulco and Puerto Vallarta, I visited prehistoric sites and small village markets. On these trips I became aware of—and enamored with—the distinctive cultures of different regions. I wondered why cultural history, regional distinctiveness, and people's daily lives were never topics covered in my history books and classes. I returned home with newfound determination to find answers to this question.

In the Honors Program at Ohio State, I was fortunate to have the flexibility to create my own program of study in addition to my major in anthropology. The course catalog was extensive enough to include such classes as the

Figure P.1 While traveling on weekends between classes at the Universidad de las Américas, the author ventured out to many Mexican cities and towns with a fellow student, including San Miguel de Allende, pictured here. The author is third from left, seated with members of a local Mexican family.

histories of American art, music, literature, and technology, as well as courses in the newly emerging field of American Studies. By taking classes like these, I structured a personalized program under the umbrella of American cultural history. It was around this time that I came across the book *Introduction to Museum Work*, by G. Ellis Burcaw.[3] I perused that book over and over and decided that this was what I wanted to do—although I wasn't sure exactly what in a museum I actually could do.

Meanwhile, my History of American Technology professor, Dr. Merritt Roe Smith, noticed my interest in the interplay between early American technology and traditional crafts and started me reading articles on American material culture. These articles completely transformed my thinking and led to the topic of my Senior Honors Thesis. I decided to interpret a group of historic artifacts—early American lighting devices—by applying the methodology that archaeologists used in analyzing and interpreting artifacts they unearthed from the ground. Archeologists, after all, had long used the term "material culture" to relate to the physical remains that people left behind and had developed strategies for analyzing and interpreting these remains. Why not bring together my studies in anthropology and American history, placing objects at the center? I was proud of this interdisciplinary approach, although my thesis review committee, comprised of very traditional professors from both the anthropology and history departments, had some difficulty understanding it. Even today, material culture takes a back seat to historians' preference for documentary sources, while anthropologists tend to study cultures from all over the world but less often look at cultural patterns within the United States.[4]

Because of my growing passion for material culture, Dr. Smith also recommended that I look into a graduate program called the Winterthur Program in Early American Culture. Held in partnership with the University of Delaware, this was a rigorous museum studies program that focused specifically on researching and interpreting American material culture.[5] I would find later that it also revolved around the collections and period rooms at the Winterthur Museum—a stately and monumental mansion that was once home to the wealthy Henry Francis duPont and housed his collection of high-style decorative furnishings. Because of this focus, most of the students who applied to this program were art history majors who expected to study decorative arts connoisseurship. I was truly out of my element, but I somehow got accepted into the program. I think the selection committee liked my somewhat alternative approach to interpreting material culture and took a chance on me.

One of the requirements of the program was that we had to guide museum visitors through the approximately 175 period rooms at the Winterthur Museum, citing minute details about the fancy furnishings in each room. Unfortunately, no matter how hard I tried, I could not recall (or care about) the details distinguishing high-style Philadelphia Chippendale chairs or New York City Federal-style knife boxes or Chinese export porcelain. I was much more interested in (and able to study, thank goodness) the museum's extensive collection of Pennsylvania German "folk art"—that is, the handcrafted objects that came out of the Pennsylvania German folk tradition.[6] On the weekends, I roamed the southeastern Pennsylvania countryside in search of these types of objects, even doing an independent study of related collections that I encountered in the many small regional museums there.

It was on one of these trips that I discovered the Mercer Museum in Doylestown, Pennsylvania.[7] It was my ultimate dream place! Henry Mercer had begun his career as an archaeologist but later shifted to collecting early American daily life artifacts. When he created a museum to house his massive collection, he brought his earlier perspective as an archaeologist to organizing them, referring to them all as "historic human tools." It was like finding a kindred spirit I didn't know existed! I simply had to delve more deeply into the wonders of this place. I managed to land an internship there and happily

Preface

spent a summer cataloging and writing interpretive labels for the collections that related to traditional basketmaking, broom making, and turpentine making—as well as, unintentionally, learning about the challenges facing a small, underfunded museum like the Mercer. During that summer, I was fortunate enough to also live at Mercer's unusual, castle-inspired home, Fonthill. During the evenings there, immersed in Mercer's unique world, I began working on what would become my masters' thesis focusing on Mercer's collection and collecting philosophy. I spent the second year of the Winterthur Program commuting between Newark, Delaware, and Doylestown, Pennsylvania, to research and write my thesis.

During my second year in the Winterthur Program, I also took an influential course called "Inside the Victorian Home." This class was taught by one of the more popular professors, Dr. Kenneth Ames. I loved the way that Dr. Ames made the Victorian era come alive through the artifacts that people used in furnishing their homes. It was like he gifted us with a key that unlocked a door to another world—a world that had been a mysterious "black box" until he explained to us the role of these artifacts in people's daily lives. This laid a road map for what I wanted to do in my future museum career (if I was, indeed, going to have one): to make people's lives from the past come alive through the objects they made and used. When it came time to do a paper for this class, my colleagues chose to study elaborate objects like hall stands and dining accoutrements. But I decided to focus upon the kitchen—not only the most common and ordinary room of the house but also a place that had always buzzed with activity and the presence of people. Dr. Ames was surprised, but also delighted, by my choice, and he soon became enthralled with hand-cranked apple parers—an interest that I had elicited through my paper (see figure P.2).

When I graduated from the Winterthur Program with an M.A. in Early American Culture, I knew that I needed a job. What could I do? Where would I go? Finding a job in the late 1970s was perhaps a bit easier than it is today. But it wasn't automatic. First, I applied to job openings at historic houses, but got turned down at every place. Not enough experience, I was told. I wondered whether I should look into registrars' jobs, as it seemed that curators needed to have deep expertise in something and I felt that I had none.

Then, from a friend, I found out about an opening for a curator at The Henry Ford (then Henry Ford Museum & Greenfield Village) in Dearborn, Michigan, working with a collection called Home Arts.[8] This huge, one-of-a-kind collection consisted of row upon row of stoves, sewing machines, laundry equipment, and spinning wheels on display in the museum (mostly acquired during Henry Ford's era of the 1920s and 1930s), and more of the same in storage. Museum administrators desperately needed someone to make sense of these artifacts and select items for a new display to commemorate the museum's fiftieth anniversary in 1979. I applied for the job and, miraculously, got called for an interview. My kitchen paper helped, as did my interest in everyday life,

Figure P.2 The apple parer, a hand-cranked device for peeling apples, emerged as an iconic object in the author's study of Victorian kitchens and kitchen labor-saving devices. From the collections of The Henry Ford.

approach to interpreting objects, schooling at Winterthur, and internship at the Mercer Museum. By the end of my interview, I was offered the job of curatorial assistant working with the Home Arts collection.

I happily served as the curator of this unusual collection for more than twenty years. I became a national expert on kitchens. I delved into food history, helping start cooking programs in Greenfield Village. I researched and helped create the menu for a new historic restaurant in Greenfield Village, Eagle Tavern. I soon branched out, developing exhibitions on streamlined design and vacationing; working on a National Endowment for the Humanities (NEH)-funded project documenting the museum's collections related to childhood; acquiring major collections related to soda fountains and kids' meal toys; and reinstalling and reinterpreting several historic structures in Greenfield Village. Most notably among these was the 1880s J. R. Jones General Store, which involved a complicated and challenging—but wonderfully satisfying—combination of primary source research about J. R. Jones and the people who shopped at this store; cataloging thousands of artifacts and acquiring numerous others; researching, then obtaining thousands more reproductions; creating and implementing a furnishings plan; interviewing descendants of J. R. Jones; writing interpretive training materials; and, ultimately, training interpreters. Aspects of this work are still ongoing today.

Another major early project was researching and writing an NEH-funded book that drew heavily from the museum's collections, entitled *Leisure and Entertainment in America*.[9] In those days, we were told to write for a "broad public audience." This meant writing in everyday (i.e., not scholarly) language, with no footnotes or index. When the book was finally published, after four years of diligent work, I wasn't sure whether anyone was actually reading it! Without footnotes, scholars kind of dismissed it. The popular audience seemed to enjoy the images and image captions but that was about it. From that experience, I resolved that from then on, I would try to understand who my audience was before starting a new project. The desire to know more about museum audiences soon became a passion, ultimately taking me down a somewhat different path from most curators, and even leading to a career shift.

The timing was right for this. A lot of change was happening in museums in the 1990s, as they began to look outwardly for possibly the first time. I joined in, delving deeply into learning about museum visitors, through workshops, articles, and conferences (the Visitor Studies Association was founded in 1990) and trying out small on-site visitor studies. All of this dramatically changed my outlook. By the late 1990s, I could not work on a new project without considering the visitor perspective. As a result, I found that I no longer fit neatly into my traditional curatorial shoes.

I decided to act on that, leaving my comfortable curatorial world behind to join a newly formed department at the museum called Experience Design. There I got to be involved with every new exhibition, working with different curators as well as cross-functional teams, stakeholders, and outside vendors. This position also put me at the center of a major renovation in Greenfield Village, involving several historic structure reinstallations and new interpretive signs for every structure. In Experience Design, I learned to develop engaging visitor experiences while also working strategically, leading groups, serving as a liaison to outside vendors, establishing processes for collaboration, and experimenting with strategies gleaned from outside the museum field (particularly from the so-called "Experience Economy," which is what inspired the name of the department).[10] And, after some formalized training, I spearheaded lots and lots of visitor studies. This innovative new department went through some rocky times and eventually ceased to exist (though it was recreated again later). Virtually everyone who had initially worked in that department would soon leave the museum—everyone except me, that is. Never fully leaving behind my curatorial roots, I returned to the curatorial department—this time taking on a collection related to public and community life, which incorporated many topics that I had worked on over the years.

It was weird. I felt like I had changed. Other curators weren't sure what to make of me, especially when I would get out the clipboards for a new visitor study or champion visitors at an exhibition meeting. Some of them joined me in these ventures; others welcomed my visitor-focused comments on their exhibition labels. Still others considered me a mere curiosity. Inevitably, there were those who were downright hostile to me, insisting that curatorial work should be based purely on the individual curator's perspective. But I stuck to my guns. I felt that my experiences over the previous several years had actually made me a stronger, more multi-faceted, more empathetic curator. In everything I did from that time—exhibitions, interpretation, tours and presentations, and writing—I happily returned to my old skills of rigorous research and material culture interpretation, but I integrated these with my newfound knowledge of a much larger body of collections (from working on all those exhibitions), as well as an understanding of the need for being strategic, having a process to get past roadblocks, embracing teamwork and collaboration, and championing visitors' perspectives. All of this came in handy when I spent the final four-and-one-half years of my career at The Henry Ford as the senior curator (along with my regular curatorial duties)—mentoring, coaching, and guiding the rest of the curatorial staff on their goals, projects, and own curatorial paths.

Although I had worked on topics related to diverse groups of people for many years, the museum field—and curatorial work along with it—dramatically changed in 2020.[11] Conference sessions, books, articles, collecting—truly everything related to what curators do—increasingly focused around social justice issues, decentering White perspectives, being more inclusive, and sharing authority. New scholarship on both older topics and previously untold stories continually revealed new and different perspectives, while curators also stepped up their collaborations with diverse communities.

I went through a real wake-up call about my work, my mindset, and my biases. In some ways, it was like starting over. One advantage of the COVID-19 pandemic was that I could attend virtual conferences of museum organizations from across the country. I absorbed the new perspectives and embraced the call to action within the museum field. Much of my work after that time came to involve revisiting, reframing, and updating content at the museum that

Preface

now seemed outdated; championing new, previously hidden or untold stories; assisting in newly created community engagement projects; and helping to define and support new collecting initiatives.

In 2021, my teaching a class on museum curatorial practice to both undergraduate and graduate students at Michigan State University underscored how much the world and the field had changed. While interested in core aspects of curatorial practice, students expressed a strong desire to learn about and discuss such current issues as decolonization, repatriation, community and contemporary collecting, and controversial topics. It was the syllabus for that class that led directly to the writing of this book.

As seen in the following descriptions, each chapter of this book focuses upon a key competency that curators in history organizations must possess in order to get the job done. But getting the job done is merely the first step. Thinking like a curator involves *mastering* each of these competencies, which promises an ever greater chance of success, influence, and impact—on colleagues, the public, and the larger museum field.

CHAPTER DESCRIPTIONS

Chapter 1 explores what it means to be a museum curator. What is the role of the curator in a history organization? How might this vary whether it is at a large or small museum, an indoor or outdoor museum? What is the role of the specialist versus the generalist curator? What are the core competencies of curators, and how are these represented in a job description? Finally, how has the role of museum curators changed with the increasing focus on social justice issues and DEAI (Diversity, Equity, Accessibility, and Inclusion) perspectives?

Chapter 2 is about gaining proficiency in interpreting material culture objects. A core competency of museum curators is the ability to understand and interpret objects, from the detail to the bigger picture, and from different lenses. This chapter will cover approaches to looking at objects as a key to understanding broader, inclusive cultural context.

Building and shaping collections—the subject of chapter 3—is another core competency of curators. This involves both rigor and creativity. How do curators go about doing this? This chapter will include such foundational curatorial tasks as developing collecting plans, creating acquisitions rationale, working with donors, ethical issues, cataloging, and deaccessioning. Current issues such as repatriation, decolonization, and community and contemporary collecting will be covered.

Chapter 4 discusses the topic of historical thinking, basically the "history" part of public history. This is also sometimes referred to as "applied research"—that is, synthesizing and interpreting a variety of historical sources to support the museum's public offerings. This chapter describes a wide range of useful sources, each source's pros and cons, and tips for getting started in doing in-depth historical research with a special focus on researching marginalized groups whose history is often hard to find.

Exhibitions, the topic of chapter 5, are an important and expected part of curatorial work, but these should not be created in a vacuum. What is the curator's role in exhibition planning and implementation? What are some constraints? How might curators navigate the murky worlds of teamwork and collaboration, controversial issues, community engagement, and sharing authority? How can curators work toward more inclusive and equity-oriented exhibitions in today's world?

As covered in chapter 6, historic sites and structures offer opportunities for curators to bring together research, collecting, exhibitions, and interpretive writing and training. What are the special qualities and tasks for curators doing historic house museum interpretation? How might outdated content be recognized as such and upgraded to align with current scholarship? How might curators navigate controversy and social justice issues at these places? How might they uncover hidden history and previously untold stories?

As explored in chapter 7, curators are not only expected to possess special expertise but be able to represent their institutions as knowledgeable experts through presentations, tours, interviews, and published materials. Over the last decade, digital content has exploded—vastly increasing curators' opportunity to disseminate their knowledge on various topics, but also necessitating new writing styles and approaches. More recently, virtual tours and talks have been added to the expectations of curators' work. How might curators prepare for all of these? How can they gear their presentations to ensure that these are as engaging as possible to their intended audience(s)?

In chapter 8, the book wraps up with a discussion of leadership opportunities and strategies for curators. This is not the same as leadership at the head of an organization. Nor is it about management (although this will be covered). It is about leading from the middle of an organization, which involves positive influence aimed outward in every direction. The chapter covers, first, leading oneself, then leading (or managing) up (to one's boss or supervisor), leading teams, mentoring, and—for curators who are also managers—leading direct reports. It concludes with a discussion of what it means to be an inclusive leader in today's world.

In summary, I believe that curatorial thinking is a mindset that curators must embody in approaching work that is—at the same time—rigorous yet creative, detail-oriented yet conceptual, both concrete and abstract, based upon personal knowledge and insights while also aligning with institutional goals and considering audience perspectives. It includes both core competencies and a willingness to adapt to and embrace change. Thinking like a curator requires a passion for objects, history, and people; empathy and respect for others; a willingness to share authority and collaborate; and—perhaps most importantly—a boundless curiosity and a questioning mind.

Preface

Acknowledgments

When I completed my book, *Spaces that Tell Stories: Recreating Historical Environments* (Rowman & Littlefield, 2019), I was already wondering what my next book could be about. John Neilson, former vice president of venues at The Henry Ford and a longtime colleague, suggested that I write about my career-long work as a history museum curator. I initially dismissed the idea. It would take too long, be too complex, and I would have to deal with too much recent change in the field. But a few years went by until, at the 2022 AASLH meeting in Buffalo, New York, I broached the idea to Charles Harmon, senior executive editor at Rowman & Littlefield. He immediately encouraged me to polish off my half-written proposal and submit it. The book ultimately got accepted, and here it is!

First, I would like to thank several curators at The Henry Ford (THF) who provided encouragement, support, and ideas for this book: Jeanine Head Miller, Charles Sable, Matt Anderson, Katherine White, Amber Mitchell, and former curators Saige Jedele and Ryan Jelso. Special thanks to Katherine, Saige, and Ryan for reading and commenting upon each chapter as I completed it.

I would like to also thank staff members at The Henry Ford who supplied missing bits of information—Lisa Korzetz, Mary Fahey, and Andy Stupperich; cheerfully followed up on my inter-library loan requests—Sarah Andrus and Mollie Gordier; and processed my requested images for this book—Brian Wilson and Jim Orr. Also, thanks to THF staff who kindly allowed me to use photographs they had taken—Debra Reid, Jim Johnson, Caroline Braden, and Melissa Foster. I would like to additionally thank other staff members at The Henry Ford—past and present and too numerous to mention—who helped shape this book in some way.

Much appreciation to those who enthusiastically helped me with and/or allowed me to use images from outside The Henry Ford—Ted Ligibel, Dean Weldon, Dr. Gaia Sims, and staff at The Indianapolis Children's Museum and the Erma Hayman House. Additional thanks to the five descendants of Dr. Alonson B. Howard who visited Greenfield Village—Corey Washburn, Sue Gillies, Dawn Gunther, Fiona Lynton, and in memoriam of Angela Karaka—who allowed me to use an image of them standing by their ancestor's medical office.

xvii

Authors of books and articles, especially in recent years, have faced the challenges of researching, exhibiting, interpreting, and otherwise championing diverse, inclusive, truthful history. This book could not have been written without all the wonderful work that's being done in the field right now. My special thanks to all of these authors.

Knowledge does not spontaneously generate; it always comes from somewhere. Writing this book brought to mind many of my early mentors, who taught me the ropes of this work, gave me opportunities, and instilled in me a lasting desire to pass knowledge along to others: Dr. Merritt Roe Smith, then at Ohio State University; Dr. Kenneth L. Ames, then at the Winterthur Program of Early American Culture; Lynne Poirier-Wilson, then-Mercer Museum curator; Harold K. Skramstad, The Henry Ford's president from the 1980s into the mid-1990s; and Peter H. Cousins, The Henry Ford's curator of Agriculture when I first arrived and the best mentor that anyone could ask for. This book cannot replace real people and real situations but hopefully it can begin to lay a foundation of knowledge and experience for readers who may not have had the types of advantages that I had.

Thanks to Rowman & Littlefield staff, especially Charles Harmon—who has been continually supportive—and to Lauren Moynihan for answering all my questions about the book production. Thanks, also, to AASLH staff who championed the writing of this book, especially Aja Bain, and to the anonymous reviewers who encouraged me to reach further than I ever thought possible to add, revise—and ultimately, I believe, improve—the scope and quality of this book.

Finally, thanks to my husband, Curt, and my daughter, Caroline, for being patient as I wrote this book as part of my personal "reinvention" of retirement.

1
The History Museum Curator

Today, the word "curated" seems to be everywhere. Websites boast of "curated" book lists, playlists for discerning listeners, clothing selections for the fashion conscious, snack boxes organized around themes, health food products chosen by wellness experts, and gift selections supporting socially responsible businesses. Within the context of today's world of information overload, particularly online, the word "curated" is meant to calm and reassure. It suggests editing, culling, aggregating, and organizing so the user does not have to bother. "Curated" also implies that the selected items have been carefully chosen by knowledgeable experts—thus, hinting at a discerning eye, good taste, the latest trend, and prestige.

With social media, the terms "curate" and "curated" have, in fact, now gone mainstream. Anyone can be a curator these days. It's easy. It's fun. You can curate your stuff, your experiences, your vacation, your very life. All by taking selfies and posting them online.

Has the mainstreaming of the word "curator" helped or hindered the understanding of what museum curators do?[1] Are we all curators now? Is there a way to define and delineate museum curators from marketing gurus, other types of specialists, or just anyone who wants to "curate" content for others' enjoyment and edification? What is truly involved in museum curatorial work, and particularly, what is unique about the work of the history museum curator? That is what this chapter is about.

The chapter starts with some basic definitions of museum curators and then delves into the specifics of "Curator Core Competencies"—a noteworthy and extremely useful reference document created by CurCom (the American Alliance of Museums' (AAM) former Curators Committee).[2] Next, it delineates the distinctions between curators at different types of history museums and explores how the work of history museum curators has expanded and evolved to meet today's needs and expectations. It goes on to describe different aspects of the job itself, from strategies for obtaining a curatorial position, to mastering core competencies and growing new skills, to assessing one's career. Finally, several activities for discussion and reflection are included to help readers apply the topics covered in this chapter to their own unique situations.

DEFINING MUSEUM CURATORS

Traditional definitions of museum curators tend to focus on their work with collections. In the seminal book *Introduction to Museum Work*, G. Ellis Burcaw simply stated that a curator is "a person who is in charge of a museum's collection."[3] More recently, Mark Walhimer, author of *Museums 101*, shifted this definition to focus more on public impact, maintaining that "the work of the curator is to organize the objects in the collection" in order to prepare content for visitor enlightenment, education, and inspiration.[4]

Other definitions hint at the central and vital role that museum curators play in their respective museums. The book *Museum Careers and Training: A Professional Guide* states that "curators are considered the heart of many museums. They usually determine what a museum collects, studies, and exhibits, and they provide the cultural, aesthetic, and intellectual foundation for the institution."[5] Similarly, the authors of the book *Museums: A Place to Work: Planning Museum Careers* maintain that, since "curators are often the major subject-matter experts in a discipline in the museum, they have an important responsibility in keeping the museum on track toward its goals and objectives."[6] CurCom succinctly defines curators as "highly knowledgeable, experienced, or educated in a discipline relevant to the museum's purpose or mission."[7]

Most would agree that the key differentiators between museum curators and just anyone are the levels of scholarship and intellectual rigor that go into museum curatorial work. These provide curators with the unique expertise "to study objects and to put together exhibitions for cultural and educational purposes."[8] They enable museum curators to communicate an unparalleled "understanding about historic objects, past and present lives and culture."[9] Ultimately, they ensure the highest degree of authenticity and accuracy.

CURATOR CORE COMPETENCIES

As curators have become central to the outwardly focused strategies of museums, a primary part of their role has become the meaningful contribution to "philosophical issues that guide their institutions."[10] This evolving role is embedded in the "Curator Core Competencies" written by members of CurCom in 2014.[11] This is still, I believe, the best reference for describing the work of museum curators. The document outlines the knowledge, skills, and experience required of today's curators and addresses what curators need to be successful in their profession. It contains a comprehensive and detailed description of the three primary domains in which curators work—collections, research, and communication, as well as the duties they perform and the applied skills that they must possess to be successful in today's profession. Although it is broad-based and applicable to all museum curators, it is an excellent foundation for understanding the core work of history museum curators (see figure 1.1).[12]

Figure 1.1 When the donor sent the author this photograph, showing a sampling of products from his family's specialty-import grocery store in Toledo, Ohio, it led to a multitude of curator core competencies: selecting objects; developing a long-term relationship with the donor and his family (including conducting oral interviews); historical research; writing an acquisitions rationale; cataloging for online digital records; and even giving a public presentation in which family members were invited. Photo courtesy of Ted Ligibel.

The following is a synopsis of this document:

Domain 1: Collections—Acting with uncompromising integrity and ethical standards, curators advocate for, supervise, oversee, champion, and develop the museum's collections. This domain, which includes object authentication and advising on acquisitions, is subdivided into three functions:

1) Collections Development—the assurance of a well-balanced collection through the development of a strategic collection plan that supports the institution's mission and reflects the best scholarship on the subject. Core competencies involve:
   - Possessing or collecting knowledge, information, and data regarding those objects.
   - Knowing the collection and identifying gaps and duplication.
   - Championing these perspectives to administrators.

- Expanding and/or reducing the size, significance, and complexity of the collection.
- Creating a statement on the scope of the collections.
2) Collecting—seeking objects to fill gaps in the collection that fit the needs of the institution and align with its mission. Core competencies involve:
    - Locating and authenticating collection items.
    - Addressing new research questions.
    - Building networks of potential donors, community members, dealers, and vendors to aid in this process.
    - Checking with other curators and collections.
    - Negotiating for acquisitions.
    - Serving as a public advocate for the collection.
3) Collections Care—ensuring and advocating for the care and preservation of the collection. Core competencies include:
    - Working with collections managers, registrars, and conservators if they are on staff.
    - With no support staff, carrying out the fundamental requirements of collections care and preservation, which might include: best practices for collections record management and documentation, working knowledge of object handling and storage, understanding the risks of loaning and traveling objects, and the ability to recognize objects that need professional conservation along with the coordination of this work.
    - Having digital literacy skills in terms of digitization and establishing and maintaining databases.

Domain 2: Research and Scholarship—providing the museum with credibility as trusted sources of information while expanding knowledge and performing relevant research. The focus is on accuracy, authenticity, and credibility. This domain is subdivided into three functions:

1) Scholarly Research—rigorous study and investigation that contributes to the sum of new knowledge and advances museology and curatorial practice. This can relate to objects, content, process, or larger context. Core competencies involve:
    - Engaging in original research and writing using accepted scholarly methodology aligning with the curator's academic discipline.
    - Using a professional writing style.
    - Ability to synthesize data into an orderly narrative based around a thesis.
    - Sharing insights and knowledge with the museum field, other curators, and the academic community through publications, conference participation, and so on.

2) Object Research—applying rigorous research methodologies to determine the authenticity, importance, and quality of museum objects. Core competencies include:
   - Knowing how to look at an object with scrutiny and critical thinking.
   - Ability to categorize, classify, and document objects into taxonomic systems.
   - Ability to conduct research to determine the authenticity, importance, quality, and context of museum objects.
3) Applied Research—synthesizing and interpreting facts, scholarly research, data, and related objects to support educational and public offerings. Core competencies include:
   - Ability to interpret scholarly and object research in accessible ways for public exhibitions, programs, and so on.
   - Ability to develop an interpretive narrative.

Domain 3: Communication—building trust and rapport with communities and intended audiences by facilitating access to knowledge through exhibitions, outreach and advocacy, and public programs. Involves the ability to communicate effectively with a variety of people from different backgrounds. Interpersonal skills are vital, and leadership/management and digital literacy skills are helpful. This domain is subdivided into five functions:

1) Exhibitions—serving as subject matter and object experts, and often working collaboratively with internal teams and external partners. Core competencies include:
   - Determining what stories to tell.
   - Determining what objects to use to illustrate those narratives.
   - The ability to create descriptive outlines and narrative scripts.
   - Might lead or manage the exhibition planning group, which involves managing people, time, and resources; inspiring others by providing purpose, motivation, and direction.
2) Writing—creating coherent written words from ideas, thoughts, and plans. Core competencies include:
   - Communicating to internal staff and external partners.
   - Creating scholarly work for publication.
   - Engaging in interpretive writing, involving the synthesis of complicated information for intended audiences.
   - Writing exhibition labels.
3) Object Interpretation—using objects to illustrate an idea or series of ideas. Although visitors make their own meaning from objects, curators can help them make sense of objects, opening windows of possibility and actualization. A core competency of this function is:

- The ability to reframe rigorous research about objects into understandable, accessible narratives geared to intended audiences.
4) Outreach and Advocacy—championing the museum and specific curatorial efforts by actively engaging with diverse publics and constituents. Core competencies include:
   - Possessing interpersonal skills.
   - Using empathy to relate to others.
   - Having a willingness to collaborate and share traditional responsibilities/authority with others.
5) Education—communicating on subject and object specialties to various audiences, including lectures, gallery talks and tours, publications, classes, and mentorship. Core competencies include:
   - Ability to reframe rigorous research about subject specialties in understandable, accessible, engaging ways geared to intended audiences.
   - Familiarity with online approaches and strategies and an ability to communicate through this format.

ONE SIZE DOES NOT FIT ALL

Just as history museums vary in size and scope, curatorial roles and responsibilities can vary widely and differ radically from one museum to the next. Here are some major distinctions.

Specialist Curators

These are the most traditional of all history museum curators.[13] Today, specialist curators tend to work at large institutions, with massive collections that are then subdivided into narrower segments. Specialist curators may be able to spend more time on original research than other types of curators. They are expected to have in-depth knowledge of their collections. These curators understand and appreciate each object's significance, and they maintain a working knowledge of the latest scholarship in their field. They can quickly and efficiently provide accurate information when needed, for inquiries from the media as well as for outside scholars, colleagues, stakeholders, and visitors. Specialist curators often maintain relationships with potential donors, are aware of objects' values, understand objects' travel suitability for loans, and can identify which are the most significant items for disaster planning.

While specialist curators require an institutional commitment of resources, they can also facilitate important donations, pass knowledge on to others, and easily share their knowledge with both the public and scholarly communities. While they are becoming rarer, their importance should not be overlooked—especially in collection areas that require a high degree of connoisseurship, such as decorative arts.

Generalist Curators

Generalist curators are those who cover a wide variety of subjects, collections, and tasks. The rise of digital content and online collections, broader interpretive perspectives, and the prioritization of certain collections over others have encouraged the increase of generalist curators.[14] Some museums have both specialists and generalists, working together collaboratively, with each type of curator helping the other when needed. It is good curatorial practice to have some skills in each.[15]

The term "skills-based" curator may come to replace the term "generalist" curator; in fact, this type of curator may be the wave of the future.[16] The skills-based curator relies on the transfer of skills and expertise rather than subject specialization. As museum workers move between jobs, they develop a host of skills they take with them. These skills are transferrable as workers continue to obtain curatorial roles and experience.

History Curators at Small Museums

Curators at small museums are likely generalists by default. Sometimes they are even the only paid staff member or were hired for another position and may find themselves functioning as curators. The small museum curator wears many hats, possibly even serving as the museum director.[17]

At a small museum, the curator is expected to address the curatorial core competencies. But they also might be responsible for a wide variety of other tasks, including: exhibition design and production; writing and producing museum publications; training docents and volunteers; taking school groups on tours; managing projects and budgets; overseeing digital outputs; managing the archives; coordinating outside image requests; recommending and/or evaluating merchandise to be sold in the museum store; donor relations and fundraising; and promotion.

At small museums without collections managers, registrars, and/or conservators, a major part of the curator's work might involve collections management, including: object handling; simple conservation procedures; documenting and tracking collections; taking care of loans and deaccessions; collections storage; preventative care; simple conservation treatments; disaster planning; monitoring the care and security of objects on exhibit and in storage; and possibly overseeing the activities of conservators, registrars, and collections managers.

Curators at Outdoor Museums and Historic Sites

Curators at outdoor museums and historic sites have the paradoxical problem of putting historic artifacts at risk to use for interpretation (see figure 1.2). As Tracie Evans, curator at Historic Sauder Village, wrote, "By the inherent nature of these museums, we must expect artifacts to be touched and used.

Figure 1.2 Curators at outdoor museums and historic sites must constantly weigh the value of using real objects versus using reproductions. Here, the staff at Firestone Farm (in Greenfield Village) is operating a restored ca. 1885 Johnston Self-Raking Reaper to harvest wheat. It would have been challenging and cost-prohibitive to attempt to reproduce a similar reaper to this one. Photo courtesy of Jim Johnson and The Henry Ford.

But how do we reconcile ourselves, as curators, with making those choices between using objects and the preservation policies of our institutions?"[18] Curators at these museums and sites must decide whether an object can be used. Is a reproduction available? Can the museum afford it? Is a real object replaceable? How will it be used? How often? Like other curators, outdoor museum curators must champion historical accuracy and authenticity, but—in addition to visitor engagement—they also must consider safety, comfort, maintenance, and security. Purpose statements, program objectives, and training in object handling become crucial to maintaining these curators' decisions about the placement and use of objects on-site.[19]

More than other curators, outdoor museum and historic site curators must also be adept at researching, creating, updating, and maintaining furnishings plans; communicating furnishings' intent and use; developing interpretive manuals; and training staff about interpretive messages, priorities, and presentation points.

Guest Curators

An outside guest curator might be engaged when a museum is lacking an expert on a topic it wants to explore or that person possesses a unique outlook or point of view that the museum wishes to pursue. This might involve having that person document or reinterpret an existing collection, develop a new collecting plan, acquire new collections, and/or interpret collections and topics within their area of expertise or unique perspective.

Community Co-Curators

This is an increasingly popular way of documenting, interpreting, or reinterpreting a museum's collections and/or topics. It involves sharing authority with members of an outside community with the understanding that they have accurate and authentic knowledge of the context of certain collections or topics. This is particularly becoming the norm for collecting and for creating exhibitions and public programs that incorporate Indigenous groups and their perspectives (see figure 1.3).[20]

Figure 1.3 Curators and exhibition staff at the American Museum of Natural History, New York City, worked in close collaboration with consulting curators from Indigenous groups to re-envision its Pacific Northwest Coast Hall. Enlivened with new interpretation, this exhibition showcases the creativity, scholarship, and living cultures of the Pacific Northwest. Photo by the author.

The History Museum Curator

THE HISTORY MUSEUM CURATOR IN TODAY'S WORLD

In today's rapidly changing world, the expectations of history museum curators have considerably ramped up. History museum curators today are charged with telling relevant, truthful, inclusive stories, "giving voice to the voiceless," "righting the historical record."[21] They must strive to tell stories that represent the lives of diverse people, marginalized communities, and unrepresented groups; to counter often controversial and contested histories, stereotypes, and misconceptions; and to engage contemporary audiences with stories that are relevant to their own lives.[22] Moreover, they are expected to supplement collections that are deemed insufficient for these purposes. Where can curators find strategies for guiding, steering, and inspiring this important work, for "moving the needle" in these directions?

History Relevance Initiative

The History Relevance Initiative, led by the American Association for State and Local History from 2012 to 2021, is a good place to start.[23] The group working on this initiative searched to find ways in which institutions and their audiences might connect through impactful and applicable programs that are both timely and rooted in historical quality. In 2020, the group published "Five Qualities of a Relevant History Experience"—that is, qualities to consider when developing products for the public. These are crucial to the work of history museum curators and should be seen as a constant thread running through their research, collecting, interpretation, writing, and public program development. The five qualities, and their defining characteristics, are:

1) Rooted in historical quality
   - Offers historical context and perspective.
   - Relies on scholarly expertise.
   - Primary sources are used as authentic evidence of the past.
   - Diverse perspectives of people of the past are represented.
   - Narratives that have been previously absent are present.
   - The goal is to reinforce public trust in the interpretation of historical topics.
2) Applicable
   - Relevant and useful to people's lives today.
   - Involves suggesting ways people and communities can apply these experiences to effect change.
3) Impactful
   - Challenges familiar assumptions by using new and profound pathways.
   - Offers unexpectedness and surprise.
   - Leads to memorable changes of thinking.

4) Current and Timely
   - Provides connections to current events, locally and/or nationally.
   - Underscores the idea that the present is informed by knowledge of the past.
5) Connected
   - Shows continuity between past, present, and future.
   - Builds empathy for people in the past.
   - Engages emotions to strengthen connections.
   - Relates to something personal and meaningful in people's lives today.
   - Provides entry points to topics that are absent or marginalized in community dialogue, ones that are often difficult for the audience to discuss.

DEAI (Diversity, Equity, Accessibility, and Inclusion) Perspectives

Another crucial place to look for strategies related to doing curatorial work in today's world is the plethora of DEAI initiatives, policies, and practices that currently form a core tenet of standards of excellence in the museum field. DEAI initiatives and practices offer several lenses through which curators can assess their work "to ensure that it is representative of all relevant subjects, available to all who wish to experience it, and resonant for and respectful of all stakeholders."[24] How can curators navigate the many DEAI-related statements, books, and articles that the museum field is producing right now and take away relevant, applicable, and practical strategies?

A useful place to begin is to look at the three core concepts in the American Alliance of Museums' "Excellence in DEAI" report, which are intended to pervade the work of different levels and departments within a museum.[25] They include:

Core Concept #1: DEAI is the responsibility of the entire organization—For curators, this involves the ability to fulfill explicit DEAI and equity goals as set out by their institution through its mission, vision, and strategy. These goals should also support individuals' skills.

Core Concept #2: DEAI is an ongoing journey without a fixed end point—This involves the commitment by curators and their institutions to transparency, vulnerability, trust, and—ultimately—public accountability. It relates to the stories that curators choose to tell about their own institutions; giving different people a voice; inviting input from the community, peers, the field, and other people; welcoming different types of people to the table; and being able to respond proactively and effectively to their input.

Core Concept #3: DEAI demands an ongoing commitment of resources—For curators, this involves having ample time to be able to dedicate to DEAI work, including individual and collective learning, reflection, and relationship building. It also includes being able to measure and assess one's own progress.

Another way that DEAI initiatives might be used to strategize curatorial work is to look at each of the categories included in the acronym itself.[26] This would break down as follows:

Diversity involves a representation of as broad a range of perspectives as possible. For curators, it involves a careful reflection of who's missing, whose stories are not being told. It might also include welcoming community involvement, which should be thoughtful and authentic and should run through the entire course of a project.

Equity implies a commitment to the equitable distribution of risks and rewards in a society. This is crucial in order for marginalized communities to trust curators' work and the perspectives of their institution. It includes: considering whose voices are being heard and/or silenced; providing opportunities for professional development; giving others resources, power, and hope; and/or championing a call to action to effect change within one's institution, community, or even the nation.

Accessibility is about accommodation, giving equitable access to everyone along the continuum of human ability and experience. It implies meeting people where they are, anticipating needs, fulfilling those needs, and accommodating requirements in a respectful manner. It can relate to physical, emotional, or intellectual access, or some combination of all three. In relation to curatorial work, this is particularly crucial in writing—whether through exhibition labels or writing other forms of print or digital content—as well as the development and delivery of special programs, offerings, or tours for different audiences.

Inclusion means that all people understand they are welcome, expected, and respected. For curators, this might involve story and object selection; label text and other forms of writing; and engaging in conversation, dialogue, and relationships that are authentic, generous, and respectful. Curators should aim to work inclusively and champion inclusivity from the inception of a project through its evaluation.

An action plan for looking at how DEAI principles intersect with curatorial work might involve creating a checklist of questions, like the following:[27]

General:

- What objects and whose stories are being collected and told?
- Do you value and welcome the work of excluded minorities?
- Do you make a conscious effort not to favor individuals and communities who are typically and traditionally heralded?

Collections:

- Are you representing marginalized people through collecting?
- Are you caring for and preserving their material culture with their input and consent?
- Are you revising accession records to reflect new understandings and practices that affirm non-dominant object creators and surrounding cultural context?
- Are you checking to see how object creators prefer to be named and memorialized?

Exhibitions:

- Do you include ethnically and racially diverse communities in creating the exhibitions you work on?
- Are your exhibition themes and subjects educational, enriching, meaningful, and culturally responsive?
- Do you value other staff and outside community members as experts in their own right?

Programs, Tours, Interpretation:

- Do you lead school and adult tour groups from all walks of life?
- Are your interpretive materials written and/or recorded at various levels?
- Do you consider accommodation for people with disabilities?
- Are your programs geared to various audiences, interests, cultures?
- Do you engage community members in dialogue if you are including messages about them?

Checking In with Museum Audiences

What about the reactions of museum visitors to all of this? Should curators be concerned if some visitors don't respond positively? Is it their job to care what visitors think? I believe that, yes, this is something that curators should understand, consider, and work toward in their work. An insightful aid to understanding visitors' attitudes about this work is the study undertaken by Wilkening Consulting, in the report, "Audiences and Inclusion: A Primer for Cultivating More Inclusive Attitudes among the Public."[28]

This report revealed that museum visitors are polarized, just like the United States, representing the range of current political perspectives. People at one end of the spectrum will not be interested in stories of inclusion no matter what we do. At the other end of the spectrum are the people who are already converts to these stories and attitudes. The group of people we should pay the most attention to, Wilkening argues, is that group in the middle, who need convincing but are innately curious. Wilkening's ten-step "Primer of Inclusive Practice," which follows, offers a road map for museum staff to use empathy and encourage curiosity to "crack open" these museumgoers' worldviews and attitudes:

1) Acknowledge your bias from the beginning and then encourage your visitors to do likewise. Create a plan to address your bias—for example, advisors, team approach, and so on, and be upfront about it with your audiences.
2) Reinforce visitors' aspirational identity as curious, open-minded, and/or well-rounded individuals.
3) Spark curiosity.
4) Engage in dialogic questions.
5) Give them the facts. ALL the facts.
6) Show your work. Trust cuts both ways, so you need to share your process and sources and identify advisors.
7) Mainstream inclusive content. And never apologize for being inclusive.
8) Pace your work at the "speed of trust." Some of the content you share may be difficult for some visitors, especially if it represents a change from what they thought they understood. Do not make them feel dumb. Do not preach.
9) Be a forum for civil discourse.
10) Your visitors are human, as you are. There will be bias on both sides. There will be controversy. Accept that, despite your best efforts, you will not be 100 percent successful.

There are many strategies in Wilkening's report and the preceding ten-step "Primer" to help curators with their work, including: acknowledging your biases and accepting those of others; encouraging curiosity by starting where visitors are and then taking them to new places; presenting the facts and letting visitors know where your information came from; and not talking down to people. Wilkening encourages us to keep working at developing and presenting stories of inclusion, despite potential pushback.

MANAGING YOUR CAREER

So You Want to Be a History Museum Curator

If you are trying to break into the museum field and this chapter has so far excited you rather than deterring you, you may want to consider a career as a history museum curator.[29] You can begin to prepare for this as early as high school, taking such classes as US and world history, art history/appreciation, and language arts/humanities.

After high school, you will need to earn at least a bachelor's degree. History museum curators come from a wide pool of majors, ranging from anthropology to history to art history to communications. Often, curators end up with a specialty or group of collections that they did not expect and for which they could not prepare. That's okay. It is more important to get practice in historical research methodologies, writing, and historical thinking than to gain a topic specialty. You might also want to consider courses in marketing, public relations, public administration, business, and/or communications. A foreign language mirroring your interests can be an asset as well.

In today's competitive world, it is also recommended to acquire a master's degree (some museums require it). While you might study an academic discipline, it is increasingly crucial that you be fully immersed in museology and know the role and function of museums to be a successful member of a museum team and to become a leader for the advancement of the profession.[30] A PhD might be required at some institutions, especially those expecting publishing credentials.

Future museum curators can greatly benefit from acquiring real-world experience, including on-the-job training and internships. It is also a good idea to start building your network—professional connections that you can use as you pursue a career. This might be a professor with connections to the museum field; a staff person at a local museum or archive; someone involved in a local or state museum organization; or a museum professional you might encounter at a lecture or webinar. You might even attend a professional conference.[31]

When you finally reach the point of applying for a museum curator job, a carefully prepared resume is important. And a list of trustworthy references—people who know your work and work style and are willing to champion you—is crucial. But many would argue that the single most important part of the application is your cover letter.[32] It may be the most persuasive piece of writing you have ever written. It should be brief and businesslike, listing all the qualifications you have that are important to the job for which you are applying. You are not writing about how the position meets your own needs, but how your skills, experience, and background align with the position description that is being described—task by task, function by function. As an added bonus, it can also show off your writing skills.

Mastering Competencies, Growing New Skills

Whether you are just getting started, in mid-career, or a seasoned professional, you never stop mastering competencies and growing new skills. New scholarship, technology, and resources constantly emerge; institutional goals and strategies change over time; even the museum field changes.

A career as a history museum curator is different every day. With curiosity, openness, and a willingness to learn, your job should never become boring. It will likely involve "maintaining a balance between the pragmatic and the intellectual, the practical and the theoretical."[33] Daily practice and mastery of core competencies, with added strategies taken from the History Relevance and various DEAI initiatives, will likely constitute much of your work as a curator. There are few better places than on the job to learn such "how-to" skills as: determining what collections to acquire; using collections creatively; reinterpreting an existing collection or historical topic as new information is revealed; combining collections and content together to tell a story; and interpreting collections and stories in new ways for different audiences.

In addition to mastering core competencies, there is another layer of important skills of which curators must be aware and willing to practice daily. These are the skills they don't teach you in school, but they can increase your chances of being successful throughout your career. They are the so-called "soft skills"—the intangibles that you use to accomplish tasks. These comprise the personal goals, habits, attitudes, and social graces that make you a valuable employee, someone with whom others want to work.[34]

Although you might think you are being judged on your knowledge alone, soft skills are, in fact, some of the most important criteria for success against which you are measured as an employee. Indeed, they can serve you in good stead from the time you are being assessed by a prospective employer to your last performance review. They include behaviors like teamwork, adaptability, problem-solving, creativity, leadership, work ethic, interpersonal skills, time management, and attention to detail.[35]

Leadership might seem like a surprising soft skill for curators. But it is not, as some think, the exclusive province of the executive director. Curators, in fact, have many opportunities to lead from where they are in their institution (see chapter 8, Leading from the Middle). Being successful in this requires personal vision, determination, and interpersonal skills. Leadership also might mean moving a project forward, keeping people on task. For this type of leadership, you must be goal-oriented, focused, and directed, while also being flexible and able to respond to change, challenges, and setbacks. Many curators find leadership to be innately satisfying, as it offers "the ability to create positive change, the sense of making significant contributions, and the excitement of empowering yourself and your colleagues."[36]

In addition to mastering core competencies and learning new skills, responsible curatorial practice in today's world also entails doing the internal work to build your DEAI capacity. We all have "an obligation to continue our work to center DEAI in everything that we do so we can fully realize our commitment to the whole public, not just a select few."[37] Action steps to take in this regard might include:

- Creating your own DEAI strategy.
- Facing your own unconscious bias. Understanding White privilege, supremacy, racism, your own blind spots and those of your institution.
- Developing a commitment to change.
- Learning from others. Asking a lot of questions.
- Being intentional in your efforts.
- Reading everything on the DEAI shelf. Requesting training, professional development, and skill development. Checking out online resources, webinars, and conference seminars.
- Looking for coaching.[38]

As you progress through your curatorial career, gaining expertise and experience, you should continually be asking yourself, how am I contributing to existing knowledge related to objects, historical topics, stories of people in the past and their relevance in the present, curatorial methods and processes? How am I challenging myself by being creative, innovative, and unique? How am I sharing my new learnings and insights with others, contributing to the larger field of curatorial practice and museology? How am I making a difference?

Remember that, in mastering competencies, growing new skills, and doing the necessary internal work, you are not alone. There are books, articles, online resources, webinars, professional organizations, special-interest groups, and conferences to help you.[39] Find mentors. Build your personal network. Schedule time for learning and reflection. Create a "Community of Practice"—a group of like-minded curators or individuals who want to read, discuss, and share insights together.

Ongoing Assessment

Once you are in a curatorial position, you should periodically assess whether where you are is the right place for you. Where do you see yourself in the future? What is best for your personal growth? As Anne W. Ackerson wrote, "Whether you're just starting out or you've been around for a while, there are career crossroads to be navigated, some sooner rather than later, some by choice, others not."[40] Ackerson recommends creating your own mission statement to shape your museum career—something you can steer, shape, or even throw out. What can you aim for, short term and long term, practically speaking and as stretch goals? By periodically assessing your career path, you will continue to grow. It is a sure way to control your career rather than letting it control you.

This chapter has established important groundwork for the tasks, functions, and responsibilities of history museum curators, which will be described in more depth in succeeding chapters. It explored evolving definitions of curators, CurCom's "Curator Core Competencies," distinctions between history curators at different museums, strategies for meeting the heightened expectations of curatorial work in today's rapidly changing world, and ways to manage and succeed in your own career.

REFLECTIVE PRACTICE

In the following section, I describe several activities, exercises, and topics that encourage you to apply the foundational information in this chapter to your own situation and career. You can certainly try out any of these on your own. Even better, however, if possible, is to form a "Community of Practice" (as described in the Mastering Competencies, Growing New Skills section), in which you are part of a group engaging in common readings and sharing perspectives. Not only will you feel less alone but you will also grow from this—individually and as a group. Though you may not realize it at the time, through your creative, collaborative, and critical thinking in doing this work, you are contributing to current and future excellence in curatorial practice.

1) Curatorial Alignment with Institutional Mission, Vision, and Strategic Plan

   Consider the ways in which your curatorial work aligns with your institution's mission and vision. Look at your institution's current strategic plan. How does/can your curatorial work best align with this? How might your curatorial work influence your institution's strategic plan in the future?

2) Curator Core Competencies

   Read CurCom's "Curator Core Competencies." How does your institution's perception of curatorial work align with this? Did anything surprise you? How applicable is this to your own work? What seems unreasonable to you? How might you aim what you do in the future to better align with this?

3) Five Qualities of a Relevant History Experience

   Re-read the qualities described in this chapter. What do you think you do well now? What had you not thought about before? What is the perspective of your institution about these? How might you go about changing this perspective for the better? How might you align current projects with this? What do you want to work on in the future?

4) Creating a Strategy for DEAI Work

Look over the section of this chapter on DEAI initiatives and practices (and, if you want to go deeper, refer to the citations). How do these strategies of looking at curatorial work through a DEAI lens align with your own work? How might you shift your perspective? Look over the section on DEAI self-work in the section on Mastering Competencies, Growing New Skills (and check the citations if you want to go deeper). What DEAI self-work might you want to do, now and in the future?

5) Curatorial Job Description

Curatorial job descriptions can vary widely from one institution to the next, but it is always important to have one. This is a touchstone, the basis for goal setting and professional development, an official document to rationalize and explain what you do to others, a reminder of the unique skills you have and need, and an enumeration of the exact functions you are expected to perform. Generally, a job description includes: a Summary of Purpose (a synthesis of the work in three to four sentences); a list of Essential Functions; Minimum Requirements (education, experience); and Special Skills (generally, soft skills). Look over your current job description or create one if you don't have it. How might it incorporate the "Curator Core Competencies," the qualities of a Relevant History Experience, the DEAI practices, and the soft skills covered in this chapter?

6) Soft Skills

Look at the soft skills described in this chapter (and, if you want to go deeper, refer to the citations). Set up a matrix listing these and fill in: the skills that best relate to your work as a curator; skills you already have; skills you'd like to work on; and action steps for improving certain skills.

7) Your Personal Career Plan

Read over the "Strategizing Me" article cited in note 40 of this chapter and consider (or if the article is not accessible, simply reflect upon) the following questions: What are the strengths you've got going for you now? What are the biggest personal challenges you have right now? What kind of growth opportunities do you see in your current job? What prevents you from moving forward? What growth opportunities or situations do you want to embrace more in the future? What situations do you want to avoid in the future? What are you most passionate about? What truly motivates you at work? What can you best offer the curatorial department, your institution, the field? Write a statement about your personal career plan that plays to your strengths and aims at opportunities that support your vision. Revisit it periodically and revise or update it.

2
Making Sense of Objects

I entered my new office space. It was actually a makeshift dry-walled partition on the museum floor that divided the objects on public display from those sitting in storage. But I didn't care that it wasn't a "real" office. It was my first day of work as a curatorial assistant at The Henry Ford, responsible for the museum's vast holdings of household equipment and other daily life artifacts. I was filled with anticipation.

The previous curator of these collections had retired eight months earlier and the office was, in essence, "frozen in time"—as if she had just walked out. Objects sat on shelves, tagged with notes about donor information or about places the objects needed to go. A pile of unanswered letters from potential donors sat on the desk. I recalled the list of my assigned projects that another curator had previously sent me related to the museum's upcoming fiftieth-anniversary commemoration: cull the household equipment on display; create four period settings of kitchens to serve as a "focal point" at the center of that display; and identify additional objects for a larger interpretive exhibition highlighting the museum's collections. I also needed to somehow get a handle on all the objects in my collection that were in the process of being moved to a new storage building. On top of that, the Education Department was requesting a list of kitchen equipment that I could supply for a new cooking program in several historic homes in Greenfield Village.

I started feeling kind of queasy. What did I really know about stoves and sewing machines, cooking equipment and washing machines, spinning wheels and sap buckets? I was drowning in objects, and I'd better get to work!

Hopefully, other newbie curators have not had (or will not have) similar experiences with an immediately overwhelming to-do list like I did. But it is pretty much a given that working with objects are (or will become) a major portion of every history museum curator's work. People will assume that you, as the curator, already have expertise on everything and they will expect prompt answers. Not only do you need to quickly get a handle on the objects in your collection, but you must also bear in mind that objects can be tricky. What do they really mean? Are they what they seem? What are they not telling us?

This chapter presents foundations, methodologies, and practical case studies to help history museum curators explore and navigate the myriad ways in which to make sense of objects.

THE WORLD OF OBJECTS

It is difficult to imagine a world without objects. Many of us are surrounded by multitudes of them every day. In fact, we are so used to living with them that we sometimes barely even notice them.

That is the unique calling of the objects in history museums. Sure, they can be overwhelming. There are often too many of them for a museum's needs (more on this in the next chapter). But they also relentlessly remind us of their physical existence, their pervasiveness in our lives, their significance, and their power. When used effectively, they can serve as tools to uncover stories that are filled with meaning and connection, to link the past to the present and future, and to reconnect us with what it means to be human.

It is important to recognize that, for Indigenous curators and curators working with Indigenous collections, topics, and communities, historical objects embody an entirely different meaning and context. As Amy Lonetree writes in her book, *Decolonizing Museums: Representing Native America in National and Tribal Museums*, "The objects are important because they belong to living Native peoples who maintain deep and ongoing connections to the pieces."[1] She goes on to explain that

> objects in museums are living entities. They embody layers of meaning, and they are deeply connected to the past, present, and future of Indigenous communities. In the presence of objects from the past, we are privileged to stand as witness to living entities that remain intimately and inextricably tied to their descendant communities.[2]

Objects, Artifacts, or Items?

At history museums, these terms are generally used interchangeably, especially when referencing three-dimensional "things." The word "artifact" (borrowed from archaeology) has a more formal connotation, denoting something from the past that scholars study and analyze. Conversely, policies relating to the repatriation of Indigenous materials—respectful of language and context—generally use the term "items." Paper and archival materials are also often referred to as "items," as the terms "artifact" and "object" tend to denote three-dimensionality. I'll generally be using the term "object" throughout the remainder of this chapter, with the understanding that it isn't always perfect and that it might be culturally sensitive within certain contexts.

Scholars' definitions of these terms vary. For example, in their 2017 book, *History Through Material Culture*, historians Leonie Hannan and Sarah Longair argue that the term "artifact" denotes "the hand of humankind in the making of an object in contrast to things that are produced by nature alone."[3] The authors of the 2010 book *Nearby History: Exploring the Past Around You*, write that "things" are "creations and products of culture" that come from the "bundles of knowledge, beliefs, norms, and values that compose that culture."[4] Back in the 1970s, historical archaeologist Ivor Noël Hume defined "artifacts" as "anything made by man at any time."[5] All of these, and many other attempts at definitions over the years, have one thing in common—the presence of people. People use objects. People made them or were somehow involved in their creation. Objects not only help us understand those specific people but also the social groups, communities, and larger culture within which these people lived and worked.

What Is Material Culture?

While an object, artifact, or item implies a singular entity, the term "material culture" refers to a larger assemblage of these. Art historian Jules Prown, who pioneered much work on the study of material culture, argued that the underlying premise of material culture was that these groups of human-made objects "reflect, consciously or unconsciously, directly or indirectly, the beliefs of the individuals who commissioned, fabricated, purchased, or used them and, by extension, the beliefs of the larger society to which the individuals belonged."[6] A more recent, and somewhat broader, definition of material culture is that it is "a description of any and all human-constructed or human-mediated objects, forms, or expressions, manifested consciously or unconsciously, through culturally acquired behaviors."[7]

Why Study Material Culture?

Today, many scholars would concur with Prown's claim back in 1982 that material culture offers "aspects of mind that differ from, complement, supplement, or contradict what can be learned" from traditional documentary sources.[8] As historical evidence, they present the past firsthand. They are concrete, immediate, and real—to be touched, seen, smelled, weighed, measured, and counted. They can reveal and/or elucidate such details as manufacturing techniques, inscriptions, dates, size, weight, texture, and materials.

Objects can also serve as key documents to represent the lives of people for whom written documents do not exist, were not saved, or were erased from the record. On the downside, they can embody cultural and individual biases as well as fail to represent aspects of culture for which objects either did not exist or were not considered important.

For the most rigorous and comprehensive analyses, objects should always be paired, if possible, with written documents and other types of sources such as visual images and oral histories.

FOUNDATIONS OF OBJECT STUDY

Today's approaches to analyzing and interpreting objects are built upon many still-significant layers of previous approaches, dating from at least the middle of the last century. There is a plethora of books and articles on each approach so they will only be summarized here. Key published sources for each approach are mentioned in the citations at the end of this book.[9]

"Manufacts" (1950s to 1960s)

Academic historians were, in fact, some of the more recent scholars to consider using objects in their research. Most of them were quite satisfied with their longtime use of documents to address historical questions and issues (and many still are). "Pots and pans" history, they dismissively called object studies. Nor did museum curators of the 1950s and 1960s do much to advance the field of object study. Sure, they collected and stewarded collections of objects, but these tended to represent the lives of the elite.[10] Moreover, curators of these collections often focused on connoisseurship—not only authenticating these objects but also judging their merits in terms of design and workmanship.

The major influencers of using objects to interpret the lives of people were archaeologists, who had long classified groups of objects and analyzed this material to interpret human behavior. Historical archaeology was an early crossover field, in which scholars studied the lives of past people through both the things these people left behind and related written documents. Anthropologists, who analyze changes in cultural behavior, also looked to objects for clues, as did folklorists, who tended to study groups of people for whom few written records existed.[11] The American Studies field, just emerging and inherently interdisciplinary, was additionally receptive to analyzing "things" along with other sources.

Historians of technology, who understood the key role of objects in studying the intricacies of technological change, were early champions of using objects as historical evidence. In his now-classic 1964 article, "Manuscripts and Manufacts," Smithsonian Institution curator Wilcomb E. Washburn challenged the concept that there was a dichotomy between the written word and the material object. "The specific fact," Washburn wrote, "may be either in the form of a written document—a manuscript—or a material artifact or 'manufact.'"[12]

A handful of academic historians picked up the mantle and put the notion of using objects as historical documents into practice. One of the most exciting books to emerge at the time—and frequently referenced when I was in graduate school—was *A Little Commonwealth: Family Life in Plymouth Colony*, written by academic historian John Demos in 1970.[13] Demos was the rare historian at the time who combined material culture—specifically, the physical objects that remained from the seventeenth century—with wills, inventories, and other written records to offer an analysis of daily life in Plymouth Colony.[14]

"History from the Bottom Up" (late 1960s to 1980s)

In the late 1960s and 1970s, a field emerged in academia called "new social history."[15] Tracing their discipline's origins to the 1920s-era "Annales School" in France, the new social historians asserted that everyone's history—not just that of the more traditionally studied political, social, and economic elite—was important in understanding historical change through time. These social historians focused new efforts on studying people who lived ordinary lives and did ordinary things—what came to be referred to as "history from the bottom up" or "grassroots history." They argued that these people's lives often offered a truer lens through which to understand the culture of the time than the lives of the elite.

Although these ordinary people (e.g., working classes, women, enslaved African Americans, impoverished and/or illiterate groups) did not leave much in the public record (or their records were not considered valuable enough to save by people in positions of power), the new social historians began to dig more deeply and more imaginatively analyze primary source records. Bringing new questions to the analysis of such data, they could draw conclusions about beliefs, customs, and values of individuals, families, and communities as well as about broader societal questions like how people responded to change and disruption.

The new social historians came to look at manmade objects as tangible, concrete evidence of past lives and events. They invested ordinary historical objects with new meaning, using them to reveal clues about not just everyday life but about such complex ideas as attitudes, values, social conventions, and human relationships.[16]

In 1975, the twenty-first annual Winterthur Conference veered from its long-standing focus on a single decorative arts topic and chose the theme "Material Culture and the Study of American Life."[17] The introduction to the subsequent publication explained that this conference, planned in time for America's bicentennial, was intended to explore the question of "How has our study of artifacts altered our perception of American history?" An interdisciplinary group of speakers explored this question from several different angles. Conference speaker Cary Carson, a social historian and coordinator of research for the Historic St. Mary's City (MD) Commission, proclaimed that "the interests of some historians for the first time are converging with those of the 'thing' people."[18]

Material Culture Studies (1980s to the present)

By the mid-1980s, material culture had become a scholarly field, a serious area of study that was incorporated into such disciplines as social and cultural history, American Studies, folklore, and cultural geography.[19] In 1982, the scholarly journal *Winterthur Portfolio* (begun in 1964) was given the additional subtitle *"for the Study of Material Culture"*—thereafter encouraging innovative scholarship specifically on material culture studies.

Groundbreaking research was undertaken during this time, combining objects with primary documents to shed new light on the previously lost, silenced, hidden, or forgotten lives of African Americans, women, Indigenous people, and other marginalized groups. Innovative work was especially accomplished at outdoor museums in which historians were on staff, such as Colonial Williamsburg, Plimoth Plantation, and Old Sturbridge Village. Computer-based statistical methods were beginning to aid in these studies, helping scholars crunch data to analyze patterns that would quantify continuity and change in different communities.

In 1993, Winterthur once again held an important material culture–related conference, "American Material Culture: The Shape of the Field," to "canvas the current state of American material culture study, explore emerging questions, and see how the field has changed since 1975."[20] The conference, and the resulting publication, focused attention on the ways in which material culture could contribute to a more nuanced and accurate cultural history. The speakers, again drawn from many different disciplines, combined theory with practice in their varied presentations. Reflecting a maturing field, they emphasized a broadening concern with exploring the lives and experiences of individuals and groups who had often been omitted from traditional cultural narratives.

The conference launched deeply into theoretical underpinnings and approaches, which would become increasingly important in twenty-first-century material culture studies. What was the role of power and ideology? How was meaning "constructed"? How did power distort social consciousness? How can we know anything from or about objects? Most speakers agreed that objects should not be taken at face value, that their meaning depended upon the context in which the object was made and used, the context within which social relationships took place. Material culture, they argued, did not simply mirror culture. It was symbolic, active, and communicative.

Since that time, academic material culture studies have increasingly focused on theoretical underpinnings to analyze the role of material culture in understanding what it means to be human and what we value as individuals and as a society. These studies remind us that, while objects can offer a beacon to new knowledge about families, communities, individuals, and our own lives, we must consider the more ambiguous and negative values of such themes as materialism, objectification, consumerism, global sustainability, government/political impacts, and religious laws and tenets.[21]

Digital Transformation (1990s to the present)

While material culture studies were maturing as a scholarly field, something momentous was occurring in museums. Beginning in the 1990s, the impact of the internet would utterly transform the ways in which curators and the public interacted with museum objects. Relatively primitive websites and online information services evolved into increasingly sophisticated research databases, websites, online collections management systems, and, more recently, the emergence of online communications platforms.[22]

The advantages of online collections quickly became obvious in terms of accessing, analyzing, and interpreting museum objects. Digitized objects in museum collections were now findable, searchable, viewable, replicable, and manipulable. Objects in storage found new life online, as did particularly valuable or fragile objects that could not stay on exhibit for long. Curators could now share stories using objects in the collections that had been previously all but hidden. They were able to compare similar objects and enhance their object studies by zooming in on details. They could more easily find, sort, and track down objects for exhibitions, programs, online articles, and presentations. Online collections also contributed to greater inclusivity, helping curators to uncover and highlight marginalized or silenced voices and "to incorporate them into our work in ways not possible in print or the space of an exhibition gallery."[23] Beyond using databases of digitized collections, the opportunities for researching objects through online sources (with caution) also expanded exponentially.

In his 2011 essay, Matthew MacArthur, director of New Media at the National Museum of American History, claimed that the so-called "digital revolution" also gave museums the opportunity to "enhance the relevance of our collections in the lives of the public that we serve."[24] Users could enjoy digitized objects on museum websites, in both self-directed ways and through more mediated experiences. Ultimately, online communication platforms allowed them to express their opinions, "publish" their perspectives alongside that of the museum, and share their experiences with others. Some museums even encouraged them to contribute to online museum collecting projects or submit their own memorable objects and related stories for online exhibits.[25] Unfortunately, negative aspects of online collections also emerged, as the public came to believe that what they were perusing online constituted the entirety of a museum's collections and it became easier to misinterpret or misconstrue the meaning of objects that were digitally reproduced.

Of course, despite the initial concern that no one would ever visit museums again, we also learned that digital representations of objects could never actually replace the real thing. Digital versions of objects simply could not replicate the size, scope, texture, and dimension of real-life objects. And it became clear that there were ongoing challenges to funding, staffing, and prioritizing digitization initiatives.

While digital collections have, for the most part, offered wonderful advantages for making collections accessible and visible, from the perspective of curatorial practice and material culture studies, they are often missing a key piece of information—the interpretation, the context, the meaning of the object—arguably the most important part of curators' work! These tend to appear in exhibition labels (both on-site and online) and in online articles. But they have failed to find their way into most digitized collections databases. These databases tend to identify the objects, include their dimensions, describe their materials, supply a date or approximate date, and identify a maker (if known). Fortunately, a visual image is usually included. But this is where these usually stop. In fact, in some cases, curators don't even supply this information anymore, as much of it has transferred to registrars' office staff or digitization specialists.

To combat this dearth of interpretive information on records of digitized collections, some museums have made efforts to embed or link this type of information with the catalog records. Sometimes these appear as introductions to groupings of objects organized around exhibit sections or themes.[26] Less frequently, each individual catalog record includes or is linked to interpretive information.[27] This is particularly popular when groupings of objects have been created for online educational offerings, to help teachers and students.[28]

"Active" and Inclusive Objects (about 2012 to the present)

The title of the 2018 book *Active Collections* is an appropriate manifesto for history museum curators working with objects today.[29] The authors of the collected essays in this book argue for the effective use of objects, which, in today's world, could mean everything from reconsidering what stories are being told to asking different questions, seeing objects in a new light, and/or reinterpreting them in a new way that provides insight into the lives and experiences of those who have traditionally been ignored, dismissed, or bypassed.

A succinct summary of interpreting objects in today's world can be found in Masum Momaya's essay in the *Active Collections* book, "Ten Principles for an Anti-Racist, Anti-Orientalist, Activist Approach to Collections."[30] These include:

1) Openly acknowledging colonialism, racism, inequality, oppression, and privilege in museum objects, as the objects that a museum possesses often reflect the collecting decisions of White, wealthy, powerful patrons and collectors.
2) Establishing opportunities for community engagement and co-construction of meaning of objects.
3) Aiming for as many divergent perspectives as possible rather than a consensus of a singular narrative.
4) Rejecting definitions of value based on a grand narrative of White European supremacy.

5) Considering how digital tools and social media shift the balance of power and voice.
6) Considering how objects might be used to reinforce equity, welcome, and mutual respect.

MATERIAL CULTURE METHODOLOGIES

In attempts to bring rigor, consistency, and standards to the study of material culture, numerous scholars from different disciplines have offered approaches to object analysis and study.[31] Of all of these, I believe that one specific methodology emerges as particularly salient to the study of historical and cultural objects and will be described in detail here.

"Artifact Study: A Proposed Model"

E. McClung "Mac" Fleming—a cultural historian and professor in the Winterthur Program in Early American Culture—published his now-classic article with the above title in the *Winterthur Portfolio* in 1974.[32] His creation of this methodology, however, actually dates from ideas that he developed as far back as 1958.[33] While this article may seem like it's out of the Dark Ages, Fleming's methodology continues to be cited as relevant and useful.[34]

In the article's introduction, Fleming admitted that there had already been both academic discussion and methodology about objects in the fields of art history, archaeology, and history of technology, but that there were no models or methodology for an approach in cultural history. Moreover, while there had been progress in analyzing the physical properties of cultural and historical objects, there was as yet no methodology for "differentiating this information from a more conceptual-level interrelationship between the artifact and its culture"—a true "discipline of artifact study."[35]

Fleming's first step in his proposed model for artifact study involved accumulating a body of concrete facts about the object itself. This step, which he called "Classification," included:

- The object's history—where it was made, when it was made, by whom and for whom it was made, why it was made, and successive changes in its ownership and condition.
- Material—what the object was made of.
- Construction techniques.
- Design.
- Function.

With this basic information in hand, his subsequent four steps involved increasingly deeper and more conceptual levels of analysis.

1) Identification—deeper research to make sure that the above information was accurate:
   - Classification—How was this referenced in its own era, over time, and today?
   - Authentication—Was it what it claimed to be?
   - Description—How might you describe in words and sentences the physical aspects of the object? This ideally involved both looking at the object, doing extensive research in both secondary and primary sources, and understanding how the object was made/constructed. It should describe maker, purchaser, owner, place of origin, materials, techniques of construction, design motifs, and meaning of iconography.
2) Evaluation—comparison with other objects:
   - How did this object compare to other objects that were similar or were made by the same maker?
   - Was the object part of a group or genre of objects? What features distinguished the group as a whole? What features were unique or distinctive to this object?
3) Cultural analysis—examining in depth the relation of the artifact to aspects of its own culture:
   - Reasons for its initial manufacture.
   - Various intended uses and unintended roles.
   - The essential importance and meaning of the object and how it conveyed that meaning. This could include such ideas as visual delight, utility, communication; its use as a symbol of social status, ideas, values, and feelings; and its relation to religious beliefs, standards of living, politics, family life, and economics.
   - The object as seen through the lens of "product analysis" (the ways in which a culture leaves it mark on the particular artifact) or "content analysis" (the ways in which the particular artifact reflects its culture).
4) Interpretation—the relation of the object to larger cultural themes, trends, and patterns, which could include:
   - Describing the object's relevance in our culture and our lives today.
   - Pinpointing key aspects of our current value system.
   - Incorporating universal themes like American nationalism, urbanization, ecology, democracy, mechanization, mobility, innovation, and empowerment.
   - Acknowledging that there could be many interpretations.

Critiques of Fleming's model have called out such omissions as his not incorporating fluctuations of the marketplace and economic depressions, not taking marketing and advertising into account, and missing political, social, and economic influences.[36] And, of course, it also lacks today's more inclusive consideration of makers, users, materials, and larger cultural context. Despite these omissions, this model has proven remarkably resilient. It can be added to or subtracted from as it fits the object, the needs, the era within which the object was made, and the era within which it is being interpreted.

Fleming's model may seem overly complicated. But it really boils down to four steps: observing an object's physical attributes, comparing the object with others, researching the object's history, and assessing its larger context. Several methodologies developed since that time have followed essentially this same sequence.[37]

Six Practical Steps

With Fleming's and similar models in mind, here are my suggestions for a series of practical steps to take when analyzing and interpreting an object (see textbox 2.1):

TEXTBOX 2.1: SIX PRACTICAL STEPS TO ANALYZING AND INTERPRETING AN OBJECT

1) Ask yourself, what is this thing?
2) Identify basic attributes, such as maker, user, maker location, material, date, and use.
3) Assess fit for your museum collection.
4) Engage in deeper research on object attributes.
5) Assess the object's historical and cultural significance.
6) Cite your sources.

---

1) Ask yourself, what is this thing? Do whatever you need to identify the object, whether it involves physically handling it (highly recommended, as this can reveal details that aren't always visible at first glance or through images), checking other collections, and possibly even perusing the internet for similar items (with caution because the information can be inaccurate).
2) Undertake initial research to identify the object's basic attributes: makers, users, maker locations, methods of construction, estimated dates, and use. This might involve online research (using reputable sources) and looking at books or articles that quickly supply information on company histories, methods of manufacture, or these types of objects. You might want to get initial input from other curators or other experts at this point.
3) If the item is being offered as a donation, you will want to determine what else you have, how it compares, and if it aligns with existing collections

plans and/or institutional strategy. These points will be covered in the next chapter.

4) Engage in deeper research on all the object attributes listed in item number 2. This will likely involve delving into the history of makers, users, and/or the promotion and dissemination of that object. Sources might include online databases and other reputable online sources, scholarly books and articles, archival materials such as trade catalogs and ledgers, such visual documentation as prints and photographs, and oral histories and written reminiscences. This is the step in which you might also involve individuals or community members who originally made, owned, or used the object and can provide important context. (See chapter 4, Thinking Historically, for more detail on sources.)

5) Assess the object's historical and cultural significance. The specifics of this, and the amount of time you spend on it, will vary, depending upon the need. But it is a crucial step—the all-important "cultural analysis" in Fleming's model and the most important part of "thinking like a curator" in all of your work with objects. You will also want to consider Fleming's final step, "Interpretation." This will get at the broadest, highest-level cultural themes as well as the object's contemporary relevance. Finally, you will want to make sure that you are checking the object for what might be missing or less obvious—issues about inclusion, omission, erasure, hidden history, or racism. This might inevitably lead to multiple interpretations.

6) List your sources, both to back up the validity of your analysis and for future reference.

EXAMPLES OF OBJECT STUDIES

Finding practical, real-world examples of object studies that curators might use as models can be elusive. Here are some of my favorites, gleaned from books, articles, and websites, and followed by a few of my own examples.

I begin with four scholarly articles in which the authors have analyzed categories of objects in such groundbreaking and substantive ways that I place them in a category of their own: Fleming's study of a seventeenth-century New England court cupboard, Kenneth L. Ames's analysis of Victorian hall furnishings, Alison J. Clarke's cultural analysis of Tupperware, and Rebecca K. Shrum's work on Mr. Coffee.[38] These are often singled out as exemplary examples in books on material culture studies. Unfortunately, they are quite lengthy—lengthier than most curators can attempt, given schedules and priorities.

A highly recommended resource for material culture interpretations is AASLH's "Exploring America's Historic Treasures" book series.[39] The intent of this series is to "bring to life topics and themes from American history through objects from museums and other history organizations." Each item chosen for inclusion in these books is carefully selected for diversity, relevance, and significance. Books that feature "greatest hits" from a museum's collections offer another approach to material culture interpretation.[40]

Other useful examples of object analysis and interpretation can be found in the many recent academic books on material culture study, such as the essay on coffee cups in *Object Studies: Introductions to Material Culture* and the chapter on smartphones in *What Objects Mean: An Introduction to Material Culture*.[41] Some of the best examples of object analysis come from books on general social and cultural history topics whose authors have a natural inclination toward interpreting objects in both rigorous and insightful ways. I include here the work of art historian and American Studies scholar Karal Ann Marling, whose book, *As Seen on TV: The Visual Culture of Everyday Life in the 1950s*, contains delightful studies of such objects as 1950s paint-by-number kits and *Betty Crocker's Picture Cookbook*.[42]

Two additional excellent examples of more recent object studies are described in the online source *The Inclusive Historian's Handbook*. In the essay "Material Culture," Rebecca Shrum recounts the uncovering of a story about a group of early-twentieth-century foil milk caps excavated by historical archaeologists in African American neighborhoods in Indianapolis.[43] After contacting community members, researchers learned that these were actually used as admission tokens when African Americans were allowed into the city's Whites-only Riverside Amusement Park one day each year. In her essay "Exhibitions," Gretchen Sullivan Sorin references the book *Mahogany: The Cost of Luxury of Early America*, which describes not only the conspicuous consumption involved in purchasing and using mahogany chairs at that time, but also the destruction of trees in the Caribbean, the slave trade, and the nature of dangerous occupations involved in this industry.[44]

This brings us to short, yet still substantive, examples. Beyond the concise interpretive summaries of digitized collections on museum websites (as mentioned earlier), excellent examples of brief material culture interpretations appear on the Smithsonian Institution's website feature entitled "Looking at Artifacts, Thinking about History."[45] Created for Advanced Placement US History teachers and students, this several-part essay looks at four universal characteristics of artifacts and describes a well-chosen example for each one. These include:

- Artifacts Connect People (example: eighteenth-century silver teapot).
- Artifacts Mean Many Things (example: 1937 Negro Leagues All-Star Game baseball).
- Artifacts Capture a Moment (example: Kodak Brownie camera used to photograph survivors of the *Titanic*).
- Artifacts Reflect Changes (example: 1875 typewriter).

This website feature also includes the longer analysis "What Barbie Dolls Have to Say about Postwar American Culture," written by child's play historian Miriam Forman-Brunell, and several additional examples of objects with interpretive descriptions.

Finally, the following includes three additional examples of object studies from The Henry Ford's collections.

1) 1950s Cleanser Dispenser[46]

This first example shows how the Six Practical Steps previously described can be put into practice. The Henry Ford was offered as a potential donation a hollow, cylindrical, pink plastic item, about five inches high and three inches across (see figure 2.1).

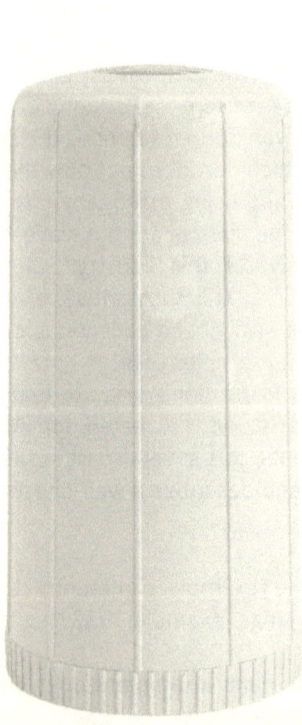

Figure 2.1 What started out as a mystery object was eventually identified as a 1950s Bab-O Cleanser Dispenser. From the collections of The Henry Ford.

The color and material dated it from around the mid-twentieth century. Upon its receipt, I picked up the object and turned it over. This revealed the first real clue—an inscription on the bottom that read, "This dispenser exclusively designed for Bab-O Cleanser." This implied that the item was intended to be used to cover cans of Bab-O Cleanser, presumably when the cleanser sat out on a shelf or sink in the home.

I perused online sources for additional clues, including company histories and advertisements for Bab-O Cleanser (primarily in Google Images, though I knew that these are often not dated). From the ads, I learned that Bab-O Cleanser was advertised as a cleaner for porcelain bathroom tubs and sinks, as well as for ceramic bathroom tile. Persuasive ads attempted to convince housewives that Bab-O transformed mere cleaning into "home beautifying," particularly in that room in the home in which the least beautiful functions took place. One ad showed a bathroom with a beautifully coordinated pink porcelain sink and bathtub. That explained the pink color of this cleanser dispenser!

Obtaining a reminiscence from the donor about the use of this dispenser cover placed everything into context. The item was purchased by the donor's mother about 1954, when the new home they moved into was accented with pink appliances and their bathroom had pink accents. The donor's mother was a meticulous housekeeper and preferred the look of this dispenser to the "dreary," "industrial" look of the cleanser packaging.

The cleanser dispenser speaks to many values and attitudes of middle-class consumerism during the mid-twentieth century: the increase of manufactured goods for the home; the ideal of convenience; the role of women; evolving standards of cleanliness, health, and hygiene; marketing strategies and the industrial design profession's emphasis on color and styling during this time; the use of chemical mixtures to create "miracle" products that were later found to be detrimental to the environment and even toxic for humans; and the negative environmental impact of mid-twentieth-century plastics.

2) Savannah Gray Brick, made between 1820 and 1850[47]

A clay brick. Plain and undistinguished in and of itself. But, with this object, the context is everything (see figure 2.2).

This brick, once called "Savannah Gray Brick," likely originated from the clay on Henry McAlpin's Hermitage Plantation located on the Savannah River near Savannah, Georgia. It would have been hand-formed by McAlpin's enslaved workers there. In 1850, 201 enslaved African Americans provided the skills and manual labor required to produce clay bricks on this industrial plantation, along with lumber and cast and wrought iron. Brick manufacturing yielded the largest profits for owner McAlpin—especially after a fire wiped out many of Savannah's wooden structures in 1820. These bricks can still be found today forming the walls of many historic Savannah homes and public buildings.

Making Sense of Objects

From the Collections of The Henry Ford (2019.113.2/THF177048)

Figure 2.2 This hand-shaped gray brick was made by enslaved workers on an industrial plantation near Savannah, Georgia. Brick was in high demand when a fire wiped out many of the wooden buildings in Savannah at the time. From the collections of The Henry Ford.

This clay brick was acquired to supplement the history of two brick structures brought to Greenfield Village in 1934 that had originally been located in an area of the Hermitage Plantation where enslaved workers lived. It helps to reinforce the specific history of that plantation as well as to expand upon a lesser-known aspect of the labor of enslaved African Americans on Southern plantations. This individual brick provides a visceral connection to the enslaved workers who labored day after day in the brick manufacturing operation at the Hermitage Plantation.

3) United Auto Workers Union Cap, made in the late 1930s[48]

This oilcloth cap was offered to The Henry Ford as a potential acquisition by the nephew of the man who had once worn it (see figure 2.3).

It is a striking document of one person's pride and feeling of empowerment during the early, heady days of union activity among Detroit auto workers. The cap is covered with thirty-six buttons related to the UAW (United Auto Workers). In fact, the cap itself was made for UAW Local 203, whose members belonged to the "Motor Products" division.

The earliest button on the cap is dated October 1937—only one year after the UAW separated from the CIO (Congress of Industrial Organizations). Headquartered in Detroit, the UAW was especially known for gaining high

Figure 2.3 This oilcloth United Auto Workers labor union cap from the 1930s is covered with buttons depicting several years of union membership. An interview with the donor—the original owner's nephew—revealed stories of his uncle's pride in union membership, his ongoing involvement, and his union activism. From the collections of The Henry Ford.

wages and pensions for its members. It rapidly found success by organizing sit-down strikes. The donor's uncle worked for both the Chrysler Corporation and Ford Motor Company during this time and would have witnessed (and perhaps even been part of) the union activism that occurred in and around Detroit. The donor relayed to us that his uncle proudly wore this cap to UAW meetings, adding buttons to the cap as he received them. Many buttons were added as he paid his monthly dues.

VISITORS AND OBJECTS

I had just completed the four kitchen settings from different eras for the museum's fiftieth-anniversary commemoration (as referenced at the beginning of this chapter). I wrote brief labels that described how these kitchens changed over time, from the one representing the eighteenth century to the one representing the 1930s. But I was flabbergasted when I overheard visitors, who were often gathered in front of the 1930s kitchen, excitedly talking about their own family experiences and memories in kitchens like this. Why didn't anyone read, or seem to care about, my labels?

More recently, I wrote an online article entitled "The Real Toys of *Toy Story*," highlighting the many different toys in The Henry Ford's collection that resembled those that had appeared in the Pixar Animation Studios movie

Toy Story.⁴⁹ I excitedly checked readers' comments when this was posted on Facebook. But, alas, I was again disappointed that people's comments were not about what I had written but about how these toys evoked personal memories of the toys people had when they were kids!

What Is Going On Here?

The fact of the matter is that most visitors engage with historical objects in museums in ways that have little to do with material culture studies and curators' methodologies for analyzing and interpreting objects.⁵⁰ Instead, they connect with objects primarily to seek personal meaning. At least in their initial encounters, they tend to draw upon a bank of prior knowledge, experience, and memory. This response is so automatic and so commanding that many visitors will shy away from stories that conflict with their own identity and understanding of the world.⁵¹

Some visitors' responses to objects do go beyond personal meaning, especially those that elicit strong emotional responses. Some examples of this include: the so-called "witnessing object," which was there at a pivotal moment in history and serves as a tangible link to that history, enabling people to feel connected to a specific moment or event; the numinous object, so emotionally transformative that it causes in some people a transcendent experience—connecting them to something higher, more reverential, and more sacred than they find in their ordinary everyday lives; and objects that are so powerful they can contribute to enhancing the "whole self"—improving physical and emotional well-being; inspiring conscientious civic engagement; and encouraging social bonding, play, creativity, and spiritual reflection.⁵²

Objects and their interpretive messages can also have a negative impact on visitors. Those that represent the elite, White privilege, colonizing, or male dominance, may—consciously or unconsciously—send the message to certain visitors that they are not welcome.⁵³ Studies have also shown that many visitors tend to favor stories of triumph over stories of pain and failure.⁵⁴ In addition, a proportion of visitors do not like difficult or controversial history, which can trigger defense mechanisms, shock, or disturbance from the new knowledge and can prompt resistance to learning.⁵⁵

How can curators, in their work with objects, encourage visitors to embrace historical and cultural contexts along with personal ones? Here are some ideas:

- Make sure that visitors feel welcome and comfortable in their encounters with objects. This might include use of language, an accessible writing style, and/or an invitational tone.
- Be open to the diverse interpretations that individuals bring.⁵⁶

- Encourage visitors to discover something new about their own personal understandings of the objects.[57]
- Actively encourage people to bring their own stories, emotions, connections, and perspectives.[58]
- Engage visitors by appealing to their emotions—evoking awe and wonder, inspiring a call to action, contributing to a feeling of uplift and rejuvenation.[59]
- Consider the power of "social objects" to attract visitors. According to participatory design specialist Nina Simon, these spark conversation because they are active (in motion, draw attention), provocative (surprising), or relational (an invitation to be interactive, which brings people together).[60]
- Leave things unsaid. Let some objects remain open for more interpretation and investigation.[61]

This chapter has presented definitions, historical foundations, methodologies, practical examples, and clues to visitor engagement with objects. These topics provide a grounding for how curators will work with objects in relation to collecting, research, and interpretation—topics to be discussed in subsequent chapters.

REFLECTIVE PRACTICE

Chances are that you will be spending most of your time working with real-life objects rather than wanting to engage in additional activities. So, the activities I describe here are short, simple, and tried-and-true—but all in some way deepen your ability to "think like a curator" as you make sense of objects.

1) Object Mind Map

One way to expand your thinking about the multiple interpretations of an object is to create a mind map. On paper (or there are online versions), start at the center of the paper (or the top of the screen) with the name of the object, then surround it with (or list and group) all the related ideas and topics that come to mind. Keep adding ideas and topics—to both the initial object and to the ideas and topics that have spun off it—until you run out of ideas or your page is filled up. You will be amazed at how many ideas you have come up with.

2) The Power of a Personal Artifact

A good way to understand how important people are to the context of an object is to pick an object of your own that has personal meaning to you. Follow steps one, two, four, and five of the "Six Practical Steps" mentioned earlier in this chapter, from physical handling and description to cultural analysis. Your personal reminiscence about it should reinforce to you why the people stories are so important to understanding the context of objects!

3) Interpretive Statements for Objects

If you have never done these, it's easy to start practicing. Think of these as you would a picture caption in a book. What is the thing? Why is it significant? Write these down in a narrative form, then hone your draft to about sixty words. This practice will help you both develop interpretive statements for objects in catalog records and write object ID labels for exhibitions.

4) Further Reading and Reflection

There is new scholarship on material culture coming out all the time. Take time to read the old classics as well as the newer material mentioned in the citations and discuss and/or reflect upon how these can help you advance your own skills and those of others in your Community of Practice.

3

Shaping and Developing Collections

The responsibility of shaping and developing collections is perhaps the most important core competency of history museum curators. It can be wonderfully satisfying. Working with friendly, cooperative donors. Being offered a collection that neatly fits your existing Collections Plan or expands the Collections Plan in an unexpected way. Tracking down an object that enhances an underrepresented story. Finding the exact documentation you need to provide context for a donation that's been offered.

Shaping and developing collections can also be hard. Really hard. Torturously hard. Anonymous donations that arrive on your doorstep. Difficult donors. Fruitlessly searching for items for your Collections Plan. Spending countless hours piecing together all the details you need to justify a proposed acquisition. And did you ever imagine that deaccessioning objects would be so difficult? How can you really know what's "out of scope" or "redundant"? What if something is in marginal condition but it's one of a kind, or you unwittingly deaccession an object that turns out to be more significant than you had initially thought? It's enough to make you lose sleep at night.

But that's not all. There's more pressure than ever to actively reduce some collections and add others. Get rid of all that stuff in storage that doesn't fit your mission statement. Work on a responsible plan for repatriation of Indigenous material in your collection. Figure out a faster, more efficient deaccessioning process. Develop a strategy to collect more inclusively. And if an important local or national event occurs, be ready to drop everything to run out and collect significant things related to it. Indeed, as more than one writer has noted, collections can be both a blessing and a curse.[1]

WHAT DO CURATORS BRING TO COLLECTIONS WORK?

I considered at length what to include in this chapter and how to organize it. I initially assumed I would start with fundamentals—such as how to accession, how to catalog, how to deaccession, and so on. But, as I perused a huge stack of published material on these things, I realized—there's a huge stack of published material on these things! What could I contribute here that is different? What topics truly embody the essence of curatorial work? Which are most closely aligned with the core competencies of curators? Where is "thinking like a curator" most visible, valuable, and necessary in collections work? CurCom's "Curator Core Competencies" document (described in chapter 1) establishes a firm foundation for addressing this question by calling out two of curators' primary responsibilities: Collecting ("seeking objects to fill gaps in the collection that fit the needs of the institution and align with the mission") and Collections Development ("assuring a well-balanced collection through the development of a strategic collection plan").[2]

So where to begin? After an initial introduction to the topic of collections, I decided to start with a call to action. Usually—at least in exhibitions—the call to action comes at the end. But the topics covered here seem too important to be lightly skimmed over after reading a lengthy chapter. Next, I discuss what I believe to be curators' most crucial work with collections and, in fact, their most unique contribution—collections planning. I cover this in depth—the why, the what, the how. I do this not only because it is hard to track down good sources for this information, but also because I want to underscore the fact that, while collections planning is easy to bypass when one becomes consumed with daily tasks, it is *foundational* to everything else. Some examples of recent collecting initiatives are included at the end of this section.

Finally, I get around to collections fundamentals, especially those related to the curator core competency of collecting. I warn readers, however, that my descriptions of most tasks are brief. You can find everything you need about collections policies and procedures in other books and get answers to your questions in relevant workshops, webinars, and conference sessions. What I highlight here are the ways in which curators bring their unique skills and expertise to these tasks. The chapter concludes with a checklist of best practices for curators working with collections.

COLLECTIONS: ESSENTIAL, ETHICAL, MISSION-ALIGNED

For most history museums, collections are the foundation of everything that takes place there. Collections communicate a museum's character. They define its purpose. They can even be the predominant reason for a museum's existence.[3]

In addition to being essential, the museum's collections are also held in public trust, so their management entails legal responsibilities and ethical obligations. These relate to ownership as well as to how objects are used, cared for, obtained, kept, documented, accessed, and responsibly disposed of.[4] The standards, ethics, and best practices that have been established for the field are meant to ensure that a museum's collections will be treated ethically and responsibly and will be maintained for the public good.[5]

Curators are at the heart of this work, considered the authorities for identifying, documenting, authenticating, and determining the significance of existing and new collections. Because they interact both physically and intellectually with the collections, curators must act with uncompromising integrity and ethical standards.

All this responsibility might seem daunting. And it *is* daunting, even to an experienced curator. Nothing is black and white, and each aspect of this work needs to be thoughtful and rigorous. But don't fear. Your institutional mission statement can guide you. Just as your mission statement serves as the guidepost for all institutional planning, development, and positioning, it should provide the purpose and direction for assessing current collections as well as planning and building new collections.

Unfortunately, not all mission statements work this way. Those that incorporate the phrase "collect, preserve, and interpret" are too vague, too broad, and too general to be effective for developing and shaping collections (as well as not being effective for many other aspects of strategic planning and positioning). Instead, your mission statement should be written in such a way that it establishes the distinctiveness and importance of what your institution does—the essence of why it exists and how it makes a difference in society. This is the kind of mission statement that will greatly facilitate the assessment of past, present, and future collecting.[6]

A CALL TO ACTION: COLLECTIONS AT A TIPPING POINT

For a chapter focusing on curators' work with collections, it seems appropriate to begin with two current hot topics that are significantly impacting curators' work. The first is facing the reality that many history museums are becoming overwhelmed by continually adding to existing collections, increasingly without the means to adequately care for them. The second is that the collections of many history museums do not adequately reflect "the full record of the nation's past"—specifically, they do not possess items related to marginalized groups or groups whose history has been erased from the written record.[7] To sum up, many history museums have too much of what they don't need and too little of what they do need! This has been true for quite a while. But these issues have reached a tipping point, with COVID-19 pandemic-related financial strains added to enhanced DEAI (Diversity, Equity, Accessibility, and Inclusion) initiatives that emerged from a greater reckoning by society about systemic racism and White supremacy. After years of sticking with the status quo—of doing "what we've always done"—these issues have reached crisis levels and need the immediate attention of curators and others who work with collections. As Rainey Tisdale writes in her article "Do History Museums Still Need Objects?":

Shaping and Developing Collections   43

The world is rapidly changing, and so is museums' role in it—that's a blessing and a curse. But objects are worth the extra effort, as centerpieces for dialogue and as loci of meaning; as delights and surprises, as enigmas, as touchstones, as treasures. Yes, history museums need them. We also need passionate and imaginative professionals who will make tough but inspired choices about the collections in their care.[8]

Too Much Stuff

As called out in a string of articles dating from 2008 and leading to a "Manifesto" in the book *Active Collections*, modifications to how and what museums collect have lagged behind other areas of museum practice.[9] Traditionally, museum mission statements have been fundamentally based upon the conviction that the museums will "collect, preserve, and interpret" the museum's collections "in perpetuity." Much time has been spent establishing collections policies and procedures, developing complex legal and ethical frameworks for accessioning and deaccessioning, and setting professional standards for collections records, environments, and security with this same assumption—that the collected objects will stay in the museum's collections "in perpetuity."

Over time, it has become a great deal easier for most museums to add to their collections than to trim, refine, or reduce what they already have. With little or no plan in place, it is also easy to accept what has fallen in their laps, to take things rather than offend donors, to accept new items that "arrive on the doorstep" without ensuring proper documentation. Often, collections staff are not sure how numerous items in their collections even got there.

Meanwhile, professional standards and practices related to collections have focused on treating every object "as if it were a Rembrandt"—all given the same level of attention despite the high cost of preservation, management, and access. As a result, many museums are holding on to and stewarding collections that are poorly maintained, inadequately cataloged, and kept in overcrowded storage areas that are neither climate-controlled nor secure—never seeing the light of day. Moreover, museums are often dealing with legacy collections—from the museum's founder or based upon the collecting whims of past directors or curators—that are now redundant, in poor condition, out of scope, or lacking relevance. These are not only taking up valuable storage space but also are accompanied by a reluctance to do anything about them because of the rationale that "we promised to care for them forever!"[10] Furthermore, with a mission to preserve objects in perpetuity, museums grapple with repatriation and other ethical dilemmas posed by objects in their collections.

In their introduction to the book *Active Collections*, authors Trevor Jones, Rainey Tisdale, and Elizabeth Wood strongly recommend that museums take a good hard look at the collections they currently possess, considering the high costs of cataloging, storage, and care.[11] They warn readers that these issues will get only more oppressive. Deaccessioning is particularly called out as a major barrier to developing leaner, more sustainable collections.

What can be done? In "A Manifesto for Active History Museum Collections," Jones and Tisdale offer several suggestions for ways in which museums can deal with these issues and, as a result, "better serve the public good."[12] These include:

- A tiered system of collections objects to be able to spend time, effort, and funding on the most compelling and mission-aligned collections. A system of this type acknowledges that not every object is precious and irreplaceable (more on this later).
- Deaccession policies and procedures that are easier, including streamlining the basic guidelines for mass deaccessioning—especially for items that don't support the mission.
- Being selective about acquisitions, with the help of a Collections (or Acquisitions) Committee and a Collections Plan (more on these later).
- Changing the conversation from preserving objects to using them—doing "something imaginative, experimental, or amazing" with the collections that ensure that they will have a viable life beyond the hidden storeroom, including visible or open storage.
- Considering the idea of sharing collections across different institutions, especially within a local area or region.
- Using online digital surrogates for user tagging, commenting, and curation.[13]

Not Enough of the "Right" Stuff

The second current hot topic impacting curators' work with collections is the imperative to build collections that are more diverse and inclusive, more meaningful and relevant to all visitors, and more responsive to community needs. As referenced in Tisdale's article "Do Museums Still Need Objects?" Gretchen Sullivan Sorin related that, back in 2000, when she guest-curated the exhibition "Bridges and Boundaries: African Americans and Jewish Americans" for The Jewish Museum in New York City, the museum mostly borrowed materials from private collections, as it was hard to find anything relevant in its own collections.[14] Ten years later, Tisdale reported that the history museum field had not made much progress in addressing the problem Sorin described, even though diversity in the United States had continued to increase. Certainly, curators and other staff could think about how to creatively use objects (or the lack of them), but they were still not enough to cover important topics or connect to current audiences. Even today, efforts to make museum collections more diverse and inclusive have been slow and often problematic, fraught with racial, cultural, or individuals' sensitivities. In his *History News* article, "Museum Collecting in the Age of Black Lives Matter," Charles E. Bethea, Andrew W.

Mellon director of Collections and Curatorial Affairs at the Chicago History Museum, stated that, "When it comes to what objects many mainstream museums choose to collect, exhibit, or discuss in programs, a large portion of society and their stories are unfortunately far too often left out of the conversation."[15]

But progress *is* being made, especially with the increasing embrace of community-related, contemporary, and rapid response collecting. More museums are simply accepting the fact that they should play an active role in a society fraught with issues of social justice, including race and gender inequality. Bethea remarked that, while museum decolonization had been a topic of discussion for many years, it reached a fever pitch during the COVID-19 pandemic, when so many people's consciousness was raised about systemic racism and White supremacy.[16] Numerous museums have followed up with mandates to implement change, including revising collecting agendas "not as acts of tokenism but legitimate efforts in moving in a new direction of honest inclusion with proper meaningful support."[17] (See examples in this chapter's sections on Community-Based Collecting and Contemporary and Rapid Response Collecting.)

COLLECTIONS PLANNING

Of all curators' work with collections, I would argue that collections planning is most crucial. It directly addresses a museum's public service mandate, encouraging "critical thinking about the scope, purpose, and future of our collections and collecting goals to ensure that what we do with our collections has value to our mission and the communities we serve."[18]

Collections planning allows curators to measure the relative strengths and weaknesses of the collection, to continually question and clarify the value of existing and needed collections. It prevents individualized, idiosyncratic, and haphazard collecting. By articulating a shared vision and strategic objectives, it also builds institutional capacity—ultimately maximizing resources and facilitating collections management and care.[19]

With all these benefits, the authors of the *AAM Guide to Collections Planning* express surprise that collections planning is among the rarest of museum activities because it "is surely one of the most critically needed."[20] In fact, museum accreditation reviewers have identified recurring problems due to the lack of collections planning, resulting in collections that are both unrelated to mission and poorly cared for, and leading to a general inability of museums to succeed.[21]

A Collections Management Policy

The foundation of collections work and collections planning is the creation of a Collections Management Policy (or Collections Policy). This is an organization's document (or series of documents) that "outlines the internal policies and procedures used to govern the development and care of the organization's collections."[22] It is approved by the organization's governing authority. The Collections Management Policy:

- Establishes control and accountability over the collections.
- Outlines the general scope of the museum's collections and the activities related to it.
- Is designed to ensure proper development, care, preservation, and use of collections while minimizing potential risks (e.g., controversial or unexpected eventualities like deaccessioning issues or natural disasters).
- Serves as a formal delegation of responsibilities, defining areas of responsibility and setting forth guidelines for those charged with making certain decisions.[23]

The Collections Plan

With a Collections Management Policy in place, a more in-depth Collections Plan can now be created. There is no one standard, but here are some strategies and tips for creating one.

A Collections Plan is a plan guiding the content of the collections. It leads the staff in a coordinated and uniform direction over a period of years to refine and expand the value of the collections in a predetermined way. It provides the context for making decisions about the future of the collections—defining, limiting, expanding, and clarifying what the museum collects within the context of its overall mission and goals. According to the *AAM Guide to Collections Planning*, some reasons for planning might include:

- Identifying the important pieces missing from the collection, so the museum can pursue them.
- Making decisions about how the museum can reduce the size of the collections, so that it can live within its means.
- Finding unifying themes to ensure that collecting is coordinated across departments and supports the museums' interpretive goals.
- Preparing a compelling case statement to leverage funding for acquisitions.[24]

The most critical part of the Collections Plan is its intellectual framework, which is, not surprisingly, guided by the institutional mission statement. This framework provides the compelling vision for why the museum collects, what collections it currently possesses and what it needs to collect, why that is so important, and why the museum is uniquely suited to fulfill this role. The authors of the *AAM Guide to Collections Planning* recommend starting with this and letting the rest of the plan flow from there.[25]

Contents for a "Model Collections Plan" include (see textbox 3.1 for a summarized version of this):

TEXTBOX 3.1: CONTENTS FOR A "MODEL COLLECTIONS PLAN"

- Executive Summary
- Preamble
- Setting the Stage
- Relationship of Plan to Other Policy and Planning Documents
- Intellectual Framework
- Analysis of Existing Collections
- Strength and Weaknesses
- Shaping the Ideal Collection
- Implementation Strategy
- Evaluation
- Revision and Renewal of Plan

Source: James B. Gardner and Elizabeth E. Merritt, *The AAM Guide to Collections Planning*, AAM Professional Education Series (Washington, DC: American Association of Museums, 2004).

- Executive Summary—both encapsulates the plan for those who may never read the whole plan and serves as a useful overview and orientation for readers who will study the whole document.
- Preamble
  - Purpose of the plan—establishes why you are doing this planning and the purpose of the resulting plan.
  - Audience for this document.
  - Authorship—how the plan was developed, who participated, and who wrote it.
- Setting the Stage
  - Museum's mission and vision statement.
  - Overview of relevant points in current strategic plan.
- Relationship of Collections Plan to other museum policy and planning documents.
- Intellectual Framework—vision for the collections; collecting philosophy for the plan reflecting the museum's unique lens; museum audiences and how their needs will be served by the collection.
- Analysis of Existing Collections
  - Description/scope.
  - History of the collections.

- Strength and weaknesses—gap analysis, comparing the real to the ideal collection.
  - Strengths might be gauged, for example, by: significance, quality (of the objects and their associated documentation), quantity, completeness, condition, and existence of ancillary collections (manuscripts, photographs, etc.).
  - Weaknesses might include: gaps (missing material), lack of fit with the museum's intellectual framework and mission, insufficient quality or significance, inappropriate provenance, or duplication and redundancy.
  - For each collections category, the plan should outline what the museum intends to do, which can include: acquiring additional material, deaccessioning existing material, or keeping the collection as it is.
  - Identification of "complementary collections" held in other museums and organizations.
- Shaping the Ideal Collection
  - Priorities for acquiring additional material, deaccessioning existing material, and/or keeping the collection as it is.
  - Strategies for above.
  - Criteria for above.
- Implementation Strategy—taking into account existing/needed resources, priorities and strategies that reinforce the intellectual framework.
  - Action steps—specifying how the museum will accomplish these goals.
  - Assignment of responsibilities for these action steps.
  - Identification of existing and needed resources (time, space, money, and how the museum will acquire them).
  - A timeline for implementation.
- Evaluation
  - How the museum will measure whether the plan is succeeding.
  - Who will perform this measurement and on what schedule.
  - How the museum will use the results of the evaluation.
- Revision and Renewal of the Plan
  - Plan for when and how often the evaluation data will be reviewed and by whom.[26]

As institutional priorities change, Collections Plans can and should be updated periodically. They should never be considered finished or "cast in stone."

Creating a Collections Plan may seem like it is taking time away from your "regular" work. It should not be seen as a burden but "embraced as an important opportunity to refocus the museum and re-engage the staff, to move collecting from routine to energized."[27] In the end, it can be not only wonderfully satisfying but will also serve you well time and time again. When you have one in place, you will wonder how you ever did without it.

Unfortunately, in creating a Collections Plan, you might also run into resistance—from curators who are used to "doing their own thing," from collections staff who prefer the status quo, or from members of senior management who think this is just an intellectual exercise and has limited practical use.[28] You will need the support of all these people to move forward. So, help them understand that, in fact, a Collections Plan is a benefit rather than a hindrance.

To meet certain predetermined needs (exhibitions, programs, DEAI initiatives, targeted community collecting, etc.), specific topics, themes, time periods, or object types might also be pulled out of the larger plan to create smaller, more focused "Collecting Initiatives." These tend to be action-oriented and timebound.

Community-Based Collecting

As mentioned in the previous section, A Call to Action: Collections at a Tipping Point, curators are being increasingly pressured to build collections that are more diverse and inclusive, more meaningful and relevant to all visitors, and more responsive to community needs. This invariably involves working directly with the keepers of the stories and objects—that is, specific individuals, families, and community groups. The "sobering realization" is that collecting this way can be slow and difficult, involving time and many steps to build trust, raise awareness, and create sustainable relationships in the community as well as to gain institutional buy-in.[29] It involves flexibility, patience, transparency, empathy, and a willingness to share authority.[30]

The following describe real-life examples of community-based collecting initiatives that have been developed to address missing stories and underrepresented groups. They have also facilitated the establishment of ongoing and sustainable community relationships. These examples will hopefully provide direction for—or at least inspiration to—curators just getting started with this type of work.

1) The authors of the book *Introduction to Public History* recount a multiyear community collecting initiative that took place for the exhibition "Latinos in Baseball: In the Barrios and the Big Leagues."[31] This exhibition was co-sponsored by the Latino Initiatives Pool and the National Museum of American History. First, the planners looked for similar collecting initiatives and projects. They found that California State University, Los Angeles, had previously reached out to its local community for an earlier exhibition entitled "Mexican-American Baseball in Los Angeles: From the Barrios to the Big Leagues." To develop that exhibition, planners had asked people to share memories, pictures, baseballs, uniforms, and other memorabilia

related to the rich history of Latinos in baseball in Los Angeles. As part of this project, the university had hosted an event in their library, inviting the public to attend and asking if people had anything to donate. They also collected oral histories. The planners for "Latinos in Baseball" next searched for other similar projects and public events, reunions of ballplayers and their fans, and publications. They invited the public to donate items at community collecting events and offered to digitize photographs if families wanted to keep them. They found that, through this process, family and community members felt that the project both honored their communities and gave them opportunities to see how their own experiences were part of a larger historical narrative.

2) Staff members at the Washington County Museum in Oregon increasingly became aware that the museum's collections and stories were largely White-dominated and that local communities of color mistrusted the place.[32] In January 2020, they decided to change their name to Five Oaks Museum (connected to a nearby historic site of trees where Indigenous Kalapuya had once gathered) to begin to repair harm and rebuild trust. They also realized that the only way to move forward in establishing a relationship with the community was to give community members the power to tell their own stories. They invited guest curators from the community to help identify glaring gaps in the collections. As a result, the collection has been revised and now represents multilayered stories.

3) A dramatic shift in the collecting approach at Chicago History Museum (CHM) occurred in 2019, when a group of twenty-five high school students from the Instituto Justice and Leadership Academy (a predominantly Latinx school located ten miles from CHM) started a campaign to raise awareness of the fact that there was little to no meaningful representation of Chicago Latinx history on display (33 percent of the current population in Chicago is Latinx). This set in motion an ongoing collaborative project that is intended to reach beyond the more common one-off temporary community exhibitions. To facilitate this initiative, CHM contracted with independent curator Elena Gonzales, known for her pioneering work with social justice and anti-racist stories and collecting. As a result, "Aquí en Chicago" is an upcoming exhibition on Latino/a/x resistance to White supremacy and colonialism in Chicago over the last hundred-plus years. It is a community-driven initiative, only one part of the museum's effort to redress a long history of omitting Chicago's marginalized communities from its central narrative.[33]

4) Many museums are currently collecting LGBTQ+ materials. Among these are the collections that have been (and are continuing to be) amassed at History Colorado by Aaron Marcus, Gill Foundation associate curator of LGBTQ+ history (see figure 3.1).

Figure 3.1 The entrance to the "Rainbows and Revolutions" exhibition at History Colorado. Photo courtesy of Debra A. Reid.

    Marcus spent three years collecting materials for the exhibition "Rainbows and Revolutions," which opened June 2022 as History Colorado's first LGBTQ+-themed exhibition.[34] With each artifact, Marcus collected the personal stories of the people connected with it. Topics, which cover both past and present, explore secret societies, community leaders, political milestones, art, and the continued fight for equality. The purpose of the collection and the resulting exhibition, according to Marcus, is not only to encourage people in the LGBTQ+ community to see themselves and know their history, but also to allow allies to see the people behind this community. His intent for the future is to create a "much more inclusive archive."

5) The Brooklyn Children's Museum (BCM), recognizing that its collections did not fully represent the Central Brooklyn community, created a collaboration between BCM's teen program and its collections department.[35] A cohort of ten to fifteen teens, trained to go into the community, engage with local residents using a framework they created to identify objects to add to BCM's collection. Past themes in this collecting initiative have included immigration, criminal justice, gender identification, and gentrification. Objects they source and the interpretation they generate will become integrated into the museum's collections and will remain there in perpetuity.

6) Many museums are also currently working toward greater inclusion and balance in their collections by posting on their websites special collecting initiatives related to local minoritized communities and to individuals who self-identify as part of marginalized groups.[36]

Contemporary and Rapid Response Collecting

A significant number of history museums have long hesitated to collect contemporary materials, arguing that it is too difficult to know what will be significant in the future. The constraints of small budgets and the challenges of storage, preservation, conservation, and access have often reinforced this reluctance. But arguments for recent and contemporary collecting have become increasingly convincing. More museums are realizing that they might miss out on significant events, technologies, and examples of social transformation by not collecting in this manner. The ephemeral nature of today's material culture also means that, if not acquired now, it might disappear completely and not be possible to find later (see figure 3.2).

Figure 3.2 In early June 2020, the non-profit letterpress organization, Signal-Return, responded to the civil unrest that followed the death of George Floyd by producing free protest posters for the Detroit community. Several of the posters captured in these images became part of an acquisition made at the time by the curator of information technology at The Henry Ford (#2020.73.0). From the collections of The Henry Ford.

Shaping and Developing Collections

Moreover, this approach makes it easier to collect the stories of the people from whom these items came. As a result of debates and discussions, more museums have developed clear and purposeful policies aimed at ensuring the acquisition of significant and representative contemporary objects while simultaneously being conscious not to overextend themselves or their resources.

So-called "rapid response" collecting—that is, capturing and documenting aspects of an event as it rapidly unfolds and/or in the days or weeks that follow—is proactive and often happens quickly, with many spur-of-the-moment decisions.[37] However, it needs to be strategically aligned with institutional priorities and collecting plans. The authors of the *History News* article "Grappling with Unfolding Events" recommend, if possible, planning in advance to get buy-in; defining your scope as it relates to mission; and understanding what the institution's extent of responsibility to the community is related to the event.[38]

The Victoria and Albert Museum in London, England, is often considered the first museum to proactively collect materials in this way. In 2014, it opened its "Rapid Response" gallery, containing "objects collected in response to major moments in history that touch the world of design and manufacturing."[39] Rapid response collecting gained considerable momentum during and throughout the COVID-19 pandemic. Hundreds of collecting projects emerged around the country, as it seemed as if virtually every museum was collecting stories and objects from their local communities related to the pandemic. As a result, the previous reluctance to collect current materials has lessened, as many more museums are beginning to understand the advantages of collecting recent materials and materials related to unfolding events.

Here are some additional examples of museum collecting initiatives related to contemporary and rapid response collecting:

1) A well-documented example of rapid response collecting was the initiative by the Orange County Regional History Center (in Orlando, Florida) to document and collect materials from the terrorist murders at the Pulse Nightclub (a popular gay nightclub) on June 12, 2016—the country's deadliest mass shooting to that date.[40] Facing a storm of controversy about pursuing this initiative (including high public emotion, local politics, media scrutiny, and already full exhibition schedules), the staff determinedly moved forward and drafted a plan called the "One Orlando Collecting Initiative" to preserve items, news articles, digital images, and oral histories. Near the beginning of the project, staff compared notes with other museums that had worked with memorial items left after episodes of violence to see if they were on the right track. They then sent out press releases and posted bilingual signs (Spanish and English) to alert people to the project. They collected (and continued to collect in subsequent weeks) thousands of relevant items, then evaluated and stored them. According to Emilie S. Arnold, author of the article "The Wound is Fresh: Exhibiting

Orlando's LGBTQ History in the Shadow of the Pulse Nightclub Massacre," this project proved that it is possible for a museum to serve a role in both a community's grieving and its healing.[41]

2) In the aftermath of the terrorist attacks on September 11, 2001, The New York Historical Society launched a "History Responds" collecting initiative.[42] They have since sent out "history brigades" to document and collect materials related to major unfolding events, such as the Black Lives Matter and Occupy Wall Street protests, the 2017 Women's March, the 2018 March for Our Lives, and the 2019 Climate Strike.

3) Before the museum was even open to the public, the National Museum of African American History and Culture sent curators to Ferguson, Missouri, after the 2014 killing of Michael Brown and the ensuing protests.[43] Missouri Historical Society responded to this unfolding event by collecting relevant materials as well.[44]

4) Especially since 2020, an increasing number of other museums have undertaken rapid response collecting projects related to social and racial justice protests and activism in their communities. For example, the Museum of the City of New York has collected materials relating to an initiative called "Activist New York." The National Museum of American History also collects materials related to protest and activism in its Center for Restorative History.[45]

COLLECTIONS FUNDAMENTALS AND THE CURATOR'S ROLE

As mentioned in chapter 1, some curators carry out the fundamental tasks of collections management, care, and preservation themselves. Others might supervise staff who do this work. For becoming proficient in each of these tasks, there is a plethora of books and articles to which to refer. What I will focus upon here are the uniquely curatorial aspects of this work, which include: identifying, researching, and authenticating objects; helping to create object names and keyword search terms for cataloging purposes; determining an object's significance based upon its value to the museum; and communicating with collectors, donors, and dealers. For deeper, more detailed information on any of the collections fundamentals described here, please refer to the citations at the end of this book.[46]

Acquisitions

An acquisition is "something obtained by a museum through gifts, purchases, bequests, exchanges, transfers, and field collecting."[47] Items can come from private sources, dealers, or auctions. The acquisition process involves a legal transfer of ownership. Curators are core to many aspects of the acquisition process.

First, curators are generally the point people who communicate with the person (or people) offering the item (or items). Donors and collectors can perform great services for museums. They might preserve objects of immense historical importance. They tend to be quite knowledgeable about the items in their possession—whether they are personal or family items or whether they have collected the items based upon criteria of their own.

Working with donors can range from wonderful to a little nightmarish. Often, collectors' criteria are different from a museum's (e.g., one-of-a-kind, idiosyncratic attributes). When you look at items in their possession, you are likely to be in their private space. As such, you often become—willingly or not—a "captive audience" to their lives and their stories. In addition, while your assessment of these items is routine—part of "all in a day's work"—these same things are special, sacred, and full of memories and emotion to those offering them.

Donors also might disagree with restrictions and conditions set forth by the museum in the legal transfer of ownership. They might counter with restrictions and conditions of their own. Don't be surprised if they change their minds about these during the negotiations. This might occur as they, for example, learn more about their item's value or significance or hesitate about giving the item to the museum. This can be excruciatingly frustrating, but worth the effort if the object or objects are of great value to the museum and align with your collections planning. Curators are often involved in the discussions that take place during these negotiations.

Like collectors, dealers can also be helpful, particularly in determining authenticity and provenance. But keep in mind that they are in the business to make money. Unsolicited donations—that is, items dropped off or mailed to the museum with little or no documentation—can also become a significant problem. It is important to have policies in place on what to do when this happens, and curators are often involved in these discussions as well.[48]

Next, curators determine whether an object is worthy of adding to the collection and create a justification for this that they will ideally present to a formalized internal group who reviews the acquisition. This involves identifying and authenticating the object, determining the object's historical significance, and judging its uniqueness and value to the institution and its connection to existing Collections Plans. (See the section Six Practical Steps in chapter 2 for more tips and details.) Curators will also want to work with other collections staff to confirm title and ownership of the object as well as appropriate resources (storage space, staff time for processing and managing, conservation needs, overhead, insurance) to care for the object in the long term. Proper gift or purchase documentation is of the utmost importance.

When all of this is confirmed, the curator ideally completes a standardized "proposed acquisition" template that documents the curator's research and rationale for acquiring the object. This should include the following categories (see textbox 3.2 for a summary of this list):[49]

TEXTBOX 3.2: PROPOSED ACQUISITION TEMPLATE

- Basic acquisition information
- Name and contact of donor(s)
- Object description
- Maker and user stories
- Personal reminiscences
- Significance
- Justification

- Basic acquisition information—including whether the item is a gift or purchase, its purchase price, and the date it was received.
- Name and contact information of the person or people offering the object.
- Object description—object name, maker, maker location, made date, and tier or rank if you have this system in place (see section on Tiering/Ranking Collections).
- Maker and user stories—brief statements on the background and history of known makers and/or users, if possible.
- Personal reminiscence(s)—Ranging from one sentence to an extended oral history or written reminiscence, this can provide crucial background and context to the object(s). It also personalizes the object. (See chapter 2, Examples of Object Studies: 1950s Cleanser Dispenser, for an example of this.)
- Significance—What is the historical and cultural significance of the object? What is its relevance today?
- Justification—Why should this item be added to the collection? What else in the collection is like it? How does it relate to existing Collections Plans?

In addition, documentation should be provided on condition, special conservation or storage needs, and any restrictions set forth by the donor. As mentioned before, the curator should present their proposed acquisitions to a formalized group—a Collections (or Acquisitions) Committee—composed of designated museum staff members who review, approve, or deny acquisitions. The institution's governing authority gives the final approval on all proposed acquisitions. After donor agreements are signed, the legal transfer of ownership to the museum can take place.

Museum ethics play a major role in museum acquisitions. Curators, who interact both physically and intellectually with the collections, must recognize, agree with, and abide by strict ethical standards. These include standards about personal collecting—that is, not collecting what the museum employing them collects. Museums also have an ethical obligation to assure that collections have accurate and timely documentation as well as proper care, storage, and access.

Cataloging

When I started my museum career in the late 1970s, catalog records were printed on cardboard index cards and cross-referenced in file drawers under several different categories, such as object name and accession number. Learning that there might not be a photograph of every object in these catalog records, we became adept at writing out physical descriptions of the objects. The goal was to describe each object in such a way that readers of the catalog card could picture it in their mind's eye.

The first time I worked with a full-fledged collections database was when I set up my own in the 1980s, with a Macintosh home computer, working on the museum publication *Leisure and Entertainment in America*. For this publication, I had to peruse several different three-dimensional, paper, and archival collections at The Henry Ford, and I wanted to perform searches in such a way that a wide range of items could be grouped together according to different leisure- and entertainment-related topics.

I don't want to belabor my experiences from the Dark Ages. I mention these because they gave me valuable lessons and practice in aspects of object cataloging that have stuck with me to this day. First, I learned how important words are—words for naming objects, describing attributes of objects, relating to the objects' context. Second, I learned how important accuracy and consistency are. I might make one typo and a search would not find that object. I might call two similar objects by slightly different names and, again, a search would not find one or the other object. I had to go back and refine keywords many times, for more accurate and nuanced searches. In the course of this work, I fell in love with the whole logic of databases. You only had to input the basic information once and it would result in multiple outputs. This is still the logic behind collections management systems (as are also, unfortunately, the pitfalls related to the lack of consistency in data—leading to the dreaded "garbage in–garbage out" syndrome). When it works, it's like magic, and I have never taken that "magic" for granted.

Cataloging involves classifying an object according to certain pre-established criteria.[50] Catalog records consist of several "fields," or discreet categories of information that answer the questions of what the object is, who made it, where it was made, when it was made, and usually something about its context (increasingly these days, through keywords). Measurements and materials are often part of a catalog record as well. Ideally, a catalog record is accompanied by a visual image or images as well as the object's location.

Museums (and curators) inevitably have to deal with cataloging both current acquisitions and what's often referred to as the "uncatalogued backlog."[51] Curators' roles vary in these tasks, from creating inventories and catalog records themselves to helping registrars' and collections management staff identify and authenticate objects.

Every museum is at a different stage of sophistication in cataloging, so it is difficult to generalize. Increasingly, museums have moved from manual to computerized records. Computerized collections databases make it easier to cross-reference collections information with other important collections management records, such as accession records, donor files, location files, conservation records, and exhibit use files. In addition, so many tasks become easier, including searches, reports, and locating objects' physical locations. Catalog records can be added to and revised as curators or other collections staff conduct additional research.

Using standardized naming conventions is crucial to effective cataloging output. *Nomenclature for Museum Cataloging of Man-Made Objects*—a lexicon of object names arranged hierarchically within functionally defined categories—is considered the standard system for cataloging historical collections.[52] Other standardized vocabulary lexicons can also be helpful.[53] Curators might do this work or, with a registrar on staff, they can help to enhance the catalog records by lending contextual or historically appropriate terms to object names and keywords. Artificial Intelligence (AI) can also help curators and registrars with this work.

To be more inclusive in creating catalog records, author Vickie Stone, in her essay "Question the Database!" encourages curators and other catalogers to establish "culturally responsive" database systems.[54] These would:

- Be aware of language—for example, terms that denote privilege, power, and White supremacy perspectives and points of view.
- More overtly include keywords related to identity and community characteristics, such as race, gender, sexuality, age, and the like, so these will appear more often in database searches.
- Consider sensitivity in the cultural practices of certain communities and restrict the viewing of certain objects (e.g., those related to sacred Indigenous practice).

Deaccessioning

Deaccessioning is "the process used to remove, legally and permanently, an accessioned object from the museum's collection."[55] Once considered extremely controversial, today it is widely accepted that historical organizations will periodically assess and thin their collections in this way. The goal is to use deaccessioning to improve the quality and integrity of the collection in respect to the museum's mission. It also frees up space and funds. An object might be deaccessioned because it is:[56]

- Out of scope—does not align with the museum's mission.
- In poor condition—damaged or deteriorated beyond reasonable repair.
- Redundant or a duplication of an object that is in better condition or for which more information is known.
- Acquired for an exhibition or program but no longer needed.
- Found to be forged or misrepresented by the seller—that is, altered with intent to deceive.
- Determined that the object can accomplish more good in another museum.
- Determined that the museum lacks the resources to provide proper care and/or storage space for the object.

Deaccessioning needs to be a thoughtful process, with detailed, carefully written policies and procedures as well as thorough documentation.[57] If not handled properly, deaccessioning can put at risk a museum's reputation, erode public trust, and endanger future donations. This is particularly an issue if items are sold for financial reasons other than to directly benefit the acquisition of new and/or the care and preservation of existing collections.

Curators are often the ones to make recommendations for deaccessioning, which, ideally, they propose to the Collections (or Acquisitions) Committee. The institution's governing authority gives the final approval. Once approved, deaccessioning leads to disposal, which is the permanent and physical removal of the items from the collection and from the premises. Disposal can involve a lengthy process of finding the best home for the object. Professional acceptable methods of disposal include sale, transfer of ownership, and destruction.

Tiering/Ranking Collections

Tiering or ranking objects in a collection is a way to prioritize those that deserve higher-level care and preservation over those that do not.[58] Rather than treating every object "as if it were a Rembrandt," it suggests the potential of more "relaxed" or "graduated" standards. It also leaves room for documenting objects that are for use, research, or teaching. Curatorial knowledge about objects and their significance can help greatly with tiering, in dialogue with collections management and care staff (if the museum has them). Two slightly different approaches are described here.

At the Kentucky Historical Society (KHS), Trevor Jones led an initiative to tier collections (on a scale of 1 to 5) based upon how well they supported the museum's mission. The primary question for tiering became, "How can this help tell stories about Kentucky's past that will be meaningful to Kentuckians today and in the future?"[59] Tiering collections also ended up proving useful for a range of other issues, including condition, rarity, replacement cost, use, storage, handling, loans, disaster planning, selection of candidates for conservation, improved storage, and staff being given the backing to be able to turn down donations.

Jones felt that the process of tiering collections at KHS changed the way staff and the board of trustees thought about their value. It led to better treatment for significant collections and conserved scarce resources. But he also admitted that this was not easy and that there were lots of gray areas, especially the Tier 3 designation. He suggested starting small, with objects that are being proposed as new acquisitions.

The Henry Ford's ranking system (1 to 4) began not from alignment with mission but to identify historical significance, rarity, and value (monetary) of individual objects so as to serve as a guide for their treatment, handling, storage, and management.[60] Ranking levels were established based upon a combination of national/international significance, uniqueness, rarity, and monetary value. While the idea was initiated by a conservator, curators have led the charge on ranking objects—especially with proposed acquisitions but also in handling the backlog while working on new exhibitions, loans, historic structure reinstallations, programs, and deaccessions.

The ranking policy at The Henry Ford has changed over time, and dialogue between curators and conservators continues to be crucial. Staff members feel that it successfully addresses the judicious allocation of resources by providing a framework for both ethical and practical decision-making (see figure 3.3). While not always consistent or applicable to every situation, it succeeds in helping staff think about what the museum collects, why it collects, and how the collection should be cared for and employed.[61]

Repatriation

Repatriation—the process of returning human-made items and human remains to the culture or nation of origin—has risen to the forefront of museum ethical standards and practices in recent years. While this topic covers items linked to war, looting (e.g., Nazi loot from victims of the Holocaust), and colonialism, most recent work in museums has centered around identifying and returning specific kinds of Indigenous cultural items.[62] As mentioned in the previous chapter, Amy Lonetree, author of the book *Decolonizing Museums: Representing Native America in National and Tribal Museums*, explains that, to Indigenous people, cultural materials in museums "are living entities. They embody layers of meaning, and they are deeply connected to the past, present, and future of Indigenous communities."[63] A decolonizing museum practice provides a form of healing to Indigenous people's unresolved grief, which continues to harm

Figure 3.3 Ranking objects can become particularly challenging when the decision is made to let visitors handle an extremely rare ("Rank 1") object. Such is the case with the Rosa Parks bus at The Henry Ford, which visitors can enter, sit in, touch, and move about in. Conservators keep a constant watch over the condition and use of the bus. From the collections of The Henry Ford.

people today. Human remains, funerary objects, sacred objects, and objects of cultural patrimony are all materials that may be considered for repatriation.[64]

In the United States, this work has been particularly driven by the Native American Graves Protection and Repatriation Act (NAGPRA).[65] Passed in 1990 after decades of Indigenous activism, this significant act shifted the focus from protecting the owners of the materials to more likely supporting the rights of the potential claimants. The debate swiftly moved from what museums were allowed to do to what they should do, up to and including sharing power and decision-making about the assets they steward, the return of those assets, and reparations for past harm.

Many institutions were initially slow to comply with this act, but this work has sped up since 2020, compelling museums to identify and engage in a dialogue with Indigenous constituents and descendants of people who created and used these items. Repatriation has changed curatorial work, providing a mandate for museums to collaborate with Indigenous people on the ownership of certain types of individual materials.

REFLECTIVE PRACTICE

This chapter began with a call to action about museums having "too much stuff" but not enough of the "right" stuff. It then moved on to collections planning—a crucial foundation to all other curatorial work with collections—and concluded with the many fundamental collections tasks that curators fulfill or assist others in carrying out daily. The chapter concludes with a checklist I created of best practice for curators working with collections.[66] This checklist incorporates many of the themes and topics covered in this chapter. Where can you and your institution do better? What strategies might you try? How might you begin?

Mission and Public Trust

- Does your institution have a mission statement?
- Have you assessed whether your collection is aligned with your mission statement?
- Does your institution recognize that its collections are held in the public trust?

Collections Planning

- Do you have a Collections Management Policy/Collections Policy?
- Do you have a written Collections Plan that defines past, present, and future collecting?
- Do you update the plan periodically?

Collections Fundamentals

- Do you have written criteria for accepting and refusing collections?
- Do you have a procedure for unsolicited donations?
- Do you write justifications for proposed acquisitions?
- Do you have a policy about personal collecting?
- Do you have a Collections (or Acquisitions) Committee that reviews proposed acquisitions?
- If you do not do your own cataloging, do you assist others in determining naming conventions for object names, subject names, and other keywords? Do you review others' catalog records?
- Do you use an object ranking/tiering process?
- Do you have a written policy and procedures for deaccessions and disposals?
- Is your museum currently engaged in a NAGPRA-related repatriation initiative?

Inclusive Collecting

- Does your Collections Plan encourage the acquisition of objects that reveal underrepresented or suppressed narratives?

Shaping and Developing Collections

- If your museum has primarily collected from a White perspective, what work must you do to prepare for shifting the dominant narrative your collections tell?
- How might you refine information in the catalog records to elevate hidden, underrepresented, or suppressed narratives?
- Do you invite communities who previously held ownership of an object or whose story it is telling to participate in discussions on how the object is used, displayed, conserved, or interpreted?

4

Thinking Historically

Some people think that all curators do is create blockbuster exhibitions, or maybe just spend all their time working with objects. But most history museum curators also investigate larger historical questions—questions that relate to how people lived in the past, how things changed over time, and how the past is still evident in today's world. Admittedly, sometimes they do this work to provide content for exhibitions or context for objects. Often, however, this work is undertaken for other reasons—a Collections Plan, a public program, new interpretation for a historic structure, or online content for the museum's website.

Over the course of my career as a curator, I have pursued numerous avenues of historical research for different projects to find out more about the past. I've scrutinized travelers' accounts for descriptions of tavern meals; pored over rural women's diaries and memoirs for details about domestic work; deconstructed historic recipes to create lists of kitchen equipment for cooking programs; interviewed descendants of people who lived and worked in historic buildings now located in Greenfield Village (see figure 4.2); analyzed general store merchandise by setting up a database of entries from store account books (see figure 6.2); studied the messages that vacationers wrote on the backs of postcards (to the dismay of postcard dealers who had methodically organized them by the images on the fronts); and even attended a workshop on Swiss alpine cheesemaking (tasting eight cheeses in two hours!) to better understand the original business of a family whose specialty-import grocery store contents the museum had acquired (see figure 1.1).

These research projects were all in addition to more typical research I undertook—in books and journals, local history and genealogical sources, and written and visual materials in libraries, archives, and online. Each of these projects involved asking questions, searching for the best information to reveal clues, comparing and weighing the validity of each source, and creating a summary that interpreted the findings. Often, this work was tedious and time-consuming.

Most people (including both non-curatorial museum staff and visitors) have no idea that curators do this sort of thing. Or what's involved in doing it. Or even why we do it.

So, why *do* we do it?

First, presenting accurate, authentic history is an ethical responsibility of museums, part of our museums' public service mandate. Second, it is enjoyable—or at least satisfying—as a curator to piece together the best interpretation one can of what happened in the past by uncovering new bits of data or asking new questions from existing information.

Finally, research is considered core to the work of curators. CurCom's "Curator Core Competencies" document calls out "Research and Scholarship" as curators' next most important competency after "Collections."[1] According to this document, the domain of "Research and Scholarship" is defined as "providing the museum with credibility as trusted sources of information while expanding knowledge and performing relevant research." Included under this domain are three subcategories: scholarly research, object research, and the mysteriously named "applied research." Applied research, defined in the document as "synthesizing and interpreting facts, scholarly research, data, and related objects to support educational and public offerings," is particularly relevant here. In history museums, applied research equates with public history.

This chapter focuses on the "history" part of public history (other chapters to come will focus on the "public" part). The "history" part of public history involves the process of thinking historically, which consists of "critically examining multiple accounts and perspectives of past events."[2] Even though the projects may vary widely—based upon your museum's mission, assets, strategic plan, and occasionally your own personal interests—thinking historically involves the rigorous methodology used by historians.

PUBLIC HISTORY IN MUSEUMS

The National Council on Public History (NCPH) defines public history as "the many and diverse ways in which history is put to work in the world," and the work of history museum curators certainly fits this definition.[3] As previously mentioned, the "history" part of public history involves the historical thinking of academic historians, and that is what this chapter is about. As the NCPH website states, "The theory and methodology of public history remains firmly in the discipline of history, and all good public history rests on sound scholarship."[4]

But public history in museums goes beyond this, and before moving on, it is useful to explore this dichotomy further. According to James Gardner in his article "Contested Terrain: History, Museums, and Public," public historians in museums must be advocates for *both* history and the public, constantly negotiating the gap between historians' and the public's understanding of the past.[5] The "public" aspect of museum curators' work generally diverges from the work of academic historians. First, in constructing historical questions and evaluating evidence, public historians frequently go beyond the written text favored by academic historians to include historic structures, landscapes, objects, orally transmitted memories, and visual materials. Second, they take history outside of purely scholarly debates and consider how our understanding of the past is relevant to people living in the world today. Finally, they routinely engage in collaborative work, with community members, stakeholders, the public, outside experts, specialists, and professional colleagues.[6]

Doing public history—that is, being advocates for both good history and for the public—can present many challenges for curators: relinquishing their singular control and expertise by sharing authority; realizing that they bring their own biases, unique perspectives, and personal experiences to their filtering of information; responding in a timely way to their museums' institutional strategies and priorities; working collaboratively in teams; and mediating between vastly different types of collaborators, co-creators, and stakeholders. Attempting to research assigned topics can be constrained by time, resources, skill or experience, and funding. It can be additionally frustrating because of the low-priority status and low regard sometimes given to sound scholarship and rigorous research methodology by people who don't understand what's involved and why it's important. And, finally, it can feel ultimately unrewarding because curators' work is often anonymous. These challenges might lead to compromises in accuracy, authenticity, and quality, which can ultimately threaten the public's trust in museums.[7]

On top of this, findings show that the public is just not very interested in the complexity, multiple interpretations, and changing nature of history that good public history often reveals. As Stanford University historian of education Sam Wineburg concluded, "It really is an unnatural thing" for the public to "think historically."[8] The "Reframing History" initiative, undertaken by the American Association for State and Local History (AASLH), reinforced this with the following findings:[9]

- The public thinks of history (i.e., the past) as a series of chronological events driven by the actions of key individuals.
- The public believes that history (i.e., providing an account of the past) is about recording and documenting "just the facts."
- People can't tell the difference between rigorous analysis and personal opinion.
- People think that learning about the past means absorbing facts and figures.
- There is a belief among the public that mainstream (i.e., White male) historical narratives are the default that everyone has to learn, while

narratives of historically oppressed peoples are "extras" that are, in principle or practice, unnecessary for everyone to learn.
- Many members of the public are reluctant to learn or talk about painful or troubling things that happened in the past, particularly in relation to historically oppressed groups.
- The public sees history as a nonessential hobby.
- People are fatalistic about the possibility of improving how history is taught in school.

In addition to the challenges of work realities and the public's misperceptions about history, curators doing public history often face the mistrust of curatorial research by academic historians. This mistrust is precipitated by the lack of scholarly training that some curators have; the variety of hats that curators wear; the limited time curators have to devote to a single topic; the often uncited nature of their research as presented in exhibitions, programs, and online content; and the potential skewing and compromising of research and findings due to museums' funding sources and bureaucracies. Some academic historians have long believed, and continue to believe, that public history is not "real" history.[10]

How can a history museum curator navigate all these challenges and still maintain their passion for doing sound historical research?

As far as the work goes, museums should view historical research not as tangential but core to curators' work, written into job descriptions and expected as an essential part of the job. Probably the most misunderstood aspect of doing historical research is the time it takes (some people think it is so time-consuming that it will overtake all other tasks, while others think it is magical and takes no time at all). In truth, it always takes *some* amount of time, though curators—often pressed for time—learn to be strategic about how much time to spend on any given research project. It does, however, require resources, such as access to inter-library loans and funds for purchasing books and subscription-based online databases. It takes professional development support for those who require research skills. In the end, sound scholarship can significantly inform (and should be informed by) museums' strategic plans and priorities, as it ultimately enhances the museum's validity and strength as a believable, truth-telling, and relevant institution.[11]

In response to public perceptions about history, curators might look for ways to help people better understand the curatorial process—reminding them that scholarship, interpretation, and differences of opinion are central to what curators do; that choosing objects and stories (and the perspectives they take on these) are always subjective; and that they use as much data and evidence as they can to provide insight on these. Fact- and evidence-based information works well as a basis for interpretation, but it should strive to go beyond this.[12] In his article "'People Need to Remember': American Museums Still Struggle with the Legacy of Race," Lonnie Bunch III argues that a sign of a successful exhibition or program is one in which "the audience becomes more comfortable with ambiguity and complexity."[13] In his article "Contested Terrain: History, Museums, and the Public," James B. Gardner also encourages us to:

- Share what we do, not just the end product.
- Admit it if we don't know something.
- Focus on people whenever possible, as people connect best with other people.
- Encompass multiple political and ideological perspectives. See difference as a strength, providing a fuller picture of American history.
- Appeal to visitors' curiosity by unveiling hidden stories and helping them understand that there might be more to the history than they thought.
- Demonstrate that the history we interpret is challenging, messy, and complex. It's not simple.[14]

To help appease academics' skepticism, involve them in your projects as often as possible, in appropriate and productive ways. Establish relationships with academic historians whom you find particularly helpful and who have a vested interest in your museum. Find ways (through publications, online content, etc.) to cite your sources. Don't be afraid to show contrasting perspectives and conflicting evidence and explain how you arrived at your conclusions.

HISTORICAL RESEARCH METHODOLOGY

Good public history involves "solid historical research based on a rigorous examination of available sources."[15] This is the essence of what academic historians do. They gather clues and evidence from a range of materials in order to understand the significance of a particular person, place, event, or time period, and then they use these to form a coherent argument about the meaning and significance of past events. Each historian's research brings a new, fresh interpretation of the past.

Historical research methodology involves three major steps: asking questions, identifying and analyzing sources, and constructing a reasonable argument based on evidence.

Asking Questions

To begin a historical research project, historians start with a question or series of questions. As historian Jennifer Ford wrote in the article "Chinking Between the Logs: Reinterpreting the Miller House at Meadowcroft Museum of Rural Life":

> If as a researcher you approach your source material without questions to ask, mysteries to solve, or hypotheses to test you will end up with bushels

of interesting trivia. If however you approach your data with issues to address, when you read through inventories and ledgers and diaries and newspapers you will be alert to clues. When clues string together they form patterns and when you begin to see patterns you are on your way to answering your original questions. When you find answers to questions then you are in a position to explain local history to your visitors rather than just sharing interesting trivia with them.[16]

The process of asking questions helps you determine what you want to know and where to begin looking for the answers. Do not be surprised if new questions continue to arise. Asking different historical questions also might lead you to new sources or to interrogate familiar sources in new ways.[17] Conversely, you might need to change the questions if you can't find evidence or the evidence points you in a different direction than you had intended. The more widely you read, the more questions may occur to you.

In determining questions, historians are not only interested in what happened at a certain point in time. They are curious about the larger historical context—all part of the immensely complex past. History museum curators should always aim to consider the larger context in their work as well as the minute details related to their research topic. Historians' typical categories of inquiry include:

- Cause and effect, causes and consequences.
- Historical significance, including how deeply people were affected, how many people were affected, and how great and long the impact lasted.
- Change and continuity over time.
- Historical turning points.
- Seeing the world through others' eyes, including how people from other times, places, and conditions made sense of the world, and how their experiences, needs, and worldviews affected their actions and choices.[18]

Identifying and Analyzing Sources

After determining the initial questions for which you are seeking answers, you can begin to identify research sources. Historians aim for a wide range of materials, using these to form a coherent argument that helps address their questions, as well as provide broader meaning and significance to past events.

In analyzing sources, historians look for both patterns and deviations from those patterns. They read the sources critically, analyzing for messages that were, or may not have been, intended by the creator. They aim for plausible causal claims, knowing that they likely can't prove all their assertions. This is not easy work. As mentioned in Zachary Schrag's *The Princeton Guide to Historical Research*, "Even the tiny fragment which survives in the shape of historical evidence presents the most bewildering variety of sequences, connections, relationships, parallels, contrasts, and irrelevancies."[19] Historians must learn to read and judge with equal parts efficiency and rigor. This becomes easier as you delve into multiple sources for an individual project or as you do this more often as part of your daily work.

In your search for answers, each source will uncover bits of data that will reveal new insights. Sometimes sources will conflict. In this case, you will have to evaluate each one and decide which is most valid. Historians are so used to doing this that it is almost second nature to them. To help beginning researchers work through this, it is useful to develop a "sourcing heuristic"—that is, a series of steps that historians intuitively work through before analyzing the content of a document.[20] A critical assessment of the source's strengths and weaknesses provides a road map for weighing the evidence revealed by each source, helping to establish its authenticity, credibility, accuracy, and usefulness. These questions can include:[21]

- When, where, and how was it created?
- By whom was it created? What is the authors' authority?
- Why and for whom was it created?
- How was it used at the time of creation?
- Does it seem accurate, complete, and reliable?
- What kind of evidence does it offer?
- What are its strengths and advantages?
- For a secondary (book or journal article) or online source, are citations and documentation included?
- What are its weaknesses, limitations, and biases?
- Knowing that mistakes, omissions, personal prejudice, and social norms might skew how an event, person, or place is perceived and reported, what (or who) seems missing?
- In comparing sources, do you find things that are contested or inconsistent?

Bringing a healthy skepticism to assessing each bit of evidence is a good habit to adopt. Compare sources. The more different types of sources you find in agreement, the more you can likely trust them, especially if you can track down the original source of the information. Remember that it is impossible to ever know what actually happened in the past. So you must make a best guess based upon what seems most probable by weighing all the evidence. This is why going to a wide range of sources is desirable.

Interpreting the Evidence

This step involves knitting together the pieces of evidence you have collected to tell a coherent and meaningful story. This might take the form of a single overarching statement, an outline, a more substantive research report, an online article, an interpretive manual, or a published book or article.

In this step, you are constructing a narrative out of many different pieces of evidence and will have to deal with conflicting sources or even an absence of information and sources. You may reorganize your original plan, discover new questions, reach dead ends, have to frame new questions, or need to pursue more information. The way you arrange your data might reveal different associations and different analyses. In fact, the same evidence often leads different historians to different conclusions, depending upon the mix of primary source evidence, new considerations, research questions, and the individual's perspective.[22]

RESEARCH SOURCES: A DEEPER DIVE

Sources for researching different topics vary widely. The following is a summary of key sources that are useful in doing historical research. Get to know the sources you need for your specific purpose.[23]

Online Research

Because it is so convenient, your research might start with—or at some time involve—online research. But beware. As Jenny L. Presnell attests in *The Information-Literate Historian: A Guide to Research for History Students*, "The Internet is perhaps the best and the worst reference resource available today. It has the ability to connect you to an established authority in the field you are studying, as well as a self-proclaimed authority who knows very little."[24]

A basic rule of thumb for doing online research is that a website is appropriate for historical research if it leads you to an original work that is responsibly based on primary sources and intelligently informed by relevant scholarship. Like other sources (perhaps even *more* than other sources), it is important to evaluate the quality of a website before using it as a reliable source of information. This includes assessing:

- The author's/creator's credentials
  - Does the author have credentials that convince you that his or her information is/findings are valid?
  - Does there seem to be a persuasive, marketing, political, or otherwise skewed point of view being taken that warns you to avoid these sources?
- Audience and purpose
  - For whom was it created? If for a fourth-grade class or the general public, it might help you understand the basics of an idea or topic, but it likely won't provide the research value of a more scholarly piece.
- Accuracy and content
  - Does it appear accurate based upon your other research? Make comparisons with other websites as well as journal articles and books.

- Internet sites often copy each other, and the original information might be inaccurate. Watch, as well, for inaccuracies with dates.
- If it appears sloppily written or cited, be suspect of the entire piece.
- Are sources listed, or can you track the content to a reliable source?
• Publication date
  - When was it last revised? Information preceding the last two to three years may be outdated and inaccurate. This older information might be helpful in tracking down original source material on the topic or deeper specifics on sources than more recent articles, but tread with care.
• Navigability and structure
  - Do the links lead to dead ends? Are the images of marginal quality? These are signs that the website is inactive and cause for more careful perusal.[25]

Google is currently the most accepted search engine for doing historical research online. But keep in mind that Google's primary asset is to make information—past and present, printed and digital—easily accessible to as wide an audience as possible. Therefore, your search might be filled with a chaotic range of websites.

Two other free Google search engines may help in your research as well. Google Books contains digitized books and magazine articles and advertisements (fully before 1923, in part after 1923 because of copyright issues). Google Scholar provides access to academic literature.

Often, Wikipedia, a popular online encyclopedia, will appear near or at the top of a search.[26] Although Wikipedia can get a bad rap, especially among history professionals, it is an easy site to check to get a general overview of a topic. Because it is operated by a nonprofit organization, it stands apart from many of the online for-profit entities. The rules for submitting entries to Wikipedia require that they have a neutral point of view, and all entries are organized in a consistent, easy-to-follow way. Wikipedia also flags contentious issues and is often updated. It is particularly useful for tracing sources listed in the "References" section, as it can provide leads to many primary sources of which you might not have been aware. But Wikipedia is *never* the whole story. The content can be skewed by its (often male) writers, and it can be edited by anyone. Most importantly, it has often been criticized for lack of reliability. In the end, it is an adequate site to start your research journey, but it is only the beginning.

Also hugely important for curators at smaller institutions with small budgets are free, accessible, online resources such as Open Access (OA) journals and Open Educational Resources (OER's), both supported by Open Knowledge Foundation (OKF), as well as Creative Commons (CC).

Digitized materials from libraries, archives, and other repositories have made possible easy access to a vast array of additional hard-to-find or previously inaccessible materials, including historical journals, government documents, genealogical records, newspapers, magazines, books, and visual images. This is, for the most part, a wonderful boon to researchers. But one must proceed with caution through this material. There are no universally accepted standards for placing documents and other materials online. Lacking context or provenance, documents can be misleading, purposefully skewed, inaccurate, impossible to identify or date, or totally fabricated. It is important to know exactly what the document is, where it came from, and whether it is a reliable source. To check for reliability, go through the same checklist as described previously for websites. Also keep in mind that, at least at this point, documents accessible online still present only a fraction of all the material available in archives, county courthouses, universities, public libraries, and elsewhere.

For additional guidelines related to online research, see the section on Getting Started: Suggested Research Steps.

Secondary Sources: Published Books and Articles

It is a comfort, particularly to beginning researchers, to know that—sometime, somewhere—something was probably written about the topic you are researching. New research projects often involve referencing what are called "secondary sources"—that is, published scholarly books and journal articles that analyze the past from a later time in an attempt to synthesize, provide perspective to, or make sense of, that place and time.

Surveying the secondary literature on a topic is often the most straightforward way to start and involves the easiest sources to track down. Online bibliographies—that is, collections of references to secondary source material—can be helpful here. These will include journal articles, books, and some websites. If you're lucky, they will contain an internal search engine or full-text articles. Periodical indexes (in libraries and online) can also be helpful. *America: History and Life* (which is subscription-based) is considered the definitive index of literature covering the history and culture of the United States and Canada from prehistory to the present. Indexing hundreds of journals, it is an invaluable bibliographic database for curators. Online indexes *JStor* and *Project Muse* (also subscription-based) provide digital access to major academic journals in the humanities and social sciences. Their strength is in providing full-text articles if you already know the title and author. They are also keyword searchable.

In using secondary sources, it's always best to seek out the most current scholarship. Current publications, if well cited, will lead you to previous books, articles, primary source materials, and the repositories for these. You can get a good idea of up-to-date scholarship by checking bookstore holdings and online booksellers such as Amazon and Barnes & Noble, which might include "Look Inside" features and brief reviews of the books. Other websites will sometimes include longer book reviews, particularly for books by better known authors or books aimed at a popular readership.

While convenient to access, published books and articles can be fraught with research problems, especially if they are older. When was the source written? What are the author's credentials? What is his or her point of view? Did the author use sources taken directly from the era? How are these interpreted? Are the author's claims footnoted? A good research methodology will incorporate up-to-date secondary sources but might need other kinds of sources as well, to validate, reinforce, and confirm those sources and to provide greater specificity and detail. Footnotes and bibliographic references in these will lead you on the path to many of these.

Secondary Sources: Graduate Theses and Dissertations

Graduate theses and dissertations can be incredibly valuable and insightful sources of information, often involving the collection and analysis of primary sources with attempts to piece together a bigger picture and reach broad conclusions. Many of these explore historical topics at specific places and times. The main drawback of these sources is that their authors tended to create them early in their careers, exploring new, unfamiliar topics and perhaps even using unfamiliar sources and methodology. In fact, the purpose of these is often to gain familiarity with such methodologies as using primary sources, synthesizing information, and drawing larger conclusions. Since 1938, dissertations have been available on microfilm at University Microfilms International in Ann Arbor, Michigan, and are indexed on Dissertation Abstracts International. Full-text access to graduate theses and dissertations is available online through PQDT (ProQuest Dissertations and Theses) Global.

Primary Sources: A General Overview

Primary sources are firsthand accounts of an event or topic. They are the most direct evidence of a time or event because they were created at that time or event. As mentioned previously, these have become increasingly available online from historical societies, museums, archives, universities, and research agencies.

This myriad group of sources—created during or around the time period being studied—is usually harder to access, both physically and conceptually, than secondary sources. But familiarizing yourself with the range of primary sources that is available for the time, place, and situation you are researching can open up a vast world of opportunity for telling richer and deeper stories. Keep in mind that each primary source will usually reveal only small bits of data. These need to be collected and compared with each other, with other primary sources, and with other types of sources, to build a more complete picture. It may seem frustrating at first to find little fragments that do not seem to add up to much, but every bit of data contributes a potentially crucial piece to the larger picture you are assembling.

Because they were created at or near the time period being studied, primary sources give the impression of being accurate. But, like secondary sources, they can also contain biases. Primary sources were intended for many different purposes, almost none of which were to be used as later historical documents! They can be inaccurate, muddled, hearsay, or intended to persuade or mislead. Some were intended for personal use while others were created for strictly documentary purposes—and even then filled with misinformation. One must constantly assess the origin of the source, evaluate its worth and accuracy, and compare it with other sources.

Primary Sources: Published Primary Documents

Published primary documents are sources of which multiple copies were printed for wide dissemination. These include:

- Period literature such as advice books, etiquette books, home furnishings books, how-to books, and cookbooks.
- Published journals, diaries, memoirs, biographies, and travel accounts. These are fantastic records of people's lives, offering personal thoughts and ideas as people react to the world around them and interact with others in their communities. Their insight is both private and authentic. These personal narratives can be a powerful and illuminating way to discover multiple truths, as they might counter documents that are in the public record. Still, it is important to ask who is writing them, how accurate they are, and if using them might "ruffle feathers" among the original writers' descendants.
- City and county directories, generally published annually with listings of local residents and often including their occupations.
- Periodicals and/or magazines of the period, useful for both articles and advertisements.
- Newspapers of the period, for articles, advertisements, community news, and obituaries. Obituaries are a valuable source, highlighting facts about a person's life that are not revealed elsewhere. Many newspapers have been digitized on the subscription-based online source newspapers.com. Obituaries also often appear on genealogical websites such as ancestry.com.
- County atlases. Many of these bound collections of maps and supplementary local information were published around the time of America's centennial celebration in 1876, then again in the early twentieth century.
- City and county histories, published during similar eras as county atlases. These in-depth sources are valuable especially for details about the early (mostly White founders' and settlers') history of these places. Use caution here, because their purpose was to commemorate the settlement and survival stories of these residents as they began to pass on. These histories can be racist, particularly offensive in their descriptions of Indigenous people, and filled with both purposeful and unintentional inaccuracies. Many of these can be found on Google Books.
- Published business histories. The intent of these is celebratory but, when used with caution, they can provide invaluable information about a business's origins and evolution not found in other sources.

- Ephemera, including booklets, pamphlets, and programs.
- Government reports. Secondary sources can often lead you to these.
- Trade literature, including trade catalogs and mail-order catalogs (see figure 4.1).

These are extremely helpful for providing visual images of objects that people used in the past, as well as looking at the range of choices, styles, and prices of a given time. Some of these are online, such as those at the Hagley Digital Archives (a collection of hundreds of trade catalogs and pamphlets from the collections of the Hagley Library in Wilmington, Delaware, https://digital.hagley.org/tradecats).

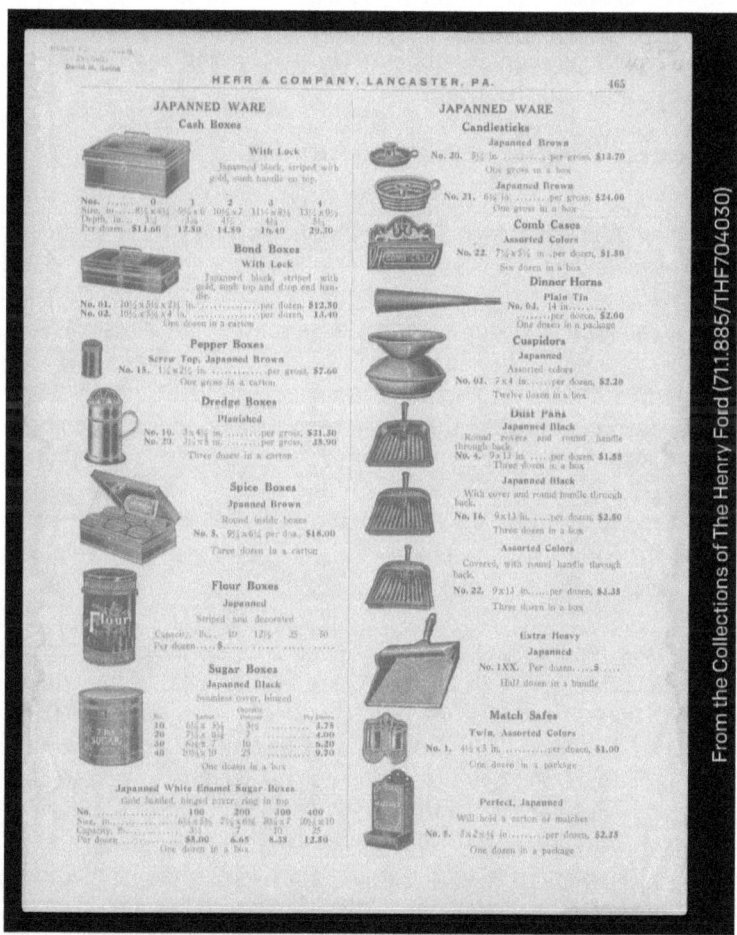

Figure 4.1 Trade catalogs provide an invaluable source for what objects looked like (and cost) from different eras. This page of tin household items appeared in the 1926 Herr & Co. trade catalog from Lancaster, Pennsylvania. "Japanned" tin items were coated in a shiny black varnish that was intended to be an inexpensive imitation of fine European lacquerware. From the collections of The Henry Ford.

Thinking Historically

Published primary documents can be extremely useful links to the past, as they were produced for wide distribution at the time. But they must also be evaluated for bias. What is the context? Who created it? What was the author's intent in creating it? What was his or her motivation and point of view? For example, published biographies and memoirs were often skewed to present the person in a positive light. Newspapers were often slanted toward a particular political party as well as being produced so hurriedly that they often omitted or distorted facts. Period advice, etiquette, and furnishings books were all intended to persuade the reader to the author's point of view. The images of prosperous farmsteads in county atlases usually appear because the farmers who owned them paid to have them published. Trade catalogs list wholesale prices, leaving customer prices to each retailer's discretion. Community brochures and programs promoted boosterism. Everything comes with bias, so always be cautious and skeptical.

Primary Sources: Unpublished Primary Documents

These are unique documents that were created for a specific purpose, such as recordkeeping. A major category of unpublished primary documents is public records, which are documents or pieces of information that are not considered confidential and generally pertain to the conduct of government. This is a large and crucial category of documentation, especially for local history research. Much of this information is filed in Public Records offices, often county courthouses. Many of these documents are now accessible online on searchable databases, often on websites that have been created for researching family genealogy (such as the subscription-based sites ancestry.com and FamilySearch.org). Historians have heavily used these in their research, so leads to them—and the repositories in which they reside—often appear in secondary sources. Particularly useful public records for researching time, place, and people include:

- US Census records, collected at the end of each decade. Population census records began in 1790 and are available for public viewing up to 1950 (except those from 1890, most of which were unfortunately destroyed by fire in 1921). Some states also collected census information. Agriculture and manufacturing census records were also collected through various decades of the nineteenth and twentieth centuries. Census records are incredibly valuable to research time, place, and people. But they can be hard to read because they were often handwritten, and they can contain inaccurate spellings of names. They also often missed people or inaccurately described people's heritage, especially members of marginalized groups. Primarily because they are difficult to read,

census records that have been transcribed for online databases often contain errors as well.
- Land and property records, proving ownership and transfers of property.
- Tax records showing increases in land values, which often denoted the building of a structure on a property.
- Wills and probate records, which can include inventories of personal belongings at the time of one's death.
- Vital records, including births, marriages, divorces, and deaths.
- Court records of lawsuits, criminal activity, and other transactions.
- Military records.
- Records of the US Patent and Trademark Office, since 1790 (available online).
- Records of the US Post Office Department, with listings of postmaster appointments and names and locations of post offices (on microfilm at the National Archives, searchable via an online index).
- Records of the US Customs Bureau (on microfilm at the National Archives, searchable via an online index).

Other useful unpublished primary documents for researching historical topics include:

- Personal and family papers, letters, journals, diaries, and scrapbooks. As mentioned under Published Primary Documents, these can offer insightful personal thoughts and ideas as people react to the world around them and interact with others in their communities. But, it is important to ask who is writing them, how accurate they are, and if using them might "ruffle feathers" among the original writers' descendants.
- County and municipal government records.
- Community organization records, including those from churches, labor unions, political parties, service clubs, philanthropic and fraternal organizations, and the Social Register. (Founded in 1887, this is a directory and a network of socially prestigious members of society in selected cities.)
- Business records, including accounts, inventories, meeting minutes, and correspondence.
- Records of Dun and Bradstreet (originally R. G. Dun), providing detailed information on American businesses in order to rate the suitability of these businesses for credit, 1841-1892 (online finding aid at the Baker Library, Harvard Business School).
- Cemetery records, some of which appear on https://www.findagrave.com/.

Unpublished primary documents are advantageous for many reasons. They often include data on demographics, social stratification, occupations, and household composition. They also have disadvantages. They are all simply bits of data that need to be assessed, analyzed, and compared with other sources. Furthermore, they provide little insight into attitudes, mindset, and potential ways in which individuals within groups responded to social, economic, and political changes. These sources can contain factual inaccuracies as well.

Visual Documents and Media Sources

These types of primary documents can be incredibly valuable tools for researching time, place, and people, as they can reveal emotions, context, and unexpected details.

Visual images and media sources comprise:

- Maps, which are rich sources of information, include plat maps showing the exact dimensions and layout of a piece of land (often part of a deed or land record); Sanborn Fire Insurance Maps depicting layout, shape, and use of structures in cities and towns, published beginning in 1867 (online access through Library of Congress); county atlas maps; hand-drawn property maps; and bird's-eye-view lithographs of towns and villages, popular between the 1870s and 1920s. The detail of some of these is quite extensive, while others will likely leave you disappointed because of their sketchiness and inaccuracies.
- Sketches, paintings, and other artwork (particularly useful during the era before photography).
- Architectural drawings and plans.
- Photographs, beginning earlier but particularly from the 1860s onward.
- Personal home movies or videos.
- A plethora of historic media on YouTube. Be sure you pinpoint the original sources for these because they are often not cited.

Visual documents such as paintings and photographs are excellent sources for showing how people dressed, the settings within which they lived and worked, how they conveyed proper etiquette and deportment of their time, and the accoutrements of their daily lives. Visual sources make extremely valuable complements to written sources. But keep in mind that they are mediated documents. People usually consciously dressed and posed for them. Artists and photographers brought their own biases to the subjects and the ways in which they portrayed their subjects. Caution must be used to assess what they are, why they were created, and who created them. Always question how accurate, manipulated, altered, and documented the visual source is.

Also, beware of historical advertisements and other visual documents on sites like Google Images (which offers a useful "reverse image" feature that allows users to search for related images by uploading an image or copying the image URL) and Flickr, as many do not mention date or provenance. These sites are, however, occasionally useful for offering leads through keyword searches that can take you to better documented information.

Oral Histories

These types of primary documents involve "the systematic collection and recording of personal memories as historical documentation."[27] They have the advantage of supplementing written records by filling in gaps (see figure 4.2).

Oral histories usually involve recording a live, in-person interview in audio or video format and then transcribing and summarizing the interview. They can also take the form of written reminiscences, such as enslaved people's narratives, Great Depression oral history projects, and regional local history initiatives. Some of these have been transcribed and are available online or through online databases and finding aids. If you can't find anything online as part of an oral history initiative, you might try contacting the library or historical society where this material seems most likely to reside, or try seeking out the actual descendants or acquaintances of the person you are researching.

Figure 4.2 Descendants of the people who originally lived and/or worked in a historic structure can offer rich primary source information. This was the case when we interviewed five descendants of Dr. Alonson Howard when they came to Greenfield Village to visit the 1860s office where their ancestor had practiced medicine. From the collections of The Henry Ford.

The advantages of oral histories are many. They can be highly engaging to the public because they express how people feel about something and convey a level of detail not available in other sources. As eyewitness accounts of events that took place in the past, oral histories can be informative, vivid, and colorful. They can enliven a larger narrative, add a touch of humor, show common or contested threads among groups, and provide a welcome change of pace to the often dry data of statistics and demographic information. They are, of course, particularly valuable for recent history, where synthesized versions of the history do not yet exist but people are still around to recount an era and supply missing information if records are incomplete.

But oral histories are highly subjective as well. They can conflict with written sources, presenting a problem to the researcher. It is not unusual for people being interviewed about the same event to disagree with each other over the details, as personal memories of the past can be greatly divergent. Oral history interviews are fraught with bias, as interviewees might purposely leave out part of the story, focus on trivial details, show disregard for following a standard chronology, compress or telescope time, or change the story for their own purposes. In addition, personal memories are imprecise and can even change over time. Interviewers can also add their own biases, asking leading and loaded questions and bringing certain attitudes, beliefs, preconceived notions, and personal interests of their own. Like the use of other documentary materials, it is best to combine the use of oral history sources with additional sources.

Also keep in mind that recording, transcribing, and summarizing oral histories take a great deal of time and resources (there are now AI- or Artificial Intelligence-powered transcription tools but these still require time to review). One must consider the value of undertaking a project like this before getting started. It is best to check for any previously implemented oral histories related to your topic, in published form or online. Before starting an oral history project, it is crucial to know exactly what you are trying to find out. In the course of interviewing someone, it is easy for the conversation to veer off track. It takes as much rigor to get what you want out of an oral interview as out of other research sources—just a different kind of rigor. Useful books exist on planning and implementing oral histories.[28]

Objects as Evidence

Objects, or groupings of objects, can reveal insights into socioeconomic conditions, political circumstances, and cultural norms with an immediacy that documents do not.[29] Whether they are archaeological specimens excavated on a site or historical items that have survived, objects provide powerful windows into both the past lives of individuals and the beliefs and mindset of the larger culture and society to which individuals belonged. Keep in mind that there is a dearth of objects for marginalized groups. Both community involvement and archaeological evidence have helped to supplement the missing record in this regard.

As a research source, objects should be approached similarly to other sources—with a series of questions. What is it? Who made it? Why was it made? How does it relate to other material culture evidence of its time and place? What does it reveal about individual and cultural mindsets? How does it complement other research sources to reveal these things? Consider inherent biases. Are you certain that it is an authentic object from that era? Does it truly reflect the time, place, and people you wish to represent (as opposed to coming from outside of the region, from a different era, or from a different socioeconomic level than you are intending)?

Physical Structures and Historic Landscapes as Primary Documents

Finally, the careful examination of a physical structure or a historic landscape can provide vast amounts of information to help inform research topics related to different groups of people.[30] Materials, design, construction techniques, and layout can reveal much about the attitudes, mindset, traditions, and values of people living in a time and place. It is helpful to get input from experts in "reading" the details and features of these, as they can pinpoint, interpret, and help reconstruct changes over time.

See table 4.1 for a summary of pros and cons for each of these research sources.

LIBERATING THE NARRATIVE: RESEARCHING MARGINALIZED GROUPS

Using the aforementioned sources will allow you to create adequate narratives related to mainstream history. But it is important to remember that mainstream historical narratives are founded upon long-created social systems designed to advantage dominant ideologies and groups and disadvantage others.[31] Within this structure, it is easy to exclude (either intentionally or unintentionally) historically marginalized groups, to overgeneralize, to stereotype, or to lump all people together into these narratives. In researching historical eras, people, and topics, it is convenient to choose to interpret only materials that reside and are accessible in known and well-traveled repositories. It is easy to steer away from the idiosyncratic and atypical, opting instead for general trends.

A standard rationale for excluding marginalized groups goes something like, "We *want* to tell these stories, but there just isn't any [or enough] information." People might also worry that bringing in new stories means throwing out the old, rather than adding to the greater picture. Or it causes discomfort and fear of pushback. Dr. Hasan Kwame Jeffries calls this tendency "creating a false narrative"—that is, "leaving out key aspects of the story in our purposeful historical amnesia, . . . [particularly the] stuff that makes us uncomfortable."[32]

Thinking Historically

Table 4.1 Types of Research Sources with Major Pros and Cons

Source	Pros	Cons
Secondary	Convenient	Dependent upon author's interpretation of information
Primary—Published	Original intent of wide distribution makes these easy to find and often quite in-depth	Original purpose for their publication contains potential bias
Primary—Unpublished	These date to actual time being studied	Contain bits of data that may conflict and/or not add up
Visual	Provide rich pictorial representations	May have been manipulated
Oral History	High level of detail and emotion	Likely contain factual errors because based upon memory
Material Culture Evidence	Offers concrete evidence of past time, place, people, and mindset	Needs expertise to understand how to interpret
Structure/Landscape	Offers concrete evidence of past time, place, people, and mindset	Good chance of change over time, which requires expertise to interpret

But this attitude is rapidly changing, especially since 2020. Academic historians are crafting new historical narratives using different sources and asking different questions. Meanwhile, public historians in museums are seeking to tell richer, more inclusive stories—attempting to repair years of erasure and a legacy of mistrust among members of local communities.

As marginalized individuals and communities have often been erased from the public record—or, at the very least, have been hidden and difficult to find—historians and public historians have had to be particularly creative in finding, considering, and using research sources. Sometimes these were previously overlooked; other times different questions are being asked of known sources. Some people call the results of these new approaches, findings, and interpretations "changing the narrative," "correcting the narrative," or "comprehensive content." I prefer the term "liberating the narrative," as it implies that the narrative was bound, held captive, restricted, constrained, and this new work is finally freeing it—to be truthful, to be accurate, to be what it should have been all along.[33] "Liberating the narrative" involves expanding or rethinking sources, methodology, and questions to see the same subject matter with new eyes. In doing so, it reveals the previously untold stories of those who have been missing, erased, lost, hidden, marginalized, unacknowledged, stereotyped, misrepresented, or mythologized.

The following includes a sampling of some of the groundbreaking strategies and research sources currently being used to liberate the narrative for three traditionally marginalized groups: enslaved Africans/African Americans, women, and LGBTQ+ individuals and communities.[34]

Enslaved Africans/African Americans

In their publications related to interpreting slavery, Kristin L. Gallas and James DeWolf Perry admit that the interpretation of slavery has for many years been neglected, interpreted incompletely, perpetuated by myths, downplayed, overgeneralized, simplified, misleading, or just plain wrong.[35] But, as Lonnie Bunch III argues, accurately researching and interpreting this history is crucial, as "for nearly 250 years, slavery not only existed but was one of the most dominant forces in American life."[36] Bunch goes on to explain that

> the history of slavery matters because it has shaped so much of our complex and troubling struggle to find racial equality. There is a great need to help Americans understand this. And until we use the past to better understand the contemporary resonance of slavery, we will never get to the heart of one of the central dilemmas in American life—race relations.[37]

In order to attain an accurate, balanced, and sensitive understanding of slavery and its role in our history, Gallas and Perry recommend undertaking fresh research and developing a well-rounded narrative informed by individual stories with rich, personal details. Individual stories both lend humanity to the lives of enslaved people and highlight their broader role in history. This new scholarship will not only feed programming and exhibition topics, but it also gives museum staff necessary information to feel confident in working with this difficult topic and conveying challenging material to visitors.

Particularly useful sources for liberating this narrative include:[38]

- Connecting with descendant communities (groups of people whose ancestors were enslaved at a particular site), enslavers, and former residents from the place being researched.[39]
- Family histories of enslavers and slave owners (e.g., correspondence, journals) that intersect with the lives of people who were enslaved.
- Listings of enslaved people in archival repositories (see figure 4.3) (see more detail at https://www.familysearch.org/en/blog/researching-formerly-enslaved-african-americans).

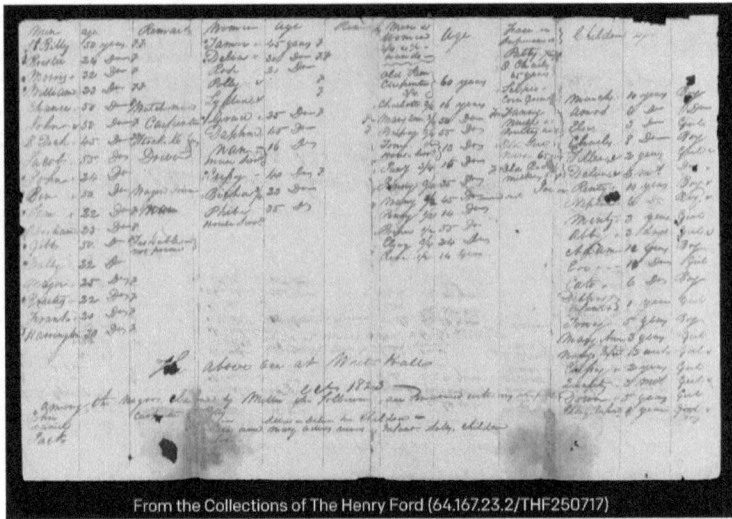

Figure 4.3 This handwritten inventory from Mulberry Hill and White Hall Plantations, Bryan County, Georgia, provides clues to names, ages, and capabilities of the more than 130 enslaved African Americans that plantation owner Richard James Arnold took over in 1823. The plantations were part of Arnold's wife's dowry. From the collections of The Henry Ford.

- Period newspapers, especially those with "runaway slave" notices. Many of these have been collected for the online database "Freedom on the Move" (https://freedomonthemove.org/).
- Town and church records.
- Legal documents in local courthouses, including lawsuits involving enslaved people resisting captivity.
- Structures and landscapes.
- Archaeological remains.
- Cemetery research.
- Information related to enslaved people living near the place being researched.
- Secondary sources for assembling the bigger picture of slavery, both regionally and nationally.

Increasingly, many of these sources are available online. Some museums and researchers have created their own websites to request and collect new information.

Women

For researching the history of women, it is important to note that women's history is often subsumed under men's history.[40] Such historical documents as census data, government records, court accounts, and legal papers lead a researcher to believe that men initiated change and the course of history, as these documents render women's lives almost invisible. Moreover, most libraries and archives have collected papers that were heavily biased toward men's endeavors and were cataloged to make the records related to women difficult to locate (e.g., "family papers—misc"). References to women are often omitted from finding aids or hidden beneath fathers' and husbands' names, while databases and book indexes lack keywords to identify women.

According to Heather Huyck in her book *Doing Women's History in Public: A Handbook for Interpretation at Museums and Historic Sites*, these "challenge us to understand women on their own terms, to unravel the mysteries and to discover missing parts of their lives."[41] She encourages researchers to always assume a female presence and actively go find it. In her article "Interpreting Women's Lives at Historic House Museums," Mary A. van Balgooy recommends asking different questions of the same material, using unconventional resources, and trying out subject headings (in archival finding aids) and search terms that may not seem obvious. Both authors advise researchers to be aware that documents related to women were often not saved by archives or descendants, as their lives were not believed to be sufficiently interesting or valuable enough to save. Moreover, the women themselves were often reluctant to document their own lives or save materials related to their lives.

Recommended sources for researching women include:[42]

- Secondary sources. There is always new scholarship on women's history emerging, so check for the most recent. These can provide the framework, context, and leads for additional secondary sources and the types and locations of primary resources.
- Extensive archival collections at three major women's history archives: the Sophia Smith Collection of Women's History, Smith College; the Schlesinger Library, Radcliffe Institute for Advanced Study, Harvard University; and the Sallie Bingham Center for Women's History and Culture, Duke University. Local repositories of women's materials also exist, such as the Mujeres Latinas Project, containing collected material of Latinas and their families in Iowa history.
- Women's diaries, journals, memoirs, and personal correspondence are invaluable resources, though they tend to be written by wealthier, formally educated women.
- Primary written sources such as: census records and other genealogical material, legal documents such as divorce proceedings, voter records, shop

accounts and ledgers, architectural plans, cemetery records, town and city directories, and documents from women's clubs.
- Oral histories of the women themselves, as well as of relatives and acquaintances, especially when supplementing written sources or providing new insights in the absence of written sources.
- Visual sources, including photos, postcards, maps, films, and videos.
- Tangible resources, such as objects, structures, and landscapes.
- For researching African American women's public and community activities, church newsletters and bulletins are particularly helpful.[43]

Be careful of idiosyncratic spellings, antique handwriting, and differences in language from current words and phrases. (For example, women who agitated for the vote during the late nineteenth and early twentieth centuries did not often identify as "suffragists.") Question findings and revise research parameters, as some materials might lay outside traditional research repositories. Look for everyone who knew or had been associated with the person you are researching.

LGBTQ+ History

Researching the stories of queer and gender non-conforming people can reveal a great deal about society as a whole.[44] But, given cultural taboos, it can be quite difficult to find information. Historical sources can be scarce. Many sources have been destroyed by individuals worried about the problems that could arise by "outing" themselves in an unaccepting (or intolerant) society.

Recommended sources for researching individuals and communities within this topic include:[45]

- Personal diaries and letters.
- Legal documents, such as laws criminalizing certain activities and court records that detail arrests. (These are sometimes published in newspapers. Keep in mind that published court cases will likely show bias in testimonies.)
- Religious writings and sermons.
- Songs, literary writings, and medical writings of the era.
- Subtle (or unsubtle) features in newspaper and magazine articles.
- Oral histories.
- Photographs, often containing subtle clues.
- With increasing activism in the late twentieth century, the amount of material evidence has increased from the 1960s onward—including political flyers, leaflets, buttons, posters, documented legal protections, evidence of subcultures, and AIDS-related materials.

According to scholar Susan Ferentinos, historians must be vigilant about studying evidence of LGBTQ+ history within the context of the time and not simply applying modern categories to behavior in the past. The use of language has changed, as have the meanings of certain types of behavior and expression. Use caution in referring to people in the past by modern labels they would not have recognized or chosen for themselves. Researching this history requires perseverance, creativity, and a love of sleuthing.

GETTING STARTED: SUGGESTED RESEARCH STEPS

If you weren't trained in historical methodology before becoming a curator, and/or you don't have anyone showing you the ropes, this can all be pretty confusing, even daunting. How do you start? Where do you start? While the answers to these questions—and perhaps the order in which you follow the sources—will differ by project, I provide here some basic practical steps (see textbox 4.1 for a summary of this list):[46]

TEXTBOX 4.1: GETTING STARTED: SUGGESTED RESEARCH STEPS

1) What is the expected end product?
2) Begin with your research questions.
3) What do you currently have?
4) Whose stories are *not* being told?
5) Look to other museums and historic sites.
6) Determine the sources you need.
7) For online research, evaluate carefully for reliability.
8) Check published sources.
9) Identify primary sources and find where they reside.
10) Read with intent.
11) Check non-documentary sources (oral histories, objects, structures, and landscapes).
12) Keep your needs list current.
13) When you feel ready organize your information and write it up.
14) Show your work to others.

---

1) What is the expected end product? Whether you are writing a 60-word statement of historical significance for a newly digitized object, a 100-word exhibit label, an 800-word online article, a lengthy interpretive manual for a historic structure, or an academic research report for a new initiative, this will determine the amount of time and depth you should dedicate to your research. But, even with the briefest of end products, you need to use reputable sources and apply rigor to your research methodology.
2) Begin with your research questions. These will help you determine what kind of information to look for.

3) What do you currently have? Do you have previous research reports, site reports, historic structure reports, object descriptions? View this information from a practical perspective. Be skeptical as you carefully evaluate this information for accuracy and bias. Does it seem to ring true? Do you know where the information came from? Remember that local history is often based upon hearsay and folklore, while oral histories (especially those undertaken long after the time period you are pinpointing for your research) can be inaccurate and lacking in details. Decide what you need to do with this current information. Should you revisit it? Elaborate upon it? Start from scratch?
4) Whose stories are *not* being told? "Listen for the silences" and think critically about why documentation might not exist.[47]
5) Look at other museums and historic sites doing similar work and dealing with similar issues—in journals, in books, or by contacting them directly. If needed, consult experts, specialists, other curators, and community members.
6) Determine the sources you need (or, at least, those you can access within your project timeline, noting others for future reference), and document where to find them. Be strategic as you search for answers to your research questions and be creative in identifying new sources to uncover.
7) If you choose to start with online research, first reference the earlier section on Online Research, then peruse the following tips. Knowing how to do keyword searches is crucial but it takes practice before it becomes intuitive. Search words and phrases can be tricky to create, especially when language, spellings, and phrases have changed over time. Always try alternate ways of wording your searches. Boolean search techniques (that is, methods of using operators and symbols—such as quotation marks, asterisks, and "plus" signs) can help refine your web searches. Each search will garner listings of numerous websites. Check their domains, looking especially for .edu (related to colleges, universities, and other educational institutions), .org (for museums, historic sites, and history organizations), and .gov (government-administered sites). Domains ending in .com (commercial websites) can be especially useful for company histories. Go through the results of your search findings until you find enough websites of value. If you find nothing (which often happens), try searching on a different word or phrase.
8) Check published sources, through library catalogs, archival finding aids, and online bibliographies and databases. Start with current scholarship, checking footnotes and bibliographic references to expand your sources.
9) Identify primary sources and track down where they reside. If doing local history research, check with your local public library, local and/or state historical society or archives. Some sources may be digitized, or at least

can be located through online finding aids. If not sure, contact librarians and archivists to help you.
10) Read with intent. Be critical as you sift and sort, evaluate, and analyze until you feel satisfied with your findings. Learn how to process information quickly and efficiently. Be continually open to new leads. Every source is a tool for filtering information. It is easier to judge the quality of a source if you have been immersed in it for a while. Your internal lens will improve over time as you get to know the material and the topic. Be open to asking new questions and then delving once again into available research sources.
11) In addition to written sources, don't forget the often key documentary sources of oral histories, objects, structures, and landscapes.
12) Keep your needs list current. Cross off sources you have used and add more as you find them. Organize the information you have accumulated and document where it came from (saving untold amounts of time later).
13) When you feel ready, organize the information and write it up. As mentioned before, it will take different forms depending upon the end product. Cite footnotes and include a bibliography or source list.
14) Show your work to others, to review and comment. Be open to others' suggestions. Revise accordingly.

PUSHBACK STRATEGIES

In doing good public history—particularly when you liberate the narrative—you might get pushback—that is, a negative or unfavorable response that prevents your findings from being publicized or from being incorporated into a public offering. This pushback might come from board members, senior staff, vocal stakeholders, other museum staff, or the general public. Pushback is tough. It feels like you have fallen short of your ideals—that is, to tell history closer to what it really was rather than what others wish it had been. It might discourage you from researching and presenting these stories, and from future research projects.

But don't despair! Strategies to help surmount these challenges include:[48]

- Listening to/understanding the perspectives of those giving pushback, or from whom you expect pushback.
- Establishing project goals that are consistent and frequently communicated.
- Identifying important audiences and understanding what engages them.
- Seeing where the public stands through community engagement and visitor studies.
- Communicating updates to staff and helping frontline staff feel supported.
- Reminding yourself that doing something is better than doing nothing!

WHY HISTORICAL THINKING MATTERS

So, why go through all the trouble of doing this work? Admittedly, both academic historians and public historians believe that accurate history is important. And doing this aligns with the public service mandates of our museums. But it's a lot of work. It takes time and energy. You might have to defend your rationale for doing this work. And, in the end, you might get not only no credit but aggressive pushback. This work clearly can seem thankless at times. So, in the bigger picture, why does it matter? What good does it do for our public and for society at large?

In an era of false news, personal bias, half-truths, conspiracy theories, partisan agendas, and manipulated data, history matters because the past informs the present. According to AASLH's Value of History Statement:[49]

- History nurtures personal and collective identity in a diverse world. People discover their place in time through stories of their families, communities, and nation. These stories of freedom and equality, injustice and struggle, loss and achievement, and courage and triumph shape people's personal values that guide them through life.
- History is the foundation for strong, vibrant communities. A place becomes a community when wrapped in human memory as told through family stories, tribal narratives, and civic commemorations as well as discussions about our roles and responsibilities to each other and the place we call home.
- History is a catalyst for economic growth. Communities with cultural heritage institutions and a strong sense of historical character attract talent, increase tourism revenues, enhance business development, and fortify local economies.
- History helps people envision a better future. Weaving history into discussions about contemporary issues clarifies differing perspectives and misperceptions, reveals complexities, grounds competing views in evidence, and introduces new ideas; all can lead to greater understanding and viable community solutions.
- History provides today's leaders with role models as they navigate through the complexities of modern life. The stories of persons from the past can offer direction to contemporary leaders and help clarify their values and ideals.
- History, saved and preserved, is the foundation for future generations. By preserving authentic and meaningful documents, artifacts, images, stories, and places, future generations have a foundation on which to build and know what it means to be a member of a civic community.

In short, history is essentially a "training ground for democracy."[50] Democracy thrives when individuals convene to express opinions, listen to others, and take action. Inevitably, our work can help support a more tolerant, diverse, and inclusive society by generating a better understanding of the diversity of human experience across time and place.[51]

It is truly important work!

REFLECTIVE PRACTICE

After reading this chapter, do you think you have what it takes to think historically, using rigor and sound methodology to pursue the many avenues of research necessary to ensure that your museum is as truthful and inclusive as possible? Consider the following questions to find out:[52]

1) Are you insatiably curious? Do you have a passion to dig for clues, leaving no stone unturned until you have pieced together the facts that make up a cohesive story? Are you willing to creatively search for and keep an open mind when considering new avenues of information? Are you an avid reader, conference-goer, information gatherer—always hungry to learn more?

2) Do you insist on historical accuracy, as much as that is possible? Do you carefully and critically weigh evidence for accuracy and bias? Do you aspire to "tell the truth" even though you might have to settle for simply avoiding obvious falsehoods? Are you willing to work with the many contradictory, fragmentary bits of information that will turn up and sometimes admit you don't know something? Do you report your findings as accurately as possible?

3) Are you analytical and skeptical? Are you willing to question everything until you find out more? Can you decide who should be trusted/believed/held accountable for their words and deeds? Are you willing to reject cherished myths and stereotypes and aim for a more realistic assessment? Do you look for what's missing? Can you avoid confirmation bias (the tendency to ignore evidence that challenges your original assumptions)?

4) Are you empathetic? Are you able to step in the shoes of another person and see the world as they do? Do you strive to understand a person's motivations for a decision or action?

5) And, perhaps most difficult of all, are you willing to give up your power and singular place of privilege as a curator to share authority with others, in the spirit of collaboration and inclusion?

5

Curating Exhibitions, Large and Small

I was fresh out of graduate school, starting my job as a curatorial assistant. I spent much of my time familiarizing myself with my collection of household equipment, learning how to navigate the massive campus at Henry Ford Museum and Greenfield Village, and—on a daily basis—trying to figure out who could answer all my questions. Meanwhile, the decorative arts curators were periodically meeting about a new exhibition called "Taste in America, 1830-1910," focusing on changes in home furnishing styles through those decades.[1] Eventually, I was invited to attend the meetings because one of the younger curators in the group decided it might be useful to consider the design of kitchen equipment in this exhibition. The other curators all smiled at me politely, then proceeded to ignore me. Our director, who led the meetings and was a specialist in decorative glassware, seemed to be fine when I quietly assumed the role of meeting notetaker.

Amid this exhibition planning, Harold Skramstad—a noted changemaker in the museum field—became president of our museum. And did he make changes! From day one, he established new standards and ways of doing things that, for the first time, professionalized the museum.[2] Nothing went unnoticed. Not even that exhibition. He swept away the concept of a bunch of curators sitting around a table making all the decisions about an exhibition and he set up a cross-functional team, with a designer, an educator, a marketing specialist, and one curator to represent all the others. That curator, it turned out, was me! When I heard about his plan, I was trepidatious. What did I really know—about this topic, about the collections related to it, about creating exhibitions? Yet, confident that I had senior-level support behind me, I forged ahead.

Years later, when I asked Harold Skramstad what he had been thinking when he put me in charge of that exhibition, he said he "saw something in me." That "something" turned out to be a passion for exhibition creation. After that experience, I was forever hooked. Creating exhibitions has always been my favorite work as a curator.

94

I have been involved in so many different exhibitions—contributing content expertise, collections expertise, and later, exhibition development process and visitor expertise, that I had to think hard about how to approach this chapter. How do I "peel back the layers" to reconstruct those transformative moments, experiences, and learnings that influenced and inspired me? How do I customize the complex and varied nature of exhibition creation to highlight the curatorial role—a role that, in and of itself, has great potential for producing powerful, resonant, and engaging exhibitions at the same time that it requires a sharing of authority with others. I will delve into this dichotomy throughout this chapter.

All exhibitions are different, as all museums are different. But I would argue that there are some core attributes that connect them—steps in the process, the nature of collaboration, and a focus on audience. This chapter is about all those things, specifically as they relate to the curatorial role. It first revisits the topic of public history—this time from the perspective of the "public" part of public history and what that truly means. It goes on to delineate the steps of the exhibition process—especially the crucial but often downplayed (or completely bypassed) planning phase that occurs before the design ever happens—and notes what curators can and should contribute each step of the way. Finally, this chapter turns to how history-based exhibitions are changing in today's world, how this impacts the process, and what curators should be thinking about in developing current exhibitions or upgrading outdated ones.

EXHIBITIONS AND THE "PUBLIC" PART OF PUBLIC HISTORY

In the creation of any exhibition, curators are generally considered the content and collections experts, the go-to people to ensure the historical and scholarly integrity of everything that goes into it. They may share their enthusiasm and expertise with others on the team—for example, by suggesting readings or welcoming everyone's presence in meetings with outside experts. But curators remain the champions, the advocates, the ultimate "quality control" for well-researched, accurate content and for the selection, research, and interpretation of objects that best convey the ideas being presented in the exhibition.

Significantly, though, CurCom's "Curator Core Competencies" document categorizes exhibitions under the domain of "Communications."[3] The document defines this domain as "building trust and rapport with communities and intended audiences by facilitating access to knowledge," which involves the "ability to communicate effectively with a variety of people from different backgrounds." This categorization reinforces the fact that curators are not developing exhibition content for themselves, for their colleagues, or even for others like themselves. Exhibitions are created *in* public spaces, often *with* the public, and always *for* the public. They embody the essence of the "public" part of public history.

In Public Spaces

Most obvious to their connection with public history, exhibitions (unless they are virtual) are installed in the public spaces of museums, intended for public viewing. As independent exhibition designer and developer Kathleen McLean claims, "Museums are not museums without exhibitions, the most prominent and public of all museum offerings."[4]

As museums shift and change over time—taking on new leadership, developing and shaping collections, revising mission statements, and looking to form new partnerships and attract new audiences—exhibitions serve a wide variety of purposes. These can include:[5]

- Highlighting an object or objects from the museum's collections.
- Exploring a new topic.
- Revisiting a previously treated topic with new insight.
- Telling a unique or previously untold story.
- Increasing museum attendance and revenue.
- Raising the institution's prestige or positioning.
- Attracting a new audience or audiences.
- Declaring a position or point of view.
- Embracing the opportunity to form new partnerships and/or work with new advisors.
- Demonstrating a willingness to be a vital part of the community and society by showing a desire to be more inclusive.
- Providing a place for social interaction.
- Experimenting with new exhibition methods and techniques.

Each exhibition has its own qualities, distinctive style, and methods of presentation. But they all share the quality of existing in the public space of the museum.

With the Public

Increasingly, museums are working with the public to develop exhibitions that reflect perspectives other than those of the curator. Much has been written about community engagement that can help in this regard.[6] Whether curators coordinate and lead these discussions or are simply included in the process, this requires sharing authority and authorship of the content with external collaborators. In any of these encounters, curators must hone their facilitation and listening skills. Most importantly, they must leave their ego behind and let go of the assumption that they will have the last word.

Sharing authority with the public in creating exhibitions has become an important way of representing multiple voices and perspectives—especially those of members of communities who have traditionally been under-represented or misrepresented in museums. Often it is a good idea to form advisory groups (long term) or focus groups (short to longer term) to offer guidance on key elements of the exhibition in an ongoing way. If your topic involves the history of a certain community, it is crucial to engage members of, or advisors from, that community and invite their participation in exhibition development. Sometimes these individuals are what the authors of the book *Introduction to Public History: Interpreting the Past, Engaging Audiences* refer to as "experients"—that is, "community members who have gained knowledge through their own living experiences."[7] They can appreciate the museum's attention to people and events they know well but also perceive that the curator or other content expert may not be getting it completely right.

Museum audiences are also being invited and empowered to partner with museums in content creation—by leaving comments or voting within exhibitions, providing input through social media, or being formally invited to join a community or visitor advisory group to shape or direct the course of the exhibition content.

In *The Participatory Museum*, Nina Simon describes three distinctive tiers of visitor/community participation in advisory or focus groups.[8] These relate to the type of commitment that is intended, the amount of control the museum maintains, the relationship between the museum and the participants, and the overall goals for the collaboration:

- *Contributors* provide feedback and potentially contribute objects, photographs, stories, and memories. They might loan something, write a response, attend a single meeting, or answer interview questions, but the internal exhibition team drives the ultimate vision and goals. Community voices may or may not be incorporated into the final product.
- *Collaborators* ensure accuracy and authenticity of the exhibition by participating in the design, creation, and production of their own content or research. The museum helps them feel like partners or co-owners of the content. Community members and the team work together to develop ideas and share some decision-making. The community voice is visible in key elements of the exhibition.
- *Co-creators* are an integral part of the decision-making, design, interpretation, and media experiences of the exhibitions. They are integral to the planning. Their voices are a key piece of the narrative, visible throughout the exhibition (see figure 1.3).

For the Public

A third aspect of the "public" nature of exhibitions—and I would argue the most passed-over aspect by curators—is the fact that exhibitions are for the public and, as such, need to be planned with the public in mind. Curators have many excuses for ignoring or dismissing this aspect of exhibition development. Some consider it exclusively the work of educators. Others claim that they simply don't have time to deal with this aspect of the exhibition when they're focusing upon their core work with content and objects. An all-too-common assumption by curators is that the public has (or should have) the same level of knowledge and interest that they do. This includes the specialized "jargon" that they have learned while gaining their expertise, not realizing that most of the public does not use or know this language. This assumption, unfortunately, leads to the dismissive attitude that making their content understandable to visitors is "dumbing down."

It is important to be cognizant here of the placement of exhibitions under "Communications" in the Curator Core Competencies document. As McLean argues, "If we want exhibitions to be truly engaging, then all exhibit professionals, not only the educators and evaluators, will have to be communicators and audience advocates."[9] Doing this, she explains, involves experiencing our exhibitions from a visitor's perspective:

> We must be interested in what visitors think, and interested in their questions. We must truly want them to enjoy themselves, and to come away from an exhibition with a sense of competence and satisfaction.[10]

Once you start putting yourself in visitors' shoes, you realize that they are dealing with a lot of stuff when they visit a museum exhibition—much of which has little to do with the actual content of the exhibition. Fortunately, many specialists have studied and written about museum visitors and their behavior in exhibitions, and we can take advantage of their writings to gain insight into visitors' patterns of behavior. Here are some basics:

- Visitors bring a wide variety of abilities, knowledge, and learning styles to an exhibition.[11]
- They explore exhibitions at their own pace, in their own way, and on their own path according to their own interests.[12]
- They come looking for personal meaning, confirmation of their personal identities, and relevance to their own lives.[13]
- They visit museums for many reasons that extend beyond learning—for example, relaxation, escape, entertainment, and social interaction.[14]
- They want to feel comfortable, welcome, and competent—not stupid.[15]
- Some visitors seek more contemplative experiences or opportunities to connect with objects, without the interference of interpretation or interaction.[16]
- The physical environment plays a crucial role in their visit, which can include such elements as crowd size, noise, wayfinding, seating, light levels, and temperatures.[17]

- Personal needs are often much on their mind, such as the need for food, drink, restrooms, the needs of children accompanying them, time limits on parking, and other things they have to do that day.[18]
- Many visitors *do* come to museums seeking encounters with real, authentic objects. There is great appeal and intrinsic power in viewing the real thing—seeing something rare, wondrous, and awe-inspiring that they can't experience elsewhere.[19]

As curators, of course we want to share our passion for and expertise about historical topics and objects. But we need to remember what got us interested in them in the first place. I believe that you can bring your interest, passion, and knowledge into museum exhibitions in ways that create deeply meaningful and memorable experiences for visitors. But you must start where they are! As exhibition specialist John Summers says, "You could create an exhibit with well-researched content and engaging interactives, but unless you have also given consideration to these fundamental elements of the visitor's experience, all of your hard work could come to naught."[20]

STORIES AND STORYTELLING IN EXHIBITIONS

In creating exhibitions, the word "story" gets bandied about a lot. In the context of exhibition creation, it usually implies significant content or content specifically selected by the curator for the exhibition. It can apply to a single topic, theme, message, or thesis, or it can relate to all of these in combination. It can also indicate a larger narrative, script, or storyline for the entire exhibition.

But "storytelling" is something else entirely. Telling a story has ancient roots and comes out of an oral tradition. It involves the storyteller's flair for creating a coherent, unified, logical narrative that emotionally grabs the listener. Why is storytelling such a powerful and effective medium? Stories help us make sense of the world. They teach us what is possible. They let us know that others have struggled before us. They encourage us to empathize with people of other times and cultures while, at the same time, helping us to understand, remember, and share our own experiences. Finally, because stories can touch us on a deeply emotional level, they provide a fundamental key to learning and problem-solving.[21]

Unfortunately, the art of storytelling was not covered in most history curators' education or training. As museum scholar Daniel Spock explains, "In history class, we got good grades for presenting well-reasoned arguments supported by facts and generalized to larger societal trends over time."[22] Stories, on the other hand, do not start with facts. They more often begin at an intimate, personal level.

It is easy for curators to be suspicious of the idea of storytelling. It sounds made up. It sounds like fiction. It seems to fly in the face of everything I discussed in chapter 4, Thinking Historically. But Benjamin Filene, associate director of curatorial affairs at the Smithsonian's National Museum of American History, disagrees. In chapter 1 of the book *Storytelling in Museums*, Filene tells us that good storytelling is not at odds with solid research or facts.[23] It is not making up history. A good story, in fact, works from the building blocks of sound historical practice—people, tensions, uncertainties, change over time—and connects them to the foundation of good public history. Furthermore, Filene argues that emotional engagement—so central to effective storytelling—is a powerful tool for visitor exploration and meaning-making, providing personal connections so essential to successful engagement, enjoyment, and learning. In his book, he offers numerous examples of how this approach has proven effective in museum exhibitions.

According to Filene, common attributes of storytelling in exhibitions include:

- The best stories are about people.
- They have tension, beyond basic illustration and simple fact.
- They are particularly rooted in time and place, which is what makes them resonant and human.
- They connect to something bigger, animating broader ideas or tensions.
- They are purposeful about voice, attuned to perspective and tone.
- They don't mind showing that they *are* stories.
- They connect us.[24]

Storytelling has many applications in museum exhibitions: as a tool for teamwork and collaboration; in developing the content framework; as a way to get feedback during visitor evaluations; as an essential element in collecting oral histories; in gathering information about objects for the exhibition; in framing discussions with advisory groups; in creating the design approach and experiential elements of the exhibition; and, of course, in writing labels. Furthermore, this approach has gained increasing favor as a powerful tool in developing exhibitions for social justice and social change in today's world.

Admittedly, it is hard to switch from a didactic model of communicating information that curators are used to and were trained to do to telling stories in an oral storytelling tradition. It takes practice and a different mindset. But, in the end, it is rewarding. And quite effective at engaging visitors. Filene provides added encouragement for us, telling us that

> if we approach storytelling in museum exhibitions with intentionality, a spirit of experimentation, and a determination to listen and respond to how our audiences experience our efforts, then "storytelling" can become more than a postmodern metaphor. It can guide us in our efforts to make museums the relevant, transformative gathering places that we want them to be.[25]

In developing exhibitions related to Indigenous groups and topics, stories and storytelling are not afterthoughts. Instead, they play a central role in the shaping of exhibition themes and topics, relegating objects to a tangential role. Approaching exhibitions through this lens supports Indigenous communities in their efforts toward decolonization, "through privileging Indigenous voice and perspective, through challenging stereotypical representations of Native people that were produced in the past, and by serving as educational forums for our own communities and the general public."[26]

TEAMWORK AND COLLABORATION

The small size of some museums, or the small scale of certain exhibitions in larger museums, will mean that some curators will work more or less alone. But most exhibitions of medium to larger scale, and those at medium to larger museums, will involve curators as part of a larger exhibition team. This will require collaboration with internal team members and often with external partners—from designers and media specialists to outside scholars and community partners.[27]

Curators often love to work alone. That's why some of us got into this field in the first place. Moreover, some curators assume that, because they are experts on the content and collections, theirs should be the last word on the exhibition that focuses upon their topic. But, as mentioned before, exhibitions can have multiple purposes. Furthermore, they can be complicated endeavors. Who exactly makes up an exhibition team and what are some of the inherent challenges to successful teamwork and collaboration? How might curators navigate this murky (often) and challenging (sometimes) world?

In history museums, the core team on an exhibition usually includes, at the very least:

- A curator or content expert.
- One or two designers, including a 3D designer, who is a specialist in how visitors navigate the space and how the exhibition is organized, and a graphic designer, who determines the overall look and feel of graphics in the exhibition, from banners to labels.
- An educator, who, as the audience advocate, links content to intended audiences and might also spearhead visitor evaluation.
- A project manager, who is responsible for setting and maintaining the schedule, budget, and workflow.

Numerous other staff members might also be involved in the creation of an exhibition. In fact, sometimes, by the time the exhibition opens to the public, almost everyone at a museum needs to be acknowledged for their involvement!

The team approach to exhibition creation implies that, while everyone has a particular area of expertise and is responsible for representing a particular point of view, team members share common goals and objectives created for the exhibition, together champion the project's vision, and share responsibility for the outcome.

This all sounds great. If it works. Often it doesn't. It can be a difficult, time-consuming experience.[28] Putting people in a group does not automatically make them function as a team. Working across departments can be frustrating, especially if people are used to working within their own areas. Strong points of view can take over or derail a group process. Unclear roles and undefined final authority for decision-making can slow things down and frustrate people. Territoriality, or loyalty to a discipline, can intrude. Teams can devolve into "groupthink," in which team members avoid their own best judgments and agree with each other for convenience, to not appear stupid, for conformity, because of group pressure, or because of the chaos that ensues when too many people are expressing their opinions at the same time. As a result, everyone becomes too invested in agreeing with each other and they don't consider outside alternatives or input. All these challenges are amplified for people who lack power or status on a team.[29]

The literature on teamwork (both in the museum and business worlds[30]) tells us that teams function most effectively when:

- Everyone understands their roles, responsibilities, and obligations.
- Everyone works toward the common, shared, and understood goal of creating an effective and engaging visitor experience.
- An atmosphere of mutual respect is ensured, in which team members truly listen to, trust, and respect each other.
- Senior management establishes a climate of experimentation, in which it is acceptable for the team to take risks and make mistakes.
- A clear structure for decision-making and conflict resolution has been established.
- Flexibility is embraced as a value among all team members.

The appointed team leader has a great deal to do with the effectiveness of exhibition teams. Often, but not always, this is the project manager. Sometimes this can be the designer or even the curator (more on this in chapter 8, Leading from the Middle). But everyone contributes to the team's success or must suffer its ongoing challenges.

CURATORS AND THE EXHIBITION PROCESS

Initial Planning[31]

Once the decision has been made to begin working on a new exhibition, the excitement is palpable. People want to get started and quickly move forward. But that is not as easy as it sounds. It is inevitable—and human nature—that people working together on a new project will have different ideas and opinions about what it entails and where it is headed.

The planning process lays a firm foundation for everything that will follow. Initial planning will: promote team cohesion by helping get members of the team working together and on the same page; help prevent conflict later; help the team communicate clearly with staff, stakeholders, and consultants; and save time, money, and resources. It provides a road map to follow and increases the likelihood of the success of the exhibition. Of course, the length, time, and depth of the planning process will differ for every institution and every exhibition. The important thing is to engage in a planning process, however it works for you, even if the exhibition is small and you are the sole person working on it. It will help you focus, make decisions as you move forward, and explain your vision to others.

The following steps are recommended in this planning process (see textbox 5.1 for a summary of the role of curators in the exhibition process).

TEXTBOX 5.1: CURATORS AND THE EXHIBITION PROCESS

Initial Planning:

- Identify the topic.
- Understand the charge of the exhibition.
- Develop the preliminary content framework.
- Check in with the public.
- Focus the experience with a Big Idea.
- Create visitor-related goals.

Design to Installation:

- Determine look and feel.
- Evolution of floor plan.
- Refine content and object list.
- Plan experiential elements.
- Write labels, select images.
- Post-installation assessment.
- Create auxiliary materials.

---

1) *Identify the Topic*

The exhibition process starts with identifying a topic or focus. This can come from any number of people or places—the curator, the director, another staff member, members of the community—and serve any number of different purposes. This is a great time for you, the curator, to start reading about the topic. What are the classics? What work is new in the field? What do scholars agree or disagree upon? What are the points of contention? What ideas are fundamental to understanding the topic? If working within a team structure, you can suggest readings for others on the team so you can all start with a shared foundation of knowledge about the topic. This is also the time to do a preliminary check on what collections you have (or might need) for the exhibition and start thinking about experts and potential collaborators who might assist in the exhibition. It is also useful to see what else is being done in the field to help hone your thinking.

2) Understand the Charge of the Exhibition

The official project charge might range from an in-depth written "Project Charter" to an informal conversation between director and curator. Knowing the following crucial information up-front will have an impact on many later decisions: space, location, size, length of the exhibition, budget, and timetable. If working in a team structure, knowing the roles and responsibilities of exhibition team members is critical. This is also a good time to understand or define how this exhibition relates to the museum's mission, vision, and strategic goals. Why is your museum creating this exhibition? What value does it serve to your museum? Knowing the answers to these questions will help in many ways as you move forward with the exhibition planning.

3) Develop a Preliminary Content Framework

This is where you, as the content expert, will begin to identify major topics, themes, and ideas related to the exhibition. What are the accurate, important, and compelling historical stories you want to/should/can tell here? What is your historical point of view, your thesis? How might you divide your essay or content outline into discreet topics? What themes cut across the entire content framework? Turn your research findings into a written report, essay, content outline, or a story-based narrative. The written piece can vary in length, depending upon the scope of the exhibition. Reports might also be written by scholars and other advisors that you involve at this point.

Also at this time, as the collections expert, you will begin to define the collections you might want to use to inform, shape, and deliver the stories. What collections might reveal previously untold stories? Where do you need to do deeper research to ensure that an object is what it purports to be? This is not a final object list (this will come later), but a good first stab. Also begin to identify object conservation needs, loans, and acquisition needs as well as possible supportive images if you plan to include them.

4) Check In with the Public

While knowing about general visitor behavior can help exhibition teams make educated guesses, visitor knowledge, misperceptions, attitudes, and opinions about a specific topic can surprise even the most knowledgeable among us. It helps to check how visitors understand a given topic and how this aligns with the expectations of the exhibition team before much work is started and much money is spent. One of the best ways to get visitor input for an exhibition is through a formal visitor evaluation. Front-end evaluation, appropriate at this phase of the exhibition, involves gathering information about visitor knowledge, perceptions, interests, and expectations.[32] The team might need to involve evaluation experts in this phase. It is easy for curators to dismiss this step or say this is not part of their role. But I have seen some curators' attitudes become utterly transformed as a result of taking part in the evaluation process.

This is also the time to begin to involve community members and advisors. This involvement will likely take time, money, and resources, but, in today's world, involving community members in exhibitions is often crucial and something that curators are frequently involved in. For more on this, see the sections With the Public and Curating Exhibitions in Today's World in this chapter's Exhibitions and the "Public" Part of Public History.

5) Focus the Experience with a Big Idea

With a topic selected, clarity on the charge of the exhibition, a preliminary content framework and object list, and an initial understanding of visitor knowledge, interests, and expectations, it is time to focus your exhibition. In the exhibition development world, the generally accepted way to do this is by creating a "Big Idea."[33] As label-writing expert Beverly Serrell tells us, "Exhibitions that lack a big idea are very common. And they show it because they are overwhelming, confusing, intimidating, and too complex."[34] According to Serrell, the Big Idea should be:

- The key idea you want people to know in your exhibition.
- One sentence—and one sentence ONLY!—stating what the exhibition is about. One sentence forces people to focus and it is much easier to remember than multiple sentences. Often, this sentence includes a subject (the topic), an action (what is the subject about?), and a consequence (why should people care?).
- An internal statement that sets the tone, limits the content, and unifies the team vision moving forward. Visitors may never see this statement, or they may see part of it, but when you ask them later what they thought the exhibition was about, their comments should in some way reflect back on

this statement. This is very helpful in assessing the success of the exhibition after it is open.
- BIG! It should have fundamental meaningfulness. It should not be trivial.
- Written in concise, everyday language that can be easily understood by internal staff, external consultants, and stakeholders.

Even if you are the only person developing an exhibition, and it is small, you should still go through the exercise of determining what is my major point here?

After you have your Big Idea, it helps if you revisit your content framework and consider how you might organize (or reorganize) your ideas into discreet themes, topics, or sub-stories. Each of these should now relate back to and reinforce the Big Idea.

6) Create Visitor-Related Goals

In exhibition planning, visitor-related exhibition goals have been construed in many ways, such as cognitive/affective goals and thinking/feeling/doing goals. Often, educators lead this discussion. Based upon my readings and experience in studying visitor agendas, I like to create what I call "visitor experience" goals, which consist of two questions:

- What do we want visitors to know more about?
- How do we want visitors to feel inspired by/personally connect with in the exhibition?

For curators contributing to this conversation, it is helpful to think back and remember, what did you *not* know when you started studying this topic? What hooked you, got you interested, helped you understand it better, incited your passion for it? How might you simulate that experience for visitors who likely come in with that same lack of knowledge you had when you started?

From Design to Installation, and Beyond

Except for label-writing—the most important curatorial work during these phases—much of the work for curators at this point consists of refinement and the application and alignment of existing content to experiential elements. You will continually find that the work you did during the planning phase will come in handy.

During these phases, curators can or should play a role in these tasks (see textbox 5.1 for a summary of the following list):

1) The Look and Feel of the Exhibition

If you are working on a larger exhibition in which colors, scenic or architectural elements, and graphic design style are important, you might be involved in providing historic reference images that will help inform the overall look and feel of the exhibition. This will also be needed for any immersive spaces or other exhibition components that specifically reference historical eras and/or locations.

2) Getting to the Floor Plan

If you are working on a small case display, doing a preliminary layout on paper that is sized to the case(s) is useful. It will help you determine juxtapositions, whether there are too many or too few objects, and how much space can be devoted to labels. If you are working on a larger exhibition with an exhibition team, I have found this to be one of the most challenging parts of developing an exhibition—that is, turning over your nice, clear content framework and preliminary object list to the messy, chaotic process of creating an exhibition layout.

For a larger exhibition involving a team, sometimes the designer will draft a preliminary layout that you can then respond to. But, other times, you will work together to create the physical layout of the exhibition. Collaborative tools help with this, like arranging Post-it Notes or providing input while a team member makes rough sketches. My favorite collaborative tool for developing exhibitions as a team is the "bubble diagram" (see figure 5.1).

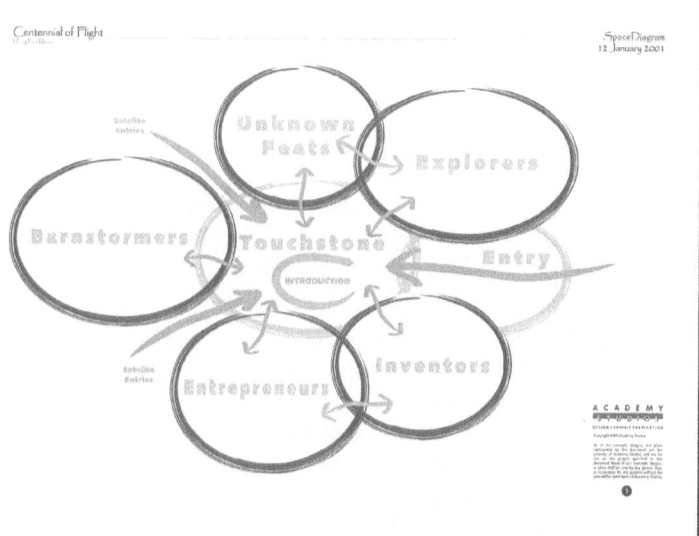

Figure 5.1 This "bubble diagram" represents the first iteration of ideas that emerged during a group brainstorming for the "Heroes of the Sky" exhibition in Henry Ford Museum of American Innovation. Although many more complex and detailed bubble diagrams followed, the final exhibition design still adhered to this basic approach. Credit: Weldon Exhibits/Academy Studios/John Chiodo.

This conceptual "idea map" encourages the entire team to think spatially, to consider how ideas, themes, topics, and objects form patterns and relate to each other. As each idea or key object is placed inside a discreet circle drawn on a page (or created on a screen), the circles' positions to each other start to show linkages, relationships, and juxtapositions. The relationships establish a rough layout of space and provide the foundation for developing the floor plan of the exhibition. A thoughtfully conceived bubble diagram can lead directly to a real-life floor plan. At this point, the exhibition begins to transition away from being just the presentation of knowledge to becoming a three-dimensional experience.

3) Ongoing Refinement of Content Framework and Object List

Having a preliminary floor plan leads to a continual process of refinement of content and object lists. You, as the curator, will need to assure that the history is accurate and credible; to "speak" for the objects and their groupings and juxtapositions; and to champion the presentation of the stories they tell. At this point, you can also be researching and gathering images (if you are using them) that support the exhibition's themes, objects, and stories, provide context, and are visually clear and eloquent. Be mindful of each image's tone, connotation, and potential emotional impact on visitors as well as images that reinforce cultural myths and stereotypes. Document the sources of your selected images, as you will need to know these when you seek rights to use them and determine how to credit them in the exhibition.

4) Addition of Experiential Elements (media, interactives, immersive environments)

As experiential elements are added to enhance the visitor experience—including tactile and other sensory elements, hands-on activities, interactive stations, and media—the curatorial role continues to be important in assessing their alignment with the content. Curators might help supply objects and props for hands-on activities or immersive spaces; be involved in the development of interactives that reinforce exhibition concepts; and help identify, select, and review appropriate media—always ensuring that the elements reinforce the exhibition Big Idea and are true to the content.

If historical or immersive environments are planned as part of an exhibition, curators will likely oversee the creation of these to ensure that they are historically accurate, sensitive to the care and use of objects, and appropriately nuanced in their interpretation (see more detail in chapter 6, Interpreting Historic House Museums) (see figure 5.2). Planning and creating these might occupy a curator's time all the way up to the installation of the exhibition.

Figure 5.2 The 1973 "Back to the Land" commune is a richly detailed immersive environment in the "Your Place in Time" exhibition in Henry Ford Museum of American Innovation. The furnishings plan was based upon primary research as well as personal reminiscences by people who lived in spaces like these at the time. From the collections of The Henry Ford.

5) Writing Labels and Selecting Images

Labels offer a concrete way of making sense of everything in an exhibition. This is the most important and time-consuming task for curators during the design phase of an exhibition. Early in the project, find out when label drafts are due, who is going to review them, when final label copy is due, and whether there will be someone researching image rights. Before writing the labels, you (if working alone) or the exhibition team (if working collaboratively) should determine:

- The overall label objectives (intent, audience).
- The hierarchy of labels and word lengths for each type of label in the hierarchy. This sequence of labels—for example, introductory label, section labels, area labels, and object ID labels—provides a way to visually organize the information into a logical structure and then communicate it in a consistent way for visitors.
- The voice, style, tone, and point of view of the labels. Sometimes your institution will have a style guide with standards for spelling, grammar, and institutional voice.

Writing label text is such a key part of the curatorial role in creating exhibitions that I have devoted an entire section to this (following this section). At this point, you will also be honing your final decisions on images to be turned into graphic panels or graphics on labels.

Be sure that you read label proofs carefully after they have been produced, as they will sometimes still contain errors even if you thought you'd already proofread them. During installation—even with the most modest case display—ensure that the labels are placed correctly and that they are all there. I have experienced cases in more than one situation in which there are inaccuracies and labels missing. You, the curator, are the best advocate for making sure that everything looks correct and is placed appropriately.

6) Post-Installation Assessment

A curator's work on an exhibition does not end when it opens. After opening, take the chance to review your work, make notes if changes are needed from your perspective, and capture lessons learned about what might be improved next time. What went well? What were some of the successes and challenges during the project? Try to resist wanting to change objects or rewrite labels—chances are the budget can't support this unless the errors are egregious. You might again be involved (or want to be involved) in visitor evaluation. The main thing you want to know at this point with these evaluations is whether the exhibition accomplished for visitors what you or the exhibition team had intended at the beginning. Again, you will find that the initial planning you did comes in handy.

7) Auxiliary Materials

Moving forward, you will find that there are many ways in which your knowledge and expertise as a curator can help further ensure the success and impact of the exhibition. Here is where you can bring back some of the content that, by necessity, had to "fall off the wagon" during the exhibition development process. This might include:

- Preparing interpretive materials for, and helping train, interpreters or tour guides.
- Reviewing press releases about the exhibition, checking for accuracy.
- Granting interviews to the media when the exhibition opens.
- Providing content for the preparation of K–12 curriculum materials and family guides.
- Producing a written exhibition catalog, writing a piece for a mobile app, or writing online content related to the exhibition for your museum's website and social media platforms.

- Helping to conceptualize and/or review merchandise related to the exhibition.

WRITING LABELS

Label-writing is one of the most important curatorial tasks in creating an exhibition. This is your chance to communicate the content that you've been researching and applying to the development of themes and messages; using as the context for the selection of objects, documents, and images; and aligning with exhibition elements and experiences. At the same time, as mentioned earlier, you are using these labels to communicate effectively with the public—a wide range of people who are likely *not* like yourself.

It is important to understand that museums are not like being in school. Visitors feel under no obligation to study, memorize, and learn labels so they'll get a good grade on a test. They are there on their own time, for their own reasons. Labels should enhance the overall visitor experience in a place where visitors voluntarily devote time and effort and expect positive rewards, such as confirmation of existing knowledge, uplift, enlightenment, inspiration, and provocation.

Visitors' Label-Reading Behaviors

It is second nature for some curators to assume that visitors will read all the labels in an exhibition. But, when they inevitably find that visitors wander, read some labels, skim others, and completely ignore still others, they are disappointed. Or frustrated. Or annoyed. The fact is that some visitors will seek out and read all the labels in an exhibition while others won't read any of them. But most visitors will read at least some labels, sometimes for lengthy periods of time—if the conditions are right. What are the conditions that encourage label-reading behavior?

Of course, what and how you will be writing your labels depends upon your museum, the exhibition, and its Big Idea, so there are no hard-and-fast rules. What follows is a summary of visitor label-reading behaviors and tips for writing effective labels, drawn from a vast literature of studies about this topic.[35] According to studies of visitors' label-reading behaviors, labels that attract the most label-reading attention:

- Address what visitors want to know, providing concrete information and answering questions that visitors have on their minds.
- Help visitors feel like "experts," explaining things in a way they can understand it, encouraging them to feel like competent and knowledgeable "insiders."
- Shift visitors' thinking by reinforcing existing knowledge and perceptions, but also correcting misconceptions and offering a different perspective.

- Address larger questions that are relevant to visitors, like what's in it for me, why should I care, and how will knowing this improve my life?
- Have a lasting impact on visitors by being highly memorable and/or motivating an active response.

The literature on visitors' label-reading behavior further reveals that:

- Different visitors (or the same visitors throughout their visit) spend vastly varied amounts of time reading labels—from no time at all to a few seconds to an average of nearly a minute.
- Visitors read a larger proportion of shorter labels than longer ones. But they *will* read more lengthy text if it is presented in smaller chunks.
- Most concentrated label-reading occurs during the first twenty to thirty minutes of a visit. Then, museum fatigue sets in. This can include such challenges as standing up for a lengthy period of time, the jostle of crowds, the attraction of other exhibitions or exhibition components, the onset of hunger, and other practical problems. At this point, visitors become more selective in their reading, more likely paying attention to only those labels that satisfy their curiosity or answer a specific question.
- Visitors want to learn new things, but they also rely on their conceptual frameworks—their previous knowledge and experience—to understand what they encounter.
- Most visitors deal with exhibition topics and concepts on a concrete level as opposed to an abstract one—that is, what it is, where it is from, or what it is for, rather than how it changed the course of history.
- Visitors tend to be very attentive to objects and will often read more about the specifics of an object than about general or more abstract concepts.
- The "average" visitor is generally unwilling to exert a lot of effort to read a label but will stop if something catches his or her interest or attention. This relates directly to Bitgood's Attention-Value Model, which posits that visitors weigh the costs against the benefits of everything they decide to do during a museum visit.[36] "Costs" preventing label-reading can include the many elements of museum fatigue (described earlier), as well as poor lighting, inconvenient or confusing placement of labels, long and wordy text, and unfamiliar language. "Benefits" that encourage label-reading include finding a personal connection, emotional engagement, an attention-grabbing headline, evocative visuals, active involvement, and sharing with others.

Admittedly, some of these findings relate to more than just the text that curators write. Design factors can also influence label-reading. The most important thing to realize about labels is that they are a visual medium. When visitors encounter a label that *looks* dense, wordy, or hard to read—whether it's well-written or not—they may steer clear of it. Some labels also suffer from such design factors as too-small type, difficult-to-read fonts, or not enough contrast between type and background.

Tips for Writing Effective Labels

Despite these challenges, there is much that curators can do in their writing to improve the chances that visitors will read labels. Studies have shown that labels possessing these qualities have proven particularly effective (see textbox 5.2 for a summary of the following list):

TEXTBOX 5.2: TIPS FOR WRITING EFFECTIVE LABELS

- Readable
  - Clear, concise, coherent.
  - Direct, vivid, focused.
  - Well organized.
  - Stick to word count.
  - Appealing.
- Understandable
  - Avoid jargon, abstract concepts.
  - Use shorter sentences, visual references, pronunciation guides.
  - Put main points first.
  - Consistent placement of technical language.
- Relevant
  - Ask so what, then answer.
  - Begin where visitors are.
  - Connect to visitor experience, interests, worldview.

- They are readable. This is because:
  - The writing style is clear, concise, and coherent.
  - The writing is direct, vivid, and focused, using active voice and active language.
  - The structure is well-organized, with a consistent style, tone, and voice.
  - The text aligns to a predetermined number of words.
  - The writing is appealing, not preachy or pedantic, not simplistic or condescending.
- They are understandable. To achieve this:
  - Don't use jargon.
  - Avoid abstract concepts. Focus on what visitors can see, feel, and understand in terms of their own experience. Correct misconceptions visitors may have.

- Replace long words and sentences with shorter, equivalent ones.
- Use visual references.
- Use pronunciation guides if a word is not common or in a foreign language.
- Put main points up front, background further down.
- If technical language is deemed necessary (like car specs or quilting stitches per inch), place them in a consistent location on each label.
- They are relevant to people's lives. This is achieved by:
  - Asking so what, then answering this question for visitors.
  - Beginning where visitors are, then proceeding to where you want them to be.
  - Connecting to visitors' own experience, interests, and ways of viewing the world by giving them information that's useful to them, offering context and connections, and aiming to increase the social interactions that naturally occur during a museum visit.
  - Asking questions in a label only if you intend to answer them, if the purpose is to encourage open-ended conversation, or if you know that they are specifically visitors' questions.

A prime challenge for many curators is that they suffer from what exhibition specialist John Summers refers to as "the curse of knowledge."[37] As Summers explains, "The more you know about a given subject, the harder it can be to communicate, because the more you know, the further away you are from the audience with which you need to communicate."[38] A second challenge for some curators is that they equate the writing of clear, understandable, visitor-focused labels with the specter of "dumbing down." Serrell confirms that "many curators voice their fear and repulsion of dumbing down their content."[39] But, exhibition designer and developer Kathleen McLean strongly believes that having the mindset of, "If the visitor cannot comprehend the label, the visitor is at fault," is an "elitist stance" that is "inexcusable."[40] As Serrell reminds us, there is a huge difference between simplification and clarity, and the goal of labels at all times is clarity.[41]

Labels That Tell Stories

Writing labels in a narrative format—inspired by the tradition of oral storytelling—can be extremely engaging to visitors if this format seems appropriate for the exhibition.[42] Storytelling elements that can be incorporated into labels include:

- An overt beginning, middle, and end. The first sentence is evocative, drawing the reader in by raising an unanswered question or otherwise provoking curiosity.

- An air of suspense and/or tension that continues to engage the reader.
- A framework that traces a journey through time and/or distance.
- Details and sensory impressions that immerse readers so they can imagine the action or circumstance in their mind's eye.

Testing (Prototyping) Labels

When you have drafted a set of labels (or even one or two), this can be a great time to check back in with your community advisory group or re-engage with the public through visitor evaluation. This phase of visitor evaluation, called formative evaluation or prototyping, focuses on refinement.[43] Its purpose is to detect and isolate problems before too much time, resources, and money are used. Formative evaluation in label-testing lets you spot weaknesses in the label's ability to attract, hold attention, involve, and communicate. You can quickly make versions of label copy, test them with a small sample of visitors (five to twenty), and modify and retest the prototypes.

CURATING EXHIBITIONS IN TODAY'S WORLD

Following the groundbreaking exhibition "Mining the Museum" at the Maryland Historical Society in the early 1990s, an increasing number of history museums used exhibitions as a platform to take a stance, tell the hard history, connect with current social issues, and work toward inclusion, equity, and justice.[44] Particularly since 2020, as "the ground under our feet has shifted," more museums than ever have been refocusing their efforts in these directions.[45]

Independent scholar Elena Gonzales has been a particularly articulate spokesperson for museums' mandate to develop inclusive, anti-racist, and equity-oriented exhibitions in today's world.[46] Through her work on "The African Presence in Mexico" exhibition at the National Museum of Mexican Art in Chicago, Gonzales became captivated by the idea that "museums are a tremendous force that can help us create the just societies that we need to live sustainably on the planet."[47] She feels that museums working for social justice can help "learners of all ages" gain the tools they need "to examine problems, find solutions, act pro-socially, and engage in respectful, inclusive behavior that is rooted in an understanding of historical and cultural diversity."[48] By recognizing the inequities of the past and present, by elevating the voices of historically marginalized people, and by building relationships with stakeholders, community members, and other collaborators, curators can help museums "emerge as leaders in a more civic domain and as respectful keepers of a great diversity of culture and expertise."[49]

Gonzales suggests three elements that curators and other exhibition team members can incorporate into exhibitions to help accomplish these goals—resonance, empathy, and a call to action.

Resonance

The concept of resonance implies that exhibitions in today's world need to incorporate both truthful content and emotional relevance. Related to content, resonant exhibitions involve multiple vantage points and voices, admit that there are multiple truths, reveal previously untold and hidden history, and claim a position—refuting the false notion that museums are neutral.

Emotional resonance is achieved through connections to people's own lives and identities, offering multiple points of entry and making sure that visitors of all backgrounds see themselves reflected in the exhibition. Exhibitions using this principle are designed with people of all abilities in mind and ensure that everyone feels invited and welcomed.

Empathy

Elif M. Gokcigdem, who pioneered the establishment of empathy as a field of inquiry for museums, defines empathy as "our inherent ability to feel the emotion of another."[50] It involves perspective-shifting, with the understanding that everyone makes sense of the universe in their own way and that there are multiple ways of looking at and seeing a particular issue or problem. Empathy has increasingly become an essential life skill, with the enhanced need for it to help us connect with each other and find our purpose in a complex world.

Museum exhibitions are uniquely equipped platforms to foster empathy. In developing exhibitions in today's world, cultivating empathy is essential to motivating people to work toward change in our society. Dina Bailey—an independent consultant who champions systemic change in museums so they can positively impact their communities—also advises us to encourage empathy in today's exhibitions. As Bailey explains, we need to be more self-aware, more culturally aware, and more sensitive than ever before to be more accepting and more inclusive of those we deem to be different from ourselves.[51]

Call to Action

According to Gonzales, the combination of resonance and empathy leads to a sharing of perspectives which in turn inspires collective action—that is, it empowers individuals to take steps toward making positive change. The Big Idea is a perfect place to include a call to action—providing a continual reminder for the exhibition team to incorporate this into their planning and inspiring the positive action that the team hopes visitors will want to take after experiencing the exhibition. The call to action can continue to be encouraged beyond the exhibition, through public and educational programming, social media, collaborations with partners, and opportunities for visitors to extend their learning after their museum visit.

Refinements to the Exhibition Process

Working on exhibitions in today's world might necessitate refinements to certain aspects of the exhibition process described in the section Curators and the Exhibition Process. These include:

1) Understanding the Charge of the Exhibition—From the start, these types of exhibitions require institutional support, and their presence should be found in the museum's strategic goals. They might be a direct outgrowth of a DEAI (Diversity, Equity, Accessibility and Inclusion) Statement and/or a more in-depth Statement of Foundational Truths, Non-Negotiables, or Grounding Virtues.[52] Having these connections makes it easier to align the exhibition with institutional strategy and to explain how it fits the institution's mission and vision to staff, stakeholders, community members, the media, and the public. It also leads to easier alignments during exhibition planning.
2) Teamwork and Collaboration—These exhibitions open the door to the incorporation of multiple voices and perspectives. Beyond the creation of the exhibition narrative, these might be included in exhibition planning and decision-making—empowering and elevating voices among staff, community members, and other stakeholders who have previously been silenced or rendered invisible.[53]
3) The Content Framework—The framework needs to be inclusive, truthful, and anti-racist. Curators should pay close attention to choosing inclusive language that "disrupts the perpetuation of unjust power dynamics" by "bringing to light non-dominant narratives, avoiding exclusionary false consensus, and clarifying meaning embedded in coded terms."[54] Creating the object list might involve searching the collection for objects that, either subtly or overtly, represent marginalized individuals or groups, expose hidden history, and tell untold stories. Relevant objects might have to be acquired or borrowed.
4) Checking in with the Audience—Sharing authority is frequently considered essential in these exhibitions. Community engagement is often involved, with the assurance that the partners—not just the institution—will benefit in ways that matter to them. Visitor evaluations must work to center equity and justice in their creation and execution.[55]
5) Big Idea—The Big Idea should reveal important inclusive and truthful content points while also including a call to action.
6) Images, maps, guides, and experiential elements such as interactives and media—These can help reinforce 3D objects or fill in empty spaces left by the lack of objects in telling stories about marginalized individuals or groups.

7) Labels—The exhibition labels should communicate the inclusive, truthful content developed in the content framework. Attention to language is crucial. A storytelling approach can work well (see the section Stories and Storytelling in Exhibitions).

Real-Life Examples

Several examples of real-life exhibitions are described and summarized here. Drawn from both large and small institutions, with topics both broad and narrow in scope, each of these case studies represents a benchmark example of a curator or exhibition team working toward sharing authority, truth-telling, equity, and justice.

Heart Mountain Interpretive Center, Powell, Wyoming[56]

The Heart Mountain Interpretive Center opened in August 2011, dedicated to passing on the Heart Mountain story to future generations. It tells the story of the uprooted Japanese and Japanese American internees to this location during World War II, from their lives before the war to the reverberations of illegal imprisonment upon successive generations of Japanese Americans. The primary goal of the exhibition was to take the position that the forced relocation and confinement of Japanese Americans was unambiguously wrong. The injustice of the entire internment camp program, and specifically that at Heart Mountain, is communicated through the singular voices of the actual people who had been imprisoned here. Outside experts and members of the Japanese American community were extensively consulted.

Two immersive barracks spaces are particularly powerful—with furnishings and stories recreated from diaries, camp newspapers, government documents (scrutinized for propaganda), memoirs, oral histories, and detailed photographs that internees had surreptitiously taken.

"Native New York" Gallery, The Smithsonian's National Museum of the American Indian, New York City[57]

This exhibition explores the question of what makes a place Native and who is a Native New Yorker. The scholarship for this gallery was informed by years of consultation with Indigenous communities and an advisory board of tribal nation representatives and community members. The story-based narratives of actual Native New Yorkers, past and present, are told through the medium of comic art, which was created by Native writers and illustrators steeped in the world of Indigenous comic creation and critique. These creators felt that this approach could disrupt expectations among the general audience (both locals and tourists) about traditional museum text. It also aligned with a 2018 study by the racial and social justice organization IllumiNative, which found that "accurate information, authentic representation, and narrative disruption are essential to ending racism, bias, and discrimination against Native people."[58]

"Finding Our Voice: Sister Survivors Speak,"
MSU Museum, Lansing, Michigan[59]

For this temporary exhibition, Michigan State University Museum turned to community co-creators to tell the stories of female survivors of sexual violence on campus. The staff talked to survivors and family members and decided that an exhibition was needed to "unflinchingly document institutional failures across the decades while stressing survivors' agency in charting our healing journeys."[60] Based upon advice from specialists on sexual violence, trauma, and recovery, the exhibition team formed an advisory group of sister survivors, parents, and the university detective who broke the case. The team allowed the survivors to tell their own story in their own words, plus play a major decision-making role in the exhibition. Through this exhibition, the team's intent was to enhance a feeling of unity between survivors and remind anyone who has been victimized that they are not alone. It also issued a call to action to help prevent things like this from happening again.

Cellblock 4, Eastern State Penitentiary, Philadelphia, Pennsylvania[61]

The long-term exhibition "Prisons Today" asks visitors to grapple with the complicated history of mass incarceration while being immersed in the stabilized ruin of the Eastern State Penitentiary (the world's first true penitentiary, in use from 1829 to 1971). The exhibition starts with what is referred to as "The Big Graph"—that is, a larger-than-life sculptural visualization of the astronomical growth of people incarcerated since 1970, which also dramatically shows that the number of Black inmates has been six times higher in number than White inmates. The exhibition includes a mix of interactive panels, objects, and media interactives. Individual stories that humanize difficult, abstract concepts build empathy and emotional connections. The museum chose to be inclusive in developing the exhibition by using community brainstorming to change and improve initial prototypes. Some tour guides had themselves been previously incarcerated.

"The Power of Children: Making a Difference" Exhibition, The
Children's Museum of Indianapolis, Indianapolis, Indiana[62]

This exhibition features immersive storytelling spaces and components, dynamic environments, and live theater that focus upon the achievements of four extraordinary children who touched the world in unique ways: Anne Frank, Ruby Bridges, Ryan White, and the recent addition of Malala Yousafzai (see figure 5.3).

Figure 5.3 Section of "The Power of Children" exhibition, featuring Malala Yousafzai. Image courtesy of The Children's Museum of Indianapolis.

The exhibition explores issues of intolerance, fear, and prejudice as experienced in the lives of these children, with the hope that they can inspire children today to fight discrimination and intolerance and make a positive difference in the world.

Planning, visitor evaluation, family focus groups, expert advisors, and strategic partners were all key to defining and developing the experience of this potentially sensitive topic aimed at children and families. In addition to formative testing, testing was also conducted in the museum with random families accompanied by children in the target age range on successive iterations of the prototypes, reactions to selected artifacts (e.g., Nazi objects with swastikas), and label phrasing and content.

TENACITY: Women in Jamestown and Early Virginia, Jamestown Settlement, Virginia[63]

This temporary exhibition explored the little-known, captivating personal stories of real women in Jamestown and the early Virginia colony—women who are continually left out of the narrative. It provided a gendered lens toward a more complete story of English colonization, its impact on Virginia's Indigenous people, women involved in Virginia's tobacco economy, and African women who experienced enslavement in Virginia.

The team involved staff, visitors, outside experts, and leading academics. Members of the Pamunkey Tribe of Virginia (whose seventeenth-century ancestors inhabited these lands) helped determine word choice, illustrations, and objects. All of this was done with the intent of creating an accurate, inclusive, and relevant exhibition.

"A Monumental Weight: The Auction Block in Fredericksburg, Virginia"[64]

In 2022, a 1,200-pound block of sandstone associated with the sale of enslaved people became the focus of a new interpretive exhibition in the Fredericksburg Area Museum (see figure 5.4).

Figure 5.4 The auction block as located in the interpretive exhibition, "A Monumental Weight." Credit: *A Monumental Weight: The Auction Block in Fredericksburg, Virginia*, curated by Dr. Gaila Sims. Opened November 2022 at the Fredericksburg Area Museum.

The auction block, located on a downtown street corner in Fredericksburg since the 1840s, was the documented site of at least twenty sales of more than three hundred enslaved individuals between 1847 and 1862. The block had immense historical and emotional significance (often widely diverging) for members of the local community, climaxing in its role during the Black Lives Matter protests of 2020 as a contested symbol of racial justice. Following the move of the auction block to the museum, the staff worked with local scholars and educators, connected with a diverse group of community members, and conducted a front-end evaluation with visitors. The intent of the resulting exhibition was to have people leave with a better understanding of the historical and emotional "weight" of this monumental object.

"Mimi's Family: Photographs of Matthew Clowney," Boston Children's Museum, Boston, Massachusetts[65]

This temporary traveling exhibition, which displayed a series of photographs of local transgender woman Erica Tobias with her children and grandchildren, presented one of the most difficult and controversial topics to present and interpret in a museum exhibition for children and families—that of queer narratives. Since it emphasized the idea that gender is important to a person's identity, many strategies were devised to both counter arguments that themes of gender and sexuality are inappropriate for children and to make sure that families felt as welcome and comfortable as possible in the exhibition.

The exhibition team worked with community partners with trans experience and expertise to create a resource guide with a glossary for use both in the gallery and for visitors to take home. The exhibition also included interactive story stations, a book nook, explanatory text, and welcoming and knowledgeable staff. Throughout the exhibition, caregivers were encouraged to be the narrators, helping guide the children's learning experience.

"Chinese Medicine in America: Converging Ideas, People, and Practices," The Museum of the Chinese in America, Chinatown, New York City[66]

This exhibition framed the context of Chinese medicinal practice in America and how these traditions are still in use in contemporary culinary and medical practice. A member of the Chinese community who had deep expertise in modern Chinese herbal practices and traditions served as the guest curator of this small-scale exhibition. She collaborated with colleagues, scholars, teachers, friends, members of the community, and a formal advisory board to gather multiple perspectives. The exhibition re-created the interior of a traditional Chinatown neighborhood store from the past and included a series of stories of people who were familiar with the uses of these ingredients and concoctions. This modest, community-based collaboration was intended to engage both those who were steeped in expertise from lifelong scholarship and practice and those who were new to the stories.

"The Sand Creek Massacre: The Betrayal that Changed Cheyenne and Arapaho People Forever," History Colorado, Denver, Colorado[67]

This exhibition, which opened in 2022, presents a powerful account of the atrocities that occurred in southeastern Colorado on November 29, 1864, when the US army murdered more than 230 Cheyenne and Arapaho people. The history of that betrayal is told from the perspectives of Cheyenne and Arapaho tribal representatives, drawn from oral histories that have been passed down through generations. Cheyenne and Arapaho people continue to live with the unresolved trauma the massacre left behind on their communities and families. The exhibition was a decade in the making, since the museum's first exhibition recounting the tragedy, open in 2012, quickly closed after tribal representatives criticized the museum for excluding their input, arguing that, because of this, "It had no sense of trauma."[68] Every aspect of the exhibition has been reviewed and approved by members of the Cheyenne and Arapaho tribes.

"¡NUEVOlution!' Latinos and the New South," Levine
Museum of the New South, Charlotte, North Carolina[69]

In September 2015, the Levine Museum launched a bilingual, interactive traveling exhibition portraying diverse Latino experiences in the South. It involved a collaborative effort with input from a broad spectrum of participants to focus on the effects of the transformative influx of Latino newcomers to the southern states in the past two decades. Inspiration for this project began in 2011, when the Levine Museum brought together a cross-section of Charlotte's population to spark a dialog with Latino newcomers, called the LATINO NEW SOUTH project. The collaborative team subsequently spent nearly three years developing the content to tell this complex, changing, and current history. Community feedback informed the title of the exhibition; the inclusion of stories of success not just struggle; more focus on language, race, and ethnicity; and a greater number of experiential elements. It also brought more interest in flattening the traditional hierarchical structure of exhibition development.

"WINIKO: Life of an Object," First Americans
Museum, Oklahoma City, Oklahoma[70]

At First Americans Museum, an all-Native curatorial team preserves and interprets the histories of the state's thirty-nine tribes. "WINIKO: Life of an Object" offers "a new model of culturally informed care, shared authority, and cultural sovereignty and reclamation in the museum."[71] This exhibition unites historical objects long held at the Smithsonian's National Museum of the American Indian collection in Washington, DC, with their Indigenous relatives and cultures in Oklahoma, providing the opportunity for both communities and descendants to contextualize and treasure them.

In the unique object labels, all object names are written in their original Indigenous language, with an English translation in parentheses, along with the object's tribe of origin, its user or maker, and the circumstance under which it left its community. Each object label is written in first-person by a representative of the original tribe and many of them pair photographs of original creators/users with contemporary descendants to highlight the continuity of these families and cultures as embodied in the objects.

REFLECTIVE PRACTICE

As a curator, you are probably already knowledgeable about content- and object-related tasks in creating an exhibition (covered in chapters 2, 3, and 4). But what about the other parts of exhibition creation, the kinds of things that have been discussed in this chapter? Here are a few activities that will help you expand your knowledge in these areas and ensure that you are contributing to future exhibition planning in the most positive and productive ways possible.

Getting to Know Visitors

- The two seminal (and still groundbreaking!) readings that initially sparked my interest in learning more about visitors were the article by Mihályi Csikszentmihályi and Kim Hermanson, "Intrinsic Motivation in Museums: What Makes Visitors Want to Learn?" and the book *The Visitor Experience* by John Falk and Lynne Dierking.[72] These are easy reads and they will truly change your thinking. After reading these, if you're hooked like I was, check out the other sources on this topic that are listed in notes 11 through 19. If you can, do the readings with others and discuss your thoughts together.
- Take part in a visitor evaluation, helping frame questions, interviewing visitors based upon standard protocols (see sources in note 32) and actively participating in the discussion of findings. It just might transform your thinking forever!

Exhibition Roles and Process

- Talk to other members of the team, at least to an exhibition designer and an educator. Ask them what they think about, what's important to them when they work on an exhibition. It helps to walk through an exhibition while you're doing this.
- *Exhibition* is a journal of exhibition theory and practice for museum professionals, published by NAME, the National Association for Museum Exhibition. The table of contents for each issue, and many of the articles, are available online at https://www.name-aam.org/past-issues-online. If you get really hooked on these articles, you can purchase past issues as well as subscribe to the journal itself.

Writing Labels

- If you'd like to brush up on studies of visitors and their label-reading behaviors, check the related books and articles listed in note 35. For basics, start with the label-writing sections in McLean, *Planning for People in Museum Exhibitions*, and Summers, *Creating Exhibits That Engage*. For an in-depth read, see Serrell, *Exhibit Labels*. If you can, do the reading with others and discuss your thoughts together.
- Narrative, or creative, nonfiction provides a useful model for exploring storytelling techniques in label-writing. Narrative nonfiction writers begin with well-researched historical information and then apply such story elements as strong character portrayals, a dramatic unfolding of events, descriptive settings, and active verbs to make the reading experience vivid, emotionally compelling, and enjoyable. Read (or re-read) a narrative nonfiction book, such as: Isabel Wilkerson's *The Warmth of Other Suns: The Epic Story of America's Great Migration* (New York: Random House, 2010); Timothy Egan's *The Worst Hard Time: The Untold Story of Those Who Survived the*

Great American Dust Bowl (Boston: Houghton Mifflin Co., 2006); or David Laskin's *The Children's Blizzard* (New York: Harper Perennial, 2005). Think about (or discuss with others) how these elements might apply to how you'd write an exhibition label. Better yet, try writing some labels in this style, either reworking the labels in an already existing exhibition or drafting a set of new ones for an exhibition you're working on.

- It's always informative to check in with visitors about new labels you're writing. With help from others on staff (such as the education staff or an experienced evaluator), try writing a label in a few different ways and ask visitors which they prefer, why, and what they don't understand. You can also try having different team members write their own labels for the same topic and test visitors' opinions that way.

Exhibitions in Today's World

- If your museum is on board and working on exhibitions that are inclusive, anti-racist, and equity-oriented, that's great. But if not, you might still be able to do some pre-work on this. One way to do this would be to go through your museum and do an audit of current exhibitions, noting what could use upgrading and what might be involved in doing this (new collections, new research, etc.) to bring this more updated perspective to your institution. Think about how you might begin this work on your own.

6

Interpreting Historic House Museums

For a curator, bringing a historic structure back to life through research, objects, and interpretive strategies involves determination, rigor, and an ability to connect seemingly disparate dots. It can be tedious and, at times, frustrating. But it can also be highly rewarding and deeply satisfying. Here are two examples from my own experience that reinforce both the rigor and the revelation involved in this work.

Back in the 1990s, I worked on reinstalling and reinterpreting a historic general store in Greenfield Village (see figure 6.2).[1] I diligently did all the research I could to reconstruct the history of the storekeeper, the customers, the local community, and the broader context. But the *real* challenge was determining the appropriate stock for an 1880s store—which ended up consisting of some six thousand items of every shape and kind. This involved studying historic store photographs, reading oral reminiscences and local newspaper columns, analyzing entries in store account books, researching the existing items that had sat in the store for more than half a century, acquiring new ones, and determining appropriate reproductions. I created a shelf-by-shelf template of what the installation would look like. I imagined the space by writing out the experience as if visitors were walking through it. I even worked with an exhibition designer to mock up each shelf on cut-to-size brown butcher paper. But nothing prepared me for what it was like to install the real shelves of the real building with real objects. I felt like I witnessed this inanimate building actually spring to life and become a real working store again! Apparently, visitors agreed—and *still* agree, at least according to the interpreters who work there, with whom I have continued to meet to review and refine interpretive materials.

In late 2020, at the height of the COVID-19 pandemic, I revisited and expanded the written interpretive manual for the 1860s-era Dr. Howard's Office in Greenfield Village (see figure 4.2).[2] I did my due diligence researching this country doctor, his family, the local community, his patients, and his medical practice. Then one day while I was working on the manual, it hit me. At the time Dr. Howard was practicing medicine, people didn't understand the nature of germs and contagion, nor that diseases were transmitted in these ways. As a result, infectious diseases—such as cholera, typhoid, and yellow fever (or malaria)—were the leading causes of death at the time. These often reached epidemic proportions and people constantly feared that they, or members of their families, might contract them. But, without knowledge of what caused and spread disease, along with the lack of modern pharmaceuticals (including vaccines), safe drinking water, and improved sanitation facilities, nineteenth-century country doctors constantly fought an uphill battle.

How relevant this was, I thought, to our lives in 2020—to the COVID-19 pandemic; to people fearing they or members of their family might contract the virus; to our knowledge of germs and our understanding that washing our hands, cleaning surfaces, and wearing masks reduced its spread; and to our hopes for combatting this disease through the application of successful vaccines. Suddenly, the story of a country doctor practicing medicine in the nineteenth century took on a much more relevant connection to modern times.

This chapter explores the meaning of interpretation, describes three key issues that influence curators' interpretive work, and lays out a series of steps for curators doing this work. It concludes with several real-life examples and strategies for getting started.

Admittedly, interpreting historic structures and spaces can be a lot of hard work. But I like to think there's a bit of magic in it too!

WHAT IS INTERPRETATION?

After looking at numerous definitions of interpretation, I believe that a good working definition for the purpose of this chapter is that interpretation is "a mission-based approach to communication aimed at provoking in audiences the discovery of personal meanings and the forging of personal connections with things, places, people, and concepts."[3] This definition contains several key words and phrases that are worth further exploration:

- "mission-based"—Reinforcing the necessity that all interpretation aligns with an organization's mission statement.
- "communication"—Although many interpretive techniques can be employed, traditional interpretation has generally involved live communication between a knowledgeable staff person and visitors.
- "provoking in audiences"—This comes directly from the most influential writer and champion of interpretation, Freeman Tilden. More on him in a bit.

- "the discovery of personal meanings and the forging of personal connections"—Effective interpretation consciously (or unconsciously) inspires personal meaning-making that incorporates both emotion and intellect. Sometimes simply stepping inside the historic structure or space can inspire these connections.
- "things, places, people"—Traditionally, the term interpretation is used in connection with concrete, tangible things—structures, sites, or spaces that were inhabited by people in the past. While the term is occasionally applied to exhibition planning, I will use it here to relate strictly to uncovering and communicating the meanings behind these concrete, tangible things.

Interpretation is a term that has been embraced by the history museum field, especially by outdoor and living history museums.[4] But, in fact, the term originated not with museums but with parks.[5] From the philosophy of naturalist John Muir in the 1890s to that of his protégé Enos Mills in the early twentieth century, interpretation became connected with the role of the nature guide—that is, someone who translates, who "illuminates and reveals" what is seen and experienced in the parks to others with less knowledge and experience.[6] This approach was—and still is—intended to inspire people to want to care for, protect, and champion America's cultural and natural resources, ensuring their sustainability and long-term preservation.

In 1957, writer and environmental educator Freeman Tilden set down for the first time the principles and theories of interpretation in his book *Interpreting Our Heritage*.[7] Drawing heavily from Mills's earlier writing, Tilden's "Principles of Interpretation" continue to inspire outdoor museum and living history practitioners today. They are summarized as follows:

- *Relate* what is being displayed or described to something within the personality or experience of the visitor;
- *Reveal* the main concept or theme, through a creative, unique, memorable viewpoint;
- *Provoke* thought among visitors so they actively seek to discover for themselves rather than simply passively receiving cold facts;
- *Unify* the message by organizing information, presenting the whole picture rather than fragments, and making connections;
- Interpretation is an art which combines many arts, whether the materials presented are scientific, historical, or architectural. Any art is in some degree teachable; and
- Interpretation addressed to children should not be a dilution of the presentation to adults, but should follow a fundamentally different approach.

THREE KEY ISSUES INFLUENCING CURATORS' INTERPRETIVE WORK

Issue #1: The Sustainability of Historic House Museums

In recent years, historic house museums (a term now used to comprehensively refer to historic structures, spaces, and sites) have received a great deal of scrutiny. Most of it has not been positive. Many historic house museums were initially preserved because of their association with prominent White men. In addition to numerous already existing historic house museums, many new ones were created during the bicentennial era of the late 1960s and 1970s, citing as their rationale an association with patriotism and/or the founding of our country. Often, these places were created with no long-term plans for funding or staffing. Furthermore, the interpretation tended to be static.

In 2002, Richard Moe, then-president of the National Trust for Historic Preservation, posed the question: Are there too many historic house museums? This ignited a field-wide response.[8] Two symposia (referred to as Kykuit I and II because they were held at the majestic Rockefeller Estate of that name) explored common assumptions, traditional approaches, and the consequences of professionalization. Among the conclusions drawn at the first symposium (Kykuit I, held in 2002) were that, while historic house museums could be emotionally powerful settings contributing to community stability, pride, and sense of place, they seemed to be stuck in a rut. They needed to move beyond a one-size-fits-all approach.

The conversation continued at Kykuit II (held in 2007), which focused upon standards and best practices, models of innovation and success, alternative uses of historic sites, and expectations of historic sites and funders.[9] Donna Ann Harris's groundbreaking 2007 book, *New Solutions for House Museums: Ensuring the Long-Term Preservation of America's Historic Houses*, described several successful alternatives to the one-size-fits-all approach.[10]

Meanwhile, AASLH's Historic House Affinity Group Committee (now the Historic House Museums Affinity Community) took seriously the challenge to establish a set of standards and best practices for the ongoing sustainability of historic house museums. This committee's work resulted in the 2008 Technical Leaflet, "How Sustainable Is Your Historic House Museum?"[11] This article identified eleven signs of a healthy, thriving historic house museum, which included the eight points listed below (specifically chosen because of their connection with curators' interpretive work):

- Serving its audience and being valued by the community.
- Being inspiring.
- Leaders adhering to a standard of excellence.
- Leaders embracing a culture of learning and a spirit of inquiry.
- Leaders being proactive stewards of their buildings, collections, and landscapes.

- Being interpreted in innovative and creative ways that extend well beyond the traditional house tour.
- Leaders being strategic in their thinking and in their activities.
- Being well prepared for the future by adapting current technologies to enhance the understanding of their resources, expand public access, and improve efficiency and effectiveness.

But change is hard and reluctance to rethink or abandon traditional historic house museum approaches continued. The 2015 book *Anarchist's Guide to Historic House Museums: A Ground-Breaking Manifesto* painted a bleak picture of the static and insular state of many historic house museums at the time.[12]

Fortunately, an increasing number of enlightening new models and examples were being described at conference sessions, workshops, and webinars as well as being featured in books, journal articles, and blogs. Many of these examples were captured in the highly acclaimed 2019 book *Reimagining Historic House Museums: New Approaches and Proven Solutions*, which reflected an indication that historic house museums were finally turning a corner.[13] But, for some, the future has remained uncertain.

Despite "the passage of time, global pandemics, seismic political and societal shifts, and an economic roller coaster," most of the advice from the 2008 Technical Leaflet still rings true.[14] But the field has also changed since then. This topic was revisited in a 2023 Technical Leaflet, with a more explicit call for diversity, equity, inclusion, and accessibility.[15] Once thought merely important, these are now considered *critical* to all aspects of historic house museum operations. Key points in this new updated list of standards included the importance of:

- Tying the interpretation directly to the museum's mission and vision.
- Correcting previous interpretation that is inaccurate, biased, and/or out of date.
- Creating collaborations to share authority with communities and ancestors represented.
- Including multiple perspectives.
- Utilizing the museum's unique strengths, including sense of place and ties to the local community.
- Connecting with visitors in meaningful ways, through current issues and events as well as visitors' lived experience.

My suggestions for what curators can do related to Issue #1:

- Align your work with your institution's mission, vision, and strategic plan.
- Determine who your audience is (or might be) beyond general visitors and consider involving them in the process.

- In developing interpretive themes or story points, consider how these might be relevant to audiences in today's world.
- Review your original interpretation (including content, furnishings, etc.) over time so it continues to be fresh, accurate, and up to date.
- Contribute content and collections expertise if there are changes or upgrades to technology, interpretive techniques, or the interpretive program in general.

Issue #2: Uncovering and Interpreting Previously Untold Stories

Attitudes toward interpreting historic house museums have shifted. Many of these places were founded to preserve the history of the dominant culture and do not reflect the full story of the people at that site or in that community. Moreover, the interpretation often uses the records of those who were in positions of power to tell their histories. The words and knowledge of people who have been historically oppressed—women and children, people of color, Indigenous people, LGBTQ+ people, individuals who were differently abled, enslaved workers, domestic servants, immigrants, working class and poor people—were often not saved and, for the most part, were not transmitted through site interpretation. When these people were included, their interpretation often conveyed a great deal of misinformation, shaped by racism, prejudice, gender bias, and a desire to ignore or conceal unpleasant stories about America's past. Moreover, many historic house museums have continued to perpetuate these historic silences.[16]

The advantages (strategic and otherwise) of uncovering and interpreting the histories of people who have been traditionally marginalized or silenced are many, including:[17]

- Lending credence and authority to your institution.
- Tying your institution closer to the community.
- Exposing audiences to new ideas and perspectives, creating energy and building excitement.
- Connecting your institution to the national conversation, through both historical and contemporary issues.
- Broadening your audience to include people who may have never visited a museum, much less *your* museum.
- Showing that museums have the potential to be a force for the public good.
- Providing reparative responses to historical injustices, thereby engendering hope through healing, affirmation, and reflection.
- Teaching empathy and concern for others.

Over the past several years, there has been a particular surge of new attention paid to reinterpreting spaces devoted to honestly and authentically representing the lives of enslaved workers who, in most older interpretations, were ignored, treated anonymously, or considered inconsequential.[18] The many books and articles published about this topic in recent years affirm the crucial importance of this work in:

- Offering tremendous value in helping visitors understand the institution of slavery—not only in the South or with the wealthy elite, but as a cornerstone of the nation's economy and society and an engine of upward mobility for millions of American families.
- Expanding visitors' understanding of the major contributions of slavery, and the lives of enslaved Africans and African Americans, to the political, economic, and social life of the entire nation.
- Providing more comprehensive and balanced stories about *all* who lived and worked at a site, including the voices of marginalized people.
- Dismantling old narratives and replacing them with new, more historically accurate alternatives that are healthy and productive.
- Acknowledging that plantation sites (and other places where enslaved people were forced to labor for others) can be "spaces of brutal terror" and trauma.[19] Too often this has been overlooked in favor of generalized interpretation, but these sites continue to bring immense pain to people whose ancestors lived and worked on them. The truthful interpretation of slavery at these sites takes the depth and breadth of this pain seriously, recognizing that this history has a long footprint that extends to our present day.

Unfortunately, these new interpretations of slavery can also generate outright disbelief and active resistance, as they counter some people's preconceived notions and existing beliefs.[20] Difficult history in general can disrupt long-held personal and collective memories. It can also involve personal suffering, trigger painful reactions, and raise intense emotions. Choosing to present new history of this type requires careful thought and planning; sensitive handling and training; overt alignment with museum mission and vision statements, strategic plans, interpretive master plans, and DEAI (Diversity, Equity, Accessibility and Inclusion) statements; strong leadership; and ongoing institutional commitment and support.

My suggestions for what curators can do related to Issue #2:

- Be aware of your own biases.
- Compare notes with colleagues in the field working on similar projects and dealing with similar challenges.
- When doing community engagement, ensure that input is treated with respect.

- Apply rigorous research methods to get to the truth behind the myths, the legends, and the oft-told stories that can be embedded in long-existing historic house museum interpretation.
- Use your expertise in research to show how history changes, shifts, and is relevant today.
- Use objects in creative ways to interpret untold stories or to interpret absence.
- If experiencing pushback, explain your research process, findings, and interpretive rationale in a way that works for those pushing back. If need be, defer to senior management for support.

Issue #3: The Power of Historic House Museums over Visitors

Studies show that historic house museums can have an almost mystical power over many visitors (see figure 6.1). These places grab ahold of people's imaginations, elicit emotional responses, and stay in people's memories longer than many other aspects of museum visits. A key reason for this is that "historic sites and house museums have at their core the unmistakable advantage that their visitors stand in a place where history happened—where someone from the past lived, where a battle was fought, where important political decisions

Figure 6.1 It doesn't matter that Elvis Presley's birthplace in Tupelo, Mississippi, was moved down the road from its original location, or that the porch swing did not exist at the time, or that the interior décor is not entirely accurate to the era. Places like this hold a mystical power over people. Photo by the author.

Interpreting Historic House Museums

or daily labor took place."[21] They are seen by many as tangible links to the past, where visitors can stand within the same places as real people who lived and breathed.

In their study of visitors to historic sites, anthropologists Catherine M. Cameron and John B. Gatewood estimated that more than one quarter of visitors to these places were active "numen seekers"—that is, people who sought "visceral, emotional responses to an earlier event or time" in order to achieve a connection with the "spirit" of the times or persons past.[22] Numen seekers, according to Cameron and Gatewood, develop deep engagement, empathy, or spiritual communion with people or events of the past.

Unfortunately, numen seekers are particularly susceptible to mythologized and romanticized understandings of the past, as they desire stories that appeal to their emotions and to their urge to connect spiritually with places and objects that inspire awe and reverence. Revealing stories that counter their existing narratives can have a "backfire effect," hardening their preexisting biases, especially when new information challenges their worldviews and sense of cultural identity.

A particularly important characteristic of historic house museums to visitors is the perception of authenticity. In a national study, museum visitors equated authenticity with "stepping back in time and immersing myself in the past" while many of them referred to wanting "an authentic respite in an unreal world."[23] Objects seem to be particularly powerful in conveying a sense of authenticity to visitors. Indeed, in their classic book, *The Presence of the Past*, historians Roy Rosenzweig and David Thelen reported that the respondents in their study felt that objects were direct links to the past, allowing people to imagine experiencing that time and place without mediation.[24]

The power that historic house museums hold over visitors brings with it both positive and negative attributes that history practitioners doing interpretive work should bear in mind. Positive attributes can include:[25]

- Creating a sense of continuity that helps people feel more balanced, stable, and healthy.
- Eliciting personal memories, which help visitors better understand themselves, others, and their place in the world.
- Embodying individual identity, which contributes to people's sense of who they are.
- Enhancing people's civic, state, national, and universal identities, which shifts their sense of history, acknowledges difficult aspects of our collective past, and provides places where reconciliation can happen.
- Providing deep spiritual and psychological benefits of peace, serenity, and inspiration.
- Encouraging creativity and entrepreneurship.

- Supporting learning in a social context, in which the group produces a shared approach to the museum visit, drawing upon common history and knowledge of each other to fill in gaps, learn new things, and create content and meaning together.
- Connecting people with their ancestors, which reinforces their sense of continuity and belonging.
- Fostering mental restoration and well-being, both of which can improve the quality of life and enable individuals and communities to thrive rather than just survive.

The power of historic house museums over visitors can also have negative attributes. These include:[26]

- Visitors' tendency to take things literally. While we museum professionals know we can never truly re-create the past, visitors generally assume that that is exactly what we are doing.
- Details being too subtle. Studies of visitors at historic house museums reveal that they often miss or do not understand the details that curators and other museum practitioners bring to them and potentially miss major points that were intended.
- Personal meaning-making leading to misconstrued history. As visitors attempt to place what they encounter within the context of their previous life experience, they can take away an entirely different meaning of something than what the museum intended.
- Visitors having mixed feelings about uncomfortable history. While these attitudes show signs of changing, many respondents in the 2008 Reach Advisors study expressed mixed feelings about museums presenting difficult and uncomfortable issues of the past, such as slavery, racism, and religious intolerance.[27] They want experiences that make them think deeply, but they also want museums to consider how interpretation at these places will affect their children's and their own ability to confront these more complex issues. As mentioned in Issue #2, presenting difficult and uncomfortable history takes thoughtful planning, effective leadership, and institutional support.

My suggestions for what curators can do related to Issue #3:

- Do not dismiss or discount either the positive or the negative attributes related to visitor engagement with historic house museums. Some things you can control, others you cannot.
- Incorporate a strong presence of people in your content and interpretation. Use objects as a vehicle to help make the people come alive.

- Make sure that your research is beyond reproach and that you are ready to convey it to different audiences as needed.
- Be creative and expansive in using objects and other concrete evidence, to interpret both obvious and untold stories, to enliven both what is there and what is missing.
- Do not assume that your visitors just "get it." Find ways to clearly communicate the stories through interpretive strategies that best fit your goals, your budget, and the experience itself.
- Although your interpretive information is informed by scholarship, write up your findings in an accessible and interesting way. This does not mean "dumbing down." It is the opposite—you want to challenge the audience and encourage them to engage fully in the content, especially when the content contains difficult topics and complex ideas.

THE INTERPRETIVE FRAMEWORK

A strong and effective interpretation of a historic house museum generally involves thoughtful planning. This might be undertaken as part of a team, by a lone curator, or even by a group of volunteers. All historic house museums are different, as are their governing bodies, so it is impossible to generalize. But there *are* steps in the process that ensure the best chance of success:[28]

1) Alignment with Institutional Strategy

The reason for engaging in an interpretive planning or reinstallation project should be closely related to your museum's mission, vision, and strategic plan. What needs does your interpretive framework address? Is it related to preservation goals, an institutional mandate to tell more inclusive stories, ADA (Americans with Disabilities Act, passed in 1990) compliance, new interpretive priorities, and/or new audience goals? After determining this, you or the team should draft an interpretive statement of purpose for the project. This conveys the museum's position clearly and transparently and helps ensure institutional commitment and support.

2) Community Engagement

An important strategy early in the process is connecting with stakeholder communities, especially when the interpretation relates to that group's history.[29] This might involve engaging expert advisors, organizing focus or advisory groups, holding community forums or conversations, or even community co-creation (that is, directly involving members of stakeholder communities in interpretive planning). As the curator, you might be involved in coordinating, leading, or simply listening to these conversations. Consider how these shape your approach to the history, help determine the type and use of objects, and relate to possible interpretive themes and messages.

3) Historical Research

All good interpretation "rests on a bedrock of good scholarship," undertaken by the curator and sometimes with input from outside scholars, student researchers, community members, and/or other experts or specialists.[30] The rigorous attention to detail you pay in historical research provides a firm backbone of believability and authenticity to the final interpretation. This is particularly important for projects involving marginalized individuals and groups, because of the need to get the history right and the many misconceptions that visitors can bring. See chapter 4, Thinking Historically, for in-depth descriptions of different sources, with their pros and cons.

It is useful to start a new interpretive project by checking existing reports in your museum's files along with current scholarship and other sites doing similar work. Usually, because the site or structure you are researching is a known entity, this will involve primary source research, especially local history sources. But, in fact, a range of sources—secondary, primary, visual, oral, material culture, and the physical structure—usually all aid in the creation of a solid interpretive framework.

In your research, determine who is not included and whose stories need to be recontextualized and reframed—or require completely new research. Focus as much research as possible on the stories of specific people, the people who lived and worked in these spaces. This is also a good time to start assessing your collections, particularly what objects and/or structural elements best represent the stories of people. Determine what you do not know and why. How might you make a plan for further research? At all times, consider multiple perspectives and a variety of lenses, and keep in mind that all historical research is evolving and dynamic, subject to new research and scholarly debate.

Write up your research findings into a report, an essay, an outline, or a narrative that articulates the historical significance of the site and synthesizes both its specifics and broader context. Sometimes you have only fragments to go on or must go with representative research. Write the best and most accurate history you can. This key document will lay the foundation for determining the specific time and place upon which to base interpretation, as well as for creating the interpretive themes and techniques.

4) Thematic Interpretation

It is now time for you or the team to begin to shift from information to interpretation. The most common and widely accepted communication strategy for historic house museums is what interpretation experts refer to as "thematic interpretation."³¹ Themes are the central messages or key ideas that both guide you to home in on the main points you want to communicate and help visitors get a focused understanding of what is unique or significant about your historic house museum. Themes make the communication easier to follow and more meaningful to visitors because they connect all the ideas, topics, stories, and physical evidence together. They also steer you away from just giving lists of facts.

The most effective, memorable learning often occurs when big ideas are used as an umbrella for smaller, related ideas. This hierarchy of ideas becomes easy for both interpreters and audiences to follow because, no matter what is being communicated, everything should relate back to the same core ideas. By using this organizing structure, an interpretation can bring in many different topics or pieces of information that illustrate and reinforce a limited number of essential concepts.

In planning thematic interpretation, a main, or primary, message (which serves the same purpose as the Big Idea in exhibitions) should be followed by a series of interpretive themes. While the number of themes varies among different interpretive planners, I find that three themes present a nice symmetry. These become the key ideas that will both guide you through the planning process and ultimately help visitors get a focused understanding of what is most unique or significant about your historic house museum (see textbox 6.1 for a real-life example).

TEXTBOX 6.1: BIG IDEA AND INTERPRETIVE THEMES FOR DR. HOWARD'S OFFICE, GREENFIELD VILLAGE

Big Idea:

Dr. Alonson B. Howard Jr., a country doctor practicing in rural southwest Michigan around the time of the Civil War, combined varying approaches to treating sick patients when little was known about what caused infectious diseases.

Interpretive Themes:

1. People at the time didn't understand that germs and unsanitary conditions caused illness and could lead to death and they were anxious to try just about anything to cure what ailed them.
2. Dr. Howard would have been considered an "eclectic" doctor at the time, choosing from three approaches that he thought would work best for each illness: "conventional" (also called by other names: orthodox/ allopathic/heroic), homeopathic, and botanic medical practice.

3. Dr. Howard used this modest building for multiple purposes, including: a public waiting/examination room, a private office, and a "laboratory" and "pill room" for mixing and storing medicinal ingredients.

Source: Dr. Howard Presenter Training Manual, The Henry Ford, Dearborn, MI.

Each theme should:

- Present one discreet idea.
- Be specific enough to have focus but not be too narrow.
- Give unity and coherence to multiple things.
- Serve as a "basket" for other smaller concepts.
- Be inherent in, illustrated by, or supportive of the material culture and physical evidence at the site.

5) Past-Present Connections

According to Timothy Glines and David Grabitske in their *History News* Technical Leaflet, "Telling the Story: Better Interpretation at Small Historical Organizations," historical interpretation translates human stories from the past into meaningful thoughts for people in the present.[32] Doing this makes past experiences relevant to modern audiences. Although making contemporary connections for visitors is not always intuitive or top-of-mind for curators, it is important for curators to oversee, provide input, or give feedback to these, as I have found that undertaking this part of the interpretive framework involves nuances that only practice in historical methodology can bring. It is very easy for someone lacking experience in this practice to leap to myths, stereotypes, and overgeneralizations.

6) Audience Evaluation and Visitor Outcomes

As with exhibitions, audience evaluation and visitor outcomes will likely be spearheaded by staff members other than curators, although the creation of visitor outcomes is a valuable team activity that will influence everyone's—including curators'—interpretive work.

While your work with community members should be ongoing, this is a good time to check back with general visitors. With evaluation, you can better understand visitor expectations and preconceptions. At this stage, you also might check the understandability and engagement factor of your themes.[33]

Evaluation is particularly important when dealing with difficult and potentially traumatic topics. Evaluator Conny Graft suggests several strategies for gaining visitor feedback on historic house museums interpreting slavery.[34] Topics deemed potentially controversial at this early stage can help staff members be better prepared in furnishing the space and interpreting it to the public.

Visitor outcomes—that is, specific visitor-focused goals—should also be developed at this time. What do you want your audience to take away from the experience—in thoughts, feelings, memories, or actions? Visitor outcomes are not simply learning objectives, although these can be considered, especially in relation to school-age audiences. From my perspective, they should involve strategies for how your interpretation can be made more relevant and meaningful to your audience by:

- Providing context, giving meaning to the ideas.
- Bridging the familiar with the unfamiliar, letting people understand what you're saying by connecting to something they already know.
- Making emotional connections, thereby giving the intellectual information more importance.
- Bringing the ideas down to a personal level, to something people care about and will most likely remember.

7) Interpretive Approach

At this point, you or the team are ready to begin thinking about the actual experience at your historic house museum. As a curator, you should be considering such questions as, how literal will you be in recreating time and place? Will real artifacts be used? Will they be accessible to visitors? Will you be encouraging visitors to touch things? Should you consider reproductions? What further research is needed? What objects need to be further researched or acquired? What stories have you missed?

FURNISHINGS PLANS

The furnishings plan documents in two dimensions what the three-dimensional environment will look like.[35] Though some historic house museums do not use furnishings, these are a core curatorial responsibility and will be treated in some detail here.[36]

In a good furnishings plan, all objects have a purpose. They are there to support the story. In the absence of human presence, objects (as well as structures, structural details, and landscapes) represent the people who made, owned, used, worked at, and went about their daily lives in these spaces. According to Laura C. Keim, in her essay "Why Do Furnishings Matter? The

Power of Furnishings in Historic House Museums," objects are essential to bringing the past alive for visitors.[37] They:

- Structure the experience.
- Reinforce the character and meaning of a structure or space.
- Represent a complicated past, or many pasts, and tell complex stories.
- Embody human action.
- Convey layers of meaning.
- Incorporate both the everyday and the beautiful.
- Create visually compelling spaces.[38]

According to Keim, furnishings in historic house museums have been criticized in recent years for being elitist and off-putting, for representing the past through an idealized lens. While this was certainly true when many historic house museums were founded and initially furnished, many museums are now making efforts to rethink, recontextualize, reinterpret, and refurnish their spaces so that they become gateways into a more complicated past. Keim recommends not devaluing or disposing of collections that were previously saved or acquired to suit ostensibly aesthetic or nostalgic cultural values. Instead, consider layering on additional or alternative understandings of furnishings in wider, even global, contexts to a more multifaceted comprehension. She gives the example of a mahogany parlor chair, which can be interpreted as both a status symbol and the product of enslaved labor and of an industry that was harmful to the environment. In a similar example given by Ken Turino and Nina Zannieri in their essay "Historic House Museums" from *The Inclusive Historian's Handbook*, a sugar cone in the kitchen can reflect both the owner's sweet tooth and evidence of an economy based upon enslaved labor.[39] Many objects have multiple layers of meaning. Ask new questions to uncover new meanings.[40]

Furnishings Rationale and Inventory

For the first time, you are imagining in real terms what the concrete, physical space will look like. Be as disciplined and rigorous as possible, and document everything along the way. In the end, you will probably have to take some leaps of faith and have confidence in your ability to both analyze and imagine. As William Seale claims, "Almost every restored interior represents a combination of fact and supposition."[41] Similarly, Nancy Bryk encourages curators to apply "disciplined imagination" by combining knowledge of the time, place, and material culture with what is known or implied about the people who inhabited the space.[42]

I have found that the most advantageous way to both guide your own decisions about furnishings and to help you explain those decisions to others is to write a brief rationale that describes the overall vision for your arrangement.[43]

An item-by-item inventory of furnishings should follow your rationale, grouped by location and noting such details as:

- Whether the item is an authentic object or a reproduction.
- The date, provenance, and accession number of real objects.
- If applicable, what objects were originally in this place or were owned by the people whose stories are being told here.
- If a reproduction, its source and cost.
- If applicable, structural and setting details such as lighting fixtures, floor covering, window treatments, wall and ceiling treatments.
- Important visual references that support your decisions, with captions and identification numbers. If these references are not from your collections, cite your sources.

Props and Reproductions

Whether called props or reproductions, facsimiles of objects that were made and used in the past should be considered logical and important additions to the furnishings plan of a historic house museum. In her article "But They're Not Real! Rethinking the Use of Props in Historic House Museum Displays,"

From the Collections of The Henry Ford (2008.171.820/THF53774)

Figure 6.2 To get across the concepts of object quantity and newness at a real working store, the furnishings plan for the J.R. Jones General Store in Greenfield Village called for a combination of historical objects (like the showcases, boots and shoes, and tin spice canisters) and reproductions (like the wooden boxes and labels, tin food cans, posters and signs, and barrels). See Textbox 6.2 for Reproduction Criteria for this historic general store. From the collections of The Henry Ford.

Bethany Watkins Sugawara advises that "used effectively, props can provide a vital link between the static objects of a past life and the visitor's understanding of what that life must have been like."[44] Props can draw the eye, lend interest and atmosphere, bring the past to life, and serve as excellent interpretive tools when real objects are lacking or are too rare or fragile to display. These can include such items as letters, sheet music, food, clothing, accessories—anything that reinforces a lived-in atmosphere and enhances the impression that real people inhabited this space.

How does one decide whether to use historical objects or reproductions? This depends upon a number of factors, unique to each project. For the J. R. Jones General Store in Greenfield Village, we created a list of criteria, which proved helpful in determining which to use in each case (see textbox 6.2 for this criteria) (see also figure 6.2).

TEXTBOX 6.2: REPRODUCTION CRITERIA FOR THE J. R. JONES GENERAL STORE, GREENFIELD VILLAGE

- Replace objects of organic materials such as paper, cardboard, and textiles that are fragile or in too poor condition to put back on display.
- Include products in the store for which we do not have originals and cannot easily acquire them.
- Simulate quantity and newness of products to help give the impression of a working store.
- Provide interpreters, actors, and sometimes visitors with the opportunity to handle store products as part of special programs.

Source: J. R. Jones General Store Training Workbook, The Henry Ford, Dearborn, MI.

It is always a good idea to have a plan in place for choosing, tracking, and maintaining these non-collection items. This includes determining:

- How you are defining the terms reproduction and prop.
- What criteria you are using to determine the need for such items.
- Who is responsible for choosing and acquiring them.
- How these will be documented, tracked, and moved.
- How these will be displayed (e.g., because these are not real artifacts, they can be affixed to a surface or modified in some way to keep them in place and intact).

- How these will be treated, repaired, or replaced if they wear out, break, or become missing.
- From what budget these will be purchased, maintained, and replaced.

It is best if props and reproductions are tracked through a special numbering system, on both the objects themselves and in the museum's records.[45] These records become crucial documents over time when items need to be replaced, questions arise about them, or staff members change.

Layout, Installation, and Accessibility

In planning the layout, it is helpful to imagine the people who once inhabited this space (or a space like this).[46] How might they have made the space their own? How can you make it look as if these people have just left the room? Even though you always want to aim for historical accuracy, keep in mind that this space also needs to tell a story in a three-dimensional way—a way that transforms all your rigorous research and creative thinking into a cohesive and emotionally compelling three-dimensional environment (see figures 5.2 and 6.2).

Beyond three-dimensional storytelling, the layout should also address such logistics and operational requirements as:

- How lighting, sound, and tactile elements will work.
- How interactives will be integrated.
- How natural and designed barriers will fit the space, considering pros and cons of each of these.
- Additional seating that might be needed for visitor comfort.
- Visitor flow.
- Staffing needs.
- Cleaning and maintenance requirements.
- Visitor and staff safety (such as uneven floors, low lights, and low ceilings).
- Care of collections (such as the need for low light levels, environmental controls, and window treatments).
- Artifact security issues (including potential theft as well as damage by weather, vibration, and falls).[47]

As a result of assessing these, such controls as alarms and locks, barriers, safety wire, security systems, and smoke alarms might be needed. Also keep in mind that any of these decisions might have to be adjusted later as you observe the space when it opens to the public.

Historic house museums must also consider physical accessibility wherever possible. The 1990 Americans with Disabilities Act (ADA) prohibits all museums from discriminating against people with disabilities by calling for removal of barriers in buildings "if readily achievable." However, if barrier removal threatens or destroys the historic significance of the building, it is not considered "readily achievable." Instead, museum staff should consider offering interpretation in other ways—through such techniques as video, touchable objects, interpretive panels, and/or tactile models. In determining what physical accessibility opportunities are possible, it is useful to determine the historical significance of the structures on your museum's property, conduct an accessibility audit to determine the current level of access of each structure, and then create a transition plan for changes within a preservation context.[48]

INTERPRETIVE TECHNIQUES AND THE CURATOR'S ROLE

Determining the interpretive strategy for your historic house museum—that is, the right mixture of interpretive techniques, programs, offerings, and auxiliary products—is key to both helping get your message(s) across and creating an experience that is engaging and memorable to your visitors.[49] This will likely be determined by a larger team, but curators need to stay closely involved to ensure that the content being communicated through the chosen technique(s) adheres to the research and aligns with the interpretive themes and messages. Sometimes, as the curator, you will be creating interpretive information directly for the public (e.g., interpretive signs, audio excerpts, exhibitions); other times you will be preparing background information to hand off to others to communicate to the public (e.g., for guided tours, dramatic presentations). Interpretive techniques should, like the components of any engaging visitor-focused experience, encourage discovery and exploration while, at the same time, help visitors avoid confusion, boredom, overload, and fatigue.

The following describes several interpretive techniques, programs, and offerings to consider.

Interpretive Staff

Using staff to deliver interpretive information is perhaps the most common technique at historic house museums. This means that you, as the curator, will have to hand off your content to these staff members so they can communicate it to the public in accurate and engaging ways. Guided tours, or having interpretive staff stationed in particular places, are especially common in historic house museums.[50] In tours with expert and engaging docents, visitors can ask questions leading to new insights, make comments, and get immediate responses. These tours can be enhanced by such additions as audio snippets; video clips; showing or passing around reproduced documents, photographs, or objects; and engaging in guided conversation with visitors.

Living history interpretation—that is, "an attempt by people to simulate life in the past"—has been suggested as a possible strategy for interpreting more inclusive history.[51] Through it, historic house museums can reassert missing voices and repopulate historical landscapes with a more accurate depiction of its inhabitants and its relevance to today. Living history interpretation also offers opportunities to personalize and respond to visitor interests. Keep in mind, however, that this type of interpretation brings with it challenges in hiring, funding, and training.

A newer interpretive technique for encouraging more inclusive interpretation is what is referred to as a dialogic approach, which involves—rather than a tour guide—a trained facilitator who actively involves visitors in conversation. Championed by the International Coalition of Sites of Conscience, this approach encourages visitors to find their voice, consider multiple perspectives, and empathize with others.[52]

Self-Guided Experiences

Interpretation at unstaffed historic house museums may be enhanced by printed or downloadable brochures, maps, or guides; information at digital kiosks; or smartphone apps that describe the main points of each stop. These can all be effective vehicles for conveying stories, interpretive themes, and research findings—especially if they are visually appealing, well-written, and easy to follow. Scripted audio can add to the immersive quality of these, especially if it is written in a narrative format.

Exhibitions and Interactives

Exhibitions—ranging from graphic panels to modest case displays to entire interpretive centers—offer many opportunities for historic house museums to provide deeper content. They can come in handy for displaying particularly fragile or valuable objects, putting archaeological fragments on public view, providing broader context beyond what is possible in a furnished space, and presenting more inclusive content—especially when there are no real objects to flesh out the stories.

Interactives can greatly enhance the experience within a historic house museum. One category of interactives is low-tech, hands-on activities that are especially engaging to families and younger audiences.[53] Media and technology-based interactives can also help reinforce the content and concepts of the interpretation, attract new audiences, and potentially extend the experience beyond the museum after the visit. But keep in mind that technology changes quickly and will be more costly to implement, monitor, and update.

Interpretive Signs and Labels

Interpretive signs should, above all, address the unique aspects of the historic house museum. What is its significance? Why should people care about it? Signs should reinforce people stories, both obvious and more hidden. Who lived here? What was their role? What was life like for them? In place of a typical didactic label, you might consider going in a more story-based direction. Incorporate historic images if possible.

Exterior signs should additionally convey, in an easy-to-locate place, what the structure is, when it dates from, where it came from (if not the original site), and its construction date.[54] The content and approach of interior labels in historic house museums depends upon the label's location and intent. If describing an interior space, much the same guidelines for exterior signs would apply. Labels describing the people who lived and worked there as well as broader context should follow the guidelines of label-writing in chapter 5, Curating Exhibitions, Large and Small.

Theatrical Performances

With their richly textured settings, historic house museums can serve as perfect backdrops to the staging of theatrical performances.[55] Because of theater's traditional focus on storytelling and emotion, visitors are easily drawn in, feel that they are being entertained rather than talked at, and are willing to suspend disbelief as they become participants themselves in this imagined world. Moreover, studies have shown that visitors not only enjoy these performances but see meaning and relevance in the issues being presented, often more clearly than through the more traditional methods of presenting historical information.

Public and Educational Programs

In addition to the previously described interpretive techniques and components, various forms of public programming—for both general and special audiences—can also be considered at this time.[56] Daily programs can be augmented through enhanced programming during special events or special themed days or weekends.

The objects and stories of historic house museums also have rich potential for both school-age audiences (preschool, K–12, home school, after school, and university) and their teachers. Educational programs for these groups should align with curriculum goals established by the teachers working in concert with museum educators. The objects and stories of historic house museums also lend themselves to activities, tours, and storytelling opportunities for scout groups, special classes, summer camps, and community outreach programs.

Offerings for Audiences with Special Needs

Today, many museums are going beyond the legal obligations of ADA to provide opportunities and educational offerings for people of all abilities—including people who are blind or have low vision, are deaf or hard of hearing, or have developmental or cognitive disabilities (e.g., autism and dementia).[57] Historic house museums offer many opportunities for these audiences to engage with the stories, and the interpretive techniques you choose can be geared toward meeting their needs, cognitive abilities, and interests. This can involve multiple modes of presenting and receiving information, such as tactile maps and models, audio description to complement visual and tactile experiences, large-print versions of interpretive labels, and customized tours and activities.

Auxiliary Interpretive Products

As mentioned previously, historic house museums are among the more memorable aspects of museum visits, potentially leading to longer-term interest and learning. They might inspire visitors to dig deeper into a topic through reading or travel, to take action to effect societal change, or to pursue a different path in their personal lives. For these reasons, it is worth providing opportunities to extend visitors' personal encounters through such auxiliary products as digital content on websites and social media, brochures, and publications.

IMPLEMENTATION AND FOLLOW-UP

Training and Interpretive Manuals

Whether interpreters are expected to give tours or be stationed in a specific space of a historic house museum, you will want to communicate your content and furnishings rationale with them through formal training sessions.[58] You should be prepared to answer their questions and offer updated information when it becomes available.

As part of their training, interpreters should be provided with an interpretive manual that they can reference in an ongoing way. Curators should take on the responsibility of writing at least the content portion of this. In my *History News* Technical Leaflet, "Not Just a Bunch of Facts: Creating Dynamic Interpretive Manuals," I argue that manuals for interpretive staff should not be simply a fragmented collection of information but a hierarchically organized grouping of materials that, at all times, aims to facilitate effective interpretation.[59] Interpretive manuals can help to:

- Provide consistency for staff at all levels of the institution about the goals and themes of the project.
- Document the rigorous and creative work that went into the planning of the project.
- Provide updated information for interpretive staff as it becomes available.
- Provide a concrete tool for training, program assessment, and staff evaluation.

The following is my recommended organizational plan for a written interpretive manual based upon the approach of a hierarchical structure of information. Following the table of contents, the front section contains the most important information for interpreters to know and provides the framework for everything that follows in the rest of the manual:

- Main Message and Interpretive Themes
- Mission Connection
- Past-Present Connections
- Visitor Outcomes
- List of Interpretive Techniques and Program Elements

The rest of the manual should build upon the information in the front section, organized in a way that is keyed back to these elements, easy to locate, and written in a straightforward and readable manner. For this portion, you as the curator should be responsible for writing a deeper dive on each of the interpretive themes, using historical research information that you have pulled together; the furnishings rationale and inventory; and any additional historical background that is deemed important (biographies, broader context, appendices with primary source data, etc.).

Immediate Adjustments and Ongoing Refinements

Sometimes after opening to the public, it becomes apparent rather quickly that something you planned (furnishings, interpretive themes, interpretive techniques) is just not working.[60] You might notice this yourself or get feedback from staff or visitors. Be open to revision and refinement.

Moreover, you may think that once you have installed the spaces of your historic house museum, trained interpreters, provided them with an interpretive manual, and even made some adjustments to the installation, you are finished. But you are never really finished. Things fade. Things break. Things mysteriously "walk off." Your attempt to purposefully "mess up" a space to make it look lived-in might inadvertently get "tidied up" by well-meaning cleaning staff. Because of these likely possibilities, it is crucial to communicate your intent to all staff members who will be coming in contact with this installation and to plan ahead for replacements.

You should also be open to refinements that enhance and improve the visitor experience over time. This might be due to changing institutional priorities, evolving programs, and newly targeted audiences.

REAL-LIFE EXAMPLES

Recent museum books and journals abound with examples of new and reimagined interpretations of historic house museums. I include just a sampling here, chosen for their relevance to curators' interpretive work. These vary in size and scope.

1) Erma Hayman House, Boise, Idaho[61]

This modest nine-hundred-square-foot sandstone house is a historic site and cultural center that preserves, contextualizes, and interprets the history of Boise's River Street Neighborhood. The stories of the people who once called this neighborhood home—immigrants, African Americans, and members of the working class—had been largely omitted from the standard historical narrative. Erma Hayman, who lived in this house from 1948 until her passing in 2009, was a vital advocate for her community during her lifetime.

To uncover the history and formulate the interpretive plan for this house, the Boise City Department of Arts and History created an advisory task force with the key goal of reestablishing trust with members of this once-thriving neighborhood. As part of this initiative, the staff collected oral histories and family and community photographs and conducted an archaeological excavation at the site. The resulting interpretation involved a blend of furnished spaces that evoked Erma Hayman's "spirit," an "artistic timeline" that traced the history of the land and neighborhood—starting with Indigenous people; and community spaces devoted to "culturally mindful," mission-aligned public programs (see figure 6.3).

2) Codman Estate (Lincoln, Massachusetts) and Phillips House (Salem, Massachusetts)[62]

These two sites, administered by Historic New England, present compare-and-contrast examples interpreting the presence of domestic workers. The

Figure 6.3 This image inside the Erma Hayman House, Boise, Idaho, captures the spirit of the original installation—a partially furnished space and the "Threads of Land" artistic timeline that traced the history of the land and neighborhood. Credit: Gabe Border-ErmaHaymanHouse-6.jpg – *Threads of Land: A History of the Site the Erma Hayman House Resides On* by Stephanie Inman, a temporary exhibition on view at the Erma Hayman House, September 22, 2022 – September 16, 2023. 2023. Photography by Gabe Border (Border Media, LLC). © Boise City Department of Arts & History.

Codman House, interpreting the late-nineteenth-century era, tells complex and individualized stories that convey both the realm of the sizable staff of domestic workers and the interrelationships of these workers with the family who lived there. These worker-family dynamics are suggested through the interpretation of specialized spaces and objects. Research sources such as family papers, photographs, and census records helped flesh out the stories of specific domestic roles, while also hinting at the oft-discussed "servant problem"—that is, the challenge of engaging and retaining staff at the time.

The Phillips House, which interprets the early-twentieth-century era, is filled with a "veritable treasure trove of domestic machinery," reflecting the downsizing of domestic workers by this time and the replacement of domestic staff with mechanical devices and appliances. Census records, family photographs, and oral histories with relatives of past domestic workers helped provide documentation, while objects (many obtained for the program), the house's spaces, and the structure itself provide concrete evidence of domestic workers' lives and daily tasks.

3) Crane House and Historic YWCA, Montclair, New Jersey[63]

When this structure became a historic house museum in the 1960s, the intent was to re-create its early history (1796-1840) through decorative arts and the story of Israel Crane (a prominent local businessman) and his family. Since 2017, the house has been reimagined, not only to tell a more inclusive story of enslaved workers and domestic servants who lived and worked there, but also to include the significant story of the segregated YWCA for African American women that existed here from 1920 to 1965.

Incorporating this story took research into archival documents, a scholars' panel, touching base with other historic sites telling diverse stories, and reestablishing trust with the local community, especially with women who had belonged to that YWCA and felt that the interpretation had been "whitewashed" when the structure became a historic house museum in the 1960s. This involved collecting oral history interviews, many of which were recorded and incorporated into a documentary (with selected audio sound bites used in public tours of the house). Through furnished and community spaces, a graphic timeline, tours, and conversations, visitors see the evolution of a historic house museum, with the overarching theme of "it takes a thousand voices to tell a single story" (see figure 6.4).

4) Cook's Cabin at Exchange Place Living History Farm, Kingsport, Tennessee[64]

Many Southern historic house museums are bringing previously untold stories of enslaved workers into their interpretation. One modest example is this living history farm in northeast Tennessee, which attempts to break down

Figure 6.4 YWCA Club Room in the Crane House and Historical YWCA, Montclair, New Jersey, after the reimagining of this historic house museum. Credit: YWCA Club Room 1940-1965, Montclair History Center.

the popular misconception that slavery did not exist in Appalachia. A group of volunteers undertook the research, restoration, furnishing, and interpretation of what was originally a one-room log dwelling that housed an enslaved cook during the mid-nineteenth century, when James and Catherine Preston operated a farm here with diversified crops using enslaved and tenant labor.

Research sources included slave schedules and family memoirs as well as current scholarship and similar work being done at other historic house museums. Clues to furnishings were gleaned from an 1850 inventory of Exchange Place as well as archaeological and structural evidence and current scholarship about the material culture of enslaved laborers in the South. As one interpretive technique, the group commissioned silhouettes of what the women who labored here might have looked like, helping visitors imagine and connect with real people.

5) Levi and Catharine Coffin State Historic Site, Fountain City, Indiana[65]

When created in 1967, this site (originally called the Levi Coffin House) interpreted only the life of White male Quaker Levi Coffin and his role in the Underground Railroad that went through the area during the mid-nineteenth century. The interpretation was primarily based upon Levi Coffin's 1876 memoir. The presence and voice of Levi's wife, Catharine, was lost to history, as she left no letters, interviews, or autobiography. As the result of an institutional mandate to become more inclusive, the interpretation now includes the life and contributions of Catharine, who worked in partnership with her husband to welcome and aid freedom seekers along the Underground Railroad. The interpretation also reflects the lives of freedom seekers who spent time in the Coffins' home, gleaned from references in Levi Coffin's memoir and oral histories from descendants of these people.

In 2016, the name of the site was officially changed to the Levi and Catharine Coffin State Historic Site. A new interpretive center also opened at that time. Its exhibition "Souls Seeking Safety" elevates the role of Catharine, expands upon the lives and risk-taking of freedom seekers heading north, and discusses how the local community worked together to help them—including free Blacks who worked side by side with the Coffins and other Quakers in the area. Through guided tours, the furnished home provides context for this couple's commitment to antislavery. The site also offers a changing calendar of mission-aligned talks and programs.

6) The Tenement Museum, New York, New York[66]

The Tenement Museum has been called "one of the most innovative and compelling interpretive sites of immigrant and urban history in the United States."[67] Through re-created apartments and businesses of real families in two historic tenement buildings, the museum tells the stories of individuals and families who came to America and started their lives anew on Manhattan's Lower East Side.

The Tenement Museum truly delivers on authenticity. Visitors feel utterly transported through time when they enter restored tenement apartments that have been re-created through painstaking historical research. An abundant use of reproduction and representative objects (rather than solely unique collection items) means that no stanchions or barriers are required, so visitors can easily imagine family members inhabiting the spaces. Apartments are lit using period fixtures and natural lighting while each apartment is furnished to represent a precise moment in time.

The Tenement Museum's offerings have shifted and expanded since its opening in 1988, from tours related specifically to immigrants who resided at 97 Orchard Street to its "Under One Roof" tour at 103 Orchard Street, which highlights three post-World War II families and a re-created Chinatown garment factory, to its most recent tour, "A Union of Hope: 1869," about an African American family who lived in a nearby tenement during the turbulent aftermath of the American Civil War.

REFLECTIVE PRACTICE

This chapter raised a series of issues, described a step-by-step process, and offered best-practice examples and recommendations for curators doing interpretive work at historic house museums. Hopefully, it has encouraged you to assess the interpretation and perhaps implement some changes at your own historic house museum. But what if you lack time, funds, or resources to make this happen? Here are some initial steps I've developed to get you started.

Assess what you have by asking these questions:

- When was the interpretation last updated?
- Is the current interpretation inaccurate or biased?
- Does it include multiple perspectives?
- What is missing?
- How might you begin to attempt some changes?
- Can you meet with your interpreters to find out and answer their questions and get input into what questions visitors ask? Or, if you do not have interpretive staff, consider how you or other staff at your museum might gather information or questions from visitors.

Take initial steps to telling more inclusive stories by asking these questions:

- Are there existing documents in your files (historic structure report, interpretive master plan, archival primary documents collected when the building was acquired or that accumulated over time) that you can revisit to provide new insight into previously overlooked stories?
- Can you pinpoint new avenues of research?
- What community—local or a specific group of people—might help you by providing input and insight into more inclusive stories?
- Who else in the museum field is working on similar issues with whom you can touch base and compare notes?
- How might objects—existing, in storage, or newly acquired—tell new or untold stories?
- How might existing structural elements accomplish the same thing?
- Can you create a new or revised interpretive manual that tells more accurate history, reinforces multiple perspectives, and reveals untold stories?

7

Sharing Knowledge with the Public

I was a nervous wreck. I was going to be giving my first public presentation as a curator, at Henry Ford Museum's Midwest Antiques Forum. The program was filled with august speakers—many of whom were nationally known in the antiques-collecting world. I was a young, inexperienced curator, speaking on a relatively obscure topic related to my collection—labor-saving devices for the kitchen.

I had avoided giving presentations all through school. Standing in front of the class, trying to string together coherent sentences with all those people staring at me? No, thanks! Just the thought of it had filled me with dread. I assumed that, as a curator, I would be happily spending my days working by myself.

Was I wrong! I almost immediately learned that the very word "curator" evokes in the public's mind deep (often esoteric) knowledge and people love hearing about that. Furthermore, as public service institutions, museums depend upon curators to provide credible and accurate information as well as unique access to the museum's collections and stories.

Sharing knowledge with the public is a rather untold and certainly underrated part of a curator's job, but it can take an inordinate amount of time. No one warns you about this. It may not be explicitly written in a job description. There are few places to learn or read up on how to do it. Most of the learning is gained through experience, as well as watching and comparing notes with others.

I prepared that first presentation as best I could, practicing my written notes so many times that I had basically memorized them. But, when I gave the presentation, my voice still quavered. My knees shook. My throat went dry. That haunting feeling of everyone staring at me returned from my school days, only this time it was real!

Somehow, I got through it.

That was only the first of numerous times I have been called upon to share my knowledge with the public as a curator—through talks, tours, media interviews, and various forms of public-oriented writing. In the course of doing these, I learned something immensely valuable. People often remarked that they could tell how passionate I was about my topic. That was the key, I realized. Curators bring a passion to this work. We want others to get as excited as we are about our topics. Remembering this saw me through many subsequent presentations.

If you're an introvert like me, the anxiety of doing public presentations never really leaves you. Even after countless presentations, I still get butterflies in the pit of my stomach. After numerous media interviews, I still fear that only gibberish will come out. Before I start to write, I still panic that the muse has left me forever.

My best advice is to prepare, remember to bring that passion, and then just dive in. This chapter is about what all those things entail.

LINKS TO CURATOR CORE COMPETENCIES

In understanding the nature of sharing knowledge with the public, it helps (as usual) to revisit CurCom's "Curator Core Competencies."[1] Like exhibitions (covered in chapter 5), this work falls under domain 3, "Communication," which the document defines as "building trust and rapport with communities and intended audiences by facilitating access to knowledge." It involves the ability to communicate effectively with a variety of people from different backgrounds. Three competencies listed under this domain are particularly relevant to this chapter:

1) Interpretive writing—that is, creating coherent written words from ideas and thoughts. This means synthesizing and interpreting facts, scholarly research, and complex ideas and then developing a related narrative that is relevant and accessible to museum audiences. This writing can range in tone and complexity depending upon the format, intent, and audience.
2) Object interpretation—that is, using objects to illustrate an idea or series of ideas through understandable, accessible narratives. As written in the CurCom document, "Using objects to illustrate an idea or series of ideas is at the very heart of what defines a curator." In interpreting objects for the public, curators should challenge themselves to be original, thoughtful, and unique while, of course, incorporating current scholarship.
3) Education—that is, communicating with various audiences on subject and object specialties. This can include (according to the CurCom document) "lectures, gallery or exhibition talks and tours, and classes." It involves the ability to reframe original research about subject and object specialties in understandable, accessible, and engaging ways geared to intended

audiences. It helps to possess capabilities in public speaking, interpersonal communication, and collaboration.

THE PUBLIC HISTORY CONNECTION

Sharing knowledge with the public combines rigorous historical methodology with audience engagement—in other words, it embodies the essence of public history. Like exhibition work, curators doing this work must balance the seemingly competing goals of scholarly excellence with that of effective communication. Unfortunately, whereas curators know that history is complex, multifaceted, and continually being reinterpreted, studies show that the public assumes there is only one, unchanging truth that exists "out there" in the world.[2] According to AASLH's "Making History Matter" initiative, strategies to counteract this public perspective include:

- Shifting the conversation from "truth" to critical thinking in order to change perceptions of what history involves.
- Using concrete, location-specific, solutions-focused examples to build support for inclusive history.
- Emphasizing how history helps us make progress toward a more just world in order to increase recognition of history's importance.
- Comparing historical interpretation to detective work to deepen the public's understanding of historical practice, using a range of sources and methods.
- Helping people recognize that examining the past from the perspective of different groups makes the historical record more accurate.

Sharing knowledge with the public—through writing, talks, tours, and media interviews—offers curators many opportunities to consider and incorporate these insightful strategies.

WRITING FOR THE PUBLIC

As Margot Wallace states in *Writing for Museums: Communicating and Connecting with All Your Audiences*, "Despite galleries and classrooms and space immersed in visuals, museums rely on writing."[3] Curators can contribute some of their best thinking, analyzing, and synthesizing through writing, or more often these days, pairing writing with visuals. Curatorial writing—now accessible to global audiences via online platforms—can vastly expand the reach of one's institution. It has the potential to reveal the wondrous depth of the museum's collections, offer a deep dive into historical topics, demonstrate diversity, explore interconnections between ideas and objects, and reinforce the links between past and present. Moreover, it can help curators clarify their thinking and hone their writing skills in different formats and for different audiences.

No matter what type of writing you are doing, first find out who your audience is. This determines how you will write—the language, the level of complexity, and the tone (informal vs. formal). Even if you are writing a piece that presents complex ideas and incorporates citations, remember that your audience is non-academic, and the writing should—at all times—be aimed at them. This does not mean "dumbing down" (i.e., oversimplifying) your content. Consider and respect your audience's intelligence, curiosity, and life experiences. Assume that your audience is inherently interested in, and eagerly wants to find out more about, the incredible discoveries that you have made and are revealing through your writing.

Printed Materials

Many history museum curators contribute written content for published books, articles, and other traditionally printed materials.[4] These range from exhibition catalogs and books highlighting their museums' unique collections to articles in members' magazines to brief descriptions for self-guided tours on the museum's property. Every printed publication varies, determined by its unique goals as well as the museum's resources, writing style guide, and audience. In each instance, follow the guidelines provided by your institution to determine that printed piece's purpose, word length, tone, and audience. Of course, many traditionally printed materials are now accessible through digital formats—eBooks, digital versions of members' magazines, and downloadable brochures and guides. But the writing style still adheres to that of traditional printed pieces.

Digital Content

The 2023 *Museum* article "A Digital (R)evolution" poses the question, "Has the pandemic sparked an evolutionary leap in practice?"[5] The article goes on to explain that while digital technologies have "reshaped the world" over the past twenty years with bewildering speed—transforming how people engage with entertainment, shopping, education, work, and socializing—the COVID-19 pandemic "turbocharged" that pace of change.[6] The forced closure of museums during the pandemic put immediate pressure and demands on museums to move toward digital engagement.[7] Even small to midsize museums, with limited staff and funds, and for which undertaking digital projects proved a daunting task, acknowledged the value and need for an online presence. With the subsequent reopening of museums and the return to on-site experiences, many museums have continued to find benefits in retaining online content and including it in their strategic plans.

Writing for Online Audiences

Today an increasing amount of what history museum curators write is digital content, appearing on their museum's website or another digital platform, and aimed at online users. Writing online is "a specialized world with its own rules, customs, and more than a few quirks."[8] In contrast to traditionally printed materials, digital content presents a shift from merely presenting information to more robust storytelling, visually appealing content, and linkable components. Everything you write has to be shorter, get to the point more quickly, and consider a larger profusion of visuals. This is because the audience has a much lower level of commitment than with a printed piece. They are used to browsing rather than following a linear pathway. It is challenging to attract and keep their attention when they can quickly link to somewhere else in this highly competitive environment. At the same time, we also cannot follow every whim of the public.

In his book *History Disrupted: How Social Media and the World Wide Web Have Changed the Past*, public historian Jason Steinhauer argues that the internet has essentially changed how the public views the past and knows about history, claiming that "the values that underpin the professional discipline of history are at odds with the values that underpin the social Web."[9] Whereas professional history is expert-centric, always evolving, time-consuming, and based upon the premise of intrinsic value, the social web is a user-centric, data-driven commercial enterprise—privileging extrinsic value and intended to be immediately gratifying. One does not need to be an expert or even a recognized authority to publish on the social web. Everyone is encouraged to speak, contribute, and form an opinion regardless of their credentials or expertise.

To cope with these conflicting values, Steinhauer advises historians, museum curators, and other historical experts to adapt to the conventions and formulas that are best suited for the social web and how users have been conditioned. How we *interpret* the content, he argues, is more important than *what we know*. We must hone and sharpen our writing and thinking skills to operate successfully within the broader conversation, a conversation that now includes anyone. Digital writing also means competing with whatever else the reader is doing. You have little ability to control what else is going on around your content—determined by the platform, the user's past behavior, and the algorithms that power the feed. You have a short amount of time to capture and keep someone's attention and you don't know precisely to whom you are speaking. Content can be complex, but it should always be relevant, answering the overarching questions that online users inevitably ask: "Why should I care?" and "Why should I devote my time to reading this?"

Here are some tips for engaging readers through digital offerings:[10]

1) Be personal. Personal stories bring the past to life and help people relate to history on an emotional level.
2) Be informal but expert. People want to learn from experts, but it should not be a chore. Overly academic language can put people off, but stories should not be "dumbed down." Finding the right balance is important.
3) Tell hidden stories. Bringing hidden heritage to light engages audiences and creates a sense of community, identity, and shared history.
4) Illustrate your points. Consider how visuals and text work together in the stories you share.
5) Organize your writing so that readers have a clear sense of both the narrative and digital structure. This helps keep the story coherent and will capture people's attention from beginning to end.
6) Be specific. Storytelling that focuses on specific topics can engage a broad audience. Generally speaking, it works best to proceed from details to the big picture.
7) Be evocative. History-based stories need to be based on fact, but the facts don't need to be dry. Don't be afraid to use poetic, descriptive, and evocative imagery and approaches, as these are more likely to engage people.

The explosion of digital content has vastly increased curators' opportunity to share knowledge with the public on various topics, while also necessitating new writing styles and approaches. The technology behind digital experiences is complex and constantly changing, so curators must be prepared to adapt as needed. The following digital experiences offer prime opportunities for curatorial writing.

Digitized Collections

As mentioned in chapter 2 (Making Sense of Objects), digital technology has vastly increased the reach, value, and accessibility of museum collections to the public.[11] Digitized collections have given the public knowledge of not only what is currently in museum exhibitions but also what is in storage and in the deep well of museums' archives. Digitized collections have not only proven invaluable to researchers and hobbyists searching for specific topics, makers, or groups of objects, but they have also revived the enjoyable aspects of self-discovery and serendipity.

Curators can enhance the value and deepen the appreciation of digitized objects in museum collections through their involvement with keyword designations for searches, brief interpretive narratives accompanying catalog records (see chapter 3, Shaping and Developing Collections), curated image "galleries" organized around a theme, and video clips in which curators reveal stories behind objects or groups of objects. Digitized collections can also be linked to other forms of digital content, such as online exhibitions, blogs, and social media posts.

Online Exhibitions

Traditionally, websites might have included a summary of an exhibition—its focus, its organization, and perhaps a few images of key artifacts. Today, there are numerous opportunities to enhance on-site exhibitions through online content, including:[12]

- An online version of your exhibition with interactive elements, including links to collections records and extended content.
- A live or prerecorded exhibition walk-through.
- A 3D tour of your exhibition space so that people who cannot attend your venue in person can get a sense of the space and your display in a virtual, interactive format that they can explore at their leisure.

Some museums have also created exhibition-like content that is online-only. These digital offerings allow creative experimentation with ideas and often feature objects and/or documents that cannot go on display because they are rare, fragile, or difficult to access. These might also include links to outside sources, to collections records of objects used in the online exhibition, and to other museum collections.[13]

Blogs (Online Articles)

Blogs started as opinion pieces, musings, and observations on personal websites, but they have become an invaluable asset for museums.[14] They have endured because, as a way to explore ideas and share knowledge, they continue to matter to people.

Blogs offer many advantages to museums.[15] They give the museum credibility; highlight the depth of its collections; reflect its mission, vision, and values; can be created by any size institution (sometimes in collaboration with other museums, outside stakeholders, a university, or local community members); are findable through search engines; can be posted to social media; build loyalty and engagement with online users; reach new audiences; and attract new members. Regular readers are consistently reminded of the museum's unique stories and resources. When posted on social media, blogs invite reader comments, which can create a sense of community and involvement (see example in Chapter 2, under Visitors and Objects).

Blogs are one of the best formats for curators to express themselves in writing. They provide a forum for your expertise; give you practice in analysis, synthesis, and writing; demonstrate scholarship and creative investigation; allow you to pursue a personal interest; and give you the chance to hone your writing skills. Moreover, they can encourage inclusivity, be provocative, explore emerging content and research, and correct or update outdated content.[16]

Writing a blog should follow these basic tenets:

- The blog should focus upon a single theme, topic, or thesis.
- The tone should be the voice of authority but not be overly academic. It should sound informal and conversational.
- The length is usually around five hundred to eight hundred words. This is long enough to be fully informative and thoughtful but able to be read in one sitting. This length also gives gravitas to the content, distinguishing it from the short, snappy comments on social media. But it should be concise, to the point, and full of facts that make for interesting reading. It can be longer, especially when accompanied by visuals. Consult any guidelines offered by your institution for length and tone.
- Engaging blogs often have a narrative quality, as the writer is taking readers on a journey. This involves a thought-provoking beginning that hooks the reader, a middle that moves the narrative along, and a conclusion that—while not necessarily resolving an issue or reaching closure on it—comes full circle with a takeaway that reminds readers of the theme, topic, or thesis and makes them care about it.
- It should represent the mission and perspective of the institution and be unique to that institution.
- It should be timely, using up-to-date scholarship and providing current information. Because of this, it might also need updating in the future.
- Sources are sometimes cited, but often not—due to the informal nature of the medium.
- The author's name should be cited. For curators, this helps establish their credentials as a go-to source of information at their museum.

The following presents a series of useful steps in writing a blog:

- Know the intended outcome. What is the purpose of your blog?
- Identify your research question(s). What historical "truth(s)" are you trying to uncover?
- Collect information, engage in research. (Although your blog is relatively brief, you still need to do your due diligence with the scholarship.)
- Organize and outline your thoughts. Start with a strong idea or topic, use thematic unity, and hint at larger truths.
- Select visuals (which you will probably reduce later). These should reinforce the points you are trying to make. The more visually clear/eloquent they are, the quicker your reader will be able to "get" the point(s) you are trying to make.

- Write a first draft. This draft does not need to stick to the word count yet. This will occur during the editing process.
- Editing is perhaps the most important part of the blog-writing process. Pare the writing back to its absolute essentials, removing redundancies. Make every word, phrase, and sentence count. Know what you are trying to say and what words express it. Replace passive verbs with active ones. Edit out extraneous bits of information, but make sure the writing holds together. If words are too technical, explain or simplify them. Shorten sentences if possible. (If you lose your breath by the end of the sentence, it's too long!)
- The final draft should be short, snappy, and to the point but retain all the information, complexity, and nuance of the extraneous words you have cut out along the way.
- Read it out loud. Put yourself in the shoes of your readers. Does it drag? Does it put you to sleep as you read it? If so, edit and refine it.
- Read it a final time for voice, tone, style, structure, and flow. Does it address your research question(s)? Is it cohesive? Is it engaging, informative, and unique?
- Finalize the visuals, making sure that each visual helps to reinforce your points. Add captions, if needed.

Other Website Content

The examples of digital content mentioned so far would typically appear on a museum's website. Curators' knowledge and writing skills might also lend themselves to content for other website features, such as educational resources, descriptions of on-site exhibitions and historic structures, and resource lists.

Writing for Social Media

While social media is often used for publicity purposes, it can provide a platform for curatorial writing as well.[17] As with other forms of writing, curators bring their authority and knowledge, while reflecting their institution's mission and personality. Length and tone should be adapted to the audience, situation, and social media channel.

In addition to the posting of curator-written website features, curators might spearhead or be involved in the selection of images with brief captions that appear on such platforms as Facebook and Instagram. With the institution's support, they might also engage in online conversations with users. I find it particularly interesting to check the online comments to my blog posts, and the posts of others. They can be wonderfully glowing about your writing and your topic, but they can also be sarcastic, negative, and quick to correct a perceived error. Moreover, they can have nothing at all to do with your post but are, instead, about visiting the museum or about a personal memory. Whatever the comments, they are instructive.

It is useful to get to know different social media platforms and understand how they are used, their tone, who frequents them, and what the best strategies might be for your contributions. You might even find that a short video on a highly visual platform such as TikTok serves a purpose for you and your institution.

STRATEGIES FOR GIVING TALKS AND TOURS

In the book *The New Academic: A Researcher's Guide to Writing and Presenting Content in a Modern World*, author Simon Clews tells his readers, "You're an expert. You know interesting stuff. We are interested in interesting stuff. Don't make it more complicated than it needs to be."[18] As a curator, you will inevitably be asked to give public presentations in the form of talks, lectures, "chats," and tours. While no one model fits every museum, you should be cognizant—at all times—that you are representing your institution. To the audience with whom you are sharing your knowledge, you *are* the institution. You are not only sharing your personal knowledge of a topic but are also helping to broaden the reach and awareness of your institution to its various publics.

Being asked to share your knowledge also gives you, under the right circumstances, the chance to correct public misconceptions and misinformation, to challenge audiences to engage fully with complex ideas, and to immerse them in the "messiness" of history. Moreover, it gives you the enjoyable opportunity to create your own personal spin on a topic and share your passion about it with the public. See textbox 7.1 for characteristics that talks and tours have in common.

TEXTBOX 7.1: WHAT TALKS AND TOURS HAVE IN COMMON

- Know your audience.
- Consider what you want to convey.
- Develop your narrative.
- Time it, practice.
- Be warm and welcoming.
- Try not to use notes.
- Appear confident, calm, in control.
- Be yourself.
- Plan time for questions.
- Consider accessibility needs.

Audiences for Talks and Tours

Developing and delivering talks and tours involve not only determining the appropriate content for a given audience and venue but also presenting this content in an engaging way. In contrast to digital content, for a talk or a tour you generally have the advantage of knowing exactly who your audience is, what they want to know, and how best to engage them. It is useful to get as much information as you can about the audience ahead of time from the staff member, outside individual, or group from whom you've received the request.

In my experience, there are certain audiences or audience groups that most frequently call upon curators to give talks and tours. Here are my anecdotal observations about engaging each of these groups:[19]

1) *Donors and donor groups.* They believe in the mission, vision, and value of your institution and want to feel that they are part of something important. They are looking for good, believable, truthful, thought-provoking stories and enjoy behind-the-scenes access. These people often attend programs for the social benefits of catching up with friends and acquaintances.

2) *Members.* They believe in the museum's mission, but they often feel particularly entitled to special benefits and treatment. This is ironic, as their financial contributions are significantly less than donors. They want to feel that they belong to part of a community and often attend functions as family groups. They don't mind telling you what they would do if they themselves were the curators!

3) *Collector groups.* They have deep knowledge of a topic or group of objects—often deeper and more esoteric than you yourself possess. Don't be surprised if they try to one-up you. If this happens, don't get defensive, just thank them and move on. They may request to see everything you have in their area of interest, but be aware that, once they see the scope of your museum, they may want to expand their tour. Be prepared to change course on the fly, if possible.

4) *Teachers.* They often attend a talk or tour for professional development. It is best to understand and address that reason for being there. But they are also adult visitors and many are deeply curious lifelong learners, so appeal to their natural curiosity while you are providing your knowledge about curriculum-related topics. They are also there for the social engagement, as a visit to the museum may offer a rare opportunity for them to enjoy the company of their colleagues.

5) *High school students.* They enjoy the "free" day away from the classroom, so work with the teacher to not only identify topics and approaches but also to deal with any disciplinary issues. Approaches that work well include: role-playing activities that encourage empathy; activities and conversations that involve active learning and critical thinking; stories of

people that have relevant connections to their own lives; and focusing on real objects. Always consider the presentation to be more of a two-way conversation than a top-down lecture.

6) *College students.* Although there are exceptions, they are generally there because of a personal choice to take a class of interest to them. They will likely be thrilled to meet a "real" curator, tend to ask thoughtful questions, and love behind-the-scenes access. They are often fascinated by the process of historical thinking and your work experiences. As a curator, you might also be asked to appear as a guest speaker, or even teach an entire college-level course, at a local college or university. While you might feel flattered by, and up to the challenge of, teaching a semester-long course, keep in mind (as I found) that the time involved in preparation for, and follow-up to, the actual weekly class can be daunting.

7) *Community groups.* They want to feel welcome and comfortable at your institution, a place they might seldom frequent. They are interested in stories in which their communities are represented, stories that validate the issues facing their families, friends, and neighbors. They also want to pass along an understanding of their heritage and cultural values to their children, and curator-led talks and tours can help with this. They are impressed when curators devote time and effort to their community's needs and issues, and a positive experience can lead to deeper involvement by these community members with your institution.

On-site Talks

Since talks tend to be removed from real objects and historic spaces, you must engage your audience through your communication skills, the way in which you organize your information, and the visuals you use. Here are some practical tips and steps to follow in preparing and delivering an on-site talk to public audiences.[20]

Preparing the Talk

- Knowing the audience is key to helping you determine your goals, language, tone (formal vs. informal/conversational), complexity of information and approach, cultural reference points, any sensitivities of which to be aware, and potential "difficult customers" in the room (i.e. naysayers, know-it-alls). It helps to try to put yourself in your audience's shoes as you develop your talking points.
- Logistics are important, including the expected length of time, the technology you will be using, the room layout, the seating arrangement, the sound system (or lack of it), and where you will be situated in the room when you deliver your presentation.

- With your theme in hand, consider what and how you want to convey it to your audience, through talking points, organization, and selected images, video, and/or audio.
- Develop the narrative, considering an introduction, the main body of the talk, and a conclusion.
- Time it, allowing enough time for questions. If it's too long, pay attention to phrases that are redundant or confusing and shorten them to be concise and efficient. It doesn't work to talk faster to fit your presentation in the allotted time! Practice it out loud to yourself. While not necessarily memorizing it, review it enough to feel comfortable with the material, hopefully preventing that uncomfortable filler, "um."

Delivering the Talk

- As an ambassador of your museum, be warm and welcoming to your audience.
- Try not to read a written paper, but instead go with notes or bullet points. Maintaining eye contact helps establish rapport and impart a friendly demeanor.
- Appear confident, calm, and in control, though nerves and stage fright are natural. Tell yourself it's not about you. It's about the message, and you're excited to tell people what you know. A good piece of advice is to find someone in the room who is actively engaged in your talk and feed off that energy.
- Be yourself—genuine, authentic, and authoritative. Let your passion show.
- Plan time for questions and answer them as best you can. "I don't know" is an acceptable answer.
- Regardless of what you say, be aware that audience members will bring their own opinions, interpretations, and explanations to your talk. People also might infer something counter to what you meant. Expect people's responses to be personal.

On-site Tours

Like talks, tours also involve organization and communication skills, but you have the advantage of engaging your audience through "real things." On the downside, be aware that because people are usually standing during a tour, they will get fatigued. There's also the chance that other things (objects, noises, other visitors, personal smartphone interruptions, friends and family members) might distract them. Here are some practical tips for preparing and giving on-site tours to public audiences.[21]

Preparing the Tour

- Understand your audience—ages, interests, why they're there and what they're expecting (if you can't find this out beforehand, ask at the time and adjust your tour accordingly).
- As with talks, knowing your audience allows you to determine your language, tone (formal vs. informal/conversational), complexity of information and approach, cultural reference points, any sensitivities of which to be aware, and potential "difficult customers."
- With the tour theme in mind, develop your main points, your stops, and the objects you will point out. Consider how you can pique your audience's curiosity through stops on the tour and your stories about them.
- Consider where and how you might provide seating during at least part of the tour.
- Practice. Time your presentation to allow for questions. If it's too long, refine and shorten it.

Delivering the Tour

- As an ambassador of your museum, be warm, welcoming, and friendly.
- Appear confident and in control.
- Speak slowly and clearly; avoid jargon.
- Maintain good eye contact.
- Use good vocal techniques, including vocal expressiveness, articulate diction, and voice projection.[22] Convey a pleasing and sincere tone.
- Give attendees a chance to sit during the tour to avoid fatigue, if possible.
- Be receptive to people's interests. Encourage and answer questions. Be willing to engage in conversation. If questions or conversations are lengthy, manage the time accordingly.
- Be sensitive to any special needs.

See textbox 7.2 for a summary of key differences between talks and tours.

TEXTBOX 7.2: TALKS VS. TOURS

Talks:

- Tend to be removed from objects and spaces.
- Possible use of technology (always with virtual).
- Logistics are super-important (especially when virtual).
- Images are helpful for maintaining audience interest.

Tours:

- You can show your audience real things and spaces.
- Be aware of fatigue and distractions.
- Consider stops, what to point out.
- Make good eye contact.
- Use vocal techniques.
- More than talks, you can change, adapt as you go based on interest and questions.
- Consider mobility issues.

Virtual Talks and Tours

During the COVID-19 pandemic, virtual programming was hailed as an opportune way to share content as well as to cultivate input from and dialogue with audiences. The AASLH 2022 National Visitation Report revealed that, over the course of the pandemic, history organizations offering virtual programming rose from 40 percent to 80 percent.[23] This programming reached more people, with a wider range of participants—demographically and geographically—than ever before. Exemplary offerings were creative, compelling, and complex; promoted social and shared experiences; made collections and content more accessible; and directly impacted public engagement.

Virtual tours and talks have been added to the expectation of curators' work, including live online "chats," talks, lectures, and panel discussions as well as pre-recorded content. With virtual tours and talks, the potential audience is no longer limited by geographical or physical barriers, cost issues, or transportation problems. Moreover, curators are no longer constrained by the physical parameters of a collection or exhibition. While virtual programming offers many advantages, it also presents obstacles. These include the inequitable nature of digital access, the limitations of communicating via a computer screen, and the reduced ability of people to interact and socialize—a major motivator to audiences who attend such programs on-site.

The tasks of preparing and delivering online talks possess similar qualities to on-site talks, but knowing how to use the technology becomes even more critical. Here are some practical tips for giving online talks to the public.[24]

Preparing an Online Talk

- Know the audience to whom you will be presenting.
- Pay close attention to logistics: camera, sound, lighting, your background, what you will be wearing, size of shot, how the virtual platform operates (e.g., Share Screen, Chat, and Q&A functions).

- Know the length of time you have to give the presentation.
- With your theme in mind, develop your talking points (as with on-site talks).
- Develop your narrative (as with on-site talks).
- Consider ways to vary the pacing by involving the audience.
- Images are very important with virtual talks. Use more visuals than text.
- Practice! Time it. Shorten if needed.

Delivering an Online Talk

- Be aware of how you look on the screen. Check this out before the audience "enters the room."
- Cue up documents/slides beforehand.
- Be thoroughly knowledgeable about how to use the technology of the platform.
- Communicate your passion and enthusiasm as best you can on screen.
- Try not to read your notes, as eye contact helps establish rapport.
- Be aware of "Zoom fatigue." Varying the pacing by involving the audience can help.
- Be prepared to adjust on the fly based on timing, technology issues, and audience questions.

Audio Tours

Audio tours have been around for decades. They started as on-site tools, offering museum visitors an enhanced experience in front of an object or historic space. Portable devices were lent out or rented on-site and returned after the visitor completed the tour. They tended to be geographically constrained and offer a single, directed path.

While this is still the norm in some places, technology for audio guides has advanced to offer multimedia experiences, pinpoint a user's exact location, connect to other objects on-site, include contextual materials, allow users to navigate their own pathway, and let users take "selfies" with favored objects and "like" or "share" objects on social network sites. Today, audio tours are accessible on personal smartphones, through a dedicated app or a web-based platform.[25] This has led to increasing choices and has enabled visitors to, in a sense, "curate" their own experiences. Moreover, many users can now access museum audio tours online, at home, rather than on-site at the museum.[26]

Whatever the technology, curators have actively contributed, and continue to contribute, to the creation of audio tours. Curators' involvement in audio tours provides a level of authenticity and intimacy not available through exhibition labels. Curators often do the research, write the tour stops, and even provide the actual voices to the tours—adding not only a personal touch but also assuring listeners that the information is coming from a credible expert.

Audio tours offer curators the opportunity to highlight objects, make connections elsewhere in an exhibition or gallery, explain broader context, refer to other collections not on display, and present material that is difficult or complicated.

Audio tours require skillful writing. Tour stops need to be brief, descriptive, interesting, and cohesive from beginning to end. The following suggests a series of steps for curators creating audio tours:

- Determine the theme or topic.
- Know the total length and number of stops. The ideal time length for a stop is about thirty seconds. Remember that audiences are on their feet and fatigue can easily set in.
- Select objects to feature, using criteria that relate to the theme or topic.
- Map the walk by imagining a visitor doing the audio tour while simultaneously walking, listening, and looking.
- Script out the tour stops, referencing the selected objects and remembering to incorporate how each represents the theme.
- Tell a story that keeps visitors engaged. Use colloquial language, with easy-to-understand words and short sentences that direct the eye. Depending upon intent, museum, and audience, the tone can range from scholarly to conversational to a combination of both.
- Edit to the predetermined word length or time limit.
- Add segues between stops, linking objects together conceptually and providing clear direction to listeners on where to go next.
- Test a prototype of the tour for clarity (of content and directional instructions). Revise as needed.

Talks and Tours for People with Disabilities—A Unique Opportunity

Like other talks and tours, offerings for people with disabilities involve understanding the nature and expectations of each of these audiences. While curators are not traditionally considered the staff responsible for program delivery to these audiences, I've had the privilege at The Henry Ford of delivering talks and tours both to people who are in early stages of dementia along with their care partners as well as to people who are blind/have low vision.[27] Early in the creation of these programs, I had the conviction that a skilled group of curators could prove an asset to developing and delivering these programs, so I offered to be the "guinea pig." I am happy to report that these have worked well and continue going strong. Here are a few of my anecdotal observations about giving talks and tours to these two audiences.

Despite varying degrees of memory loss, people in early stages of dementia exhibit a deep desire and ability to learn, be creative, and connect with

Sharing Knowledge with the Public

others and with their community.²⁸ They want to feel valued, be seen and heard. Moreover, they want to participate in meaningful experiences that are both educational and enjoyable, and museum programs can offer these opportunities (see figure 7.1).

For on-site programs (generally lasting one to two hours), keys to engaging this audience involve:

- Choosing topics/angles that they can relate to from their own lives.
- Understanding that this is a conversation, not a lecture.
- Using spaces that are quiet to maximize focus.
- Providing seating.
- Being ready to shorten the presentation or change direction if things slow down (because of lengthy conversations, logistics adjustments, or attendees' mobility needs). Change course or planned length, if needed.
- Snacks and drinks are a great addition, offering opportunities to sit down and to socialize—both important aspects of these programs.

My experiences with these programs have far exceeded my expectations, and other curators who have delivered these programs concur. People who attend them are warm, friendly, and appreciative. One regular attendee offered these comments:

Figure 7.1 The author giving a talk at the 1930s kitchen in Henry Ford Museum of American Innovation to people with early stages of dementia and their care partners. This monthly program is done in collaboration with the Alzheimer's Association Michigan Chapter. Photo courtesy of Caroline Braden.

It has a great positive effect on me. I can feel myself really improving in life due to my experiences here. It's not just an institution. It's friendship. It's hospitality. I've really come around to looking forward to things, to activities, rather than just staying at home.[29]

And his care partner commented:

It has directly benefitted us by [my husband] accepting the fact that he has dementia and that that does not mean it's the end of your life. Coming here has just opened our eyes to new things, both of us. . . . Not only the friendship, but the information and all the things we've learned here.[30]

While on-site programs have been popular and positively received, virtual programs for this group did not work as well. It was harder for people in this group to use the technology, to engage, and to converse. Also, the care partners often didn't stay for the program, unfortunately removing the support aspect of the program.

Virtual verbal description programs for people who are blind/have low vision are one- to two-hour virtual programs that involve a verbally communicated visual description of topics, places, and/or objects organized around a unifying theme. While The Henry Ford has a staff of presenters trained to give on-site tactile tours (during which attendees can touch real objects on exhibit that have been pre-approved by the curator and the conservator), these came to a sudden halt during the COVID-19 pandemic. During that time, the museum's accessibility manager observed virtual verbal description programs being offered by the Guggenheim Museum and the Tenement Museum in New York City. I also watched the Tenement Museum tour and was immediately reminded of the visual description I used to write when I first cataloged objects as a curator (see chapter 3, section on Collections Fundamentals and the Curator's Role: Cataloging). Based upon that experience, I suggested that a group of curators, this time practiced in visual description, could develop and deliver these—again offering myself as the "guinea pig."

These programs have also proven very successful and are still going strong, despite the return to on-site programs and in-person tactile tours. They are ideally suited to a virtual format, with attendees listening in from their homes.[31] They have even attracted a national audience—including many people from New York City who had already attended programs like these. I have found this audience to be insatiably curious. They want to know everything about the topic, object, or group of objects and will ask many questions to understand them better as well as to be able to picture things "in their mind's eye." Their insightful comments during the programs always amaze and impress me. Attendees to these programs are very complimentary about them. One attendee wrote:

I can't even begin to express the extent of the impact . . . not only have I been enlightened by each and every type of program offered, but each time, I almost feel as if I were "carried off" to a special locale surrounded by the subject matter. . . . It is uncanny how "real" your excellently detailed descriptions are . . . they make everything so close, almost touchable!![32]

As curators, we spend most of our time working behind the scenes. It is wonderfully satisfying to know that we can have this kind of impact!

TALKING TO THE MEDIA

As Clews argues in his book *The New Academic*, "There are plenty of places where your expertise will get to shine, but the acid test of a real 'expert' is how well you can work with the media."[33] Members of the media—newspaper reporters, journalists, TV and radio hosts, and podcast producers—seek out curators for the same reasons that people are drawn to curator-led talks and tours. They are looking for an expert, someone who is uniquely knowledgeable, credible, and able to speak on a topic of interest to their audience of readers or listeners. As with talks and tours, curators can provide special access to the museum's stories and collections, offering an authentic encounter that the media knows their public appreciates, even craves.

Working with members of the media positively and successfully means helping them do their job. They often work for a business—especially with the more traditional print and broadcast media—which means they answer to a higher authority who determines their work. They tend to lead hectic, deadline-oriented professional lives and are often working on several stories simultaneously. They may be called off your story at the last minute to follow up on breaking news, or they may be assigned to interview you at the last minute and be totally unprepared.

The primary goal of the media in working with you is to complete that interview. In accomplishing this, they need you to be reliable, trustworthy, low maintenance, available at a moment's notice, articulate, and to the point—in other words, to help them meet their needs, deadlines, and agendas. Responsible members of the media are interested in the truth, but editing, speed of work, limited broadcast time or print space, and alternate agendas sometimes lead to misquotes or skewed information, creating challenges for curators and the institutions they represent.

Overall, media publicity reaps positive benefits, usually increasing public awareness of your institution. Larger institutions likely have an External Relations, Public Relations (PR), or Marketing department, whose job it is to get as much positive coverage about the museum in the media as possible. They will not only contact you about interviews, but they will also serve as a good conduit to the media firm or interviewer about what you can expect, take responsibility for providing the interviewers with basic logistical information about the museum (so you don't have to), and lend support if you run into challenges. Your responsibility, as an ambassador of your institution, is to help place it however you can in a positive light.

Even more than talks and tours, being asked to talk to the media might catch you by surprise. This is generally something that is not taught in school. There are few resources to help you. For introverts, thinking quickly on your feet to provide an articulate, thoughtful response—especially if put on the spot or asked something you did not expect—can be downright hair-raising. But everyone expects that you know what you're doing, so you just have to forge ahead and learn as you go. Each experience will be different, as the interviewers, their platforms, and the topics about which they are seeking interviews vary. The good news is that you will likely recognize a consistent style if the same reporter, journalist, or host returns to interview you again. To get an idea of this, I've always loved the characterizations of two radically different media interviewers—albeit rather extreme—on the TV series *Parks and Recreation*: the gentle, accommodating newspaper reporter, Shauna Malwae-Tweep, and the abrasive, sensation-seeking hostess for a local newsmagazine/talk show, Joan Callamezzo. Even their names cleverly allude to their personalities and what the staff of the Parks and Rec department in the fictional town of Pawnee, Indiana, can expect during an interview. Real members of the media are not quite as consistent or easy to read.

Doing Interviews

Preparing for an interview ahead of time can be more challenging than preparing for talks and tours because, no matter what you prepare, you truly don't know what the actual interview will entail. But preparation is still key to a positive experience. Here are some tips and strategies for getting through it.[34]

Preparing for the Interview

First, find out whether the interview is live or pre-recorded. There is a huge difference in terms of preparation, delivery, and potential challenges. With live, you'll need to think quickly on your feet and answer questions as succinctly as possible. If live TV or video, visual appearance is also important. The good news (or, at times, the bad news) is that it will be all your own words, with no editing. With a pre-recorded interview, you might be able to take more time to answer the questions and know that anything you mess up will be edited out. Of course, this also means that anything you say can be edited—leaving, for example, a short, out-of-context snippet of a longer quote, or having a quote inserted where you did not intend it, or having a larger, significant explanation of something left out completely. You will also probably be asked to repeat the question in your answer to make the final editing easier.

Second, be aware that this is the interviewer's show. They might have an angle to a story already figured out and you are simply filling in the blanks—or they just need one juicy quote to help them complete that story. Readers and listeners are tuning in to their show, so their reputation depends upon delivering what their audiences want. It is best to familiarize yourself with the media outlet, the interviewer, and the program ahead of time, so you know what to expect.

Other tips when working with, and being interviewed by, members of the media include:

- Find out why they want to interview you, what they expect to get out of it.
- Consider (or try to discern) questions they might ask and how you want to answer them. Chances are they won't give you the exact questions ahead of time, as they might think this detracts from the spontaneity of the interview.
- If possible, understand who the audience is.
- Be aware of any technical requirements, especially with online interviews and podcasts.
- Before the interview, if possible, craft succinct and powerful answers or a list of key message points—each preferably thirty seconds or less for a pre-recorded radio or TV spot (providing less chance for the points to be edited). Try to make your points clear, consistent, interesting, and relevant.
- Practice these so that, hopefully, no question comes as a surprise to you. Also, the more prepared you are, the less likely it is that nerves will become a factor.

Giving the Interview

- If the interview is for a visual medium, follow instructions on where to stand, or where and how to sit, where to look, and what to wear.
- Maintain eye contact with the interviewer. Use natural hand gestures and facial expressions to help highlight your points. Use your voice to convey enthusiasm.
- Be clear, concise, and organized. Listen to the questions, then answer them as succinctly as possible.
- Be informative and interesting.
- Don't talk too fast or too slow. Try to maintain a conversational tone.
- It's easy to ramble. Figure out how to provide a definitive end to each of your answers through brevity and your tone of voice.
- Avoid jargon.
- Try not to insert fillers, like "er," "um," "so," and "look."
- Be prepared to answer logistical questions about your institution, if needed. (It's embarrassing to be asked about your museum's hours or admission prices and you don't know.)

Cautions/Challenges and Strategies

- If a question is out of your range of expertise, the best response is "I don't know."
- You are allowed not to answer a question if it makes you uncomfortable.
- Answer only what you know for a fact.
- If a question is getting off track, gently try to pivot the conversation back to the topic at hand.
- Sometimes a reporter will bait you with something accusatory or critical to get an emotional answer. If so, take a deep breath and answer in an even tone. Never get defensive.
- For potentially controversial issues, roughly frame your answers beforehand. If need be, ask for guidance from a superior, a marketing colleague, or a member of your PR department.
- Even though the conversation might seem friendly and informal, remember that anything you say can be used. Keep confidential information confidential. In an interview, the mic is always on and nothing is "off the record."
- Reinforce the importance of topics that can be misinterpreted. Assert how important it is to be accurate.
- Expect the unexpected and go with the flow. For example, when Matt Anderson, curator of transportation at The Henry Ford, walked a journalist through the museum's ground-level storage building and heard him refer to it as "the secret underground vault," he just smiled and moved on.[35]
- Be patient with technology issues, glitches, and mess-ups. Always allow more time in your schedule than you'd planned.

Most media requests for interviews will likely be to publicize something new at your institution, like the opening of a new exhibition or a deeper dive into something at your museum that is newsworthy (for example, I was asked to do many interviews by local media when we were collecting items related to the COVID-19 pandemic). These are fairly easy to prepare for. But occasionally you might find yourself in the unique situation in which you are interviewed for a high-profile, nationally broadcast media production. These have accounted for some of my most memorable interviews.

For example, like other curators at The Henry Ford, I spent several years involved in interviews for short segments about our collections and stories that appeared on the CBS Saturday morning TV show *The Henry Ford's Innovation Nation*.[36] No matter how well I prepared, I learned that anything could happen on set during the filming. For example, during the filming of various episodes, I experienced the museum power unexpectedly shutting down; a forklift causing a deafening noise as crates were being brought in for a new exhibition; the film crew realizing that the technology didn't work after a lengthy take was completed; a sudden rainstorm soaking my clothes on the way to the interview out in Greenfield Village; and host Mo Rocca (a humorist as well as a serious and extremely knowledgeable journalist) sending the conversation into a completely unexpected direction from the talking points that I had reviewed beforehand (see figure 7.2). But I learned that whatever I messed up (or thought I messed up) would be edited out for the final version.

Perhaps my most memorable interview was for an episode of *Behind the Attraction*, a series for the streaming TV channel Disney Plus. For this interview, I talked to the producer ahead of time about what questions she might ask about my topic—the Magic Skyway ride at the 1964–1965 New York World's Fair.[37] I prepared as thoroughly as I could and then traveled to Burbank, California, for the interview—despite a blinding snowstorm that had developed overnight in southeast Michigan. I thought I addressed the producer's questions with thoughtful, serious, and substantive answers, befitting a museum curator. Little did I know (because there were no episodes produced yet to give me a clue) that my interview would be edited to fit the show's light and entertaining tone, its humorous and tongue-in-cheek style. Much to my surprise (and horror), the hand gestures I used to make certain points and my mentions of Robert Moses (New York City's parks commissioner and planner of the fair) were inserted repeatedly as a comedic refrain! And, to add insult to injury, they referred to me as an archivist!

Figure 7.2 Anything could happen during the filming of *The Henry Ford's Innovation Nation*. During this episode, when the author was explaining the history of comic books to host Mo Rocca, the museum power went out and the interview had to be reshot. This episode was filmed inside the "Your Place in Time" exhibition in Henry Ford Museum of American Innovation. Photo courtesy of Melissa Foster.

Podcasts

Combining its origin on the Apple iPod with the word "broadcast," the name podcast implies a way to listen to content hosted online. The goal of a podcast is to make connections, foster curiosity through storytelling, and offer deep, often esoteric dives into topics that hook a niche audience of listeners.

Podcast formats can range from straightforward conversations between hosts to more interview-based shows, with the host or hosts providing commentary. Podcasts buck the trend of the usual short, snappy web-based content. Listeners will loyally take in an entire episode, often lasting between twenty and sixty minutes. The episodes are informal and accessible, with an intimate, personal quality—as if the hosts are talking directly to each listener.

Some museums have "jumped on the bandwagon" to produce and offer podcasts that are unique, distinctive, and thought-provoking—often focusing on unusual or esoteric objects in their collections.[38] If well done, they can engage audiences, extend the mission, and raise awareness of the institution.

Curators' contributions to podcasts—either at their own museum or for a privately hosted site—usually take the form of doing an interview.[39] Like interviewers on traditional media formats, podcast hosts are often looking for experts who know "the truth," the "real story," and have a deep well of substantive, often esoteric knowledge on a given topic. If asked to give an interview on a topic, do your research but expect surprises. If you think you need to research the deep history of something, you might be asked to provide broader context. Conversely, if you prepare to talk about the broader context, you might be asked to delve deeply into something. You also might be asked about your personal take on and/or connection with the topic at hand.

This is what happened to me when podcast host Alie Ward interviewed me for her "Ologies" podcast on the topic of "deltiology," or postcard collecting.[40] I brushed up on the timeline of postcard history but much of the interview was about my own personal experiences with postcards. Fortunately, Alie was an excellent interviewer, a great storyteller, and a skilled podcast host. She spun the story in such a creative and powerful way, bringing in her own humor, comments, and connections, that the show touched listeners on a deeply emotional level. I still receive unsolicited postcards with handwritten messages from listeners who say they loved and were inspired by that show. I felt that I gave a decent interview, but I give all the kudos of the final product to Alie.

WRAP-UP

I hope that I have instilled enough practical information, tips, and examples in this chapter to give you a sense of what is involved when curators are called upon to share their knowledge with the public. Whether you love it or fear it, keep in mind that your efforts in this regard can have both a considerable and a truly positive impact. Whatever happens, however you prepare—and *always* prepare—expect the unexpected, go with the flow, and know that you did your best. You might keep track of what went well and, if warranted, how you might prepare differently next time. I have been doing this work for more than four decades and I still find that the surprises—as well as the learning—never end!

8

Leading from the Middle

You may be wondering why I'm devoting an entire chapter to leadership in a book for curators. Isn't leadership something that directors do?

While leadership is certainly a topic that might be found in a book for directors, that's not the type of leadership I'm talking about. I'm talking about a form of leadership that anyone at a museum can (and should) do, a form of leadership that can mark the success of your workplace relationships, your projects, and even the attainment of your career aspirations as a history museum curator. I'm talking about leadership as positive influence, aimed outward in every direction. It is about leading from the middle of an organization.[1]

To help you better grasp this concept, allow me to give you a sports analogy from my own experience. I grew up with four brothers. They were all naturals at many sports, from baseball to soccer to table tennis. But I was terrible at virtually every sport—until I played field hockey. There I found my sport! You didn't have to be tall, or throw well, or even be particularly coordinated. You just had to be sharp-witted and alert to what was going on in every direction. As a sophomore in high school, I miraculously made the varsity team, playing left halfback. Being left halfback meant playing from the middle, helping both the front line and the defense succeed. It turned out that I was very good at that.

I have had a career-long interest in understanding how people can work together better, in both positive and productive ways. Over the course of my career, I have collected literally dozens of books about work styles, motivation, teamwork, dealing with conflict, and leading without authority (see figure 8.1). More recently, when I became the senior curator overseeing a staff of other curators, I was drawn to slightly different books—books for mid-level leaders who had both more authority and greater responsibility.

This chapter begins by contrasting leadership with management and describes qualities that all leaders have in common. Then it focuses on the

Figure 8.1 Not your usual books on leadership. Photo by the author.

form of leadership that I believe aligns best with the role and competencies of museum curators. This entails leading oneself, then leading up, across, and down. Strategies, challenges, and practical tools are included in each of the sections for curators to apply to their own situations. The chapter concludes with a discussion of attributes that are necessary to being an inclusive leader in today's world.

So, while a chapter on leadership may seem unimportant or trivial, I can assure you that knowing these things, putting these strategies into practice, and trying out these tools can lead to greater success in doing the work that is described in virtually every chapter of this book.

LEADING AT EVERY LEVEL

Leadership can be defined as "the ability of an individual to influence, motivate, and enable others to contribute toward the effectiveness and success of the organizations of which they are members."[2] Leadership differs from management. Managers are responsible for controlling, coordinating, planning, and organizing. Leaders, on the other hand, are people who inspire, motivate, unite people, and create visions for the future.[3]

Leadership is a learned set of skills that can be put into practice every day by any museum professional no matter your position or years of experience. According to Mark Sanborn, author of *You Don't Need a Title to Be a Leader: How Anyone Can Make a Difference*, leaders at any level of an organization can succeed because they:

- Believe they can positively shape their lives and careers.
- Lead through their relationships with people, as opposed to their control over people.
- Collaborate rather than control.
- Persuade others to contribute, rather than order them to.
- Get others to follow them out of respect and commitment rather than fear and compliance.[4]

While management is based upon one's positional authority, leadership depends upon relationships and the ability to influence others in the pursuit of goals. It calls for an "others-oriented" mindset, which focuses attention off yourself and places it on appreciating and acting upon the multitude of perspectives you must consider when interacting up, down, and across the organization.[5]

No matter your position, you can play a leadership role by "being attuned to the rhythm" of your museum and finding "responsive and sensitive ways to contribute."[6] In the book *A Life in Museums: Managing Your Museum Career*, Elizabeth Peña offers these keys to museum leadership at all levels (see textbox 8.1 for a summary of the following list):

TEXTBOX 8.1: LEADING AT EVERY LEVEL

- Know your museum.
- Engage.
- Contribute.
- Collaborate.
- Think strategically.
- Do your job and then some.
- Be sensitive.
- But not too sensitive.
- Understand that change is hard.

Source: Elizabeth Peña, "Leadership at All Levels," chapter 22 in *A Life in Museums: Managing Your Museum Career*, ed. Greg Stevens and Wendy Luke (Washington, DC: The AAM Press of the American Alliance of Museums, 2012), 144–46.

- Know your museum.
  - See needs and address them.
  - Take advantage of gaps and find opportunities to suggest ideas or propose solutions.

- Understand your institution's mission and vision, organizational chart (formal structure) and informal structure, and the ways in which the museum operates day to day.
- Be alert and observant.
- Engage.
  - Take an active role in the work of the institution.
  - Boldly champion causes important to the community or the field.
  - Attend internal meetings; take notes.
  - Go to professional conferences; give presentations; write articles.
  - Network with people from other museums.
- Contribute.
  - Offer your skills—for example, meeting facilitation, mastery of a foreign language, and so on.
- Collaborate.
  - Work with colleagues across the institution, in other areas and departments.
- Think strategically.
  - Create value for your museum while improving your own professional skills.
- Do your job and then some.
  - Complete all required tasks with excellence.
  - Go above and beyond. Make yourself indispensable.
  - Pay attention to developments and trends in your area of expertise.
- Be sensitive.
  - Be respectful of others. Conflicts are bound to arise if you venture too close to others' areas of expertise and they feel threatened.
- But not too sensitive.
  - Acknowledge that navigating workplace politics can be difficult.
  - Listen to others' ideas and criticism.
- Understand that change is hard!
  - Lead by example.
  - Remind yourself that you can contribute to the success of your museum's transformational process.[7]

POSITIVE INFLUENCE, IN EVERY DIRECTION

Being a leader at every level is foundational. But the real success of leading from the middle of an organization comes from recognizing that different leadership strategies are needed depending upon the direction in which you are leading. It involves approaching the entire institution as an entity and observing how the individual parts work together, establishing strong networks in all directions, and customizing each individual interaction.

Before delving into the specifics of leading in every direction, I want to underscore two key factors that are inherent in this work. The more you are aware of and embrace these, the more success I believe you will have.

Key Factor #1: People

Leadership involves dealing with people. Unfortunately, people are unpredictable, and no one is exactly like you. Each person possesses not only a unique set of talents and skills, but also long-embedded patterns of behavior and ways of thinking, processing, and relating to others. Knowing this can help you to develop and implement better leadership strategies.

People often work at museums not for financial rewards but for other, more personal reasons. Because of this, two personal attributes tend to come to the forefront and are essential for leaders in the middle to comprehend and use to best advantage. First, although the perception persists that emotions do not belong in the workplace, the fact of the matter is that people bring an inordinate amount of emotion to their work and their relationships with others. So, to lead people in all directions at a museum, it helps to possess a high degree of emotional intelligence.[8] Being able to empathize with people, becoming attuned to the underlying emotions behind their behaviors, and responding to these behaviors are every bit as key as possessing the technical skills that are required to complete your job and help others complete theirs.

Second, a highly underrated factor in leaders' ability to positively influence others involves knowing how to leverage people's motivations. Motivation is the high engagement and extra effort that come from truly enjoying what one is doing. It involves an innate propensity to engage one's interests and exercise one's capacities and, in doing so, seek out and master optimal challenges (i.e., efforts that fit a person's skill level exactly at the level of difficulty and complexity at which they are most likely able to accomplish that challenge). In leading from the middle, you are not in charge, you can't offer people raises or promotions or extra vacation days. But you can (and must) lead through intrinsic motivation—that is, the motivation that comes from within each individual. People are motivated in many different ways, but here are some intrinsic motivators that psychologists have found to be fairly universal:[9]

- Competence—People enjoy doing things that they are good at.
- Autonomy—People like to have a choice and a voice in what they do.
- Purpose—People want to feel that they are doing important work, having an impact, making a difference.
- Growth—People like to feel that they are becoming smarter, better, and more accomplished.
- Relatedness—People want to feel that they belong; they want others to accept and value them for who they are as individuals.
- Appreciation—There is perhaps nothing more motivating than having people say they believe in you, that you're doing or have done a great job.

Admittedly, conflicts are inevitable when people of varying backgrounds, identities, and personalities work together.[10] In fact, some would claim that organizations are set up for conflict. For curators, it's easy to want to stay detached, to stick to your world of collections, research, and writing. But to lead from the middle, you will be thrown into potentially conflicting situations with people again and again. To help enhance your relationships with others (beyond the strategies briefly described in this chapter), seek out books, workshops, mentors, colleagues, and senior leaders, and, of course, learn from experience.

Key Factor #2: Organizational Culture

In museums, we talk about such areas as collections, education, and administration as if they are separate, independent entities. But, in fact, museums operate as complex, dynamic systems in which all the parts are interconnected. Leading from the middle means accepting and embracing the systemic nature of museums.[11]

While all museums operate as dynamic, interconnected systems, each museum possesses its own unique organizational culture.[12] No matter how much you try to avoid it or deny that it exists, you are always going to be dealing with this embedded culture and its related norms—that is, the unwritten rules or modes of behavior that go along with that culture. The ability of an institutional culture to influence behaviors, attitudes, and interrelationships is so important that I'm not sure why people don't talk about it more—and develop strategies for dealing with it. Maybe it is because it often gets lumped with work politics, and the idea of "being political" or "playing politics" in the workplace has a negative connotation. The fact of the matter is that organizational culture is neutral, and knowing how it works, using it to your advantage, "playing politics" for positive reasons and productive ends are all crucial ways to lead from the middle. Because they are both deep-rooted and often misunderstood, I'm going to delve into organizational culture and norms a bit further.

Organizational culture involves the process of creating shared awareness and understanding out of different individuals' perspectives and varied interests. These are not just patterns of behavior. They are deeply held beliefs and jointly shared interpretations of "what is." Their critical purpose is to help orient the staff of an organization to "reality" in ways that provide a basis for alignment of purpose and shared action. It is also about the "why"—in other words, the "story" behind which people in the organization are unified, and the values and rituals that reinforce that story. Furthermore, it focuses on the importance of symbols and the need to understand them, including the idiosyncratic language people use within an organization's culture. When taken collectively, this complex pattern of variables (language, values, attitudes, beliefs, and customs) gives an organization its unique "flavor." It is "the way we do things around here."

Cultural norms are shared group expectations about appropriate behavior. They establish the behavior expected of everyone in the group and the unwritten rules that govern that behavior. They are enforced by the group, and group members regulate correct behavior. These norms must be upheld, as social sanctions are imposed on those who don't "stay within the lines." Conformity promotes feelings of group cohesion. Compliance with norms is enforced by either positive reinforcement or subtle forms of negative reinforcement (e.g., a snide remark, a dirty look, exclusion from group activities).

Institutional culture and cultural norms have a significant impact on the conduct of the staff. Individuals give up some freedom when they join an organization, and these constructs represent the ways in which freedom is limited. They are intangible but potent determinants of behavior, and they are incredibly powerful. A legacy culture can persist for a surprisingly long period of time, taking on a life of its own and pervading an organization even after the person or people who initially created it are long gone.

But cultures are also dynamic. They can shift with internal and external changes in a continuous process. Trying to assess the current culture can be complicated but it also opens up the possibility that it can be changed for the better.

While an organizational chart lays out the formal structure of an organization, the informal structure more often represents the genuine workings behind organizational culture and cultural norms. Politically savvy leaders know this. They view politics as a neutral and necessary part of organizational life that can be used constructively and ethically to advance organizational aims. This perspective allows them to be cognizant of the interests of others, find areas of common ground, bring others on board, and lead them in the pursuit of a common goal.

To gain "organizational intelligence" when leading from the middle, it is important to become a keen observer of the unique personality and character of your workplace. In learning the unspoken rules of your workplace, consider these questions:[13]

- How does work get done?
- How does communication happen?
- How are decisions made?
- Where are the gaps between policy and practice?
- Who gets along and who doesn't?
- Who has the most power?

Admittedly, leading from the middle can be messy, full of contradictions and opposing agendas, conflicts, differing points of view, ambiguity and uncertainty, and no small amount of personal risk-taking. But it also couldn't be more critical to an organization's success. You have the best chance of success if you learn how to apply the right approach in the right situation at the right time—one that's appropriate for the organization, the people you are leading, and yourself. See textbox 8.2 for a summary of the following keys to positive influence in every direction.

TEXTBOX 8.2: KEYS TO POSITIVE INFLUENCE IN EVERY DIRECTION

- Lead Yourself.
- Lead Up.
- Leading Other Senior Leaders
- Lead Across.
- Lead Down: Mentoring
- Lead Down: When *You* are the Boss

Leading Yourself

If you want to lead others, lead yourself first.[14] Understanding yourself can be a true challenge. Those unconscious or barely conscious patterns of thought and feeling, evolved over a lifetime, now influence your every choice and interaction. Despite the constant presence of these now-cemented patterns, we are usually ignorant of how they operate and why we respond in certain ways. The critical first step in leading yourself is to become familiar with, and ultimately take responsibility for, your own patterns of behavior—your style, motivation, biases, strengths, shortcomings, quirks, and preferences. Only then can you begin to interpret and respond to situations in a way that will provide value to others and to the institution. The more you model this behavior, the more chance you have of influencing others.

Tools for Self-Leadership

We are all complicated beings, made up of an almost endless combination of variables: background, age, gender, values, learning styles, and so on. Our identity forms over time, unfolding and revealing itself through events, experiences, and opportunities that come our way, and it is unique to everyone. However, several tools are available to help you better understand your patterns of behavior. No one tool, or even all the tools put together, will provide the ultimate insight.

First, it helps to get constructive feedback from other people. Don't expect this to be consistent. Everyone has their own perspective and worldview, which can only make their input richer and more interesting.

Several written tools can also help you become aware of your own patterns of behavior in the workplace. I think the Myers-Briggs Type Indicator (MBTI) is still the best.[15] Another popular and highly recommended self-assessment tool is the StrengthsFinder test, based upon the premise that we all possess natural talents that can be developed into genuine and productive strengths.[16] These go beyond the responsibilities—or "hard skills"—listed in our job descriptions. This tool is based upon the philosophy described in the groundbreaking book *First, Break All the Rules*, which encouraged leaders to focus on people's strengths rather than trying to fix their weaknesses.[17]

It also helps to have a keen awareness of your "soft skills"—those qualities that influence your attitudes, behavior, character, and interactions with others.[18] Soft skills work synergistically with—and are every bit as important as—hard skills to do your job. Interpersonal soft skills such as active listening, communication, cultural awareness, and empathy particularly enable you to understand, relate to, and influence others.

Leading Up

Leading up may be your greatest challenge. Your relationship with your manager or supervisor is probably the most crucial one that you will have as a museum professional.[19] A poor relationship is, in fact, the number one reason why people voluntarily leave their jobs, or at least mentally check out. Working at this relationship is essential and needs to be considered an ongoing process.

It's a natural tendency to want to complain about your boss, or your boss's boss. They're not like you. They look at things from a different perspective. Sometimes they seem unable or unwilling to appreciate what you do. To lead up, you must accept the fact that the relationship is essentially uneven but interdependent. It is filled with the tension inherent in a hierarchy. How do you reveal what you need when your boss is constantly evaluating and judging your abilities? You must establish a trusting relationship so that the roles of supporting and evaluating are no longer at odds.

To get started, first lead yourself exceptionally well. This includes managing your emotions, time, priorities, energy, mental processes, and personal life. Do your work with excellence. Be consistent. Always deliver your best product, despite the likelihood of a high degree of ambiguity and even if your plate is full. Welcome the challenge of responding to your boss's shifting priorities. Keep trying to improve upon your previous work. All of these send the message to your boss that you are someone who can be counted upon when the challenges multiply.

Next, leverage your strengths to help your boss succeed. This includes:

- Understanding what your boss expects of you.
- Adjusting to your boss's style.

- Knowing your boss's priorities and helping them accomplish these.
- Enhancing your boss's ability to make decisions by effectively presenting solutions or opportunities.

Challenges

Challenges are inevitable when leading up. It is easy to want to avoid conflict, but small issues can soon turn into bigger ones. Here are some strategies that can prove useful in responding to challenges:

- Ask for permission to present an opposing viewpoint; discuss intent before content.
- Use facts, not judgments.
- Be humble, respectful, and diplomatic.
- Link your position, ideas, or feedback to the organization's mission and the good of the institution.
- Acknowledge the challenges and bring actionable suggestions.
- Frame ideas positively.
- Be sensitive about when to push forward and when to back off.
- Consider your boss's perspective and know that you're only seeing part of the picture. Be mindful of their moods and triggers as well as their own challenges.
- Don't surprise or blindside them.
- Communicate with them in an ongoing and mutually agreed-upon way.

If you are having trouble connecting about or agreeing upon how to approach an assignment or issue, try to find some element of the assignment or issue that honestly aligns with your own vision or understanding of the problem at hand and go from there. When you can find common ground, you both become invested in searching for a solution.

Tools for Leading Up

You have a better chance of success if you come equipped with some leading-up tools. For personal encounters, be organized and prepared. Bring an agenda for discussion or a specific list of questions. Become a good judge of when (and how much) to report and when (and how much) to solicit input. For written reports, practice the art of the executive summary and get used to writing in bullet points. Learn how to synthesize information and cut to the chase. Be sure to come prepared with next steps, then follow up and, ultimately, deliver results.

Leading Other Senior Leaders

Leading in all directions also means that you will be interacting with and hoping to influence other senior leaders.[20] You don't want to bypass or upstage your own boss, but if given the opportunity, here are some strategies for leading other senior leaders:

- Understand their agendas, needs, and communication style.
- Be clear about what you want from the encounter and what you can contribute.
- Let them know that you have a role to play that will ultimately help them achieve their goals, that you have something to contribute, that you are there for a reason.
- Stay calm and focused.
- Feel and look confident.
- Listen and be ready to adapt your responses to a new set of circumstances.
- Be deferential. Never act like you are better than they.

Leading Across

Whether you are functioning within a relatively flat, team-based environment or a more hierarchical structure at your institution, you can make a positive impact by knowing how to lead across.[21] Leading across usually means leading cross-departmentally or at least across your own department. In leading across, you usually don't choose the people with whom you will be working. You'll have little formal authority and must manage through influence. The people you lead will have working styles, motivations, and expectations that are different from yours. You need to be prepared to work with almost anyone, regardless of how the team is set up and whether or not people like each other (and you). You'll be working in a world of conflict and consensus building—often with modest resources and a high expectation of meeting challenges. As a result, you will likely spend much time maneuvering through organizational politics, culture, and bureaucracy. Yet you have to galvanize the team around a strong sense of purpose and come out accomplishing (or exceeding) what is expected.

Leading across involves the ability to work together toward a common vision, to direct individual accomplishments toward organizational objectives, and to understand the characteristics of successful collaboration.[22] It means engaging everyone's strengths toward a mutual goal. You are ultimately responsible for the success of the project, but its completion is only possible with the contributions of the individuals in the group.

Start the process of leading across by leading yourself. This means possessing a deep knowledge of your own strengths and how to use them. Foundational to this is being trustworthy and genuine. It is also important to:

- Place team results over personal agendas.
- Be open to learning from others.

- Hold yourself accountable.
- Be credible and competent.
- Remain cool and unruffled under pressure.
- Be persistent, consistent, and determined.

Next, your success at leading across requires your ability to internalize, articulate, and integrate the institutional vision into the group's work. Leading up will help you with this. This involves:

- Making sure that you understand the assignment—how it fits not only the institutional vision but also the vision and priorities of your boss and other senior staff.
- Seeking senior input at regular, agreed-upon intervals.
- Being prepared for the likelihood of a shift in vision or scope.
- Getting things done by being political in the "right way."
- Getting clarity about information and decisions as the project progresses.

Finally, leading across is a nuanced practice, which emerges from building relationships. Here are some strategies to keep in mind:

- Consider the strengths and motivations of each individual in your group.
- Determine the most effective modes of communication.
- Accept and include ideas from others beyond the people with whom you are used to working.
- Be a good listener. Listen to everyone's suggestions and feedback.
- Remain open to new ideas throughout the process.
- Find overlaps and common ground.
- Celebrate small (and large) achievements.

Challenges

Leading across can be difficult, time-consuming, and exhausting. There might be naysayers, people who are disruptive or tend to derail the conversation, and people who want to dominate or take over. Some members of the group might resent your leadership, especially if they feel that they were passed over for this role. Give your colleagues a reason to respect you and follow your lead. Help them know that you want them to succeed, which will help the entire group succeed. Teams work best when members trust each other and hold themselves and each other accountable for the results.

Group members who are used to autonomous decision-making might misunderstand your purpose in offering suggestions to solicit group input. Describe the reasoning behind these and remind them that your goal is, above all, to move the group process forward. They might have other fears or feel threatened in other ways. Have compassion and patience.

Certainly, negative attitudes, all-or-nothing thinking, and "my way or the highway" comments can prevent progress. But sometimes conflict can also allow for the possibility of new ideas, points of view, and personal and shared growth. Healthy conflict can be a tool for individual and group learning and evolution. Successful leading across requires being attuned to these nuances.

Tools for Leading Across

At the top of every list of tools for leading across should be an understanding of how your assignment aligns with your institution's mission and vision. Next, determine the goals and objectives, and other frameworks and criteria against which the success of the assignment is being measured. It helps to understand and clarify people's roles and responsibilities from the start, although these can change over time. Without this, the potential is high for wasted time, conflicts between individuals, a work product that does not align with institutional goals, and possibly a risk to your own reputation as a leader.

As the work progresses, have a variety of other tools in your back pocket to help the group make decisions, measure individual ideas, and help internal and external groups get on the same page. These wide-ranging tools might include: creating a central framing statement or a list of criteria; suggesting that the group listen to everyone's individual assumptions or expectations before continuing with group work; and throwing out a radically different idea that will expand the group's thinking or help them get unstuck. If the group is having challenges working together, stop the work and talk about it together. Allow additional time for each aspect of the project if there are new members to the group or changed deadlines.

Leading Down: Mentoring

Chances are that, at some point in your career, you will be mentoring others.[23] Mentoring is one of the most important and rewarding aspects of the job. It might occur in any number of ways—if, for example, you are supervising the work of interns or project assistants; if you have hired new curators or other staff members who will be working for you; or if someone else on your museum's staff simply reaches out to you because of your experience and knowledge.

Mentoring can be defined as a sustained relationship between two individuals, ideally for mutual benefit and with the promise of ongoing one-on-one support. It is perhaps the best way to transfer skills from a more experienced staff member (along with personal examples of successes and failures) to a less experienced one, ensuring the continued application and development of this knowledge. Good mentoring supports the transfer of information, wisdom, and skills, providing advice and inspiration. It can advance the museum field on a long-term basis; help create the next generation of museum leaders; nurture the development of new leaders rather than recruiting more "followers"; and counter the trend of losing promising newcomers because of the lack of monetary compensation. Institutions benefit when they have leaders willing to foster the development of other people who can themselves become leaders at all levels of the organization.

Mentoring is different for everyone. It's personal. It involves discerning where people are, knowing where they want to be or are supposed to be, and giving them what they need for the journey. As a mentor, it is important to:

- Be credible. Believe that you can help mentees by bringing your own strengths, experience, wisdom, and ability to add value to theirs.
- See the world from the mentee's perspective—their personal point of view that has been shaped by their experience, values, current situation, and assumptions.
- Equip mentees to excel in their jobs by setting an example, knowing what they want to learn, discussing obstacles, working on attainable goals, and removing barriers to growth.
- Harness mentees' intrinsic motivation.
- Support and encourage them.
- Check in with them frequently.

Challenges

There are, of course, challenges to this work. A mentor might have limited time or be patronizing, impatient, or dismissive. The mentee might be undependable, fear rejection, be afraid to ask questions, or fail to act on the mentor's suggestions. The mentor or mentee might feel threatened. Conflicts might arise from generational or cultural differences. To be a mentor, you must be patient, have an open mind, and be willing to learn from everyone.

Tools for Mentoring

Tools for mentoring should be customized to everyone's needs and interests. Look for the potential that lies within each individual and start from where they are by:

- Looking for and helping them understand their strengths and talents.
- Learning about their goals and motivations and, if possible, helping them develop in these directions.
- Learning to accept and appreciate their differences.
- Trying to accommodate the various ways in which they approach their work.

Work out a mutually beneficial style of communication. Become a great listener. Be honest with your feedback to them and accepting of their feedback to you. Talk to them, ask questions, and learn about them with an open, curious mind.

Leading Down: When You Are the Boss

While many curators actively avoid management positions, others eagerly strive to attain them or simply become swept up in the potential of having more authority and working to effect change within their organization. For curators in management positions, the rules change as far as having more responsibility and at least somewhat more authority. But this form of leadership is still from the middle of the organization, involves positive influence outward in all directions, and entails bringing out the best in others.[24] In fact, it helps to have experience leading with no authority before moving into a position in which you do have some. This gives you greater empathy and insight into what it's like for the people who report to you.

The word "amplifier" aptly describes the core skill of a successful mid-level leader who supervises others.[25] Being an amplifier means being not just a mere conduit between everything and everyone, up, down, and across. It means making things that need to be heard, heard; clarifying ambiguous plans, visions, and assignments; and enhancing the quality of what people hear and do by sharing your own perspective and framing it properly. Mid-level leaders who supervise others amplify the strengths, effectiveness, and output both of their team and their peers. They also amplify senior leadership's direction, and—as a result—the entire organization's capabilities and impact.

Being a mid-level leader with direct reports involves multiple simultaneous skills, including both self-leadership and an others-oriented mindset.[26] Skills related to self-leadership involve:

- Being self-aware—knowing yourself and what you can best contribute; acknowledging your own style, motivation, strengths, shortcomings, quirks, and preferences.
- Seeing the big picture—recognizing how the parts work together; thinking and acting systemically; seeing patterns in relationships and processes; and dealing with uncertainties and trade-offs.
- Quickly picking up things (technical skills, people skills, institutional strategy) and reducing complicated problems or issues to their bare essence.
- Learning agility—seeking opportunities to learn and learn quickly.
- Resiliency—being able to handle stress, uncertainty, and setbacks; maintaining equilibrium under pressure; responding effectively to challenges with changing strategies; adopting new ideas or suggestions; and adjusting tasks.

Skills related to an others-oriented mindset involve:

- Communicating—in all directions, customized to each direction; being approachable, professional, attentive, and consistent; being able to think with clarity and express ideas and information to a multitude of audiences.
- Inspiring others to action through examples and inspiration, by helping people understand the why and knowing how to bring out the best in them.
- Influence—through organizational intelligence (including knowledge of both formal and informal structures), trust-building, and leveraging networks; and by gaining cooperation to get things done.
- Flexibility—managing the expectations of the team by being able to adapt to change.

Challenges

Leading direct reports from the middle of an organization is tough. You regularly get pushed in every direction and you must constantly switch the many hats you are wearing. The job is messy, full of contradictions and opposing agendas. Furthermore, there is an inherent tension in it. You often can't be sure of where you stand. You have some power and authority, can make some decisions, can access some resources, can direct some work. But if you overstep your authority, you may get yourself in real trouble. No wonder that mid-level leadership often takes an emotional toll, as you must absorb everyone else's issues and deal with them, along with your own!

To help combat these challenges, you should possess a keen awareness and understanding of the conditions around you, so you know exactly what actions to take at the time. It helps to admit to yourself that you don't know all the answers and that you're not perfect. But know what is expected of you. Learn what hat to put on at what time, maintain a consistent attitude, and remain flexible. Most of all, enjoy the challenge and appreciate the value of your position.

Tools for Leading Direct Reports

Leading direct reports from the middle of an organization involves tools for leading both individual staff and the team. Tools for leading individual staff members include:

- Leading everyone differently by playing to their strengths.
- Helping people to know and believe in themselves, to discover and reach their potential.
- Giving people a clear understanding of their duties and roles.
- Checking back with everyone in ongoing ways, not just at performance review time.
- Rewarding them for results and for being contributors to the team.

Tools for Leading the Entire Team Include:

- Clarifying the larger vision (of the institution or senior leadership) for the team. Help the team feel that they are a part of something larger than they would be on their own.
- Keeping your staff focused and directed with achievable goals and benchmarks.
- Showing the way by becoming a model they can follow. Model behavior, work ethic, motivation, and the ways in which you handle challenges, setbacks, and successes.
- Making yourself accessible and approachable.

In managing curators—especially if you were one yourself (or still are one along with your leadership role)—try to treat them as you yourself would want to be treated.[27] This includes:

- Helping them to succeed in any way you can.
- Allowing their experiences and ideas to inform the team's practice.
- Challenging and stretching them in ways that motivate each of them.
- Unifying them through shared work on initiatives about which everyone is passionate—for example, collections planning, curatorial alignment with the institution's strategic plan, creation of a curatorial vision statement.
- Shielding them from surrounding politics and unreasonable requests.
- Managing less! They appreciate the independence and lack of micromanagement that come along with being a curator—although sometimes you will find it necessary to have the hard conversations that involve calling out and/or correcting behavior.

You may ask yourself why you accepted this role. It might seem harder or more overwhelming than you had initially thought, especially if you are doing curatorial work at the same time. So, it comes as a wonderful surprise when one day you happen to find that, after all your hard work, your staff rewards you with their trust, loyalty, and full engagement!

CURATORS AS INCLUSIVE LEADERS

In today's world, museum leaders at all levels must actively work to become catalysts for inclusivity.[28] This involves both being fully ourselves and allowing others to be fully themselves. It means ensuring that others feel included, removing the obstacles that cause people to feel marginalized, questioning whose voices or perspectives might be missing, preventing the limitations to the current ways in which we might be seeing an issue, and assessing if our actions or decisions are truly just and fair.

Inclusive leaders center the value of human relationships. Inclusive leadership is a collaborative, collective, and shared endeavor—elevating care, relationship-building, and well-being as integral elements of an institution's values and culture. Inclusive leaders lead with empathy. They understand and utilize the power of emotions that individuals bring to work and that shapes workplace culture. They show respect for differences. They step back, set aside their egos, and actively listen.

To better grasp the attributes of this form of leadership, it is instructive to apply this lens to the previously described constructs of leading yourself, leading across, and leading down.

Leading Yourself

Inclusive self-leaders:

- Are extremely self-aware. They know who they are at the deepest level: their strengths, weaknesses, impact on others, core values, identity, emotions, motivations, and goals.
- Are cognizant of their own personal biases and how these influence their perceptions, judgments, and behaviors.
- Challenge their own norms and assumptions.
- Are accepting and respectful of differences, courteous to others, and mindful of other people's opinions and feelings.
- Possess a high degree of "cultural intelligence"—that is, an openness to learning how cultures are created, interpreted, and shared; how cultural meanings and symbols can impact behaviors and attitudes; and how this translates to workplace behavior.
- Have the ability to acquire new behaviors and skills to adapt to new cultural situations.
- Are authentic and genuine.
- Possess an abundance of empathy and emotional intelligence.
- Recognize that they may not know all the answers and are willing to learn from others.

Leading Across

Inclusive leading across involves:

- Aligning with organizational initiatives that are working to advance equity and anti-racism.
- Ensuring that others feel included by demonstrating respect for others' backgrounds and traditions.
- Building trust.
- Being accountable.

- Encouraging collaboration; working toward common goals.
- Considering shared leadership, grounded in a partnership relationship and based on co-expertise.
- Being aware of and avoiding idioms, jargon, acronyms, and offensive or "wrong" language when speaking or writing.

Leading Down

For leading a diverse workforce and for encouraging all direct reports and mentees to be aware and respectful of others, this involves:

- Developing positive relationships with those they lead.
- Paying attention to equity and the pay gap (if possible).
- Bringing a personalized management style.
- Fostering a climate and work norms that are inclusive of differences.
- Leading with intentionality.
- Being less authoritarian, more willing to seek input from their own staff, external partners, and across the levels of the organization.
- Communicating a greater awareness of the importance of equity, inclusion, and human rights.

Challenges

This work is not easy. It often runs counter to conventional organizational thinking, entrenched legacies, and traditional hierarchies and silos. You must be courageous and expect aspects of this work to be out of your comfort zone. The stakes are high, but so is the potential. In furthering this work, it helps to find mentors and/or a support system to share successes and challenges.

CONCLUSION

Any curator can choose to lead from the middle of their organization, positively influencing people in all directions. It may seem above and beyond your daily work. But once you get used to putting this form of leadership into practice, it becomes a seamless part of that daily work. And the rewards are considerable. You'll have the ability to create positive change; the chance to make significant museum- and field-wide contributions; the opportunity to exercise your creativity; the excitement of empowering yourself and others to take action; and the joy of helping turn vision into reality.

What could be better than that?

Notes

PREFACE

1. Ohio State University, the largest university in Ohio, is a public land-grant research university located in Columbus, Ohio, with an undergraduate student body of about fifty thousand.
2. Universidad de las Américas is a private university of about eight thousand undergraduate students located in San Andrés Cholula, in the state of Puebla, about 129 kilometers (or 80 miles) southeast of Mexico City, Mexico.
3. *Introduction to Museum Work*, by G. Ellis Burcaw, was first published in 1975 by the American Association for State and Local History. The third edition, published by AltaMira Press in 1997, is still in print.
4. Two exceptions to this are the subfields of historical archaeology, which involves studying the material remains of past societies that also left behind documentary and oral histories, and applied anthropology, which involves the application of the methods and theory of anthropology to the analysis and solution of real-world problems affecting today's societies.
5. The Winterthur Program in Early American Culture, founded in 1952, is today called the Winterthur Program in American Material Culture. Focused on the material world of America in historical and global contexts, the Winterthur Program addresses the complicated lives of objects, the way in which objects fostered human relationships, and how objects ranging from the seventeenth century to the modern era enable us to understand the past in all of its diversity, including the American material world created by Black, Indigenous, or people of color. For more on this program, see https://www.winterthur.org/education/academic-programs/graduate-degree-program/american-material-culture/. The University of Delaware is a public land-grant research university in Newark, Delaware, and is the largest university in Delaware. The university partners with several prestigious museums to offer such graduate-level programs as: The Winterthur Program in American Material Culture; the Hagley Program in the History of Capitalism, Technology, and Culture; and the Longwood Program in Public Horticulture.
6. Examples include decorative redware pottery, hand-carved blanket chests, and fraktur. Redware is a type of earthenware made from local red clays. The clay is soft and often pressed over a mold. Products are generally utilitarian, with decorative designs applied onto or scratched into their surfaces. Blanket chests were generally used to store blankets, quilts, and other valuable items as part of a woman's dowry, to take with her to her new home when she got married. The fronts of these chests

were often decorated with fanciful carvings and painted with bright colors. Fraktur are documents such as birth or wedding certificates that were written in calligraphy and illuminated with colorful decorative motifs like tulips, birds, and scrolls.
7. The Mercer Museum, a six-story, poured-concrete structure, was designed by Henry Mercer and is home to the Bucks County Historical Society. The museum contains some forty thousand tools and daily life objects, many collected by Mercer himself between 1897 and his death in 1930. The Bucks County Historical Society also oversees Mercer's home, today called Fonthill Castle. For more information on Mercer Museum and Fonthill Castle, check out https://www.mercermuseum.org/.
8. The scope of this combined indoor and outdoor museum complex is massive, with numerous exhibitions and historic structures covering more than three hundred years of the American experience. In 1977, it included Henry Ford Museum (an indoor museum) and Greenfield Village (an outdoor museum). Today, The Henry Ford encompasses the renamed Henry Ford Museum of American Innovation as well as Greenfield Village along with Ford Rouge Factory Tour and the Benson Ford Research Center. See https://www.thehenryford.org/ for more information.
9. *Leisure and Entertainment in America*, by Donna R. Braden, was published by Henry Ford Museum and Greenfield Village (Dearborn, MI, 1988).
10. This term was defined by E. Joseph Pine II and James H. Gilmore in *The Experience Economy: Work Is Theatre and Every Business a Stage* (Boston, MA: Harvard Business School Press, 1999).
11. It is important to note that some museum professionals were working to decenter White/mainstream perspectives before 2020. Examples of coordinated efforts included: #MuseumsRespondToFerguson, launched in 2014 after Michael Brown, a Black eighteen-year-old, was shot and killed by a White Ferguson, Missouri, police officer; MASS Action (Museum as Site for Social Action), which began in 2016 (see https://www.museumaction.org/about); and "Museums Are Not Neutral," launched in the summer of 2017, roughly coinciding with the increasing focus on Confederate monuments (see https://journalpanorama.org/wp-content/uploads/2019/11/Autry-and-Murawski-Museums-Are-Not-Neutral.pdf). Social justice and equity issues gained increasing awareness and urgency across the museum field in the summer of 2020, during the COVID-19 pandemic and following the murder of George Floyd.

CHAPTER 1

1. For a range of curators' opinions on this, see N. Elizabeth Schlatter, "A New Spin: Are DJs, Rappers and Bloggers 'Curators'?" *Museum* 89, no. 1 (January/February 2010): 49–55; and Alina Cohen, "Everyone's a Curator. That's Not (Always) a Bad Thing," *Artsy.net* (blog), December 21, 2018, https://www.artsy.net/article/artsy-editorial-everyones-curator-bad-thing.
2. From its founding in 1989 to the elimination of the American Alliance of Museums' Professional Networks in 2023, AAM's CurCom had as its mission to support the work of curators through programs, activities, and advocacy.
3. G. Ellis Burcaw, *Introduction to Museum Work*, 3rd ed. (Lanham, MD: AltaMira Press, a Division of Rowman & Littlefield Publishers, Inc., 1997), 45.

4. Mark Walhimer, *Museums 101* (Lanham, MD: Rowman & Littlefield Publishers, Inc., 2015), 4.
5. Victor J. Danilov, *Museum Careers and Training: A Professional Guide* (Westport, CT: Greenwood Press, 1994), 52.
6. Jane R. Glaser with Artemis A. Zenetour, *Museums: A Place to Work: Planning Museum Careers* (London and New York: Routledge, 1996), 80.
7. This definition, which appears in the "Curator Core Competencies" document, comes from CurCom's 2009 Curatorial Code of Ethics, https://www.aam-us.org/wp-content/uploads/2018/01/curcomethics.pdf.
8. Troy M. Livingston, vice president of innovation and learning, Museum of Life and Science, Durham, North Carolina, quoted in Schlatter, "A New Spin," 52.
9. Nicola Pickering, *The Museum Curator's Guide: Understanding, Managing and Presenting Objects* (London: Lund Humphries, 2020), 134.
10. "Curator Core Competencies," 3. "Curator Core Competencies" is a document that was published in 2014 by the CurCom Standing Committee on Ethics and accepted by CurCom in 2015. It can be found at https://www.aam-us.org/wp-content/uploads/2018/05/CURATOR-CORE-COMPETENCIES.pdf.
11. "Curator Core Competencies."
12. In January 2017, CurCom held a series of discussions to encourage meaningful discourse and feedback on this document. Members of several discussion groups concurred that, while the document encapsulates an often-misunderstood role and underscores the vital role of curators in the face of radically shifting cultures, technologies, and economies, it was considered most realistic at large institutions with sufficient funding and resources to support these efforts. At small to midsize museums, where a curator might have several different titles and carry out multiple functions, it must be seen as aspirational, a touchstone to strive for. Publishing was especially called out as difficult to achieve. Participants also agreed that it should not be static, but a living document that changes with the times. For the complete summary of this feedback, see W. James Burns and Sheila K. Hoffman, "Beyond Collections Work: The Evolving Role for Curators," *Museum* 96, no. 3 (May/June 2017): 13–15.
13. Giles Miller, "Do We Need Specialist Curators?" *Museums Association*, March 7, 2012 (discontinued blog accessed September 30, 2019); Matthew Caines, "Poll: Do We Need Specialist Curators?" *The Guardian.com* (blog), June 25, 2012, https://www.theguardian.com/culture-professionals-network/culture-professionals-blog/poll/2012/jun/25/poll-specialist-curators-museums-needed-decline; and interview with Charles Sable, curator of Decorative Arts, The Henry Ford, Dearborn, MI, April 6, 2023.
14. Burcaw, *Introduction to Museum Work*, 40; Caines, "Poll: Do We Need Specialist Curators?"
15. I have never regretted starting my career as a specialist curator, although I evolved into a more generalist role over time. Some of my earliest work entailed studying kitchen utensils in depth—examining their physical attributes, describing them for catalog records, and becoming acquainted with research sources such as patent records and trade catalogs, along with secondary sources on social and technological history. This early practice in closely examining and rigorously researching a body of objects proved invaluable throughout my career as I applied these learnings

to other collections, worked on exhibitions and interpretive projects that involved other types of collections, and eventually mentored others in how to critically look at and interpret objects rather than assuming all information could be found online.

16. Lewis Pollard, "The Rise of the Skills-Based Curator," Museums Association (blog), August 4, 2022, https://www.museumsassociation.org/museums-journal/opinion/2022/08/the-rise-of-the-skills-based-curator/.
17. For more on the tasks of curators in small history museums, see Martha B. Katz-Hyman, "Curatorial Basics 101," *Proceedings of the 2007 Conference and Annual Meeting, El Rancho de las Golondrinas, Santa Fe, New Mexico*, ed. Carol Kennis Lopez, Vol. XXX (North Bloomfield, OH: The Association for Living History, Farm and Agricultural Museums, 2008), 160–63; and Dawn Bondhus, Martha Katz-Hyman, and Mick Woodcock, "Curation 101: Curatorial Roots for Non-Curators," *Proceedings of the 2010 Conference and Annual Meeting, Old Sturbridge Village*, ed. Debra Reid, Vol. XXXIII (Worcester, MA: The Association for Living History, Farm and Agricultural Museums, 2011), 129–30.
18. Tracie Evans, "Making Choices Between Authenticity, Preservation and Programming: Curating at a Living History Site," *Proceedings of the 2021 Virtual Conference and Annual Meeting*, ed. Donna R. Braden, Vol. XLIV (Rochdale, MA: The Association for Living History, Farm and Agricultural Museums, 2022), 180.
19. These issues have been raised within the ALHFAM (Association for Living History, Farm and Agricultural Museums) organization since its founding in the 1970s. For some early discussions, see Steve Lewis, "Authenticity vs. Practicality," *Proceedings of the 1982 Annual Meeting, King's Landing, New Brunswick, Canada*, The Association for Living Historical Farms and Agricultural Museums, ed. Wayne Randolph, Vol. 6 (Washington, DC: Smithsonian, 1983), 65–66; and T. A. Brown, "The Agricultural Curator's Role in Developing and Maintaining Interpretive Programs," *Proceedings of the 1977 Annual Meeting, Tifton, GA*, The Association for Living Historical Farms and Agricultural Museums, ed. Virginia Wolf Briscoe, Vol. IV (Washington, DC: Smithsonian, 1978), 12–13.
20. See, for example, Geoff Woodcox, "Curation as an Act of Healing with Native American Communities," *History News* 78, no. 3 (2024): 28–32; and Jennifer Shannon, "The Construction of Native Voice at the National Museum of the American Indian," chapter 8 in *Contesting Knowledge: Museums and Indigenous Perspectives*, ed. Susan Sleeper-Smith (Lincoln: University of Nebraska Press, 2009), 218–47.
21. Aja Bain, "Peopling the Past: Living History and Inclusive Museum Practice," *The Museum Scholar: Theory and Practice*, Vol. 2, 2019, https://articles.themuseumscholar.org/2019/05/16/tp_vol2bain/.
22. Pickering, *The Museum Curator's Guide*, 137.
23. The History Relevance Initiative, undertaken by a volunteer group of history professionals across the United States under the auspices of the American Association for State and Local History (AASLH), had as its goal to raise the profile of history in the national dialogue. The goal ultimately changed to helping history organizations across the history field think intentionally about how to make their history products more relevant to their audiences. This initiative helped inspire the Reframing History project, an evidence-based strategic communications toolkit to help history professionals more effectively discuss what history is, how it is interpreted, and why it matters in society. Learn more about these significant projects at https://www

.historyrelevance.com/value-history-statemen and https://aaslh.org/reframing-history-blog/.
24. Elena Gonzales, "View from the Field: Equity-Oriented and Anti-Racist Curatorial Practice," *The Inclusive Historian's Handbook*, posted December 23, 2020, https://inclusivehistorian.com/view-from-the-field-equity-oriented-and-anti-racist-curatorial-practice/.
25. This report can be found at https://www.aam-us.org/2022/08/02/excellence-in-deai-report/.
26. For more in-depth descriptions of these, see Cecile Shellman, *Effective Diversity, Equity, Accessibility, Inclusion, and Anti-Racism Practices for Museums, from the Inside Out* (Lanham, MD: Rowman & Littlefield Publishers, Inc., 2022), 17–37. See also Gonzales, "View from the Field."
27. Shellman, *Effective Diversity, Equity, Accessibility, Inclusion, and Anti-Racism Practices*, 101–3.
28. The complete report can be found at https://www.aam-us.org/2021/02/09/audiences-and-inclusion-primer/.
29. A Google search reveals many articles with advice on how to obtain a museum curator job. One that I found particularly useful, and drew from for this chapter, was "How to Become a Museum Curator," Grand Canyon University (blog), May 20, 2022, https://www.gcu.edu/blog/criminal-justice-government-and-public-administration/how-become-museum-curator.
30. CurCom, "Curator Core Competencies," 4.
31. An additional networking suggestion is the online community "Made By Us," which is oriented toward Gen Z history enthusiasts. The website for this group is: https://historymadebyus.com/.
32. More on this can be found in Burcaw, *Introduction to Museum Work*, 197; the chapter by Wendy Luke, "Do I Really Need a Cover Letter? (Yes, You Do)" in *A Life in Museums: Managing Your Museum Career*, ed. Greg Stevens and Wendy Luke (Washington DC: The AAM Press, 2012), 55–57; and Michael Dove and Krista McCracken, "Get to Work: Crafting Cover Letters and Résumés for Emerging Professionals," *History News* 73, no. 1 (Winter 2018): Technical Leaflet #281.
33. Rick Beard, "If It Was Easy, Anyone Could Do It: Training Professionals for History Institutions," *History News* 71, no. 3 (Summer 2016): 9.
34. Numerous articles on soft skills can be found online. For specific applications to museum work, see Martha Morris, "Reinventing Museum Careers" (blog), November 18, 2019, https://www.aam-us.org/2019/11/18/reinventing-museum-careers/; Marsha Semmel's chapter on "The Value of 21st Century Skills" in Stevens and Luke, *A Life in Museums*, 97–100; and Donna R. Braden, "Leadership at Every Level," *Proceedings of the 2013 Conference and Annual Meeting, Hale Farm & Village, Akron, Ohio*, ed. Debra Reid, Vol. XXXVI (North Bloomfield, Ohio: The Association for Living History, Farm and Agricultural Museums, 2014), 248–53.
35. This list of soft skills, including specific examples within each skill, came from Emily Crowley, "Soft Skills: Definition & 100+ Examples for 2023," *Resume Genius* (blog), November 25, 2022, https://resumegenius.com/blog/resume-help/soft-skills.
36. Elizabeth Peña, "Leadership at All Levels," in Stevens and Luke, *A Life in Museums*, 144.

37. AAM, "Excellence in DEAI," https://www.aam-us.org/2022/08/02/excellence-in-deai report/.
38. This excellent checklist (reduced from a larger list) came from the webinar "Inclusive Museum Leadership," presented by Cinnamon Catlin-Legutko for the Texas Historical Commission on May 6, 2021. It was recorded and is archived under the category "Diversity, Equity, Access & Inclusion" at https://www.thc.texas.gov/preserve/projects-and-programs/museum-services/webinars. For more ideas, see Shellman, *Effective Diversity, Equity, Accessibility, Inclusion, and Anti-Racism Practices*, 36-37, 58, 60, the chart on 63, and 105; and Elif M. Gokcigdem, "Designing for Empathy," *Dimensions* 20, no. 5 (November/December 2018): 26-30.
39. One of the many history organizations that offers webinars is the Texas Historical Commission, which has organized and archived its numerous webinars. These are available for public access at https://www.thc.texas.gov/preserve/projects-and-programs/museum-services/webinars. AASLH also offers excellent webinars.
40. Ackerson, "Strategizing Me: Making a Personal Career Plan," *Museum* 96, no. 2 (March/April 2017): 41-45.

CHAPTER 2

1. Amy Lonetree, *Decolonizing Museums: Representing Native America in National and Tribal Museums* (Chapel Hill: University of North Carolina Press, 2012), xiv.
2. Lonetree, *Decolonizing Museums*, xv.
3. Leonie Hannan and Sarah Longair, *History Through Material Culture* (Manchester, England: Manchester University Press, 2017), 8.
4. David E. Kyvig and Myron A. Marty, *Nearby History: Exploring the Past Around You* (Lanham, MD: AltaMira Press, a Division of Rowman & Littlefield Publishers, Inc., 2010), 159.
5. Today, the term "man" would apply to all people. Quoted in E. McClung Fleming, "Artifact Study: A Proposed Model," footnote 1, *Winterthur Portfolio* 9 (1974): 153.
6. Jules David Prown, "Mind in Matter: An Introduction to Material Culture Theory and Method," *Winterthur Portfolio* 17, no. 1 (Spring 1982): 2-3.
7. Doug Blandy and Paul E. Bolin, *Learning Things: Material Culture in Art Education* (New York: Teachers College Press, 2018), 3.
8. Prown, "Mind in Matter," 3.
9. For an in-depth description of this history, see "Material Culture Studies in America, 1876-1976," chapter 1 in Thomas J. Schlereth's book *Material Culture Studies in America* (AltaMira Press, a Division of Rowman & Littlefield Publishers, Inc., 1999), 1-75. Several of these early essays are included in Schlereth's book.
10. There were, of course, exceptions to this, including Henry Mercer (who collected early American daily life objects as an anthropologist) and Henry Ford (who collected buildings and objects that either related to his own personal heroes or reminded him of his own past).
11. Anthropologist C. Malcolm Watkins (at the Smithsonian Institution) and folklorist/public historian Louis C. Jones (at Cooperstown) were particularly instrumental in championing material culture studies at the time.
12. Wilcomb E. Washburn, "Manuscripts and Manufacts," *The American Archivist* 27, no. 2 (April 1964): 247.

13. John Demos, *A Little Commonwealth: Family Life in Plymouth Colony* (New York: Oxford University Press, 1970).
14. Other early works demonstrating the use of objects as historical evidence include Ivor Noël Hume's *A Guide to Artifacts in Colonial America* (New York: Alfred A. Knopf, 1970) and James Deetz's *In Small Things Forgotten: The Archaeology of Early American Life* (Garden City, NY: Anchor Books, 1977). See other articles from this era in the anthology edited by Schlereth, *Material Culture Studies in America*, such as John A. Kouwenhoven's 1964 essay, "American Studies: Words or Things?" 79-92.
15. This section is primarily drawn from Donna R. Braden, *Spaces that Tell Stories: Recreating Historical Environments* (Lanham, MD: Rowman & Littlefield Publishers, Inc., 2019), 29-30. In addition to social historians, scholars from other fields who were influential during this era include folklorist Henry Glassie and decorative arts scholar Kenneth L. Ames.
16. Braden, *Spaces that Tell Stories*, 30.
17. Published in Ian M. G. Quimby, ed., *Material Culture and the Study of American Life* (New York: W. W. Norton & Co., Inc. for the Henry Francis duPont Winterthur Museum, 1978). The Winterthur Conference, which began in 1954, was an outgrowth of the graduate-level Winterthur Program in Early American Culture, which began in 1952. For more on the Winterthur Museum and the Winterthur Program in Early American Culture, see my narrative in the preface about being a student in this program as well as note 5 in the preface.
18. Cary Carson, quoted in John A. H. Sweeney, "Introduction," in Quimby, *Material Culture and the Study of American Life*, 2. Carson's essay in the publication was entitled "Doing History with Material Culture," 41-64. Other particularly relevant essays in the publication include Brooke Hindle's "How Much Is a Piece of the True Cross Worth?" 5-20, and Ivor Noël Hume's "Material Culture with Dirt on It: A Virginia Perspective," 21-40. Many additional scholarly essays from this era can be found in the anthology *Material Culture Studies in America*, with commentary by editor Thomas J. Schlereth. See also Steven Lubar and W. David Kingery's *History from Things: Essays on Material Culture* (Washington, DC: Smithsonian Institution Press, 1993) and chapter 2, note 16 in Braden, *Spaces that Tell Stories*, 35.
19. Like the earlier era of material culture studies (note 9), several articles from this era are also included in Schlereth's book *Material Culture Studies in America*.
20. Ann Smart Martin and J. Ritchie Garrison, eds., *American Material Culture: The Shape of the Field* (Knoxville: University of Tennessee Press for the Henry Francis duPont Winterthur Museum, 1997), 1.
21. Recent material culture studies as an academic discipline include: Karen Harvey, *History and Material Culture: A Student's Guide to Approaching Alternative Sources* (London and New York: Routledge, 2009); Arthur Asa Burger, *What Objects Mean: An Introduction to Material Culture*, 2nd ed. (Walnut Creek, CA: Left Coast Press, 2014); Hannan and Longair, *History Through Material Culture*; Blandy and Bolin, *Learning Things*; Lu Ann De Cunzo and Catherine Dann Roeber, *The Cambridge Handbook of Material Culture Studies* (New York: Cambridge University Press, 2022); and Cyrus Mulready, *Object Studies: Introductions to Material Culture* (Cham, Switzerland: Palgrave MacMillan, 2023).
22. For more on this history, see Sheila A. Brennan, "Digital History," *The Inclusive Historian's Handbook*, posted June 4, 2019, https://inclusivehistorian.com/digital

-history/; Daniel J. Cohen and Roy Rosenzweig, "Preserving Digital History," *Digital History: A Guide to Gathering, Preserving, and Presenting the Past on the Web*, Center for History and New Media, https://chnm.gmu.edu/digitalhistory/preserving/index.html; and Matthew Jones, "The Complete History of Social Media: A Timeline of the Invention of Social Networking," *History Cooperative*, June 16, 2015, accessed May 29, 2023, https://historycooperative.org/the-history-of-social-media/.

23. Brennan, "Digital History."
24. Matthew MacArthur, "Get Real! The Role of Objects in the Digital Age," in Bill Adair, Benjamin Filene, and Laura Koloski, eds., *Letting Go? Sharing Historical Authority in a User-Generated World* (Philadelphia, PA: The Pew Center for Arts & Heritage, 2011), 65.
25. See, for example, such projects as The National Museum of American History's "Community Curation Program," https://nmaahc.si.edu/explore/initiatives/family-history-center/community-curation-program; History Colorado's Museum of Memory Initiative, https://www.historycolorado.org/museum-memory-initiative#:~:text=Museum%20of%20Memory%20is%20a%20public%20history%20initiative,to%20decide%20how%20to%20remember%20its%20collective%20past; The Historic New Orleans Collection's collection of people's stories about their personal possessions, https://www.hnoc.org/publications/first-draft/incredible-stories-10-objects-chosen-and-told-you; and the National Museum of African American History and Culture's Memory Book initiative, https://nmaahc.si.edu/explore/initiatives/memory-book.
26. See, for example, the National Museum of American History's online exhibit guide to America on the Move, https://americanhistory.si.edu/visitor-guides/america-move/community-dreams; the Brooklyn Museum's "teasers" to certain galleries, https://www.brooklynmuseum.org/opencollection/objects/163980; and the Cooper Hewitt's "Collection Highlights," https://collection.cooperhewitt.org/highlights/2318806915/.
27. See, for example, the Victoria & Albert's summaries of "Rapid Response Collecting" artifacts, https://collections.vam.ac.uk/item/O1326209/hello-barbie-doll-mattel-inc/; Australia's Powerhouse Collection, https://collection.maas.museum/object/43956; Historic New England's collection, https://www.historicnewengland.org/explore/collections-access/; and essays about Syracuse University's plastics collection, https://plastics.syr.edu/page-essays.php. The Henry Ford includes a brief "summary narrative" with each individual object (though it is impossible to keep up with the pace of digitization). For an example of a summary narrative with a catalog record, see https://www.thehenryford.org/collections-and-research/digital-collections/artifact/443429.
28. See, for instance, examples on the Smithsonian's History Explorer website, https://historyexplorer.si.edu/resource/jetsons-lunch-box and https://historyexplorer.si.edu/major-themes/theme/womens-history-month. At The Henry Ford, curators create interpretive "expert sets" of groupings of objects based around themes or topics. These had started as part of online curriculum materials for teachers and students, but they have become a popular feature now part of the general offerings on The Henry Ford's website. See https://www.thehenryford.org/collections-and-research/digital-collections/expert-sets.

29. Elizabeth Wood, Rainey Tisdale, and Trevor Jones, eds., *Active Collections* (London and New York: Routledge, 2018), 21. Tisdale and Jones started the Active Collections initiative in 2012. Other useful sources for identifying, analyzing, and interpreting more active or inclusive objects can be found in Cecile Shellman, *Effective Diversity, Equity, Accessibility, Inclusion, and Anti-Racism Practices for Museums: From the Inside Out* (Lanham, MD: Rowman & Littlefield Publishers, Inc., 2022); the essays by Sven Haakanson, "Caretakers of Our Histories," and Mariah Berlanga-Shevchuk, "The Collective Collection: Active, People-Centered, and Collaborative," chapters 16 and 17 in *Change is Required: Preparing for the Post-Pandemic Museum*, Avi Y. Decter, Marsha L. Semmel, and Ken Yellis, eds. (Lanham, MD: Rowman & Littlefield Publishers, Inc., 2022), 111-15, 117-21; Rebecca Shrum, "Material Culture," *The Inclusive Historian's Handbook*, posted June 3, 2019, https://inclusivehistorian.com/?s=material+culture; and Gretchen Sullivan Sorin, "Exhibitions," *The Inclusive Historian's Handbook*, posted December 20, 2021, https://inclusivehistorian.com/?s=exhibitions.
30. *Active Collections*, 13-20.
31. Blandy and Bolin's book, *Learning Things*, contains an excellent description of "Ten Approaches to Material Culture Study," 93-101. For other approaches, see also Prown, "Mind in Matter," and essays in Schlereth, *Material Culture Studies in America*.
32. Fleming, "Artifact Study," 153-73.
33. Early thinking that shaped this article included Fleming's "Early American Decorative Arts as Social Documents," *Mississippi Valley Historical Review* 45, no. 2 (September 1958): 276-84 (referenced in footnote 17 in Fleming, "Artifact Study," 160); and an unpublished course outline for "The Artifact in American History" (History 803) that Fleming taught his graduate students in the Winterthur Program in Early American Culture in 1969, referenced in Schlereth, *Material Culture Studies in America*, 162.
34. For example, the authors of the 2010 book *Nearby History: Exploring the Past Around You*, wrote that "the general framework of that model is as useful for beginning students of nearby history as it is for the most advanced of scholars," Kyvig and Marty, 162. A recent book that uses this methodology is Dwandalynn R. Reece, ed., *Musical Crossroads: Stories Behind the Objects of African American Music* (Washington, DC: Smithsonian Institution, National Museum of African American History and Culture, 2023).
35. Fleming, "Artifact Study," 154.
36. Schlereth suggested that Craig Gilborn's essay, "Pop Pedagogy: Looking at the Coke Bottle," was an attempt to correct these deficiencies. Gilborn was a student of Fleming's at Winterthur. His essay, with Schlereth's annotated introduction, appeared in *American Material Culture Studies*, 183-91.
37. For example, Karen Harvey's "beginner's approach to fully interrogate an object" involves physical description, placing the object in historical context, and taking a broader view (as referenced in Shrum, "Material Culture," *The Inclusive Historian's Handbook*). The easy-to-use online worksheet "Twenty Questions to Ask an Object," created in 2014 by the Material Culture Caucus of the American Studies Association, includes: close scrutiny of the object, identifying the object's major attributes, looking at the object as part of a larger group of objects in its historical

context, assessing the object's sociocultural context, and looking at the object's contemporary context and relevance. This document is accessible at https://view.officeapps.live.com/op/view.aspx?src=https%3A%2F%2Fnetworks.h-net.org%2Fsystem%2Ffiles%2Fcontributed-files%2Fmcc-asa-20-questions-handout-2014.docx&wdOrigin=BROWSELINK.

38. Fleming, "Artifact Study," 161–73; Kenneth L. Ames, "Meaning in Artifacts: Hall Furnishings in Victorian America," *Journal of Interdisciplinary History* IX, no. 1 (Summer 1978): 19–46; Alison J. Clarke, "Tupperware: Product as Social Relation," in Martin and Garrison, *American Material Culture*, 225–50; Rebecca K. Shrum, "Selling Mr. Coffee: Design, Gender, and the Branding of a Kitchen Appliance," *Winterthur Portfolio: A Journal of American Material Culture* 46, no. 4 (Winter 2012): 271–98.

39. Published jointly by The American Association for State and Local History (AASLH) and Rowman & Littlefield Publishers, Inc. (Lanham, MD), the books in the "Exploring America's Historic Treasures" series each investigate the past through the interpretation of fifty material culture items. The books in this series cover: women's suffrage (published 2020), the history of childhood and play (2020), American girlhood (2021), the American Civil War (2021), America's healthcare (2022), the American presidency (2023), and American Jewish history (2024). For more on the approach of using a series of individual objects to tell a larger story, see Trevor Jones's article, "Telling Stories with Objects in the Starring Role," *History News* 69, no. 2 (Spring 2014): 23–26.

40. See, for example, William Wei's *Becoming Colorado: The Centennial State in 100 Objects* (Denver and Louisville, CO: History Colorado and University Press of Colorado, 2021).

41. Burger, *What Objects Mean*, 43–62; Mulready, *Object Studies*, 151–59.

42. Karal Ann Marling, *As Seen on TV: The Visual Culture of Everyday Life in the 1950s* (Cambridge: Harvard University Press, 1994), 50–84, 202–40.

43. Shrum, "Material Culture," *The Inclusive Historian's Handbook*.

44. Sorin, "Exhibitions," *The Inclusive Historian's Handbook*.

45. Steven Lubar and Kathleen Kendrick, "Artifact and Analysis: Essays," accessed May 29, 2023, https://smithsonianeducation.org/idealabs/ap/essays/looking.htm#:~:text=We%20suggest%20five%20ways%20to%20think%20about%20artifacts,4%20Artifacts%20capture%20moments.%205%20Artifacts%20reflect%20changes.

46. Cleanser Dispenser digital record (2014.87.1): https://www.thehenryford.org/collections-and-research/digital-collections/artifact/400029.

47. Interview with Jeanine Head Miller, curator of Domestic Life, The Henry Ford, Dearborn, MI, June 5, 2023. Digital record for Hermitage Plantation brick: https://www.thehenryford.org/collections-and-research/digital-collections/artifact/493338. Digital record for Hermitage Plantation enslaved workers' structures: https://www.thehenryford.org/collections-and-research/digital-collections/artifact/268474.

48. Union Cap digital record: https://www.thehenryford.org/collections-and-research/digital-collections/artifact/372670.

49. For the complete online article, see https://www.thehenryford.org/explore/blog/the-real-toys-of-toy-story/.

50. For more on visitors and objects, see Pauline K. Eversman, Rosemary T. Krill, Edwina Michael, Beth A. Twiss-Garrity, and Tracey Rae Beck, "Material Culture as Text:

Review and Reform of the Literacy Model for Interpretation," in Martin and Garrison, *American Material Culture*, 163; MacArthur, "Get Real!" 56-67; Mary Jane Taylor and Beth A. Twiss Houting, "Is It Real? Kids and Collections," chapter 11 in *Connecting Kids to History with Museum Exhibitions*, D. Lynn McRainey and John Russick, eds. (Walnut Creek, CA: Left Coast Press, Inc., 2010), 241-56; and Scott Paris and Melissa J. Mercer, "Finding Self in Objects: Identity, Exploration in Museums," chapter 12 in *Learning Conversations in Museums*, Gaea Leinhardt, Kevin Crowley, and Karen Knutson, eds. (London and New York: Routledge, 2002), 401-23.

51. Julia Rose, *Interpreting Difficult History at Museums and Historic Sites*, AASLH Interpreting History Series (Lanham, MD: Rowman & Littlefield Publishers, Inc., 2016), 91.
52. Shrum, "Material Culture," *The Inclusive Historian's Handbook*; Elizabeth Wood and Kiersten F. Latham, chapter 4 in *The Objects of Experience: Transforming Visitor-Object Encounters in Museums* (Walnut Creek, CA: Left Coast Press, Inc. 2016), 72-95; and Rainey Tisdale, "Objects or People?" in Wood, Tisdale, and Jones, *Active Collections*, 21-33.
53. Tisdale, "Objects or People?" 22.
54. Sorin, "Exhibitions," *The Inclusive Historian's Handbook*.
55. Rose, *Interpreting Difficult History*, 78.
56. Eversman, Krill, Michael, Twiss-Garrity, and Beck, "Material Culture as Text," 164.
57. Paris and Mercer, "Finding Self in Objects," 420.
58. Paul Bourcier, "#Meaning: Cataloguing Active Collections," *Active Collections*, 115-16.
59. Bourcier, "#Meaning," 112; Taylor and Houting, "Is It Real?" 241.
60. Taylor and Houting, "Is It Real?" 114. See also Nina Simon, chapter 4 in *The Participatory Museum* (Santa Cruz, CA: Museums 2.0, 2010), 127-81.
61. Wood and Latham, *The Objects of Experience*, 146-47.

CHAPTER 3

1. Rainey Tisdale, "Do History Museums Still Need Objects?" *History News* 66, no. 3 (Summer 2011): 19-24; and Rick Beard, "Collections: Our Curse and Our Blessing," *History News* 70, no. 3 (Summer 2015): 11-16.
2. "Curator Core Competencies" was published in 2014 by the American Alliance of Museums Curators Committee (CurCom) Standing Committee on Ethics. It can be found at https://www.aam-us.org/wp-content/uploads/2018/05/CURATOR-CORE-COMPETENCIES.pdf.
3. For definitions and basic background about collections and collecting, see Hugh H. Genoways and Lynne M. Ireland, *Museum Administration 2.0*, rev. Cinnamon Catlin-Legutko (Lanham, MD: Rowman & Littlefield Publishers, Inc., 2017), 283-84, 305; Edward P. Alexander and Mary Alexander, "To Collect," chapter 8 in *Museums in Motion: An Introduction to the History and Functions of Museums*, 2nd ed. (Walnut Creek, CA: Altamira Press for the American Association for State and Local History, 2007), 187-215; The AASLH Standards and Ethics Committee, "Valuing History Collections," *History News* 75, no. 4 (Autumn 2020): 28-33; and John E. Simmons, *Things Great and Small: Collections Management Policies* (Lanham, MD: Rowman & Littlefield Publishers, Inc., 2018), 2-3.

4. For the most in-depth books on the ethics of collecting, see Steven Miller, *Museum Collection Ethics* (Lanham, MD: Rowman & Littlefield Publishers, Inc., 2020) and Sally Yerkovich, *A Practical Guide to Museum Ethics* (Lanham, MD: Rowman & Littlefield Publishers, Inc., 2016). See also Simmons, *Things Great and Small*, 171-77; and American Alliance of Museums, *Museum Registration Methods*, John Simmons and Toni Kiser, eds., 6th ed. (Lanham, MD: Rowman & Littlefield Publishers, Inc., 2020), 446-523.
5. Standards of ethical practice continue to evolve in response to changing values, situations, and social movements. Refer to protocols and codes of ethics in: AAM's Curator Code of Ethics, https://www.aam-us.org/wp-content/uploads/2018/01/curcomethics.pdf; AAM's Direct Care of Collections: Ethics, Guidelines and Recommendations, March 2019 Update, https://www.aam-us.org/programs/ethics-standards-and-professional-practices/direct-care-of-collections/; the AASLH (American Association for State and Local History) Code of Ethics, http://download.aaslh.org/AASLH+Statement+of+Standards+and+Ethics+-+Revised+2018.pdf; and the ICOM (International Council for Museums) Code of Ethics, https://icom.museum/wp-content/uploads/2018/07/ICOM-code-En-web.pdf.
6. For tips on creating relevant mission statements, see Gail Anderson's *Mission Matters: Relevance and Museums in the 21st Century* (Lanham, MD: Rowman & Littlefield Publishers, Inc., 2019); and Harold and Susan Skramstad's "Mission and Vision Again? What's the Big Deal?" chapter 3 in *Small Museum Toolkit 1: Leadership, Mission, and Governance*, Cinnamon Catlin-Legutko and Stacy Klingler, eds. (Lanham, MD: AltaMira Press, a Division of Rowman & Littlefield Publishers, Inc., 2012), 60-76. See also "Museum Mission Statements: Some Examples" and the source list on the "Engaging Places" website, https://engagingplaces.net/2018/09/17/excellence-in-museum-mission-statements-some-examples/; and Sample Documents in the Tier 3 Members-only Resource Library on AAM's website, https://www.aam-us.org/topic/resource-library/.
7. Tisdale, "Do History Museums Still Need Objects?" 21.
8. Tisdale, "Do History Museums Still Need Objects?" 24.
9. For more on the topic of "Too Much Stuff," see James M. Vaughan, "Rethinking the Rembrandt Rule," *Museum* 87, no. 2 (March/April 2008): 33-35; Tisdale, "Do History Museums Still Need Objects?" 19-24; Beard, "Collections: Our Curse and Our Blessing," 11-16; Trevor Jones and Rainey Tisdale, "A Manifesto for Active History Museum Collections," in *Active Collections*, Elizabeth Wood, Rainey Tisdale, and Trevor Jones, eds. (London and New York: Routledge, 2018), 7-10.
10. Jones, Tisdale, and Wood, "Introduction," *Active Collections*, 2.
11. Jones, Tisdale, and Wood, "Introduction," *Active Collections*, 1-6.
12. Jones and Tisdale, "A Manifesto," *Active Collections*, 5.
13. More detail on these suggestions can be found in Jones, Tisdale, and Wood, "Introduction," *Active Collections*; Trevor Jones, "Tier Your Collections: A Practical Tool for Making Clear Decisions in Collections Management," chapter 8 in *Active Collections*, 103-9; Tisdale, "Do History Museums Still Need Objects?"; Beard, "Collections: Our Curse and Our Blessing"; and Meghan Gelardi Holmes, Steven Lubar, Jessie MacLeod, William Stoutamire, and Carrie Villar, "Telling Inclusive Stories When Your Collections Are Stuck in the Past," *History News* 75, no. 3 (Summer 2020): Technical Leaflet #291.

14. Tisdale, "Do History Museums Still Need Objects?" 21. The reference for this example, cited in note 7, was from Gretchen Sullivan Sorin's article, "Why Museums Need to Continue the Discussion about Race in America," *History News* 55, no. 4 (Autumn 2000): 7-11.
15. Charles Bethea, "Museum Collecting in the Age of Black Lives Matter," *History News* 77, no. 1 (2022): 13.
16. Bethea, "Museum Collecting in the Age of Black Lives Matter," 12-17. For more on this topic, see also Masum Momaya, "Ten Principles for an Anti-Racist, Anti-Orientalist, Activist Approach to Collections," chapter 1 in *Active Collections*, 13-20; Tisdale, "Objects or People?" chapter 2 in *Active Collections*, 21-33; and Mariah Berlanga-Shevchuk, "The Collective Collection: Active, People-Centered, and Collaborative," chapter 17 in *Change Is Required: Preparing for the Post-Pandemic Museum*, Avi Y. Decter, Marsha L. Semmel, and Ken Yellis, eds. (Lanham, MD: Rowman & Littlefield Publishers, Inc., 2022), 117-21.
17. Bethea, "Museum Collecting in the Age of Black Lives Matter," 15.
18. Nicolette B. Meister and Jackie Hoff, "Collections Planning: Best Practices in Collections Stewardship," chapter 5 in *Small Museum Toolkit 6: Stewardship Collections and History Preservation*, Cinnamon Catlin-Legutko and Stacy Klingler, eds. (Lanham, MD: AltaMira Press, a Division of Rowman & Littlefield Publishers, Inc., 2012), 129.
19. A particularly detailed source for collections planning is James B. Gardner and Elizabeth E. Merritt, *The AAM Guide to Collections Planning*, AAM Professional Education Series (Washington, DC: American Association of Museums, 2004). This content is summarized in Meister and Hoff, "Collections Planning." See also James B. Gardner and Elizabeth Merritt's earlier article, "Collections Planning: Pinning Down a Strategy," *Museum News* 81, no. 4 (July-August 2002): 30-33, 60-66; and Sample Documents in the Tier 3 Members-only AAM Resource Library, https://www.aam-us.org/topic/resource-library/.
20. Gardner and Merritt, "Collections Planning," 30.
21. Gardner and Merritt, "Collections Planning," 33.
22. The AASLH Standards and Ethics Committee, "Valuing History Collections," 30.
23. For detailed descriptions of Collections Management Policies, see Simmons, *Things Great and Small*; John E. Simmons, "Managing Things: Crafting a Collections Policy," *Museum News* 83, no. 1 (January/February 2004): 29-31, 47-48; John Simmons and Toni Kiser, eds, *Museum Registration Methods, Part 2,* American Alliance of Museums, 6th ed. (Lanham, MD: Rowman & Littlefield Publishers, Inc., 2020), 30-37; and Marie C. Malaro and Ildiko Pogány DeAngelis, *A Legal Primer on Managing Museum Collections*, 3rd ed. (Washington, DC: Smithsonian Books, 2012). For small museums, see Meister and Hoff, "Collections Planning," 131; and Julia Clark, "Do We Really Want the Bust of Jesus and What Should We Do with the Pump Organ in the Other Room? Or, Why You Want a Good Collections Management Policy," chapter 4 in Catlin-Legutko and Klingler, *Small Museum Toolkit 6: Stewardship Collections and History Preservation*, 86-107. See also Sample Documents in the Tier 3 Members-only AAM Resource Library, https://www.aam-us.org/topic/resource-library/.
24. Gardner and Merritt, *The AAM Guide to Collections Planning*, 16.

25. Gardner and Merritt, *The AAM Guide to Collections Planning*, 18. See also Gardner's entire chapter on "Building the Intellectual Framework," *The AAM Guide to Collections Planning*, 5-10.
26. For more detail, see Merritt's chapter on "Writing the Collections Plan," *The AAM Guide to Collections Planning*, 11-25.
27. Gardner and Merritt, *The AAM Guide to Collections Planning*, 37.
28. See Gardner's chapter on "Museum Politics," *The AAM Guide to Collections Planning*, 33-37.
29. Bethea, "Museum Collecting in the Age of Black Lives Matter," 16.
30. For more tips and strategies related to working on community-based collecting projects, see Porchia Moore, Rosa Paquet, Aletheia Wittman, "Opening Up to Transformation," chapter 3 in *Transforming Inclusion in Museums: The Power of Collaborative Inquiry* (Lanham, MD: Rowman & Littlefield Publishers, Inc., 2022), 47-72; Mike Murawski, "Let Your Community In," chapter 2 in *Museums as Agents of Change: A Guide to Becoming a Changemaker* (Lanham, MD: Rowman & Littlefield Publishers, Inc., 2021), 17-37; Katharine Allen and Robert-John Hinojosa, "The LGBTQ Columbia History Initiative," *History News* 76, no. 3 (Summer 2021): 19-23; Bethea, "Museum Collecting in the Age of Black Lives Matter," 16; Janeen Bryant and Kamille Bostick, "What's the Big Idea? Using Listening Sessions to Build Relationships and Relevance" (the Latino New South Project), *History News* 68, no. 3 (Summer 2013): Technical Leaflet #263; and Lila Teresa Church, "Documenting Local African American Community History: Some Guidelines for Consideration," chapter 7 in *Interpreting African American History and Culture at Museums and Historic Sites*, AASLH Interpreting History Series, Max van Balgooy, ed. (Lanham, MD: Rowman & Littlefield Publishers, Inc., 2015), 61-73.
31. Cherstin Lyon, Elizabeth M. Nix, and Rebecca K. Shrum, *Introduction to Public History: Interpreting the Past, Engaging Audiences* (Lanham, MD: Rowman & Littlefield Publishers, Inc., 2017), 72-74.
32. Berlanga-Shevchuk, "The Collective Collection," 120-21.
33. For more on this initiative, see Bethea, "Museum Collecting in the Age of Black Lives Matter," 16; and these press releases and online articles: https://www.chicagohistory.org/release/chm-grant-from-boa/; https://chicago.suntimes.com/2020/9/13/21428874/chicago-history-musuem-latino-history-exhibit-students-update; https://www.chicagohistory.org/staff-spotlight-elena-gonzales/.
34. For more on this initiative, see https://www.historycolorado.org/lgbtq-coloradans; https://www.historycolorado.org/press-release/2022/05/23/rainbows-revolutions-explores-history-lgbtq-coloradans-groundbreaking; and https://www.denver7.com/news/local-news/rainbows-and-revolutions-history-colorados-first-lgbtq-exhibit-opens.
35. For more, see "About Collections: Rapid Response Collecting Taskforce," Brooklyn Children's Museum, https://www.brooklynkids.org/collections/; and Kate Mirand Calleri, "Changing How They See: The Brooklyn Children's Museum is decolonizing its collection with the help of local teenagers," *Museum* 101, no. 3 (May/June 2022): 36-41.
36. See, for example, initiatives posted on these websites: https://mohistory.org/collecting-initiatives/; https://indianahistory.org/press-release/project-take-a-stand-expands-indiana-historical-societys-collecting-of-african-american

-history-in-indiana/; https://www.ohiohistory.org/get-involved/donate/call-for-collections/; https://www.historycolorado.org/collecting-colorado; https://kval.com/news/local/springfield-history-museum-collecting-stories-from-asian-community.
37. For more on rapid response collecting, see Elizabeth Pondolfi, "How Rapid-Response Exhibits Are Changing the Way Museums Engage Their Communities," *Next City*, May 15, 2019, accessed August 1, 2023, https://nextcity.org/urbanist-news/how-rapid-response-exhibits-are-changing-the-way-museums-engage-their-commu; Bethea, "Museum Collecting in the Age of Black Lives Matter"; Jason Crabill, Melanie A. Adams, and Kyle McKoy, "Grappling with Unfolding Events," *History News* 71, no. 3 (Summer 2016): 14–18; Sorin, "Rapid Response and Contemporary History," in "Exhibitions," *The Inclusive Historian's Handbook*, posted December 20, 2021, https://inclusivehistorian.com/exhibitions/; and Elizabeth Mariano Mubarek, "The End of Passive Collecting: The Role and Responsibility of Archivists in the COVID-19 Era," *Collections: A Journal for Museum and Archives Professionals* 17, Issue 2, December 21, 2020, https://journals.sagepub.com/doi/full/10.1177/1550190620980839.
38. Crabill, Adams, and McKoy, "Grappling with Unfolding Events," 15–16.
39. "Rapid Response Collecting," Victoria and Albert Museum, accessed August 1, 2023, https://www.vam.ac.uk/collections/rapid-response-collecting; and Sorin, "Rapid Response and Contemporary History," in "Exhibitions," *The Inclusive Historian's Handbook*, posted December 20, 2021, https://inclusivehistorian.com/exhibitions/.
40. Emilie S. Arnold, "The Wound Is Fresh: Exhibiting Orlando's LGBTQ History in the Shadow of the Pulse Nightclub Massacre," *Exhibition* 36, no. 2 (Fall 2017): 26–35.
41. Arnold, "The Wound Is Fresh," 28, 35.
42. For more on this initiative, see https://www.nyhistory.org/history-responds; and Sarah Cascone, "'People Are Unaware of Their History': Why Museums Are Collecting Artifacts from the Black Lives Matter Protests as They're Happening," *Artnet News*, June 9, 2020, accessed August 1, 2023, https://news.artnet.com/art-world/collecting-2020-black-lives-matter-protests-1878480.
43. Cascone, "'People Are Unaware of Their History,'" https://news.artnet.com/art-world/collecting-2020-black-lives-matter-protests-1878480.
44. Crabill, Adams, and McKoy, "Grappling with Unfolding Events," 16–17.
45. For more on the Museum of the City of New York's initiative, see Cascone, "'People Are Unaware of Their History,'" https://news.artnet.com/art-world/collecting-2020-black-lives-matter-protests-1878480. For more on the National Museum of American History's Center for Restorative History, see https://americanhistory.si.edu/restorative-history/projects; https://americanhistory.si.edu/restorative-history/undocumented-organizing-collecting-initiative; and https://americanhistory.si.edu/restorative-history/movement-for-black-lives-collecting-initiative.
46. For basics on all collections fundamentals topics discussed here, see Genoways and Ireland, "Collections Stewardship," chapter 11 in *Museum Administration 2.0*, 283–307; Alexander and Alexander, "To Collect," chapter 8 in *Museums in Motion*, 187–215; *Museum Registration Methods*; Simmons, *Things Great and Small*; Miller, *Museum Collection Ethics*; Yerkovich, "The Ethics of Acquiring and Managing Collections," chapter 4 in *A Practical Guide to Museum Ethics*, 31–47; and Malaro and

DeAngelis, *A Legal Primer on Managing Museum Collections*. For an Indigenous perspective on collections stewardship, see Raney Bench, "Taking Responsibility for Museum History and Legacy: Promoting Changing in Collections Management," chapter 5 in *Interpreting Native American History and Culture at Museums and Historic Sites*. AASLH Interpreting History Series (Lanham, MD: Rowman & Littlefield Publishers, Inc., 2014), 57–64; and "Award Winner Spotlight: First Americans Museum," *History News* 78, no. 3(2023): 34–35.

47. Alexander and Alexander, *Museums in Motion*, 287. In addition to sources listed in note 46, for this topic see also Steven Miller, ed., *Museum Collecting Lessons: Acquisition Stories from the Inside* (London and New York: Routledge, 2022).

48. For more on this issue, see Laura Donnelly Smith, "Dropping Off: The Blessings and Curses of Doorstop Donations," *Museum* 90, no. 3 (May/June 2011): 48–53.

49. These categories for a "proposed acquisition" template come from best practice in acquisition proposal documentation as developed by curatorial and other collections staff members at The Henry Ford, Dearborn, MI.

50. In addition to sources listed in note 46, for this topic see also Patricia L. Miller, "Collections Management: Know What You Have, Know Why You Have It, Know Where You Got It, Know Where It Is," chapter 3 in Catlin-Legutko and Klingler, *Small Museum Toolkit 6*, 63–85.

51. For more on this topic, see Angela Kipp, *Managing Previously Unmanaged Collections: A Practical Guide for Museums* (Lanham, MD: Rowman & Littlefield Publishers, Inc., 2016); John Summers, "Making Sense of Your Community Museum Collection: Strategies for Stuff Management," chapter 1 in Steven Miller, ed., *Museum Collecting Lessons*, 12–21; and Jane Radcliffe and Ron Kley, "Diving Into 'Stuff': Transforming an Accumulation into a Collection," *Proceedings of the 2016 Conference and Annual Meeting*, ed. Debra A. Reid, Vol. XXIX (Ashway, RI: The Association for Living History, Farm and Agricultural Museums, 2017), 97–104.

52. The most recent version of *Nomenclature 4.0*, as published in 2015 by Rowman & Littlefield Publishers, Inc., is accessible online at the Nomenclature website, https://page.nomenclature.info/. See also the AASLH Nomenclature Affinity Community page, https://aaslh.org/nomenclature/; and the article by Ron Kley, "Terms of Endearment: Nomenclature—How Did It Begin; Where Is It Going?" *History News* 68, no. 4 (Autumn 2013): 24–27.

53. For example, registrars' staff members at The Henry Ford use Library of Congress Authorities for many subject terms (see https://www.loc.gov/aba/cataloging/authority/). They also create local terms when necessary (that is, ones not found in the authorities but useful as search terms for the museum's collections). Local terms are generally constructed using authority terms as models. Reference materials also are used to determine local terms. For object and genre terms (that is, terms used to categorize the object, which can range from narrow terms to broader ones, like side chair, chair, or furniture), they use Getty Research Institute's Art and Architecture Thesaurus (AAT), https://www.getty.edu/research/tools/vocabularies/aat/. If not found in AAT, they use *Nomenclature 4.0* for museum cataloging. For geographic names, they use Getty Research Institute's Thesaurus of Geographic Names, https://www.getty.edu/research/tools/vocabularies/tgn/.

54. Vickie Stone, "Question the Database!" in *Active Collections*, 117–19.

55. Genoways and Ireland, *Museum Administration 2.0*, 299.

56. These criteria come from Genoways and Ireland, *Museum Administration 2.0*, 301; Alexander and Alexander, *Museums in Motion*, 205; and Nicola Pickering, *The Museum Curator's Guide: Understanding, Managing and Presenting Objects* (London: Lund Humphries, 2020), 38.
57. In addition to sources listed in note 46, for this topic see also Clark, "Do We Really Want the Bust of Jesus"; and The AASLH Standards and Ethics Committee, "Valuing History Collections." Also refer to official museum Codes of Ethics, including those from AAM, AASLH, and ICOM (see note 5 for links).
58. Jones, "Tier Your Collections," 103-9. Note chart on page 105 (table 8.1). See also Vaughan, "Rethinking the Rembrandt Rule," 33-35; and Ron M. Potvin, "Chasing the White Whale? Flexible Use of Museum Collections," *History News* 69, no. 4 (Autumn 2014): 11-16.
59. Jones, "Tier Your Collections," 104.
60. For more detail, see Mary Fahey and Clara Deck, "Responsibilities, Realities, and Ranking: How a Collections Tiering Policy Aids Conservators in Ethical Decision Making and Judicious Resource Allocation at the Henry Ford Museum and Deerfield (sic) Village," *Objects Specialty Group Postprints* 8 (Washington, DC: The American Institute for Conservation of Historic and Artistic Works, 2001), 97-105. Note charts shown in figures 1 and 2.
61. If using this system, it is a good idea to review object rankings periodically as it is likely that, over time, many items will become more valuable and harder to replace.
62. For a variety of published materials on this topic, in addition to the sources listed in note 46, see Lonetree, *Decolonizing Museums: Representing Native America in National and Tribal Museums* (Chapel Hill: University of North Carolina Press, 2012); Raney Bench, *Interpreting Native American History and Culture at Museums and Historic Sites*, AASLH Interpreting History Series (Lanham, MD: Rowman & Littlefield Publishers, Inc., 2014); Chip Colwell, *Plundered Skulls and Stolen Spirits: Inside the Fight to Reclaim Native America's Culture* (Chicago: The University of Chicago Press, 2017); "Repatriation, Restitution, and Reparations," *Museum* 102, no. 1 (January/February 2023): 31-33; Christine Lashaw, "Taking Native Lands and Lives," Center for the Future of Museums, American Alliance of Museums (blog), May 29, 2019, https://www.aam-us.org/2019/05/29/taking-native-lands-and-lives/; "20 Years and Counting: James Pepper Henry's Multifaceted View of NAGPRA," *Museum* 89, no. 6 (November/December 2010): 50-56; Elena Gonzales, "View from the Field: Equity-Oriented and Anti-Racist Curatorial Practice," *The Inclusive Historian's Handbook*, posted December 23, 2020, https://inclusivehistorian.com/view-from-the-field-equity-oriented-and-anti-racist-curatorial-practice/; Lyon, Nix, and Shrum, *Introduction to Public History*, 68-69; Rick Kriebel and Tom Reitz, "Uncovering Best Practice in Archaeological Collections, Part 2: Archaeology and NAGPRA," *Proceedings of ALHFAM's 2021 Virtual Conference and Annual Meeting*, ed. Donna R. Braden, Vol. XLIV (Rochdale, MA: The Association for Living History, Farm and Agricultural Museums, 2022), 203-7; and Yerkovich, "Restitution, Repatriation or Retention: The Ethics of Cultural Heritage," chapter 9 in *A Practical Guide to Museum Ethics*, 111-42. The National Museum of the American Indian (NMAI) has also published detailed repatriation guidelines in "A Step-by-Step Guide Through the Repatriation Process," available online at https://americanindian.si.edu/sites/1/files/pdf/repatriation/NMAI-Repatriation-Guidelines-2020.pdf.

63. Lonetree, *Decolonizing Museums*, xv.
64. Cultural patrimony means an object that has ongoing importance central to an Indigenous group or culture itself, rather than property owned by an individual.
65. The NAGPRA policy can be found at https://www.ecfr.gov/current/title-43/subtitle-A/part-10#10.4.
66. The basic questions listed here were inspired by the types that can be found in the workbook for the AASLH STEPs program, a subscription-based self-study program assessing standards and excellence for small to midsize history organizations, https://learn.aaslh.org/p/steps-community#:~:text=The%20Standards%20and%20Excellence%20Program%20for%20History%20Organizations,small-%20to%20mid-sized%20history%20organizations%2C%20including%20volunteer-run%20institutions. Additional questions related to inclusive collecting come from the "MASS Action [Museum as Site for Social Action] Toolkit," 183, https://static1.squarespace.com/static/58fa685dff7c50f78be5f2b2/t/59dcdd27e5dd5b5a1b51d9d8/1507646780650/TOOLKIT_10_2017.pdf; and Cecile Shellman, *Effective Diversity, Equity, Accessibility, Inclusion, and Anti-Racism Practices for Museums, from the Inside Out* (Lanham, MD: Rowman & Littlefield Publishers, Inc., 2022), 101.

CHAPTER 4

1. The "Curator Core Competencies" document was published in 2014 by the American Alliance of Museums Curators Committee (CurCom) Standing Committee on Ethics. It can be found at https://www.aam-us.org/wp-content/uploads/2018/05/CURATOR-CORE-COMPETENCIES.pdf.
2. This definition comes from the "Reframing History" project, an evidence-based strategic communications toolkit created under the auspices of the American Association for State and Local History (AASLH) to help history professionals more effectively discuss what history is, how it is interpreted, and why it matters in society. Learn more about this significant project at https://aaslh.org/reframing-history/.
3. For more on what public history is and what public historians do, see the NCPH website, https://ncph.org/, and the excellent book by Cherstin M. Lyon, Elizabeth M. Nix, and Rebecca K. Shrum, *Introduction to Public History: Interpreting the Past, Engaging Audiences* (Lanham, MD: Rowman & Littlefield Publishers, Inc., 2017). Additional insight can be found in Jennifer Lisa Koslow's *Public History: An Introduction from Theory to Application* (Hoboken, NJ: John Wiley & Sons, Inc., 2021), and *Public History: Essays from the Field*, James Gardner and Peter S. LaPaglia, eds. (Malabar, FL: Krieger Publishing Co., 2006).
4. For more, see https://ncph.org/what-is-public-history/about-the-field/.
5. James B. Gardner, "Contested Terrain: History, Museums, and the Public," *The Public Historian* 26, no. 4 (Fall 2004): 11.
6. For more on this topic, see Lyon, Nix, and Shrum, *Introduction to Public History*, 10–11; Zachary M. Schrag, *The Princeton Guide to Historical Research* (Princeton, NJ: Princeton University Press, 2021), 17–18; and "How Is Public History Different from 'Regular' History?" from the NCPH website (https://ncph.org/what-is-public-history/about-the-field/).

7. An insightful essay on this topic is Nicola Pickering's "The Museum Curator's Guide: The Value of Research in Museums," *Lund Humphries* (blog), August 14, 2020, https://www.lundhumphries.com/blogs/features/the-museum-curator-s-guide-the-value-of-research-in-museums-by-nicola-pickering.
8. Quote by Sam Wineburg from his book *Historical Thinking and Other Unnatural Acts*, in John R. Dichtl, "Making History Relevant," *History News* 73, no. 2 (Spring 2018): 26.
9. https://aaslh.org/reframing-history/.
10. Elizabeth Hitz, "The Continuing Effort (Perhaps Futile) to Bridge the Museum and the Academy," *Proceedings of the 1987 Annual Meeting, Ann Arbor and Dearborn, Michigan*, The Association for Living History, Farm and Agricultural Museums, ed. Peter Cousins, Vol. X (Washington, DC: Smithsonian Institution, 1989), 26; and Patricia Mooney-Melvin, "Professional Historians and the Challenge of Redefinition," in *Public History: Essays from the Field*, 15.
11. Pickering, "The Museum Curator's Guide: The Value of Research in Museums."
12. Gardner, "Contested Terrain." See also the ten-step "Primer of Inclusive Practice" (described in chapter 1) from the Wilkening Consulting report, "Audiences and Inclusion: A Primer for Cultivating More Inclusive Attitudes among the Public," https://www.aam-us.org/2021/02/09/audiences-and-inclusion-primer/.
13. Lonnie Bunch III, "'People Need to Remember': American Museums Still Struggle with the Legacy of Race," *Museum* 89, no. 6 (November–December 2010): 48.
14. Gardner, "Contested Terrain," 16-18.
15. Lyon, Nix and Shrum, *Introduction to Public History*, 2. Books aimed at teaching historical methodology to college-level students can also aid curators. These include: Schrag, *The Princeton Guide to Historical Research* and Jenny L. Presnell, *The Information-Literate Historian: A Guide to Research for History Students*, 3rd ed. (New York: Oxford University Press, 2019).
16. Jennifer Ford, "Chinking Between the Logs: Reinterpreting the Miller House at Meadowcroft Museum of Rural Life," in "Part II: Research Design and Methodology for a New Interpretation of the Miller House," of a three-part article written by Daniel J. Freas, Jennifer L. Ford, and David. R. Scofield, *Proceedings of the 1997 Conference and Annual Meeting, Staunton, Virginia*, ed. Debra A. Reid, Vol. XX (North Bloomfield, OH: The Association for Living Historical Farms and Agricultural Museums, 1998), 201.
17. The book *A Midwife's Tale: The Life of Martha Ballard, Based on Her Diary, 1785-1812*, by Laurel Thatcher Ulrich (New York: Alfred A. Knopf, 1990), is often cited as a model for interrogating familiar sources in new ways. Other well-known examples using this methodology include Doris Kearns Goodwin's *Team of Rivals: The Political Genius of Abraham Lincoln* (New York: Simon and Schuster, 2005) and Erica Armstrong Dunbar's *Never Caught: The Washingtons' Relentless Pursuit of their Runaway Slave, Ona Judge* (New York: Atria Books, 2017).
18. Lyon, Nix, and Shrum, *Introduction to Public History*, 23-24; Presnell, *The Information-Literate Historian*, 8-10.
19. Quote by John Cannon, in Schrag, *The Princeton Guide to Historical Research*, 208-9.
20. Lyon, Nix, and Shrum, *Introduction to Public History*, 26.
21. Lyon, Nix, and Shrum, *Introduction to Public History*, 26-27; Presnell, *The Information-Literate Historian*, 98-107.

22. Lyon, Nix, and Shrum, *Introduction to Public History*, 29; Teresa Goforth, "The Truth, The Whole Truth, and Nothing but the Truth: Researching Historical Exhibits," chapter 3 in *Small Museum Toolkit 5: Interpretation: Education, Programs and Exhibits*, Cinnamon Catlin-Legutko and Stacy Klingler, eds. (Lanham, MD: AltaMira Press, a Division of Rowman & Littlefield Publishers, Inc., 2012), 10.
23. This section is revised and expanded from chapter 4 (Your Research Methodology) of Donna Braden's publication *Spaces that Tell Stories: Recreating Historical Environments* (Lanham, MD: Rowman & Littlefield Publishers, Inc., 2019). Much of that chapter drew from David E. Kyvig and Myron A. Marty, *Nearby History: Exploring the Past Around You* (Lanham, MD: AltaMira Press, a Division of Rowman & Littlefield Publishers, Inc., 2010), as well as Barbara J. Howe, Dolores A. Fleming, Emory L. Kemp, and Ruth Ann Overbeck, *Houses and Homes: Exploring Their History*, The Nearby History Series, Vol. 2 (Nashville, TN: American Association for State and Local History, 1987). Additional information included here has been gleaned from Presnell, *The Information-Literate Historian*, and Schrag, *The Princeton Guide to Historical Research*. In addition, many tips and suggestions incorporated into this section come from Ryan Jelso, a talented researcher and former associate curator at The Henry Ford, Dearborn, Michigan (interviews, September 12 and 19 and October 18, 2023). Practical research tips for those working in small museums can be found in Goforth, "The Truth, The Whole Truth, and Nothing but the Truth." Kyvig and Marty's book was updated to a fourth edition in 2019 with author Larry Cebula.
24. Presnell, *The Information-Literate Historian*, 47. Also see Presnell's chapter 7, "History and the Internet," 164-88.
25. Presnell, *The Information-Literate Historian*, "Evaluation of Websites," 182-85.
26. For more on Wikipedia pros and cons, see Presnell, *The Information-Literate Historian*, 32, and Dichtl, "Making History Relevant," 27.
27. Barbara Allen Bogart, "Using Oral History in Museums," *History News* 50, no. 4 (Autumn 1995): Technical Leaflet #191. The many excellent sources describing oral history methodology include: Donald A. Ritchie, *Doing Oral History: A Practical Guide*, 3rd ed. (New York: Oxford University Press, 2015) and Bogart, *Using Oral History*. See also Kyvig and Marty, *Nearby History*, 113-32. For examples of specific case studies, see Maren Lavad and Aleah Vinick, "Creating Intergenerational Oral History Opportunities," *History News* 67, no. 3 (Summer 2012): Technical Leaflet #259; and Lyon, Nix, and Shrum, "Oral History Project for Baltimore '68," *Introduction to Public History*, 38-42.
28. Donald Ritchie's *Doing Oral History: A Practical Guide* is particularly in-depth.
29. See chapter 2, Making Sense of Objects. An insightful discussion of women's artifacts as documentary evidence appears in chapter 8, "Objects: Who Packed This Lunch Bucket?" of Heather Huyck's book, *Doing Women's History in Public: A Handbook for Interpretation at Museums and Historic Sites*, AASLH Interpreting History Series (Lanham, MD: Rowman & Littlefield Publishers, Inc., 2021), 139-68.
30. Excellent resources on this topic include: Kyvig and Marty, *Nearby History*, chapter 9, "Landscapes and Buildings," 177-92; and Cheryl A. Bachard, "Rethinking Architecture in the Realm of House Museum Interpretation," chapter 20, and Lucinda A. Brockway, "Looking Beyond the Front Door to Find Spirit of Place," chapter 21, both from *Reimagining Historic House Museums: New Approaches and Proven Solutions*, Kenneth C. Turino and Max A. van Balgooy, eds. (Lanham, MD: Rowman &

Littlefield Publishers, Inc, 2019), 217-36. For landscapes and buildings as women's spaces, see chapters 6, "Landscapes: Fields and Gardens," and 7, "Architecture: The Built Environment," in Huyck, *Doing Women's History in Public*, 87-138.
31. For more on this, see Madeline C. Flagler, "Interpreting Difficult Issues," chapter 2 in *Small Museum Toolkit 5: Interpretation: Education, Programs and Exhibits*, Cinnamon Catlin-Legutko and Stacy Klingler, eds. (Lanham, MD: Altamira Press, a Division of Rowman & Littlefield Publishers, Inc., 2012), 26-48; "MASS Action [Museum as Site for Social Action] Toolkit," https://static1.squarespace.com/static/58fa685 dff7c50f78be5f2b2/t/59dcdd27e5dd5b5a1b51d9d8/1507646780650/TOOLKIT _10_2017.pdf; Meghan Gelardi Holmes, Steven Lubar, Jessie MacLeod, Willilam Stoutamire, and Carrie Villar, "Telling Inclusive Stories When Your Collections Are Stuck in the Past," *History News* 75, no. 3 (Summer 2020): Technical Leaflet #291; and Christopher C. Martell and Kaylene M. Stevens, *Teaching History for Justice: Centering Activism in Students' Study of the Past* (New York: Teachers College Press, 2021).
32. Hasan Kwame Jeffries, "Getting the History Right," *History News* 76, no. 4 (Autumn 2021): 7.
33. This term is borrowed from the "MASS Action Toolkit," 89.
34. For the following examples, I have depended heavily upon selected essays in *The Inclusive Historian's Handbook*, https://inclusivehistorian.com/about/ (specific essays are cited with specific topics); selected essays and case studies from the excellent "Interpreting History" book series, co-published by Rowman & Littlefield Publishers, Inc. and AASLH (specific books are cited with specific topics); and selected essays in *Reimagining Historic House Museums*, Turino and van Balgooy, eds. For more on the vision behind *The Inclusive Historian's Handbook*, see "The Whole is Greater: Building the Inclusive Historian's Handbook," Modupe Labode, Will Walker, and Robert Weible, eds., *History News* 74, no. 3 (Summer 2019): 4-7.
35. See Kristin L. Gallas and James DeWolf Perry, "Doing Comprehensive and Conscientious Interpretation of Slavery at Historic Sites and Museums," *History News* 66, no. 2 (Spring 2014): Technical Leaflet #266; and "Comprehensive Content and Contested Historical Narratives," chapter 1 in *Interpreting Slavery at Museums and Historic Sites*, Kristin L. Gallas and James DeWolf Perry, eds., AASLH Interpreting History Series (Lanham, MD: Rowman & Littlefield Publishers, Inc., 2015), 1-20.
36. Bunch, "'People Need to Remember': American Museums Still Struggle with the Legacy of Race," 44.
37. Ibid.
38. I compiled this list by assessing specific research sources and methodologies described in the following essays in Gallas and Perry's *Interpreting Slavery* book: Linnea Grim, "So Deeply Dyed in Our Fabric That It Cannot Be Washed Out: Developing Institutional Support for the Interpretation of Slavery," chapter 3, 31-46; Katherine D. Kane, "Institutional Change at Northern Historic Sites: Telling Slavery's Story in the Land of Abolition," chapter 4, 47-60; and Dina A. Bailey and Richard C. Cooper, "The Necessity of Community Involvement: Talking about Slavery in the 21st Century," chapter 5, 61-70. It also draws from Flagler's "Interpreting Difficult Issues"; Julia Rose's "Expanding and Elevating Slave Life Interpretations and Uncovering Commemorative Museum Pedagogy," chapter 5 in *Interpreting Difficult*

History, AASLH Interpreting History Series (Lanham, MD: Rowman & Littlefield Publishers Inc., 2016), 135-68; Martha B. Katz-Hyman's "Furnishing Slave Quarters and Free Black Homes: Adding a Powerful Tool to Interpreting African American Life," chapter 11, in *Interpreting African American History and Culture at Museums and Historic Sites*, Max van Balgooy, ed., AASLH Interpreting History Series (Lanham, MD: Rowman & Littlefield Publishers, Inc., 2015), 105-14; and Ashley Rogers's "Plantations," *The Inclusive Historian's Handbook*, posted May 20, 2019, https://inclusivehistorian.com/?s=Plan. For a case study of how these types of sources were incorporated into a research project, see Lorraine McConaghy and Judy Bentley, "Charles Mitchell Case Study: Researching and Presenting the Marginalized," *Proceedings of the 2022 Conference and Annual Meeting, Tacoma, Washington*, edited by Carol Kennis Lopez. Vol. XLV (Rochdale, MA: The Association for Living History, Farm and Agricultural Museums, 2023), 35-40.

39. For more on working with descendant communities, see The National Summit on Teaching Slavery, "Engaging Descendant Communities in the Interpretation of Slavery at Museums and Historic Sites," *History News* 74, no. 1 (Winter 2019): 14-21; "Engaging Descendant Communities in the Interpretation of Slavery: A Rubric of Best Practices," *History News* 74, no. 1 (Winter 2019): Technical Leaflet #285; and Iris Carter Ford, Patrice Preston-Grimes, and Christian J. Cotz, "Honoring the Ancestors: Descendant Voices in Montpelier," in *Storytelling in Museums*, Adina Langer, ed. (Lanham, MD: Rowman & Littlefield Publishers, Inc., 2022).

40. For this section, I drew particularly from Huyck, *Doing Women's History in Public*; and Mary A. van Balgooy, "Interpreting Women's Lives at Historic House Museums," chapter 16 in *Reimagining Historic House Museums*, 171-82.

41. Huyck, *Doing Women's History in Public*, 39.

42. I compiled this list by assessing specific research sources and methodologies described in case studies included in the following sources: for general women's history, Huyck, *Doing Women's History in Public*, and van Balgooy, "Interpreting Women's Lives at Historic House Museums"; for female domestic workers, Jennifer Pustz, "Listening for the Silences: Stories of Enslaved and Free Domestic Workers," chapter 15 in *Reimagining Historic House Museums*, 161-70, and Kenneth C. Turino, "Historic House Museums," *The Inclusive Historian's Handbook*, posted April 12, 2019, https://inclusivehistorian.com/?s=historic+house+museums; and, for women's suffrage, Page Harrington, *Interpreting the Legacy of Women's Suffrage at Museums and Historic Sites*, AASLH Interpreting History Series (Lanham, MD: Rowman & Littlefield Publishers, Inc., 2021).

43. For strategies and sources for researching the lives of post-Civil War African American women, see the following essays in Max A. van Balgooy, ed., *Interpreting African American History and Culture at Museums and Historic Sites*: William Peterson, "Finding Sarah Bickford," chapter 6, 55-60; Bernard E. Powers Jr., "Churches as Places of History: The Case of 19th Century Charleston, South Carolina," chapter 9, 89-98, and D. L Henderson, "Imagining Slave Square: Resurrecting History Through Cemetery Research and Interpretation," chapter 10, 99-104. See also Harrington, *Interpreting the Legacy of Women's Suffrage*, 71-75.

44. For this section, I drew from Susan Ferentinos, *Interpreting LGBT History at Museums and Historic Sites*, AASLH Interpreting History Series (Lanham, MD: Rowman & Littlefield Publishers, Inc., 2015); Susan Ferentinos, "Where the Magic Happened:

Historic Homes as Sites of Intimacy," chapter 17 in Turino and van Balgooy, eds., *Reimagining Historic House Museums*, 183-95; Turino, "Historic House Museums," *The Inclusive Historian's Handbook*; and Kenneth Turino and Susan Ferentinos, "Entering the Mainstream, Interpreting GLBT History," *History News* 67, no. 4 (Autumn 2012): 21-25.

45. I compiled this list by assessing research methodologies included in case studies in the following sources: Ferentinos, *Interpreting LGBT History*; Ferentinos, "Where the Magic Happened"; and Turino, "Historic House Museums," *The Inclusive Historian's Handbook*.

46. Once again, I would like to acknowledge the input of Ryan Jelso, former associate curator at The Henry Ford, who offered many invaluable tips and suggestions for this section (interviews, September 12 and 19 and October 18, 2023).

47. Excerpted from the title of the article by Pustz, "Listening for the Silences: Stories of Enslaved and Free Domestic Workers," in Turino and van Balgooy, eds., *Reimagining Historic House Museums*, 161.

48. Useful strategies are offered in Wilkening Consulting's "Beware! The False Consensus Effect: An Annual Survey of Museum-Goers Data Story," https://www.wilkeningconsulting.com/uploads/8/6/3/2/86329422/false_consensus_data_story_-_2022_asmg.pdf. For more on this issue, see also Lyon, Nix, and Shrum, *Introduction to Public History*, 27; Turino, "Historic House Museums," *The Inclusive Historian's Handbook*; Ferentinos, *Interpreting LGBT History*, 151-59; Gardner, "Contested Terrain"; and Susie Wilkening, "Difficult Issues in History Museums: Finding Community, Engaging Audiences," Finding Community: Engaging Diverse Audiences in a Historic House (blog), December 9, 2013, https://findingcommunityengagingaudiences.blogspot.com/2013/12/difficult-issues-in-history-museums.html.

49. The complete statement, from the History Relevance Initiative, can be found at https://www.historyrelevance.com/value-history-statement. AASLH's History Relevance Initiative, which ultimately inspired the "Reframing History" project, was undertaken by a volunteer group of history professionals across the United States to help history organizations think intentionally about how to make their history products more relevant to their audiences. See the complete project description at https://aaslh.org/tag/history-relevance/.

50. Sam Wineburg, quoted in Tim Grove, "Truth or Consequences," *History News* 73, no. 2 (Spring 2018): 22.

51. For more on this topic, see Martell and Stevens, *Teaching History for Justice*; Jeffries, "Getting the History Right"; Max A. van Balgooy, "Turning Points: Ordinary People, Extraordinary Change," *History News* 68, no. 2 (Spring 2013): 7-13; Bruce W. Dearstyne, "Putting History to Work: Strategies to Increase the Visibility and Influence of History," *History News* 72, no. 4 (Autumn 2017): 9-14; "The Partisan Divide," *Museum* 102, no. 1 (January/February 2023): 24-29; Darlene Roth, "Seven Reasons the Past Never Dies," *History News* 68, no. 3 (Summer 2013): 14-18; and "Five Qualities of a Relevant History Experience" (from the History Relevance Initiative), https://static1.squarespace.com/static/57f5b3f06a49633bcbec84fe/t/5e57e6103d32fb17bb085eb1/1582818832552/Qualities+of+a+Relevant+History+Experience+2020.pdf.

52. This self-test was inspired by the section entitled, "Historians' Ethics," in Schrag, *The Princeton Guide to Historical Research*, 24-35.

CHAPTER 5

1. In history museums, the terms "exhibit" and "exhibition" are often used interchangeably. I will be using the term "exhibition" throughout this chapter.
2. This included diversifying the museum's stock portfolio, spearheading the creation of its first mission statement, establishing the first development department, expanding the membership program, laying the groundwork for a deaccessioning program, and implementing an annual giving campaign.
3. "Curator Core Competencies" is a document that was published in 2014 by AAM's CurCom Standing Committee on Ethics and accepted by CurCom in 2015. It can be found at https://www.aam-us.org/wp-content/uploads/2018/05/CURATOR-CORE-COMPETENCIES.pdf.
4. Kathleen McLean, "Museum Exhibitions and the Dynamics of Dialogue," 1999, reprinted in *Reinventing the Museum: Historical and Contemporary Perspectives on the Paradigm Shift*, ed. Gail Anderson (Lanham, MD: AltaMira Press, a Division of Rowman & Littlefield Publishers, Inc., 2004), 193.
5. This list comes from a variety of sources used in this chapter, including Eugene Dillenburg and Janice Klein, "Creating Exhibits: From Planning to Building," in *Small Museum Toolkit 5: Interpretation: Educations, Programs, and Exhibits*, ed. Cinnamon Catlin-Legutko and Stacy Klingler (Lanham, MD: AltaMira Press, a Division of Rowman & Littlefield Publishers, Inc., 2012), 71–99; and Nicola Pickering, *The Museum Curator's Guide: Understanding, Managing, and Presenting Objects* (London: Lund Humphries, 2020), 81–84.
6. Published works describing the rationale for involving communities in museum initiatives include: Barbara B. Walden, "Like a Good Neighbor: Community Advocacy for Small Museums," in *Small Museum Toolkit 4: Reaching and Responding to the Audience*, ed. Cinnamon Catlin-Legutko and Stacy Klingler (Lanham, MD: AltaMira Press, a Division of Rowman and Littlefield Publishers, Inc., 2012), 79–97; Candace Tangorra Matelic, "New Roles for Small Museums," in *Small Museum Toolkit 4*, 141–62; and the sources listed in note 30 of chapter 3 related to community-based and rapid response collecting. Published works that specifically reference involving community in creating exhibitions include: Benjamin Filene, "Letting Go? Sharing Historical Authority in a User-Generated World," *History News* 66, no. 4 (Autumn 2011): 7–12; Daniel Spock, "Museum Authority Up for Grabs: The Latest Thing, or Following a Long Trend Line?" *NAME Exhibitionist* 28, no. 2 (Fall 2009): 6–10; and Alison Jean and Swarupa Anila, "Whose Museum Is It Anyway? Toward More Authentic Community-Centered Practices in Creating Exhibitions," *Exhibition* 38, no. 1 (Spring 2019): 43–55. For additional helpful tips on creating community engagement dialogues and workshops, see Nina Simon, *The Participatory Museum* (Santa Cruz: Museum 2.0, 2010); Simon's "Community Issue Exhibition Toolkit" at https://www.ofbyforall.org/community-issue-exhibition-toolkit; Janeen Bryant and Kamille Bostick, "What's the Big Idea?: Using Listening Sessions to Build Relationships and Relevance," *History News* 68, no. 3 (Summer 2013): Technical Leaflet #263; Raney Bench, *Interpreting Native American History and Culture at Museums and Historic Sites*, AASLH Interpreting History Series (Lanham, MD: Rowman & Littlefield Publishers, Inc., 2014); and *A Museum and Community Toolkit* (Washington, DC: American Alliance of Museums, 2002).

7. Cherstin M. Lyon, Elizabeth M. Nix, and Rebecca K. Shrum, *Introduction to Public History: Interpreting the Past, Engaging Audiences* (Lanham, MD: Rowman & Littlefield Publishers, Inc., 2017), 35.
8. Summarized in "MASS Action [Museum as Site for Social Action] Toolkit," https://static1.squarespace.com/static/58fa685dff7c50f78be5f2b2/t/59dcdd2 7e5dd5b5a1b51d9d8/1507646780650/TOOLKIT_10_2017.pdf, 109-10.
9. Kathleen McLean, *Planning for People in Museum Exhibitions* (Washington, DC: Association of Science-Technology Centers, 1993, reprinted 1996), ix.
10. McLean, *Planning for People in Museum Exhibitions*, 4.
11. Andrew K. Pekarik, Zahava D. Doering, and David A. Karns, "Strangers, Guests, or Clients? Visitor Experiences in Museums," *Curator: The Museum Journal* 42, no. 2 (April 1999): 74-87.
12. Mihályi Csikszentmihályi and Kim Hermanson, "Intrinsic Motivation in Museums: What Makes Visitors Want to Learn?" *Museum News* 74, no. 3 (May/June 1995): 35-41.
13. Lois Silverman, "Making Meaning Together," *Journal of Museum Education* 18, no. 3 (Fall 1993): 7-11; and Silverman, "Visitor Meaning-Making in Museums for a New Age," *Curator* 38, no. 3 (1995): 161-70.
14. Jan Packer, "Beyond Learning: Exploring Visitors' Perceptions of Museum Experiences," *Curator* 51, no. 1 (January 2008): 33-54. For the sociocultural context of museum visits, see John H. Falk and Lynn D. Dierking, *The Museum Experience* (Washington, DC: Whalesback Books, 1992) and Falk and Dierking, *Learning from Museums: Visitor Experiences and the Making of Meaning* (Walnut Creek, CA: AltaMira Press, 2000).
15. Judy Rand, "The 227-Mile Museum, or Why We Need a Visitors' Bill of Rights," *Visitor Studies: Theory, Research and Practice* 9 (1996): 8-26. Reprinted in part in *Reinventing the Museum: Historical and Contemporary Perspectives on the Paradigm Shift*, ed. Gail Anderson (Lanham, MD: AltaMira Press, a Division of Rowman & Littlefield Publishers, Inc., 2004), 158-59.
16. Nelson Graburn, "The Museum and the Visitor Experience," reprinted in *Museum Education Anthology 1973-83: Perspectives in Informal Learning a Decade of Roundtable Reports*, ed. Susan K. Nichols, Mary Alexander, and Ken Yellis (Washington, DC: Museum Education Roundtable, 1984), 177-82.
17. See "The Physical Context," chapter 4 in Falk and Dierking, *Learning from Museums*, 53-67.
18. Evaluator Stephen Bitgood describes the importance of these in his "Attention-Value Model." See Stephen Bitgood's *Engaging the Visitor: Designing Exhibits that Work* (Edinburgh, Scotland, and Boston, MA: MuseumsEtc., 2014), 27-48; and "Exhibition Design that Provides High Value and Engages Visitor Attention," *NAME Exhibitionist* 33, no. 1 (Spring 2014): 6-18.
19. Andrew A. Pekarik, Zahava D. Doering, and David A. Karns, "Exploring Satisfying Experiences in Museums," *Curator* 42, no. 2 (April 1999): 152-73.
20. John Summers, *Creating Exhibits That Engage: A Manual for Museums and Historical Organizations* (Lanham, MD: Rowman & Littlefield Publishers, Inc., 2018), 13.
21. These ideas were inspired by: Marion Dune Bauer, *What's Your Story? A Young Person's Guide to Writing Fiction* (New York: Clarion Books, 1992), ix; Best Practice Analysis, "America on the Move" Front-end Study, implemented by Institute for

Learning Innovation, 11-27 (unpublished manuscript, September 2000); and Dale Jones, "Personal Connections and the Great Cosmic Soup," *History News* 63, no. 2 (Spring 2008): 16. For more on the advantages of stories, see Leslie Bedford, "Storytelling: The Real Work of Museums," *Curator* 44, no. 1 (January 2001): 27-34.
22. Daniel Spock, "A Practical Guide to Personal Connectivity," *History News* 63, no. 4 (Autumn 2008): 14.
23. Benjamin Filene, "The Why, What, and How of the Best Storytelling in Museum Exhibitions," in *Storytelling in Museums*, ed. Adina Langer (Lanham, MD: Rowman & Littlefield Publishers, Inc., 2022), 3-12.
24. Filene, "The Why, What, and How of the Best Storytelling in Museum Exhibitions," 5-10.
25. Filene, "The Why, What, and How of the Best Storytelling in Museum Exhibitions," 11.
26. Amy Lonetree, "Museums as Sites of Decolonization: Truth Telling in National and Tribal Museums," in *Contesting Knowledge: Museums and Indigenous Perspectives*, ed. Susan Sleeper-Smith (Lincoln: University of Nebraska Press, 2009), 334.
27. Useful works on teamwork and collaboration in museum exhibitions include: Summers, *Creating Exhibits That Engage*; McLean, *Planning for People in Museum Exhibitions;* Polly McKenna-Cress and Janet A. Kamien, *Creating Exhibitions: Collaboration in the Planning, Development and Design of Innovative Experiences* (Hoboken, NJ: John Wiley and Sons, Inc., 2013); Michael Schrage, "Collaboration and Creativity," *Museum News* 83, no. 2 (March/April 2004): 44-48; "Managing Creativity in the Exhibit Development Process" (entire issue), *NAME Exhibitionist* 18, no. 1 (Spring 1999); and Gary Ford and Greg Stevens, "Working on or Managing Teams," chapter 23 in *A Life in Museums: Managing Your Museum Career*, ed. Greg Stevens and Wendy Luke (Washington, DC: The AAM Press, 2012), 147-53.
28. For dealing with challenges in exhibition teams, in addition to the above sources, see Donna R. Braden, "Your Personal Toolkit: Easing through Friction, Fracas, and Free-for-All," *NAME Exhibitionist* 29, no. 1 (Spring 2010): 6-14.
29. For specific teamwork and collaboration strategies oriented toward DEAI awareness and practice, see Cecile Shellman, *Effective Diversity, Equity, Accessibility, Inclusion, and Anti-Racism Practices in Museums From the Inside Out* (Lanham, MD: Rowman & Littlefield Publishers, Inc., 2022); Porchia Moore, Rose Paquet, and Aletheia Wittman, *Transforming Inclusion in Museums: The Power of Collaborative Inquiry* (Lanham, MD: Rowman & Littlefield Publishers, Inc., 2022); and *The Inclusive Museum Leader*, ed. Cinnamon Catlin-Legutko and Chris Taylor (Lanham, MD: Rowman & Littlefield Publishers, Inc., 2021).
30. For an insightful example of teamwork and collaboration from a business perspective, see Adam Grant's "Mining for Gold: Unearthing Collective Intelligence in Teams," chapter 8 in *Hidden Potential: The Science of Achieving Greater Things* (New York: Viking, 2023), 177-98.
31. This section draws from Donna Braden's book, *Spaces that Tell Stories: Recreating Historical Environments* (Lanham, MD: Rowman & Littlefield Publishers, Inc., 2019), chapter 3, "Framing Your Project," 37-45. Recommended sources describing general exhibition processes include: Dillenburg and Klein, "Creating Exhibits: From Planning to Building"; Summers, *Creating Exhibits That Engage*; McLean, *Planning for People in Museum Exhibitions*; and McKenna-Cress and Kamien, *Creating Exhibitions*.

32. Keep in mind that front-end evaluation is just one of many tools that can help determine an exhibition's approach and direction. The goal is not to exactly follow the findings of a visitor study but to simply become aware of visitor perceptions at this early stage. Helpful published works on front-end evaluation include: *Introduction to Museum Evaluation*, ed. Minda Borun and Randi Korn (Washington, DC: American Association of Museums, 1999); Jill Stein, Marianna Adams, and Jessica Luke, "Thinking Evaluatively: A Practical Guide to Integrating the Visitor Voice," *History News* 62, no. 2 (Spring 2007): Technical Leaflet #238; Lynn D. Dierking, Robert Kiihne, Ann Grimes Rand, and Marilyn Solvay, "Laughing and Learning Together: Family Learning Research Becomes Practice at the U.S.S. Constitution Museum," *History News* 61, no. 3 (Summer 2006): 12-15; and Stacy Klingler and Conny Graft, "In Lieu of Mind Reading: Visitor Studies and Evaluation," in *Small Museum Toolkit* 4, 37-74.
33. See chapter 1, "Behind It All: The Big Idea," in Beverly Serrell's *Exhibit Labels: An Interpretive Approach*, 2nd ed. (Lanham, MD: Rowman & Littlefield Publishers, Inc., 2015), 7-18. (In Serrell and Katherine Whitney's *Exhibit Labels: An Interpretive Approach*, 3rd ed., this chapter appears on pages 9-14).
34. Serrell, *Exhibit Labels*, p. 13 (in 3rd ed., p. 12).
35. This section draws from Donna Braden's workshop "Exhibition Label Makeovers," presented at the Association for Midwest Museums, July 12, 2017. Useful published works on label-writing include: Serrell, *Exhibit Labels*, 2nd ed. (Serrell and Whitney for 3rd ed.); Bitgood, *Engaging the Visitor*; McLean, *Planning for People in Museum Exhibitions*; Chandler G. Screven, "Motivating Visitors to Read Labels," *Text in the Exhibition Medium*, ed. Andrée Blais (Quebec City: La Société des Musées Québécois and Musée de la Civilisation, 1994), 97-132; Dillenburg and Klein, "Creating Exhibits: From Planning to Building"; Summers, *Creating Exhibits That Engage*; Falk and Dierking, *Learning from Museums*; Judy Rand, Ann Grimes, Robert Kiihne, and Sarah Watkins, "Families First! Rethinking Exhibits to Engage All Ages," *History News* 64, no. 1 (Winter 2009): Technical Leaflet #245; Judy Rand, "Write and Design with the Family in Mind," *Connecting Kids to History with Museum Exhibitions*, ed. D. Lynn McRainey and John Russick (Walnut Creek, CA: Left Coast Press, Inc., 2010), 257-84; Judy Rand, "Less Is More. And More Is Less," *Exhibition* 36, no. 1 (Spring 2016): 36-41; and Sarah Bartlett, "The Hemingway Effect," *Exhibition* 36, no. 1 (Spring 2016): 30-34.
36. For references to more on this, see note 18.
37. Summers, *Creating Exhibits That Engage*, 13.
38. Ibid.
39. Serrell, *Exhibit Labels*, 159 (in 3rd edition, page 37).
40. McLean, *Planning for People in Museum Exhibitions*, 109.
41. Serrell, *Exhibit Labels*, 159 (in 3rd edition, pages 37-38).
42. For more on storytelling elements in label-writing, see Larry Borowsky, "Telling a Story in 100 Words: Effective Label Copy," *History News* 62, no. 4 (August 2007): Technical Leaflet #240.
43. Helpful published works on formative evaluation include: *Try It! Improving Exhibits Through Formative Evaluation*, ed. Sam Taylor and Beverly Serrell (Washington, DC: Association of Science-Technology Centers, 1992); Donna R. Braden, "Taste-Testing the Visitor Experience," *Proceedings of the 2013 Conference and Annual Meeting*,

Hale Farm & Village, Akron, Ohio, ed. Debra A. Reid, vol. XXXVI (North Bloomfield, OH: The Association for Living History, Farm and Agricultural Museums, 2014): 197-211; Borun and Korn, *Introduction to Museum Evaluation*; Stein, Adams, and Luke, "Thinking Evaluatively"; Rand, Kiihne, and Watkins, "Families First!"; and McKenna-Cress and Kamien, *Creating Exhibitions*, 124, 244-50.

44. "Mining the Museum" was a collaborative exhibition in Baltimore between The Contemporary (a "nomadic," non-collecting art museum) and the Maryland Historical Society from 1992 to 1993. It came about because the historical society staff was looking for opportunities to identify new approaches to interpreting its collections, shape future acquisitions policies and programs, and expand its audience. The museum engaged artist Fred Wilson to choose objects from its collections that spoke to him and then pair or juxtapose them. Wilson's ultimate choices confronted and challenged perceptions about history, culture, and race, as the significance of each object was heightened by its comparative relationship with other objects. For example, in a case titled, "Metalwork, 1793-1880," Wilson startlingly juxtaposed slave shackles with fine silver table service vessels. For an interview with Wilson, see *"Mining the Museum* Revisited: A Conversation with Fred Wilson, Paula Marincola, and Marjorie Schwarzer," in *Letting Go? Sharing Historical Authority in a User-Generated World*, ed. Bill Adair, Benjamin Filene, and Lara Koloski (Philadelphia: The Pew Center for Arts and Heritage, 2011), 230-41.

45. Quote from Deborah F. Schwartz, "Are We Serious about Changing the Equation?" chapter 34 in *Change Is Required: Preparing for the Post-Pandemic Museum*, ed. Avi Y. Decter, Marsha Semmel, and Ken Yellis (Lanham, MD: Rowman & Littlefield Publishers, Inc., 2022), 223.

46. Elena Gonzales's published works include: *Exhibitions for Social Justice* (London and New York: Routledge, 2020); "Social Justice: Framework for the Future of Museums," chapter 33 in *Change Is Required*, 217-21; "View from the Field: Equity-Oriented and Anti-Racist Curatorial Practice," *The Inclusive Historian's Handbook*, posted December 23, 2020, https://inclusivehistorian.com/view-from-the-field-equity-oriented-and-anti-racist-curatorial-practice/; "Emotionally Captivating Anti-Racist History," *Exhibition* 39, no. 1 (Spring 2020): 14-15; and an interview related to Gonzales's *Exhibitions for Social Justice* book, The Incluseum (blog), September 5, 2019, https://incluseum.com/2019/09/05/exhibitions-for-social-justice/comment-page-1/.

47. "Exhibitions for Social Justice," Incluseum (blog).

48. Gonzales, *Exhibitions for Social Justice*, 1.

49. Gonzales, "Social Justice: Framework for the Future," 220-21.

50. Elif M. Gokcigdem, "Designing for Empathy," *Dimensions* 20, no. 5 (November/December 2018): 26. For more on the topic of empathy in exhibitions, see *Fostering Empathy through Museums*, ed. Elif M. Gokcigdem (Lanham, MD: Rowman & Littlefield Publishers, Inc., 2016); and Victoria Edwards, "Empathy Check (and Why It's Not a Cliché)," *Museum* 100, no. 4 (July/August 2021): 14-19.

51. Dina Bailey, "Finding Inspiration Inside: Engaging Empathy to Empower Everyone," chapter 8 in Gokcigdem, *Fostering Empathy through Museums*, 131. The National Center for Civil and Human Rights in Atlanta, Georgia, which Bailey references as a model, was specifically founded upon the notion of fostering empathy.

52. For sample statements, see the Foundational Truths Document described in "Interpretive Planning at Ford's Theatre," Ford's Theatre (blog), June 24, 2019, https://fords.org/interpretive-planning-at-fords-theatre/; the statement of Non-Negotiables in the "Edsel and Eleanor Ford House Interpretive Plan," 2021, accessed December 11, 2023, https://www.thc.texas.gov/public/upload/preserve/museums/files/Ford%20House%20Resources.pdf; and the document "History Colorado Anti-Racism Work: Grounding Virtues," accessed December 11, 2023, https://www.historycolorado.org/sites/default/files/media/document/2020/Anti-Racism_Grounding_Virtues.pdf.
53. For more on this, see Joanne Jones-Rizzi and Stacey Mann, "Is That Hung White? A Conversation on the State of Museum Exhibitions and Race," *Museum* 99, no. 3 (Summer 2020): 26-31.
54. Rose Kinsley, Margaret Middleton, and Porchia Moore, "(Re)Frame: The Case for New Language in the 21st-Century Museum," *Exhibition* 36, no. 1 (Spring 2016): 63.
55. Cecilia Garibay, "The (Unfulfilled) Promise of Evaluation," chapter 29 in *Change Is Required*, 191-95.
56. See a lengthier description of this project in Donna Braden's book *Spaces That Tell Stories*, chapter 7, pages 138-41. Also see the description of the Heart Mountain Interpretive Center on the Heart Mountain WWII Japanese American Confinement Site website, accessed December 11, 2023, https://www.heartmountain.org/about/interpretive-center/; and Sarah Bartlett, "Can Museums Take a Stand?" *NAME Exhibitionist* 30, no. 2 (Fall 2011): 46-51.
57. Elena Guarinello, "Changing the Narrative," *Museum* 102, no. 2 (March-April 2023): 24-29.
58. Guarinello, "Changing the Narrative," 26.
59. Mark Auslander and Amanda Thomashow, "Sites of Healing," *Museum* 98, no. 6 (November-December 2019): 35-39.
60. Auslander and Thomashow, "Sites of Healing," 37.
61. "Prisons Today: Questions in the Age of Mass Incarceration," *Exhibition* 36, no. 2 (Fall 2017): 92-98.
62. See a lengthier description of this project in Donna Braden's book *Spaces That Tell Stories*, chapter 7, pages 141-47. Additional background information was drawn from "The Power of Children: Making a Difference" on The Children's Museum of Indianapolis website, accessed December 11, 2023, https://www.childrensmuseum.org/exhibits/power-of-children.
63. Beth Maloney, Kate Egner Gruber, Rahul Gupta, and Evelyn Orantes, "The Whole Is Greater: Democratizing Curation with TENACITY," *History News* 75, no. 4 (Autumn 2020): 6-7.
64. Dr. Gaila Sims and Theresa Cramer, "A Monumental Responsibility: Exhibiting and Interpreting the Auction Block in Fredericksburg, Virginia," *Exhibition* 42, no. 2 (Fall 2023): 56-65.
65. Margaret Middleton, "Queer Museum Narratives and the Family Audience," chapter 13 in *Storytelling in Museums*, 163-75.
66. Donna M. Mah, "Threads in the Fabric of Legacy: The Stories in the Exhibit, 'Chinese Medicine in America: Converging Ideas, People, and Practices,'" chapter 15 in *Storytelling in Museums*, 191-203.

67. Barbara O'Neil, "History Colorado Center Unveils Sand Creek Massacre Exhibit," *5280.com, Denver's Mile High Magazine*, November 21, 2022, accessed December 11, 2023, https://www.5280.com/history-colorado-center-unveils-sand-creek-massacre-exhibit/; and Megan McCrea, "A Museum Takes a New, Unvarnished Look at a Massacre," *New York Times*, October 18, 2023, accessed December 11, 2023, https://www.nytimes.com/2023/10/18/arts/design/colorado-sand-creek-massacre.html.
68. Quote by Gail Ridgely, director of the Northern Arapaho Sand Creek Resource Office on the Wind River Reservation in Wyoming and a descendant of survivors of the massacre, in McCrea, "A Museum Takes a New, Unvarnished Look."
69. Bryant and Bostick, "What's the Big Idea?"; Kate Baillon, Janeen Bryant, and Kamille Bostick, "Failing Forward: iNUEVOlution! Latinos and the New South," *History News* 73, no. 3 (Summer 2018): 14–18; and Elizabeth Merritt, "The Making of iNUEVOlution!: Collaboration, Ambiguity and a Willingness to Fail," American Alliance of Museums, Center for the Future of Museums (blog), May 18, 2017, https://www.aam-us.org/2017/05/18/the-making-of-nuevolution-collaboration-ambiguity-and-a-willingness-to-fail/.
70. AASLH, "Award Winner Spotlight: First Americans Museum," *History News* 78, no. 3 (2023): 34–35.
71. AASLH, "Award Winner Spotlight: First Americans Museum," 35.
72. Csikszentmihályi and Hermanson, "Intrinsic Motivation in Museums," 35–41; John Falk and Lynne Dierking, *The Visitor Experience* (Washington, DC: Whalesback Books, 1992).

CHAPTER 6

1. For more detail, see Donna R. Braden, "The Process and the Product: Transforming the General Store in Greenfield Village," *History News* 50, no. 3 (Summer 1995): 20–24; and Braden, "Shopping at an 1880s General Store," thehenryford.org (blog), October 30, 2019, https://www.thehenryford.org/explore/blog/shopping-at-an-1880s-general-store.
2. See Braden, "Searching for Dr. Howard," thehenryford.org (blog), January 27, 2022, https://www.thehenryford.org/explore/blog/searching-for-dr.-howard; and Braden, "Dr. Howard's Medicine Cabinet," thehenryford.org (blog), January 24, 2022, https://www.thehenryford.org/explore/blog/dr.-howard-s-medicine-cabinet.
3. Sam H. Ham, *Interpretation: Making a Difference on Purpose* (Golden, CO: Fulcrum Publishing, 2013), 8.
4. Since its founding in 1970, The Association for Living History, Farm and Agricultural Museums has been particularly active in defining and advancing the role of interpretation in outdoor and living history museums. See this organization's website at https://alhfam.org/. Published *Proceedings* of its annual meetings are invaluable resources, accessible to members on ALHFAM's website.
5. See, for example, Ham's *Interpretation: Making a Difference on Purpose*; Lisa Brochu and Tim Merriman, *Personal Interpretation: Connecting Your Audience to Heritage Resources*, 3rd ed. (Fort Collins, CO: The National Association for Interpretation, 2015); Michael P. Gross and Ron Zimmerman, "Park and Museum Interpretation:

Helping Visitors Find Meaning," *Curator: The Museum Journal* 45, no. 4 (October 2002): 265-76; and William J. Lewis, *Interpreting for Park Visitors* (Fort Washington, PA: Eastern National Park and Monument Association, 1981).

6. Quote from Graham Black, *The Engaging Museum: Developing Museums for Visitor Involvement* (London and New York: Routledge, 2005), 180.
7. Freeman Tilden, *Interpreting Our Heritage*, 4th ed. expanded and updated (Chapel Hill: The University of North Carolina Press, 1967).
8. For more on this, see introduction, *Reimagining Historic House Museums: New Approaches and Proven Solutions*, ed. Kenneth C. Turino and Max A. van Balgooy (Lanham, MD: Rowman & Littlefield Publishers, Inc., 2019), 1-4; Donna Ann Harris, "New Solutions for House Museums," *History News* 62, no. 4 (Autumn 2007): 12-16; Black, *The Engaging Museum*, 179-83; and Cherstin M. Lyon, Elizabeth M. Nix, and Rebecca K. Shrum, *Introduction to Public History: Interpreting the Past, Engaging Audiences* (Lanham, MD: Rowman & Littlefield Publishers, Inc., 2017), 118.
9. See Jay D. Vogt, "The Kykuit II Summit: The Sustainability of Historic Sites," *History News* 62, no. 4 (Autumn 2007): 17-21.
10. Donna Ann Harris, *New Solutions for House Museums: Ensuring the Long-Term Preservation of America's Historic Houses* (Lanham, MD: Rowman & Littlefield Publishers, Inc., 2007). The latest edition was published in 2020. See also Harris, "New Solutions for House Museums," *History News* 62, no. 4 (Autumn 2007): 12-16.
11. AASLH Historic House Affinity Group Committee (now the Historic House Museums Affinity Community), "How Sustainable Is Your Historic House Museum?" *History News* 63, no. 4 (Autumn 2008): Technical Leaflet #224.
12. Franklin D. Vagnone and Deborah E. Ryan, *Anarchist's Guide to Historic House Museums: A Ground-Breaking Manifesto* (London and New York: Routledge, 2015).
13. See Turino and Balgooy, *Reimagining Historic House Museums*, 1-18.
14. Quote from AASLH Historic House Museum Affinity Community, "How Sustainable Is Your Historic House Museum?" *History News* 78, no. 2 (2023): Technical Leaflet #302, 2.
15. "How Sustainable is Your Historic House Museum?" (as cited above).
16. For a good description of this issue, see Annie Anderson, Ashley Rogers, Emily Potter, Elon Cook, Karleen Gardner, Mike Murawski, Swarupa Anila, and Alyssa Machida, "Interpretation: Liberating the Narrative," chapter 5 in "MASS Action [Museum as Site for Social Action] Toolkit," https://static1.squarespace.com/static/58fa685dff7c50f78be5f2b2/t/59dcdd27e5dd5b5a1b51d9d8/1507646780650/TOOLKIT_10_2017.pdf, 89-102, 181-82.
17. In addition to *Reimagining Historic House Museums*, books and articles that address this issue include: Julia Rose, *Interpreting Difficult History at Museums and Historic Sites*, AASLH Interpreting History Series (Lanham, MD: Rowman & Littlefield Publishers, Inc., 2016); Heather Huyck, *Doing Women's History in Public: A Handbook for Interpretation at Museums and Historic Sites*, AASLH Interpreting History Series (Lanham, MD: Rowman & Littlefield Publishers, Inc., 2021); Susan Ferentinos, *Interpreting LGBT History at Museums and Historic Sites*, AASLH Interpreting History Series (Lanham, MD: Rowman & Littlefield Publishers, Inc., 2015); Madeline Flagler, "Interpreting Difficult Issues," chapter 2 in *Small Museum Toolkit 5: Interpretation: Education, Programs, and Exhibits*, ed. Cinnamon Catlin-Legutko and Stacy Klingler

(Lanham, MD: AltaMira Press, a Division of Rowman & Littlefield Publishers, Inc., 2012), 26-48; and Mary Rizzo, "Good Intentions Are Not Enough: Lessons for Inclusive Public History," *History News* 72, no. 2 (Spring 2017): 12-16. See also Peter A. Friesen's in-depth case study of reinterpretation at Historic St. Mary's City, "Unvarnished History: Creating Engaging Programs and Exhibits without the Whitewash," *Proceedings of the 2022 Conference and Annual Meeting, Tacoma, Washington*, ed. Carol Kennis Lopez, vol. XLV (Rochdale, MA: The Association for Living History, Farms and Agricultural Museums, 2023), 84-91.

18. Useful sources on this topic include: Rose, *Interpreting Difficult History at Museums and Historic Sites*; Kristin L. Gallas and James DeWolf Perry, "Developing Comprehensive and Conscientious Interpretation of Slavery at Historic Sites and Museums," *History News* 69, no. 2 (Spring 2014): Technical Leaflet #226; Gallas and Perry, ed., *Interpreting Slavery at Museums and Historic Sites*, AASLH Interpreting History Series (Lanham, MD: Rowman & Littlefield Publishers, Inc., 2015); Ashley Rogers, "Plantations," *The Inclusive Historian's Handbook*, posted May 20, 2019, https://inclusivehistorian.com/?s=Plan/; and Kristin L. Gallas, *Interpreting Slavery with Children and Teens at Museums and Historic Sites*, AASLH Interpreting History Series (Lanham, MD: Rowman & Littlefield Publishers, Inc., 2021). See also the richly detailed description of a visit to Whitney Plantation, in Clint Smith's *How the Word Is Passed: A Reckoning with the History of Slavery across America* (New York: Little, Brown and Company, 2021), 52-84.
19. Quote from Rogers, "Plantations."
20. For more on this topic, see Rose, *Interpreting Difficult History*; Kristin L. Gallas and James DeWolf Perry, "Comprehensive Content and Contested Historical Narratives," and Linnea Grim, "So Deeply Dyed in Our Fabric That It Cannot Be Washed Out: Developing Institutional Support for the Interpretation of Slavery," chapters 1 and 3 in *Interpreting Slavery at Museums and Historic Sites*, 1-20 and 31-46; Rose, "Interpreting Difficult Knowledge," *History News* 66, no. 3 (Summer 2011): Technical Leaflet #255; David W. Young, "Expanding Interpretation at Historic Sites: When Change Brings Conflict," chapter 4 in *Interpreting African American History and Culture at Museums and Historic Sites*, 37-44; and Susie Wilkening, "Difficult Issues in History Museums," Finding Community Engaging Audiences website (blog), December 9, 2013, https://findingcommunityengagingaudiences.blogspot.com/2013/12/difficult-issues-in-history-museums.html.
21. Lyon, Nix, and Shrum, *Introduction to Public History*, 119.
22. Catherine M. Cameron and John B. Gatewood, "Excursions into the Unremembered Past: What People Want from Visits to Historic Sites," *The Public Historian* 22, no. 3 (Summer 2000): 107-27. See also Ron Potvin, "Finding Numen at Historic Sites," chapter 12 in *Reimagining Historic House Museums*, 125-33.
23. From a broad-based study of more than five thousand museum visitors undertaken in 2008 by the research and predictive analytics firm Reach Advisors. Referenced in Susie Wilkening and Erica Donnis, "Authenticity? It Means Everything," *History News* 63, no. 4 (Autumn 2008): 18. On the topic of authenticity and visitors, see also Lyon, Nix, and Shrum, *Introduction to Public History*, 119-20.
24. Roy Rosenzweig and David Thelen, *The Presence of the Past: Popular Uses of History in American Life* (New York: Columbia University Press, 1998), 106-7.

25. This list was partially inspired by the chart (pp. 20-21) in Thompson Mayer's "Why Old Places Matter," *History News* 71, no. 3 (Summer 2016): 19-23. See also Braden, chapter 1, section on "Benefits of Historical Environments" in *Spaces that Tell Stories: Recreating Historical Environments* (Lanham, MD: Rowman & Littlefield Publishers, Inc., 2019), 9-13; and Braden, "The Power of Historical Environments," *History News* 74, no. 2 (Spring 2019): 24-28.
26. See also Braden, chapter 1, section on "Cautions in Creating Historical Environments," in *Spaces that Tell Stories*, 13-16.
27. See note 23. For strategies to address this, see Lyon, Nix, and Shrum, section on "Engaging Audiences through Difficult Encounters," *Introduction to Public History*, 123-27.
28. For more detail on the topics in this section as well as related references, see Braden, chapter 3, "Framing Your Project," in *Spaces that Tell Stories*, 37-56. See also Stephen Hague, "How to Plan and Implement Interpretation," *History News* 68, no. 2 (Spring 2013): Technical Leaflet #262; Elizabeth Nosek, *Interpretative Master Planning: A Framework for Historical Sites* (Lanham, MD: Rowman & Littlefield Publishers, Inc., 2021); and Lisa Brochu, *Interpretive Planning: The 5-M Model for Successful Planning Projects*, 2nd ed. (Fort Collins, CO: The National Association for Interpretation, 2014).
29. For sources related to this topic, see note 6 in chapter 5 (Curating Exhibitions, Large and Small). See also Dawn DiPrince, "Radical Renewal for Historic House Museums," chapter 13 in *Reimagining Historic House Museums*, 135-45; Heather Huyck, *Doing Women's History in Public*; Madeline Flagler, "Interpreting Difficult Issues"; and Dina A. Bailey and Richard C. Cooper, "The Necessity of Community Involvement: Talking about Slavery in the Twenty-First Century," chapter 5 in *Interpreting Slavery*, 61-70. For more on working with descendant communities, see The National Summit on Teaching Slavery, "Engaging Descendant Communities in the Interpretation of Slavery at Museums and Historic Sites," *History News* 74, no. 1 (Winter 2019): 14-21; and The National Summit on Teaching Slavery, "Engaging Descendant Communities in the Interpretation of Slavery: A Rubric of Best Practices," *History News* 74, no. 1 (Winter 2019): Technical Leaflet #285.
30. Quote from Hague, "How to Plan and Implement Interpretation," 4.
31. More detail on "thematic interpretation," with additional sources, can be found in Donna R. Braden, "Not Just a Bunch of Facts: Crafting Dynamic Interpretive Manuals," *History News* 69, no. 3 (Summer 2014): Technical Leaflet #267.
32. Timothy Glines and David Grabitske, "Telling the Story: Better Interpretation at Small Historical Organizations," *History News* 58, no. 2 (Spring 2003): Technical Leaflet #222, 2.
33. Helpful published works on evaluation include: *Introduction to Museum Evaluation*, ed. Minda Borun and Randi Korn (Washington, DC: American Association of Museums, 1999); and Jill Stein, Marianna Adams, and Jessica Luke, "Thinking Evaluatively: A Practical Guide to Integrating the Visitor Voice," *History News* 62, no. 2 (Spring 2007): Technical Leaflet #238.
34. Conny C. Graft, "Visitors Are Ready, Are We?" chapter 6 in *Interpreting Slavery at Museums and Historic Sites*, 71-83; and Conny C. Graft, "Evaluation Is Not Just Nice, It Is Necessary," chapter 3 in *Reimagining Historic House Museums*, 29-41.

35. For more detail on furnishings plans (and related references), see Donna R. Braden, "Bringing Your Environment to Life," chapter 5 in *Spaces that Tell Stories*, 87-112. See also the excellent work by Martha Katz-Hyman on furnishing Black spaces, including "Furnishing for Diversity," *Proceedings of the 2022 Conference and Annual Meeting*, The Association for Living History, Farm and Agricultural Museums, 76-82; and "Furnishing Slave Quarters and Free Black Homes: Adding a Powerful Tool to Interpreting African American Life," chapter 11 in *Interpreting African American History and Culture at Museums and Historic Sites*, 105-14.
36. Some historic house museums have determined that they can achieve their strategic goals better by specifically not incorporating furnishings in their spaces. Two benchmark examples include: Harriet Beecher Stowe Center in Hartford, Connecticut, and President Lincoln's Cottage in Washington, DC—both of which serve as gathering places for discourse around civic engagement and social justice that link to the ideals and work of the historic individuals. For more on these, see Katherine Kane, "Using Historic House Museum Audiences to Drive Change," chapter 10, and Callie Hawkins and Erin Carlson Mast, "Do Something Transformative," chapter 14, both in *Reimagining Historic House Museums*, 109-14 and 149-60; and Kenneth C. Turino and Nina Zannieri, "Historic House Museums," *The Inclusive Historian's Handbook*, posted April 12, 2019, https://inclusivehistorian.com/historic-house-museums/.
37. Laura C. Keim, "Why Do Furnishings Matter? The Power of Furnishings in Historic House Museums," chapter 19 in *Reimagining Historic House Museums*, 207-16. See also the extensive citations at the end of that essay.
38. Braden, *Spaces that Tell Stories*, 104.
39. Turino and Zannieri, "Historic House Museums."
40. Many strategies for this are described in Meghan Gelardi Holmes, Steven Lubar, Jessie MacLeod, William Stoutamire, Carrie Villar, "Telling Inclusive Stories When Your Collections Are Stuck in the Past," *History News* 75, no. 3 (Summer 2020): Technical Leaflet #291.
41. William Seale, *Recreating the Historic House Interior* (Nashville, TN: American Association for State and Local History, 1979), 16.
42. Nancy E. Villa Bryk, "'I Wish You Could Take a Peek at Us in the Present Moment': Infusing the Historic House with Characters and Activity," chapter 7 in *Interpreting Historic House Museums*, ed. Jessica Foy Donnelly (Walnut Creek, CA: AltaMira Press, a Division of Rowman & Littlefield Publishers, Inc., 2002), 163.
43. For three real-life examples of Furnishing Rationale (McGuffey Birthplace, J. R. Jones General Store, and the 1973 Commune in the "Your Place in Time" exhibition), see Braden, "Bringing Your Environment to Life," chapter 5 in *Spaces that Tell Stories*, 101-4.
44. Bethany Watkins Sugawara, "But They're Not Real! Rethinking the Use of Props in Historic House Museum Displays," *History News* 58, no. 4 (August 2003), 20.
45. Some museums assign props and reproductions to a separate Study, Education, or Hands-on Collection. These items are specifically designated for use and considered expendable within the context of educational programs in the museum. Other museums track them within their regular collections management system, which helps manage inventories and ensures that there is a record of where they were purchased or made.

46. For more on space layout and installation, see Braden, chapter 6 in *Spaces that Tell Stories*, 116-19.
47. For more detail on operational issues to consider, see: Bradley Brooks, "The Historic House Furnishings Plan: Process and Product," in *Interpreting Historic House Museums*, ed. Jessica Foy Donnelly (Walnut Creek, CA: AltaMira, a Division of Rowman and Littlefield, 2002), 139-41; and Mick Woodcock, "Physical Control for Collections: Keeping It on the Table after Bringing It All to the Table," *Proceedings of the 2013 Conference and Annual Meeting, Hale Farm & Village, Akron, Ohio*, ed. Debra A. Reid, vol. XXXVI (North Bloomfield, OH: The Association for Living History, Farm and Agricultural Museums, 2014): 105-7.
48. For more detail on this, see the very helpful book *The Art of Access: A Practical Guide for Museum Accessibility*, by Heather Pressman and Danielle Schulz (Lanham, MD: Rowman & Littlefield Publishers, Inc., 2021).
49. For more on interpretive techniques, see Braden, chapter 5, section on "Your Interpretive Strategy," in *Spaces that Tell Stories*, 95-100.
50. For general information on developing and implementing tours, see: Barbara Abramoff Levy, Sandra McKenzie Lloyd, and Susan Porter Schreiber, *Great Tours! Thematic Tours and Guide Training for Historic Sites* (Walnut Creek, CA: AltaMira Press, a Division of Rowman & Littlefield Publishers, Inc., 2001); Barbara Abramoff Levy, "Historic House Tours That Succeed: Choosing the Best Tour Approach," chapter 9 in *Interpreting Historic House Museums*, 192-209; Sandra Mackenzie Lloyd, "Creating Memorable Visits: How to Develop and Implement Theme-Based Tours," chapter 10 in *Interpreting Historic House Museums*, 210-30; and Margaret Piatt, "Engaging Visitors Through Effective Communication," chapter 11 in *Interpreting Historic House Museums*, 231-50. For a more recent take on developing and delivering tours, see Sharon Vatsky's *Interactive Museum Tours: A Guide to In-Person and Virtual Experiences* (Lanham, MD: Rowman & Littlefield, 2023), though this book is heavily weighted toward art museums. For tours related to interpreting women's history, see Huyck, *Doing Women's History in Public*. For the guidelines and special training needed for tours related to interpreting slavery and other difficult issues, see sources listed in note 58.
51. Aja Bain, "Peopling the Past: Living History and Inclusive Museum Practice," *The Museum Scholar: Theory and Practice*, Vol. 2, 2019, https://articles.themuseumscholar.org/2019/05/16/tp_vol2bain/. See also Debra A. Reid, "Making Gender Matter: Interpreting Male and Female Roles in Historic House Museums," chapter 4 in *Interpreting Historic House Museums*, 81-110.
52. See more at The International Coalition of Sites of Conscience website, https://www.sitesofconscience.org/.
53. See, for example, Robert Kiihne, "Creating Minds-on Exhibitions in Historic House Museums," chapter 24 in *Reimagining Historic House Museums*, 207-16.
54. Though primarily focused on natural history, the book *Interpretive Writing*, by Alan Leftridge (Fort Collins, CO: The National Association for Interpretation, 2006) contains many good suggestions and examples.
55. Helpful sources that describe theatrical performance as an interpretive technique include: Dale Jones, "Theater 101 for Historical Interpretation," *History News* 59, no. 3 (Summer 2004): Technical Leaflet #227; Dale Jones, "Living History in the City," *History News* 50, no. 3 (Summer 1995): 10-13; Catherine Hughes, *Museum Theatre*:

Communicating With Visitors Through Drama (Portsmouth, NH: Heinemann, a Division of Reed Elsevier, 1998); and Tessa Bridal, *Exploring Museum Theatre* (Walnut Creek: AltaMira Press, 2004). A useful case study is provided in Kandie Carle's article, "How Dare You? Telling a Cultural Story That Is Not Your Own," *Proceedings of ALHFAM's 2021 Virtual Conference and Annual Meeting*, ed. Donna R. Braden, Vol. XLIV (Rochdale, MA: The Association for Living History, Farm and Agricultural Museums, 2022), 116-24.

56. While historic house museums obviously vary widely, basic process information for developing programs is succinctly described in Jamie Credle, "Endless Possibilities: Historic House Museum Programs That Make Educators Sing," chapter 13 in *Interpreting Historic House Museums*, 269-92.

57. For basics on specific audiences and potential interpretive opportunities, see Caroline Braden, "Accessibility Evolving at The Henry Ford," chapter 8 in *An Accessible Past: Making Historic Sites Accessible*, ed. Heather Pressman (Lanham, MD: Rowman & Littlefield Publishers, Inc., 2024), 83-96.

58. For general information on developing interpretive training sessions and components, see Levy, Lloyd, and Schreiber, *Great Tours!*; the numerous insightful essays in *Interpreting Historic House Museums*; Hague, "How to Plan and Implement Interpretation"; Stacy F. Roth, *Past into Present: Effective Techniques for First-Person Historical Interpretation* (Chapel Hill: The University of North Carolina Press, 1998); and Gross and Zimmerman, "Park and Museum Interpretation." For training interpreters for tours related to difficult history and interpreting slavery, see Rex Ellis, "Interpreting the Whole House," chapter 3 in *Interpreting Historic House Museums*, 61-80; Flagler, "Interpreting Difficult Issues"; Gallas and Perry, "Developing Comprehensive and Conscientious Interpretation of Slavery at Historic Sites and Museums"; Gallas, *Interpreting Slavery with Children and Teens*; and Patricia Brooks, "Developing Competent and Confident Interpreters" and Nicole Moore, "Perceptions of Race and Identity and Their Impact on Slavery's Interpretation," chapters 7 and 8 in *Interpreting Slavery at Museums and Historic Sites*, 85-99, 101-17.

59. Braden, "Not Just a Bunch of Facts."

60. For more on these topics, see Braden, chapter 6 in *Spaces that Tell Stories*, 121-27.

61. Notes from the session "It Takes a Village: Making the Erma Hayman House," AASLH 2023 Annual Conference, Boise, Idaho, September 9, 2023; and Erma Hayman House website, https://www.ermahaymanhouse.org/.

62. Jennifer Pustz, "Listening for the Silences: Stories of Enslaved and Free Domestic Workers," chapter 15 in *Reimagining Historic House Museums*, 161-70.

63. Jane Mitchell Eliasof, "The Many Voices of History," *History News* 72, no. 1 (Winter 2017): 14-18; and Jane Mitchell Eliasof and Claudia Ocello, "Reflecting Race and Ethnicity in House Museums," chapter 18 in *Reimagining Historic House Museums*, 197-206.

64. Heather Gilreath, "Transforming Spaces and Shifting Paradigms: A New Interpretation for the Exchange Place Cook's Cabin," *Proceedings of the 2022 Conference and Annual Meeting*, The Association for Living History, Farm and Agricultural Museums, 46-62.

65. Joanne Hahn, "Finding Her Voice: The Evolution of Interpreting Catharine Coffin's Story," *History News* 78, no. 1 (2023): 20-25.

66. For more on The Tenement Museum, see Adam P. Nilsen and Miriam Bader, "The Psychology of Empathy: Compelling Possibilities for Museums," chapter 7 in *Fostering Empathy Through Museums*, ed. Elif M. Gokigdem (Lanham, MD: Rowman & Littlefield Publishers, Inc., 2016), 115–29; Miriam Bader, "Historic Sites and Universal Design: Lessons from The Tenement Museum," NAME *Exhibitionist* 34, no. 2 (Fall 2015): 28–33; and Kathryn Lloyd, "From Neighborhood to Nation: The *Under One Roof* Exhibition at The Tenement Museum," *Exhibition* 38, no. 2 (Fall 2019): 71–81. See also The Tenement Museum website at https://www.tenement.org/.
67. Russell A. Kazal, "Migration History in Five Stories (and a Basement): The Lower East Side Tenement Museum," *Journal of American Ethnic History* 34, no. 4 (Summer 2015): 77.

CHAPTER 7

1. "Curator Core Competencies" is a document that was published in 2014 by the American Alliance of Museums' CurCom Standing Committee on Ethics and accepted by CurCom in 2015. It can be found at https://www.aam-us.org/wp-content/uploads/2018/05/CURATOR-CORE-COMPETENCIES.pdf.
2. AASLH and FrameWorks, "Making History Matter: From Abstract Truth to Critical Engagement," Final Report, February 2022, https://cdn.aaslh.org/wp-content/uploads/2022/08/09101028/FWI-Reframing-History-Report.pdf.
3. Margot Wallace, *Writing for Museums*, 2nd ed. (Lanham, MD: Rowman & Littlefield Publishers, Inc., 2022), viii.
4. For more on writing for the public, see Simon Clews' excellent book, *The New Academic: A Researcher's Guide to Writing and Presenting Content in a Modern World*, Part 2: "Writing" (Naperville, IL: Sourcebooks, 2023), 17–71.
5. *Museum* 102, no. 1 (January/February 2023): 18.
6. *Museum* 102, no. 1 (January/February 2023): 19.
7. For additional articles and essays on this topic, see Nik Honeysett, "The Digital Awakening," *Museum* 99, no. 5 (November–December 2020): 32–35; Mark Breske and Liz Hobson, "Creating Digital Content for Museums and Historic Sites," *History News* 76, no. 2 (Spring 2021): Technical Leaflet #294; "Trendswatch: Digital Awakening," *Museum* 100, no. 2 (March–April 2021): 28–32; and Robin White Owen, "The Virtuous Circle: From Local to Global and Back Again," in *Change Is Required: Preparing for the Post-Pandemic Museum*, ed. Avi Y. Decter, Marsha L. Semmel, and Ken Yellis (Lanham, MD: Rowman & Littlefield Publishers, Inc., 2022), 37–41.
8. Clews, *The New Academic*, 123. See also the rest of chapter 16 in Clews's book: "Writing Online," 123–26.
9. Jason Steinhauer, *History Disrupted* (New York: Palgrave Macmillan, 2022), 9. This entire book is a recommended read.
10. This list comes from the useful online article "Seven Digital Storytelling Tips for the Cultural Heritage Sector," Europeana Foundation, July 13, 2021, accessed April 8, 2024, https://pro.europeana.eu/page/seven-tips-for-digital-storytelling#:~:text=Seven%20tips%20for%20digital%20storytelling%201%201.%20Be,Be%20specific%20...%207%207.%20Be%20evocative%20.
11. For more on this topic, see Matthew MacArthur, "Get Real! The Role of Objects in the Digital Age," in *Letting Go? Sharing Historical Authority in a User-Generated World*,

ed. Bill Adair, Benjamin Filene, and Laura Koloski (Philadelphia, PA: The Pew Center for Arts & Heritage, 2011), 56-67.

12. These ideas, and more, come from the report "The Virtual Era—From Onsite to Virtual: A Virtual Programming Playbook for Museums, Libraries, and Zoos," City of Palo Alto, 2021, https://www.cityofpaloalto.org/files/assets/public/v/3/community-services/art-center/playbook/from-onsite-to-virtual_a-virtual-programming-playbook-for-libraries-museums-and-zoos.pdf. See also Adriana Dunn, Ciara Fisk, Edward Castleman, and Francesca Manard, "The Digital Age: Technological Advancements at Small Museums," *History News* 77, no. 4 (2022): 28-33.

13. Some of the best examples of online exhibitions are those that have been created by museums in partnership with Google Arts & Culture—an online platform of high-resolution images and videos of artworks and cultural artifacts from partner cultural organizations throughout the world. To view some samples created by The Henry Ford, check out its twenty-one "online exhibits" at https://artsandculture.google.com/partner/the-henry-ford.

14. Because the term "blog" has been somewhat devalued due to the democratization of blog writing, some museum websites refer to these types of writings as articles or stories.

15. The following list of advantages, tenets, and tips for writing blogs primarily comes from chapter 13 of Wallace's book, 171-85, as well as the more content-focused chapter 2 of the first edition of Wallace's book, *Writing for Museums* (Lanham, MD: Rowman & Littlefield Publishers, Inc., 2014), 15-27. See also Clews, *The New Academic*, chapter 18: "Blogging," 131-36; and Heather Cox Richardson, "The New Social History: Finding the Time for Social Media and Blogging," *The American Historian*, no. 1 (August 2014): 10-11. Additionally, there are numerous online articles with tips for writing blogs.

16. Blogs can also be written in many different formats, from a straightforward narrative to a deeper focus on a specific object or group of objects to an update on a program or exhibition to a more personal memoir. Here is a sampling of the variety of topics, formats, and approaches that I have taken in the more than one hundred blogs I have written for The Henry Ford: "Teaching Black: An Educator's Library from the Black Power Era," https://www.thehenryford.org/explore/blog/teaching-black-an-educator-s-library-from-the-black-power-era/; "Carnegie Libraries: Democratizing Knowledge," https://www.thehenryford.org/explore/blog/carnegie-libraries-democratizing-knowledge; "Lamy's Diner Gets a Makeover," https://www.thehenryford.org/explore/blog/lamy-s-diner-gets-a-makeover; "Losing Weight, 1972-Style," https://www.thehenryford.org/explore/blog/losing-weight-1972-style; and "Remembering Marty Sklar," https://www.thehenryford.org/explore/blog/remembering-marty-sklar/.

17. For more on writing for social media in addition to Steinhauer's *History Disrupted*, see Tee Morris and Pip Ballantine, *Social Media for Writers: Marketing Strategies for Building Your Audience and Selling Books* (Cincinnati, OH: Writer's Digest Books, 2015); and "How Museums Can Use Social Media," MuseumNext (blog), April 16, 2022, https://www.museumnext.com/article/museums-can-use-social-media/.

18. Clews, *The New Academic*, 110.

19. In addition to my own experiences, I would like to thank curators Jeanine Head Miller, Charles Sable, Matt Anderson, and Katherine White at The Henry Ford for their input, ideas, and examples. Interviews took place in February and March 2024.
20. For this section, I drew inspiration from The Moth, an acclaimed not-for-profit organization dedicated to the art and craft of storytelling. This group offers many insightful strategies for engaging the public in their book, *How to Tell a Story: The Essential Guide to Memorable Storytelling from the Moth*, by Meg Bowles, Catherine Burns, Jenifer Hixson, Sarah Austin Jenness, and Kate Tellers (New York: Crown, 2022). See also Clews, *The New Academic*, Section 3: "Speaking," 75-90.
21. There are many good books and articles on giving interpretive tours at museums, including: Stephen Hague, "How to Plan and Implement Interpretation," *History News* 68, no. 2 (Spring 2013): Technical Leaflet #262; Sharon Vatsky, *Interactive Museum Tours: A Guide to In-Person and Virtual Experiences* (Lanham, MD: Rowman & Littlefield Publishers, Inc., 2023); Barbara Abramoff Levy, Sandra Mackenzie Lloyd, and Susan Porter Schreiber, *Great Tours! Thematic Tours and Guide Training for Historic Sites* (Walnut Creek, CA: AltaMira Press, a Division of Rowman & Littlefield Publishers, Inc., 2001); and Jessica Foy Donnelly, ed., *Interpreting Historic House Museums* (Walnut Creek, CA: AltaMira Press, a Division of Rowman & Littlefield Publishers, Inc., 2002), especially the essays by Rex M. Ellis, "Interpreting the Whole House," chapter 3, 61-80; Margaret Piatt, "Engaging Visitors Through Effective Communication," chapter 11, 231-50; Jamie Credle, "Endless Possibilities: Historic House Museum Programs That Make Educators Sing," chapter 13, 269-92; and Lisa Brochu and Tim Merriman, "Program Delivery," chapter 7 in *Personal Interpretation: Connecting Your Audience to Heritage Resources*, 3rd ed. (Fort Collins, CO: National Association for Interpretation, 2015), 91-100. For specific strategies on creating and delivering tours relating to enslavement, see Kristen L. Gallas, *Interpreting Slavery with Children and Teens at Museums and Historic Sites*, AASLH Interpreting History Series (Lanham, MD: Rowman & Littlefield Publishers, Inc., 2021). For tours focusing on women's history, see Heather Huyck, *Doing Women's History in the Public: A Handbook for Interpretation at Museums and Historic Sites*, chapter 10: "Interpretation," AASLH Interpreting History Series (Lanham, MD: Rowman & Littlefield Publishers, Inc., 2020), 193-220.
22. For more on vocal techniques, see Piatt, "Engaging Visitors Through Effective Communication," 242; Levy, Lloyd, and Schreiber, *Great Tours!*, 118-20; and Reyaa Agarwal, "Raise Your Voice: 10 Vocal Techniques for Powerful Public Speaking," Mentoria (blog), October 6, 2023, https://blog.mentoria.com/raise-your-voice-10-vocal-techniques-for-powerful-public-speaking/#:~:text=Raise%20Your%20Voice%3A%2010%20Vocal%20Techniques%20For%20Powerful,Intonation%3A%20Conveying%20Meaning%20Through%20Tone%20...%20More%20items.
23. "A Digital (R)evolution," *Museum* 102, no. 1 (January/February 2023): 21.
24. These tips and more come from Clews, *The New Academic*, chapter 12: "Presenting Onscreen," 90-96; Carolyn Keogh, "Out of One Story, Many: Frameworks for Making Diverse and Contemporary Connections at Olana," *History News* 77, no. 3 (2022): 20-25; Vatsky, *Interactive Museum Tours*, chapter 19: "Adapting the Tour Planning Template for Virtual Tours for Adults," 155-64; and "The Virtual Era—From Onsite to Virtual."

25. The free Bloomberg Connects app is a large (and growing) repository for expert-curated audio (and other multimedia) guides from hundreds of museums, galleries, and cultural spaces. See more at https://www.bloombergconnects.org/.
26. The advantages and steps in creating audio tours in this section come from Wallace, *Writing for Museums*, 1st ed., chapter 1, 1-13; Dunn, Fisk, Castleman, and Manard, "The Digital Age: Technological Advancements at Small Museums"; Dia Felix and Erin Fleming, "Real Talk: The Power (and Limits) of Audio Storytelling in Museums," *Journal of Museum Education* 48, no. 1 (March 2023): 21-28; "How a Mobile Application is Beneficial for Museums," Museum Anywhere (blog), November 16, 2017, https://www.museumanywhere.com/mobile-application-beneficial-museums/#:~:text=Benefits%20of%20Having%20a%20Mobile,any%20art%2C%20sculpture%20or%20portrait; and "Museums Use Mobile Apps to Enrich and Personalize Visitor's Experience," Museum Anywhere (blog), February 8, 2018, https://www.museumanywhere.com/museums-use-mobile-apps-enrich-personalize-visitors-experience/.
27. For more on these programs, see Caroline Braden, "Accessibility Evolving at The Henry Ford," chapter 8 in *An Accessible Past: Making Historic Sites Accessible*, ed. Heather Pressman (Lanham, MD: Rowman & Littlefield Publishers, Inc., 2024), 83-96.
28. For more on tours for this audience, including keys to engaging this audience, see Francesca Rosenberg, "Adapting the Tour Planning Template for Adults with Alzheimer's Disease and Other Dementias," chapter 21 in Vatsky, *Interactive Museum Tours*, 175-83; and "Dementia," Part III in *Welcoming Museum Visitors with Unapparent Disabilities*, ed. Beth Redmond-Jones (Lanham, MD: Rowman & Littlefield Publishers, Inc., 2024), 103-38.
29. Interview with John Firchau by Caroline Braden, September 2019.
30. Interview with Kathy Firchau by Caroline Braden, September 2019.
31. For more explanation of verbal description, see pages 149-50 in Heather Pressman and Danielle Schulz, *The Art of Access: A Practical Guide for Museum Accessibility* (Lanham, MD: Rowman & Littlefield Publishers, Inc., 2021), 149-50.
32. Roslyn Nadler, response to email questionnaire sent by Caroline Braden, January 2023.
33. Clews, *The New Academic*, 141.
34. The following sections, on preparing for and giving interviews, and cautions/challenges and strategies to consider in giving interviews, come from Clews, *The New Academic*, chapter 20: "Working with the Media," 141-54 and chapter 21: "Newspapers and Magazines," 155-66; Kate Paine, "Ten Tips for Media Interview Preparation," Change Conversations (blog), June 27, 2013, https://conversations.marketing-partners.com/2013/06/10-tips-for-media-interview-preparation/; and "How to Work with the Media," American Psychological Association (blog), June 2020, https://www.apa.org/pubs/authors/working-with-media.
35. Interview with Matt Anderson, March 19, 2024.
36. For an example of one of these segments, see my interview with host Mo Rocca in "The Last Remaining Horse-Drawn Lunch Wagon," https://www.youtube.com/watch?v=mn7nofcffMM.
37. The name of the episode in which my interview appeared is, "It's a Small World."

38. For more on creating museum podcasts, see Marieke Van Damme and Dan Yaeger, "How to Make a Podcast," *History News* 71, no. 4 (Autumn 2016): Technical Leaflet #276; Morris and Ballantine, *Social Media for Writers*, chapter 3: "Podcasting," 44-56; "How to Start a Podcast for Your Museum," MuseumNext (blog), February 4, 2022, https://www.museumnext.com/article/how-to-start-a-podcast-for-your-museum/; and Hannah Hethmon, *Your Museum Needs a Podcast: A Step-By-Step Guide to Podcasting on a Budget for Museums, History Organizations, and Cultural Nonprofits* (hhethmon.com/BookBonus, 2018).
39. For more on being interviewed for a podcast, see Clews, *The New Academic*, chapter 26: "Podcasts," 198-205.
40. The link to this podcast episode can be found at: https://podcasts.apple.com/us/podcast/deltiology-postcards-with-donna-braden/id1278815517?i=1000414099173.

CHAPTER 8

1. This chapter is a refined and expanded version of Donna R. Braden's essay "Leadership at Every Level," from the *Proceedings of the 2013 Conference and Annual Meeting, Hale Farm & Village, Akron, Ohio*, ed. Debra Reid. Vol. XXXVI (North Bloomfield, Ohio: The Association for Living History, Farm and Agricultural Museums, 2014), 248-53. For business books that approach leadership from this lens, I highly recommend John C. Maxwell, *The 360° Leader: Developing Your Influence Anywhere in the Organization* (Nashville, TN: HarperCollins Leadership, 2011) and Scott Mautz, *Leading from the Middle: A Playbook for Managers to Influence Up, Down, and Across the Organization* (Hoboken, NJ: John Wiley & Sons, Inc., 2021).
2. This definition comes from the GLOBE (Global Leadership and Organizational Behavior Effectiveness) study of leadership across cultures, referenced in Mai Moua, *Culturally Intelligent Leadership: Leading Through Intercultural Interactions* (New York: Business Expert Press, LLC, 2010), xii. The link to GLOBE's website is https://globeproject.com/.
3. Moua, *Culturally Intelligent Leadership*, 19.
4. Mark Sanborn, *You Don't Need a Title to be a Leader* (New York: Currency Doubleday, 2006), xiv.
5. For more on an "others-oriented" mindset, see Mautz, "The Mindset for Leading Effectively from the Middle," chapter 2 in *Leading from the Middle*, 27-49.
6. Elizabeth Peña, "Leadership at All Levels," chapter 22 in *A Life in Museums: Managing Your Museum Career*, ed. Greg Stevens and Wendy Luke (Washington, DC: The AAM Press of the American Alliance of Museums, 2012), 146.
7. Peña, "Leadership at All Levels," 144-46.
8. Daniel Goleman's work on emotional intelligence is a must-read for this. See, for example, Goleman's *Emotional Intelligence: Why It Can Matter More than IQ* (New York: Bantam Books, 1995) and *Working with Emotional Intelligence* (New York: Bantam Books, 1998) as well as Goleman, Richard Boyatzis, and Annie McKee, *Primal Leadership: The Power of Emotional Intelligence* (Boston, MA: Harvard Business School Publishing, 2002). A nice summary of Goleman's major points (with a self-test) appears in Jill Geisler, "Manage Yourself, So You Can Lead Others," chapter 4

in *Work Happy: What Great Bosses Know* (New York: Center Street, Hatchette Book Group, 2012), 61–81.
9. For an in-depth description of different intrinsic motivators, see Johnmarshall Reeve, "Psychological Needs," chapter 5 in *Understanding Motivation and Emotion*, 4th ed. (Hoboken, NJ: John Wiley & Sons, Inc., 2005), 101–29. To see how intrinsic motivation can be applied to leadership in the workplace, see Geisler, "Work Happy: Motivation that Really Works, Boss," chapter 8 in *Work Happy*, 151–70; and Lee J. Colan, *Engaging the Hearts and Minds of All Your Employees* (New York: McGraw-Hill Education, 2018), 45–152.
10. Just a few of the numerous works dealing with conflict in the workplace are Jo Owen, "Conflict Management," Part Four in *The Leadership Skills Handbook: 100 Essential Skills You Need to be a Leader*, 5th ed. (New York: Kogan Page Ltd, 2021), 97–102; Erik J. Van Slyke, *Listening to Conflict: Constructive Solutions to Workplace Disputes* (New York: American Management Association, 1999); and Kerry Patterson, Joseph Grenny, Ron McMillan, and Al Switzler, *Crucial Confrontations* (New York: McGraw-Hill, 2005).
11. Further explanation of this important concept appears in the introduction to *Flourishing in Museums: Toward a Positive Museology*, ed. Kiersten F. Latham and Brenda Cowan (London and New York: Routledge, 2024), 11.
12. In addition to Braden's essay "Leadership at Every Level," the ideas and tips in this section come from the following sources: Paul M. Muchinski, "Organizations and Organizational Change," chapter 8 in *Psychology Applied to Work*, 9th ed. (Summerfield, NC: Hypergraphic Press, Inc., 2009), 248–84; Michael D. Watkins, "What Is Organizational Culture? And Why Should We Care?" *Harvard Business Review*, May 15, 2013, accessed May 30, 2024, https://hbr.org/2013/05/what-is-organizational-culture; and Nan S. Russell, "Using Differences," chapter 4 in *The Titleless Leader: How to Get Things Done When You're Not in Charge* (Pompton Plains, NJ: The Career Press, Inc., 2012), 67–81. For an interesting essay on how to consider museums' organizational culture while working with communities, see Daniel Kertzner, "The Lens of Organizational Culture," *Mastering Civic Engagement: A Challenge to Museums* (Washington, DC: American Association of Museums, 2002), 39–48.
13. From Peggy Klaus, *The Hard Truth about Soft Skills* (New York: Collins Business, 2007), 93.
14. There are numerous books on the topic of leading yourself. In addition to Braden's essay "Leadership at Every Level," the ideas and tips in this section come from the following sources: Sheetal Prajapati, "Managing from the Middle," chapter 21 in *A Life in Museums*, 137–41; John Baldoni, *Personal Leadership: Taking Control of Your Work Life* (Rochester Hills, MI: Elsewhere Press, 2001); Owen, *The Leadership Skills Handbook*; Sanborn, *You Don't Need a Title to Be a Leader*; Klaus, *The Hard Truth about Soft Skills*; and Stedman Graham, "The Call for Identity Leaders," chapter 1 in *Identity Leadership* (New York: Center Street, Hatchette Book Group, 2019).
15. The official link to MBTI is https://www.mbtionline.com/?msclkid=09d390f5d0c511dbbacdf6ad33331f83. There are also free online tests.
16. For greater detail on the StrengthsFinder assessment, see Marcus Buckingham and Donald O. Clifton, *Now, Discover Your Strengths* (New York: The Free Press, 2001) and Tom Rath and Barry Conchie, *Strengths-Based Leadership: Great Leaders, Teams, and Why People Follow* (New York: Gallup Press, 2008). The StrengthsFinder

assessment tool (now rebranded as the CliftonStrengths assessment) can be found online at https://www.gallup.com/cliftonstrengths/en/strengthsfinder.aspx.
17. Marcus Buckingham and Curt Coffman, *First, Break All the Rules* (New York: Simon & Schuster, 1999).
18. For more on soft skills, see Graham, *Identity Leadership* and Klaus, *The Hard Truth about Soft Skills*. There are also numerous online articles about soft skills.
19. A plethora of books and articles have been written on the topic of leading (or managing) up. In addition to Braden's "Leadership at Every Level," the tips and strategies for this section come from Gary Ford, "Communicating with Your Boss," chapter 19 in *A Life in Museums*, 121-24; Prajapati, "Managing from the Middle"; Maxwell, "The Principles 360-Degree Leaders Practice to Lead Up," Section III in *The 360° Leader*, 84-157; and Mautz, "Leading Your Boss," chapter 4 in *Leading from the Middle*.
20. For more on this topic, see "Working with More Senior Leaders," in Owen, *The Leadership Skills Handbook*, 204.
21. In addition to Braden's "Leadership at Every Level," the tips and strategies for this section come from Prajapati, "Managing from the Middle"; Gary Ford and Greg Stevens, "Working On or Managing Teams," chapter 23 in *A Life in Museums*, 147-53; Martha Morris, *Managing People and Projects in Museums: Strategies that Work* (Lanham, MD: Rowman & Littlefield Publishers, Inc., 2017); Maxwell, "The Principles 360-Degree Leaders Practice to Lead Across," Section IV in *The 360° Leader*, 161-210; Mautz, "Leading Teams" and "Influencing Peers," chapters 6 and 7 in *Leading from the Middle*, 125-60; Russell, *The Titleless Leader*; and Mary Shapiro, *The HBR Guide to Leading Teams* (Boston, MA: HBR Press, 2015).
22. For good insight into the characteristics of successful collaborations, see Michael Schrage, "Collaboration and Creativity," *Museum News* 83, no. 2 (March/April 2004): 44-48; and Polly McKenna-Cress and Janet A. Kamien, *Creating Exhibitions: Collaboration in Planning, Development and Design of Innovative Experiences* (Hoboken, NJ: John Wiley & Sons Inc., 2013), especially chapter 1 on "Collaboration," 1-19.
23. In addition to Braden's "Leadership at Every Level," the tips and strategies for this section come from Amanda Kodek and Wendy Luke, "Mentoring Matters," chapter 29 in *A Life in Museums*, 181-85 (this essay also appeared as "Mentoring Matters: A Call for Backup," in *Museum* 87, no. 2 (March/April 2008): 62-69); and John C. Maxwell, *The Ultimate Guide to Developing Leaders: Invest in People Like Your Future Depends on It* (Nashville, TN: HarperCollins Leadership, 2023).
24. This section is refined and expanded from Donna R. Braden's unpublished paper for the online AASLH course on Leadership and Administration for History Organizations, entitled "Review of Recent Literature on 'Leading from the Middle,'" April 23, 2022. Thanks to instructor Anne W. Ackerson for her encouragement and support in allowing me to pursue this topic for the class.
25. The "amplifier" concept is expanded upon in Mautz, *Leading from the Middle*, 51-52.
26. There are numerous books on leading others, although most are approached from a management rather than a leadership point of view. In addition to Braden's "Leadership at Every Level," the ideas, tips, and strategies in this section come from Prajapati, "Managing from the Middle"; Maxwell, "The Principles 360-Degree Leaders Practice to Lead Down," Section V in *The 360° Leader*, 213-60; Mautz, "Leading Those Who Report to You," chapter 5 in *Leading from the Middle*; Owen, *The*

Leadership Skills Handbook; Baldoni, *Personal Leadership*; Colan, *Engaging the Hearts and Minds of All Your Employees*; and Buckingham, *First, Break All the Rules*.
27. This list was inspired by my own experience as well as the essay entitled "Managing Professionals," in Owen, *The Leadership Skills Handbook*, 91-92.
28. An increasing literature is appearing on this topic from a museum perspective. Insights and strategies in this section come from Chris Taylor, "Inclusive Leadership: Avoiding the Legacy of Irrelevance," chapter 4 in "MASS Action [Museum as Site for Social Action] Toolkit," 2017, https://static1.squarespace.com/static/58fa685dff7c50f78be5f2b2/t/59dcdd27e5dd5b5a1b51d9d8/1507646780650/TOOLKIT_10_2017.pdf, 73-88; Laura-Edythe Coleman, *Understanding and Implementing Inclusion in Museums* (Lanham, MD: Rowman & Littlefield Publishers, Inc., 2018); Cinnamon Catlin-Legutko and Chris Taylor, ed. *The Inclusive Museum Leader* (Lanham, MD: Rowman & Littlefield Publishers, Inc., 2021), especially Taylor, "Creating the Just Leader," chapter 3, 21-29, and Kayleigh Bryant-Greenwell, "How to Spot an Inclusive Leader and Choose to Work for Them," chapter 21, 205-19; Mike Murawski, *Museums as Agents of Change: A Guide to Becoming a Changemaker* (Lanham, MD: Rowman & Littlefield Publishers, Inc., 2021), especially chapter 6: "Leading Toward a Different Future," 63-80; Mike Muraski, "A Better Future for Museums," *Museum* 100, no. 6 (November/December 2021): 16-19; and Porchia Moore, Rose Paquet, and Aletheia Wittman, *Transforming Inclusion in Museums: The Power of Collaborative Inquiry* (Lanham, MD: Rowman & Littlefield Publishers, Inc., 2022), especially the preface, ix-xiv, and chapter 3: "Opening Up to Transformation," 47-72. For business perspectives on this topic, see Moua, *Culturally Intelligent Leadership* and Colette A. M. Phillips, *The Includers: The Seven Traits of Cultural Savvy, Anti-Racist Leaders* (Dallas, TX: BenBella Books, Inc., 2024).

Bibliography

"A Digital (R)evolution." *Museum* 102, no. 1 (January/February 2023): 18–23.
AASLH. "Award Winner Spotlight: First Americans Museum." *History News* 78, no. 3 (2023): 34–35.
AASLH Historic House Museum Affinity Group Committee. "How Sustainable Is Your Historic House Museum?" *History News* 63, no. 4 (Autumn 2008): Technical Leaflet #224.
AASLH Historic House Museum Affinity Community. "How Sustainable Is Your Historic House Museum?" *History News* 78, no. 2 (2023): Technical Leaflet #302.
AASLH Standards and Ethics Committee. "Valuing History Collections." *History News* 75, no. 4 (Autumn 2020): 28–33.
Ackerson, Anne W. "Strategizing Me: Making a Personal Career Plan." *Museum* 96, no. 2 (March/April 2017): 41–45.
Adair, Bill, Benjamin Filene, and Laura Koloski, eds. *Letting Go? Sharing Historical Authority in a User-Generated World*. Philadelphia, PA: The Pew Center for Arts and Heritage, 2011.
Alexander, Edward P., and Mary Alexander. *Museums in Motion: An Introduction to the History and Functions of Museums*, 2nd ed. Walnut Creek, CA: AltaMira Press for the American Association for State and Local History, 2007.
Allen, Katharine, and Robert-John Hinojosa. "The LGBTQ Columbia History Initiative." *History News* 76, no. 3 (Summer 2021): 19–23.
American Alliance of Museums. "Excellence in DEAI" Report. Accessed April 24, 2023, https://www.aam-us.org/2022/08/02/excellence-in-deai-report/.
———. *A Museum and Community Toolkit*. Washington, DC: American Alliance of Museums, 2002.
American Association for State and Local History. "History Relevance Initiative." Accessed April 24, 2023, https://www.historyrelevance.com/value-history-statemen.
———. "Reframing History Toolkit." Accessed April 24, 2023, https://aaslh.org/reframing-history-blog/.
American Association for State and Local History and FrameWorks. "Making History Matter: From Abstract Truth to Critical Engagement." Final

Report, February 2022, https://cdn.aaslh.org/wp-content/uploads/2022/08/09101028/FWI-Reframing-History-Report.pdf.
Ames, Kenneth L. "Meaning in Artifacts: Hall Furnishings in Victorian America." *Journal of Interdisciplinary History* IX, no. 1 (Summer 1978): 19-46.
Anderson, Gail. *Mission Matters: Relevance and Museums in the 21st Century*. Lanham, MD: Rowman & Littlefield Publishers, Inc., 2019.
Arnold, Emilie S. "The Wound Is Fresh: Exhibiting Orlando's LGBTQ History in the Shadow of the Pulse Nightclub Massacre." *Exhibition* 36, no. 2 (Fall 2017): 26-35.
Auslander, Mark, and Amanda Thomashow. "Sites of Healing." *Museum* 98, no. 6 (November-December 2019): 35-39.
Bachard, Cheryl A. "Rethinking Architecture in the Realm of House Museum Interpretation." In *Reimagining Historic House Museums*, edited by Kenneth C. Turino and Max A. van Balgooy. Lanham, MD: Rowman & Littlefield Publishers, Inc, 2019.
Bader, Miriam. "Historic Sites and Universal Design: Lessons from The Tenement Museum." NAME *Exhibitionist* 34, no. 2 (Fall 2015): 28-33.
Bailey, Dina. "Finding Inspiration Inside: Engaging Empathy to Empower Everyone." In *Fostering Empathy through Museums*, edited by Elif M. Gokcigdem, 131. Lanham, MD: Rowman & Littlefield Publishers, Inc., 2016.
Bailey, Dina A., and Richard C. Cooper. "The Necessity of Community Involvement: Talking about Slavery in the Twenty-First Century." In *Interpreting Slavery at Museums and Historic Sites*, edited by Kristin Gallas and James DeWolf Perry, 61-70. AASLH Interpreting History Series. Lanham, MD: Rowman & Littlefield Publishers, Inc., 2015.
Baillon, Kate, Janeen Bryant, and Kamille Bostick. "Failing Forward: iNUEVOlution! Latinos and the New South." *History News* 73, no. 3 (Summer 2018): 14-18.
Bain, Aja. "Peopling the Past: Living History and Inclusive Museum Practice." *The Museum Scholar: Theory and Practice* 2 (2019), https://articles.themuseumscholar.org/2019/05/16/tp_vol2bain/.
Baldoni, John. *Personal Leadership: Taking Control of Your Work Life*. Rochester Hills, MI: Elsewhere Press, 2001.
Bartlett, Sarah. "Can Museums Take a Stand?" NAME *Exhibitionist* 30, no. 2 (Fall 2011): 46-51.
———. "The Hemingway Effect." *Exhibition* 36, no. 1 (Spring 2016): 30-34.
Bauer, Marion Dune. *What's Your Story? A Young Person's Guide to Writing Fiction*. New York: Clarion Books, 1992.
Beard, Rick. "Collections: Our Curse and Our Blessing." *History News* 70, no. 3 (Summer 2015): 11-16.
———. "If It Was Easy, Anyone Could Do It: Training Professionals for History Institutions." *History News* 71, no. 3 (Summer 2016): 9.
Bedford, Leslie. "Forum: Working in the Subjunctive Mood: Imagination and Museums." *Curator* 47, no. 1 (January 2004): 5.

———. "Storytelling: The Real Work of Museums." *Curator* 44, no. 1 (January 2001): 27-34.

Bench, Raney. *Interpreting Native American History and Culture at Museums and Historic Sites*. AASLH Interpreting History Series. Lanham, MD: Rowman & Littlefield Publishers, Inc., 2014.

Berlanga-Shevchuk, Mariah. "The Collective Collection: Active, People-Centered, and Collaborative." In *Change Is Required: Preparing for the Post-Pandemic Museum*, edited by Avi Y. Decter, Marsha L. Semmel, and Ken Yellis, 117-21. Lanham, MD: Rowman & Littlefield Publishers, Inc., 2022.

Bethea, Charles. "Museum Collecting in the Age of Black Lives Matter." *History News* 77, no. 1 (2022): 12-17.

Bitgood, Stephen. *Engaging the Visitor: Designing Exhibits that Work*. Edinburgh, Scotland, and Boston, MA: MuseumsEtc., 2014.

———. "Exhibition Design That Provides High Value and Engages Visitor Attention." *NAME Exhibitionist* 33, no. 1 (Spring 2014): 6-18.

Black, Graham. *The Engaging Museum: Developing Museums for Visitor Involvement*. London and New York: Routledge, 2005.

Blandy, Doug, and Paul E. Bolin. *Learning Things: Material Culture in Art Education*. New York: Teachers College Press, 2018.

Bogart, Barbara Allen. "Using Oral History in Museums." *History News* 50, no. 4 (Autumn 1995): Technical Leaflet #191.

Bondhus, Dawn, Martha Katz-Hyman, and Mick Woodcock. "Curation 101: Curatorial Roots for Non-Curators." *Proceedings of the 2010 Conference and Annual Meeting, Old Sturbridge Village*, edited by Debra Reid, Vol. XXXIII, 129-30. Worcester, MA: The Association for Living History, Farm and Agricultural Museums, 2011.

Borowsky, Larry. "Telling a Story in 100 Words: Effective Label Copy." *History News* 62, no. 4 (August 2007): Technical Leaflet #240.

Borun, Minda, and Randi Korn, edited by *Introduction to Museum Evaluation*. Washington, DC: American Association of Museums, 1999.

Bourcier, Paul. "#Meaning: Cataloguing Active Collections." In *Active Collections*, edited by Elizabeth Wood, Rainey Tisdale, and Trevor Jones, 115-16. London and New York: Routledge, 2018.

Bowles, Meg, Catherine Burns, Jenifer Hixson, Sarah Austin Jenness, and Kate Tellers. *How to Tell a Story: The Essential Guide to Memorable Storytelling from the Moth*. New York: Crown, 2022.

Braden, Caroline. "Accessibility Evolving at The Henry Ford." In *An Accessible Past: Making Historic Sites Accessible*, edited by Heather Pressman, 83-96. Lanham, MD: Rowman & Littlefield Publishers, Inc., 2024.

Braden, Donna R. "Leadership at Every Level." *Proceedings of the 2013 Conference and Annual Meeting, Hale Farm & Village, Akron, Ohio*, edited by Debra Reid, Vol. XXXVI, 248-53. North Bloomfield, Ohio: The Association for Living History, Farm and Agricultural Museums, 2014.

———. "Not Just a Bunch of Facts: Crafting Dynamic Interpretive Manuals." *History News* 69, no. 3 (Summer 2014): Technical Leaflet #267.

———. "Bringing Your Environment to Life." In *Spaces that Tell Stories: Recreating Historical Environments*, 87–112. Lanham, MD: Rowman & Littlefield Publishers, Inc., 2019.
———. "The Power of Historical Environments." *History News* 74, no. 2 (Spring 2019): 24–28.
———. *Spaces that Tell Stories: Recreating Historical Environments*. Lanham, MD: Rowman & Littlefield Publishers, Inc., 2019.
———. "Taste-Testing the Visitor Experience." *Proceedings of the 2013 Conference and Annual Meeting, Hale Farm & Village, Akron, Ohio*, edited by Debra A. Reid, Vol. XXXVI, 197–211. North Bloomfield, OH: The Association for Living History, Farm and Agricultural Museums, 2014.
———. "Your Personal Toolkit: Easing through Friction, Fracas, and Free-for-All." *NAME Exhibitionist* 29, no. 1 (Spring 2010): 6–14.
———. "The Process and the Product: Transforming the General Store in Greenfield Village." *History News* 50, no. 3 (Summer 1995): 20–24.
Brennan, Sheila A. "Digital History." In *The Inclusive Historian's Handbook*. June 4, 2019, https://inclusivehistorian.com/digital-history/.
Breske, Mark, and Liz Hobson. "Creating Digital Content for Museums and Historic Sites." *History News* 76, no. 2 (Spring 2021): Technical Leaflet #294.
Bridal, Tessa. *Exploring Museum Theatre*. Walnut Creek: AltaMira Press, 2004.
Brochu, Lisa. *Interpretive Planning: The 5-M Model for Successful Planning Projects*, 2nd ed. Fort Collins, CO: The National Association for Interpretation, 2014.
Brochu, Lisa, and Tim Merriman. *Personal Interpretation: Connecting Your Audience to Heritage Resources*, 3rd ed. Fort Collins, CO: The National Association for Interpretation, 2015.
Brockway, Lucinda A. "Looking Beyond the Front Door to Find Spirit of Place." In *Reimagining Historic House Museums*, edited by Kenneth C. Turino and Max A. van Balgooy. Lanham, MD: Rowman & Littlefield Publishers, Inc, 2019.
Brooks, Bradley. "The Historic House Furnishings Plan: Process and Product." In *Interpreting Historic House Museums*, edited by Jessica Foy Donnelly, 139–41. Walnut Creek, CA: AltaMira, a Division of Rowman and Littlefield, 2002.
Brooks, Patricia. "Developing Competent and Confident Interpreters." In *Interpreting Slavery at Museums and Historic Sites*, 85–99. AASLH Interpreting History Series. Lanham, MD: Rowman & Littlefield Publishers, Inc., 2015.
Brown, T. A. "The Agricultural Curator's Role in Developing and Maintaining Interpretive Programs." *Proceedings of the 1977 Annual Meeting, Tifton, GA*. The Association for Living Historical Farms and Agricultural Museums, edited by Virginia Wolf Briscoe, Vol. IV, 12–13. Washington, DC: Smithsonian, 1978.
Bryant, Janeen, and Kamille Bostick, "What's the Big Idea? Using Listening Sessions to Build Relationships and Relevance." *History News* 68, no. 3 (Summer 2013): Technical Leaflet #263.
Bryant-Greenwell, Kayleigh. "How to Spot an Inclusive Leader and Choose to Work for Them." In *The Inclusive Museum Leader*, edited by Cinnamon

Catlin-Legutko and Chris Taylor, 205-19. Lanham, MD: Rowman & Littlefield Publishers, Inc., 2021.

Bryk, Nancy E. Villa. "'I Wish You Could Take a Peek at Us in the Present Moment': Infusing the Historic House with Characters and Activity." In *Interpreting Historic House Museums*, edited by Jessica Foy Donnelly, 163. Walnut Creek, CA: AltaMira Press, a Division of Rowman & Littlefield Publishers, Inc., 2002.

Buckingham, Marcus, and Donald O. Clifton. *Now, Discover Your Strengths*. New York: The Free Press, 2001.

Buckingham, Marcus, and Curt Coffman. *First, Break All the Rules*. New York: Simon & Schuster, 1999.

Bunch, Lonnie G., III. "'People Need to Remember': American Museums Still Struggle with the Legacy of Race." *Museum* 89, no. 6 (November-December 2010): 42-49.

Burcaw, G. Ellis. *Introduction to Museum Work*, 3rd ed. Lanham, MD: AltaMira Press, a Division of Rowman & Littlefield Publishers, Inc., 1997.

Burger, Arthur Asa. *What Objects Mean: An Introduction to Material Culture*, 2nd ed. Walnut Creek, CA: Left Coast Press, 2014.

Burns, W. James, and Sheila K. Hoffman. "Beyond Collections Work: The Evolving Role for Curators." *Museum* 96, no. 3 (May/June 2017): 13-15.

Calleri, Kate Mirand. "Changing How They See: The Brooklyn Children's Museum Is Decolonizing Its Collection with the Help of Local Teenagers." *Museum* 101, no. 3 (May/June 2022): 36-41.

Cameron, Catherine M., and John B. Gatewood. "Excursions into the Unremembered Past: What People Want from Visits to Historic Sites." *The Public Historian* 22, no. 3 (Summer 2000): 107-27.

Carle, Kandie. "How Dare You? Telling a Cultural Story That Is Not Your Own." *Proceedings of ALHFAM's 2021 Virtual Conference and Annual Meeting*, edited by Donna R. Braden, Vol. XLIV, 116-24. Rochdale, MA: The Association for Living History, Farm and Agricultural Museums, 2022.

Carson, Cary. "Doing History with Material Culture." In *Material Culture and the Study of American Life*, edited by Ian M. G. Quimby, 41-64. New York: W.W. Norton & Co., Inc. for the Henry Francis duPont Winterthur Museum, 1978.

Catlin-Legutko, Cinnamon, and Chris Taylor, eds. *The Inclusive Museum Leader*. Lanham, MD: Rowman & Littlefield Publishers, Inc., 2021.

Church, Lila Teresa. "Documenting Local African American Community History: Some Guidelines for Consideration," In *Interpreting African American History and Culture at Museums and Historic Sites*, AASLH Interpreting History Series, edited by Max van Balgooy, 61-73. Lanham, MD: Rowman & Littlefield Publishers, Inc., 2015.

Clark, Julia. "Do We Really Want the Bust of Jesus and What Should We Do with the Pump Organ in the Other Room? Or, Why You Want a Good Collections Management Policy." In *Small Museum Toolkit 6: Stewardship Collections and History Preservation*, edited by Cinnamon Catlin-Legutko and Stacy

Klingler, 86–107. Lanham, MD: AltaMira Press, a Division of Rowman & Littlefield Publishers, Inc., 2012.

Clarke, Alison J. "Tupperware: Product as Social Relation." In *American Material Culture: The Shape of the Field*, edited by Ann Smart Martin and J. Ritchie Garrison, 225–50. Knoxville: University of Tennessee Press for the Henry Francis duPont Winterthur Museum, 1997.

Clews, Simon. *The New Academic: A Researcher's Guide to Writing and Presenting Content in a Modern World*. Naperville, IL: Sourcebooks, 2023.

Cohen, Daniel J., and Roy Rosenzweig. "Preserving Digital History." *Digital History: A Guide to Gathering, Preserving, and Presenting the Past on the Web*. Center for History and New Media, https://chnm.gmu.edu/digitalhistory/preserving/index.html.

Colan, Lee J. *Engaging the Hearts and Minds of All Your Employees*. New York: McGraw-Hill Education, 2018.

Coleman, Laura-Edythe. *Understanding and Implementing Inclusion in Museums*. Lanham, MD: Rowman & Littlefield Publishers, Inc., 2018.

Colwell, Chip. *Plundered Skulls and Stolen Spirits: Inside the Fight to Reclaim Native America's Culture*. Chicago: The University of Chicago Press, 2017.

Crabill, Jason, Melanie A. Adams, and Kyle McKoy. "Grappling with Unfolding Events." *History News* 71, no. 3 (Summer 2016): 14–18.

Credle, Jamie. "Endless Possibilities: Historic House Museum Programs That Make Educators Sing." In *Interpreting Historic House Museums*, edited by Jessica Foy Donnelly, 269–92. Walnut Creek, CA: AltaMira Press, a Division of Rowman & Littlefield Publishers, Inc., 2002.

Csikszentmihályi, Mihályi, and Kim Hermanson. "Intrinsic Motivation in Museums: What Makes Visitors Want to Learn?" *Museum News* 74, no. 3 (May/June 1995): 35–41.

"Curatorial Code of Ethics," CurCom, 2009, accessed April 24, 2023, https://www.aam-us.org/wp-content/uploads/2018/01/curcomethics.pdf.

"Curator Core Competencies," CurCom, accessed April 24, 2023, https://www.aam-us.org/wp-content/uploads/2018/05/CURATOR-CORE-COMPETENCIES.pdf.

CurCom webpage, accessed April 24, 2023, https://www.aam-us.org/professional-networks/curators-committee/.

Danilov, Victor J. *Museum Careers and Training: A Professional Guide*. Westport, CT: Greenwood Press, 1994.

De Cunzo, Lu Ann, and Catherine Dann Roeber. *The Cambridge Handbook of Material Culture Studies*. New York: Cambridge University Press, 2022.

Dearstyne, Bruce W. "Putting History to Work: Strategies to Increase the Visibility and Influence of History." *History News* 72, no. 4 (Autumn 2017): 9–14.

Decter, Avi Y., Marsha L. Semmel, and Ken Yellis, eds. *Change Is Required: Preparing for the Post-Pandemic Museum*. Lanham, MD: Rowman & Littlefield Publishers, Inc., 2022.

Deetz, James. *In Small Things Forgotten: The Archaeology of Early American Life*. Garden City, NY: Anchor Books, 1977.

Demos, John. *A Little Commonwealth: Family Life in Plymouth Colony*. New York: Oxford University Press, 1970.

Dichtl, John R. "Making History Relevant." *History News* 73, no. 2 (Spring 2018): 25-28.

Dierking, Lynn D., Robert Kiihne, Ann Grimes Rand, and Marilyn Solvay. "Laughing and Learning Together: Family Learning Research Becomes Practice at the U.S.S. Constitution Museum." *History News* 61, no. 3 (Summer 2006): 12-15.

Dillenburg, Eugene, and Janice Klein. "Creating Exhibits: From Planning to Building." In *Small Museum Toolkit 5: Interpretation: Education, Programs, and Exhibits*, edited by Cinnamon Catlin-Legutko and Stacy Klingler, 71-99. Lanham, MD: AltaMira Press, a Division of Rowman & Littlefield Publishers, Inc., 2012.

DiPrince, Dawn. "Radical Renewal for Historic House Museums." In *Reimagining Historic House Museums*, edited by Kenneth C. Turino and Max A. van Balgooy, 135-45. Lanham, MD: Rowman & Littlefield Publishers, Inc, 2019.

Donnelly, Jessica Foy, edited by *Interpreting Historic House Museums*. Walnut Creek, CA: AltaMira Press, a Division of Rowman & Littlefield Publishers, Inc., 2002.

Dove, Michael, and Krista McCracken. "Get to Work: Crafting Cover Letters and Résumés for Emerging Professionals." *History News* 73, no. 1 (Winter 2018): Technical Leaflet #281.

Dunbar, Erica Armstrong. *Never Caught: The Washingtons' Relentless Pursuit of their Runaway Slave, Ona Judge*. New York: Atria Books, 2017.

Dunn, Adriana, Ciara Fisk, Edward Castleman, and Francesca Manard. "The Digital Age: Technological Advancements at Small Museums." *History News* 77, no. 4 (2022): 28-33.

Edwards, Victoria. "Empathy Check (and Why It's Not a Cliché)." *Museum* 100, no. 4 (July/August 2021): 14-19.

Eliasof, Jane Mitchell. "The Many Voices of History." *History News* 72, no. 1 (Winter 2017): 14-18.

Eliasof, Jane Mitchell, and Claudia Ocello. "Reflecting Race and Ethnicity in House Museums." In *Reimagining Historic House Museums*, edited by Kenneth C. Turino and Max A. van Balgooy, 197-206. Lanham, MD: Rowman & Littlefield Publishers, Inc, 2019.

Ellis, Rex. "Interpreting the Whole House." In *Interpreting Historic House Museums*, edited by Jessica Foy Donnelly, 61-80. Walnut Creek, CA: AltaMira Press, a Division of Rowman & Littlefield Publishers, Inc., 2002.

Evans, Tracie. "Making Choices Between Authenticity, Preservation and Programming: Curating at a Living History Site." *Proceedings of the 2021 Virtual Conference*, edited by Donna R. Braden, Vol. XLIV, 180-83. Rochdale, MA: The Association for Living History, Farm and Agricultural Museums, 2022.

Eversman, Pauline K., Rosemary T. Krill, Edwina Michael, Beth A. Twiss-Garrity, and Tracey Rae Beck. "Material Culture as Text: Review and Reform of the Literacy Model for Interpretation." In *American Material Culture: The Shape of* the Field, edited by Ann Smart Martin and J. Ritchie Garrison, 135-67. Knoxville: University of Tennessee Press for the Henry Francis duPont Winterthur Museum, 1997.

Fahey, Mary, and Clara Deck. "Responsibilities, Realities, and Ranking: How a Collections Tiering Policy Aids Conservators in Ethical Decision Making and Judicious Resource Allocation at the Henry Ford Museum and Deerfield (sic) Village." In *Objects Specialty Group Postprints* 8, 97-105. Washington, DC: The American Institute for Conservation of Historic and Artistic Works, 2001.

Falk, John H., and Lynn D. Dierking. *Learning from Museums: Visitor Experiences and the Making of Meaning*. Walnut Creek, CA: AltaMira Press, a Division of Rowman & Littlefield Publishers, Inc., 2000.

———. *The Museum Experience*. Washington, DC: Whalesback Books, 1992.

Felix, Dia, and Erin Fleming. "Real Talk: The Power (and Limits) of Audio Storytelling in Museums." *Journal of Museum Education* 48, no. 1 (March 2023): 21-28.

Ferentinos, Susan. *Interpreting LGBT History at Museums and Historic Sites*. AASLH Interpreting History Series. Lanham, MD: Rowman & Littlefield Publishers, Inc., 2015.

Filene, Benjamin. "Letting Go? Sharing Historical Authority in a User-Generated World." *History News* 66, no. 4 (Autumn 2011): 7-12.

———. "The Why, What, and How of the Best Storytelling in Museum Exhibitions." In *Storytelling in Museums*, edited by Adina Langer, 3-12. Lanham, MD: Rowman & Littlefield Publishers, Inc., 2022.

Flagler, Madeline C. "Interpreting Difficult Issues." In *Small Museum Toolkit 5: Interpretation: Education, Programs and Exhibits*, edited by Cinnamon Catlin-Legutko and Stacy Klingler, 26-48. Lanham, MD: AltaMira Press, a Division of Rowman & Littlefield Publishers, Inc., 2012.

Fleming, E. McClung. "Artifact Study: A Proposed Model." *Winterthur Portfolio* 9 (1974): 153-73.

———. "Early American Decorative Arts as Social Documents." *Mississippi Valley Historical Review* 45, no. 2 (September 1958): 276-84.

Ford, Gary. "Communicating with Your Boss." In *A Life in Museums*, edited by Greg Stevens and Wendy Luke, 121-24. Washington, DC: The AAM Press, 2012.

Ford, Gary, and Greg Stevens. "Working on or Managing Teams." In *A Life in Museums*, edited by Greg Stevens and Wendy Luke, 147-53. Washington, DC: The AAM Press, 2012.

Ford, Iris Carter, Patrice Preston-Grimes, and Christian J. Cotz. "Honoring the Ancestors: Descendant Voices in Montpelier." In *Storytelling in Museums*, edited by Adina Langer. Lanham, MD: Rowman & Littlefield Publishers, Inc., 2022.

Franco, Barbara. "The History Museum Curator of the 21st Century." *History News* 51, no. 3 (Summer 1996): 6-10.

Freas, Daniel J., Jennifer L. Ford, and David. R. Scofield. "Chinking Between the Logs: Reinterpreting the Miller House at Meadowcroft Museum of Rural Life." *Proceedings of the 1997 Conference and Annual Meeting, Staunton, Virginia*, edited by Debra A. Reid, Vol. XX, 200-205. North Bloomfield, OH: The Association for Living Historical Farms and Agricultural Museums, 1998.

Friesen, Peter A. "Unvarnished History: Creating Engaging Programs and Exhibits without the Whitewash." *Proceedings of the 2022 Conference and Annual Meeting, Tacoma, Washington*, edited by Carol Kennis Lopez, Vol. XLV, 84-91. Rochdale, MA: The Association for Living History, Farm and Agricultural Museums, 2023.

Gallas, Kristen L. *Interpreting Slavery with Children and Teens at Museums and Historic Sites*. AASLH Interpreting History Series. Lanham, MD: Rowman & Littlefield Publishers, Inc., 2021.

———. "Interpreting Slavery with Children and Teens at Museums and Historic Sites." *History News* 69, no. 2 (Spring 2014): Technical Leaflet #266.

Gallas, Kristin, and James DeWolf Perry. "Doing Comprehensive and Conscientious Interpretation of Slavery at Historic Sites and Museums." *History News* 66, no. 2 (Spring 2014): Technical Leaflet #266.

———. "Developing Comprehensive and Conscientious Interpretation of Slavery at Historic Sites and Museums." *History News* 69, no. 2 (Spring 2014): Technical Leaflet #226.

Gallas, Kristin, and James DeWolf Perry, eds. *Interpreting Slavery at Museums and Historic Sites*. AASLH Interpreting History Series. Lanham, MD: Rowman & Littlefield Publishers, Inc., 2015.

———. "Comprehensive Content and Contested Historical Narratives." In *Interpreting Slavery at Museums and Historic Sites*, 1-20. AASLH Interpreting History Series. Lanham, MD: Rowman & Littlefield Publishers, Inc., 2015.

Gardner, James B. "Contested Terrain: History, Museums, and the Public." *The Public Historian* 26, no. 4 (Fall 2004): 11-21.

Gardner, James, and Peter S. LaPaglia, eds. *Public History: Essays from the Field*. Malabar, FL: Krieger Publishing Co., 2006.

Gardner, James B., and Elizabeth E. Merritt. *The AAM Guide to Collections Planning*. AAM Professional Education Series. Washington, DC: American Association of Museums, 2004.

———. "Collections Planning: Pinning Down a Strategy." *Museum News* 81, no. 4 (July-August 2002): 30-33, 60-66.

Garibay, Cecilia. "The (Unfulfilled) Promise of Evaluation." In *Change Is Required: Preparing for the Post-Pandemic Museum*, edited by Avi Y. Decter, Marsha L. Semmel, and Ken Yellis, 191-95. Lanham, MD: Rowman & Littlefield Publishers, Inc., 2022.

Geisler, Jill. *Work Happy: What Great Bosses Know*. New York: Center Street, Hatchette Book Group, 2012.

Genoways, Hugh H., and Lynne M. Ireland. *Museum Administration 2.0*, rev. by Cinnamon Catlin-Legutko. Lanham, MD: Rowman & Littlefield Publishers, Inc., 2017.

Gilborn, Craig. "Pop Pedagogy: Looking at the Coke Bottle." In *Material Culture Studies in America*, edited and compiled by Thomas J. Schlereth, 183-91. Lanham, MD: AltaMira Press, a Division of Rowman & Littlefield Publishers, Inc., 1999.

Gilreath, Heather. "Transforming Spaces and Shifting Paradigms: A New Interpretation for the Exchange Place Cook's Cabin." *Proceedings of the 2022 Conference and Annual Meeting, Tacoma, Washington*, edited by Carol Kennis Lopez, Vol. XLV, 46-62. Rochdale, MA: The Association for Living History, Farm and Agricultural Museums, 2023.

Glaser, Jane R., with Artemis A. Zenetour. *Museums: A Place to Work: Planning Museum Careers*. London and New York: Routledge, 1996.

Glines, Timothy, and David Grabitske. "Telling the Story: Better Interpretation at Small Historical Organizations." *History News* 58, no. 2 (Spring 2003): Technical Leaflet #222.

Goforth, Teresa. "The Truth, The Whole Truth, and Nothing but the Truth: Researching Historical Exhibits." In *Small Museum Toolkit 5: Interpretation: Education, Programs and Exhibits*, edited by Cinnamon Catlin-Legutko and Stacy Klingler, 49-70. Lanham, MD: AltaMira, a Division of Rowman & Littlefield Publishers, Inc., 2012.

Gokcigdem, Elif M. "Designing for Empathy." *Dimensions* 20, no. 5 (November/December 2018): 26-30.

Gokcigdem, Elif. M., edited by *Fostering Empathy through Museums*. Lanham, MD: Rowman & Littlefield Publishers, Inc., 2016.

Goleman, Daniel. *Working with Emotional Intelligence*. New York: Bantam Books, 1998.

———. *Emotional Intelligence: Why It Can Matter More than IQ*. New York: Bantam Books, 1995.

Goleman, Daniel, Richard Boyatzis, and Annie McKee. *Primal Leadership: The Power of Emotional Intelligence*. Boston, MA: Harvard Business School Publishing, 2002.

Gonzales, Elena. "Emotionally Captivating Anti-Racist History." *Exhibition* 39, no. 1 (Spring 2020): 14-15.

———. "Social Justice: Framework for the Future of Museums." In *Change Is Required: Preparing for the Post-Pandemic Museum*, edited by Avi Y. Decter, Marsha L. Semmel, and Ken Yellis, 217-21. Lanham, MD: Rowman & Littlefield Publishers, Inc., 2022.

———. *Exhibitions for Social Justice*. London and New York: Routledge, 2020.

———. "View from the Field: Equity-Oriented and Anti-Racist Curatorial Practice." *The Inclusive Historian's Handbook*, December 23, 2020, https://inclusivehistorian.com/view-from-the-field-equity-oriented-and-anti-racist-curatorial-practice/.

Goodwin, Doris Kearns. *Team of Rivals: The Political Genius of Abraham Lincoln*. New York: Simon and Schuster, 2005.

Graburn, Nelson. "The Museum and the Visitor Experience." Reprinted in *Museum Education Anthology 1973-83: Perspectives in Informal Learning a*

Decade of Roundtable Reports, edited by Susan K. Nichols, Mary Alexander, and Ken Yellis, 177-82. Washington, DC: Museum Education Roundtable, 1984.

Graft, Conny C. "Visitors Are Ready, Are We?" In *Interpreting Slavery at Museums and Historic Sites*, edited by Kristin Gallas and James DeWolf Perry, 1-20. AASLH Interpreting History Series. Lanham, MD: Rowman & Littlefield Publishers, Inc., 2015.

———. "Evaluation Is Not Just Nice, It Is Necessary." In *Reimagining Historic House Museums*, edited by Kenneth C. Turino and Max A. van Balgooy, 29-41. Lanham, MD: Rowman & Littlefield Publishers, Inc, 2019.

Graham, Stedman. "The Call for Identity Leaders." In *Identity Leadership*. New York: Center Street, Hatchette Book Group, 2019.

Grant, Adam, "Mining for Gold: Unearthing Collective Intelligence in Teams." In *Hidden Potential: The Science of Achieving Greater Things*, 177-98. New York: Viking, 2023.

Grim, Linnea. "So Deeply Dyed in Our Fabric That It Cannot Be Washed Out: Developing Institutional Support for the Interpretation of Slavery." In *Interpreting Slavery at Museums and Historic Sites*, edited by Kristin Gallas and James DeWolf Perry, 31-46. AASLH Interpreting History Series. Lanham, MD: Rowman & Littlefield Publishers, Inc., 2015.

Gross, Michael P., and Ron Zimmerman. "Park and Museum Interpretation: Helping Visitors Find Meaning." *Curator: The Museum Journal* 45, no. 4 (October 2002): 265-76.

Grove, Tim. "Truth or Consequences." *History News* 73, no. 2 (Spring 2018): 21-24.

Guarinello, Elena. "Changing the Narrative." *Museum* 102, no. 2 (March-April 2023): 24-29.

Haakanson, Sven. "Caretakers of Our Histories." In *Change Is Required: Preparing for the Post-Pandemic Museum*, edited by Avi Y. Decter, Marsha L. Semmel, and Ken Yellis, 111-15, 117-21. Lanham, MD: Rowman & Littlefield Publishers, Inc., 2022.

Hague, Stephen. "How to Plan and Implement Interpretation." *History News* 68, no. 2 (Spring 2013): Technical Leaflet #262.

Hague, Stephen, and Laura C. Keim. "Preparing an Outstanding Concert: How to Plan and Implement Interpretation." Chapter 1 in *Small Museum Toolkit 5: Interpretation: Education, Programs and Exhibits*, edited by Cinnamon Catlin-Legutko and Stacy Klingler, 1-25. Lanham, MD: AltaMira Press, a Division of Rowman & Littlefield Publishers, Inc., 2012.

Hahn, Joanne. "Finding Her Voice: The Evolution of Interpreting Catharine Coffin's Story." *History News* 78, no. 1 (2023): 20-25.

Ham, Sam H. *Interpretation: Making a Difference on Purpose*. Golden, CO: Fulcrum Publishing, 2013.

Hannan, Leonie, and Sarah Longair. *History Through Material Culture*. Manchester, England: Manchester University Press, 2017.

Harrington, Page. *Interpreting the Legacy of Women's Suffrage at Museums and Historic Sites*. AASLH Interpreting History Series. Lanham, MD: Rowman & Littlefield Publishers, Inc., 2021.

Harris, Donna Ann. *New Solutions for House Museums: Ensuring the Long-Term Preservation of America's Historic Houses*. Lanham, MD: Rowman & Littlefield Publishers, 2020.

———. "New Solutions for House Museums." *History News* 62, no. 4 (Autumn 2007): 12–16.

Harvey, Karen. *History and Material Culture: A Student's Guide to Approaching Alternative Sources*. London and New York: Routledge, 2009.

Hawkins, Bethany L. "What Does Your Historic House Museum Value? Conveying Your Site's Values to Visitors." *History News* 78, no. 2 (2023): 11–16.

Hawkins, Callie, and Erin Carlson Mast. "Do Something Transformative." In *Reimagining Historic House Museums*, edited by Kenneth C. Turino and Max A. van Balgooy, 149–60. Lanham, MD: Rowman & Littlefield Publishers, Inc, 2019.

Hindle, Brooke. "How Much Is a Piece of the True Cross Worth?" In *Material Culture and the Study of American Life*, edited by Ian M. G. Quimby, 5–20. New York: W.W. Norton & Co., Inc. for the Henry Francis duPont Winterthur Museum, 1978.

Hitz, Elizabeth. "The Continuing Effort (Perhaps Futile) to Bridge the Museum and the Academy." *Proceedings of the 1987 Annual Meeting, Ann Arbor and Dearborn, Michigan*, edited by Peter Cousins, Vol. X, 26, 71–76. The Association for Living History, Farm and Agricultural Museums. Washington, DC: Smithsonian Institution, 1989.

Holmes, Meghan Gelardi, Steven Lubar, Jessie MacLeod, William Stoutamire, and Carrie Villar. "Telling Inclusive Stories When Your Collections Are Stuck in the Past." *History News* 75, no. 3 (Summer 2020): Technical Leaflet #291.

Honeysett, Nik. "The Digital Awakening." *Museum* 99, no. 5 (November-December 2020): 32–35.

Howe, Barbara J., Dolores A. Fleming, Emory L. Kemp, and Ruth Ann Overbeck. *Houses and Homes: Exploring Their History*. The Nearby History Series, vol. 2. Nashville, TN: American Association for State and Local History, 1987.

Hughes, Catherine. *Museum Theatre: Communicating with Visitors through Drama*. Portsmouth, NH: Heinemann, a Division of Reed Elsevier, 1998.

Hume, Ivor Noël. *A Guide to Artifacts in Colonial America*. New York: Alfred A. Knopf, 1970.

———. "Material Culture with Dirt on It: A Virginia Perspective." In *Material Culture and the Study of American Life*, edited by Ian M. G. Quimby, 21–40. New York: W.W. Norton & Co., Inc. for the Henry Francis duPont Winterthur Museum, 1978.

Huyck, Heather. *Doing Women's History in Public: A Handbook for Interpretation at Museums and Historic Sites*. AASLH Interpreting History Series. Lanham, MD: Rowman & Littlefield Publishers, Inc., 2021.

Jean, Alison, and Swarupa Anila. "Whose Museum Is It Anyway? Toward More Authentic Community-Centered Practices in Creating Exhibitions." *Exhibition* 38, no. 1 (Spring 2019): 43-55.

Jeffries, Hasan Kwame. "Getting the History Right." *History News* 76, no. 4 (Autumn 2021): 7-10.

Jones, Dale. "Personal Connections and the Great Cosmic Soup." *History News* 63, no. 2 (Spring 2008): 16.

———. "Theater 101 for Historical Interpretation." *History News* 59, no. 3 (Summer 2004): Technical Leaflet #227

———. "Living History in the City." *History News* 50, no. 3 (Summer 1995): 10-13.

Jones, Matthew. "The Complete History of Social Media: A Timeline of the Invention of Social Networking." *History Cooperative*, June 16, 2015, accessed May 29, 2023, https://historycooperative.org/the-history-of-social-media/.

Jones, Trevor. "Telling Stories with Objects in the Starring Role." *History News* 69, no. 2 (Spring 2014): 23-26.

———. "Tier Your Collections: A Practical Tool for Making Clear Decisions in Collections Management." In *Active Collections*, edited by Elizabeth Wood, Rainey Tisdale, and Trevor Jones, 103-9. London and New York: Routledge, 2018.

Jones, Trevor, and Rainey Tisdale. "A Manifesto for Active History Museum Collections." In *Active Collections*, edited by Elizabeth Wood, Rainey Tisdale, and Trevor Jones, 7-10. London and New York: Routledge, 2018.

Jones-Rizzi, Joanne, and Stacey Mann. "Is That Hung White? A Conversation on the State of Museum Exhibitions and Race." *Museum* 99, no. 3 (Summer 2020): 26-31.

Kane, Katherine. "Using Historic House Museum Audiences to Drive Change." In *Reimagining Historic House Museums*, edited by Kenneth C. Turino and Max A. van Balgooy, 109-14. Lanham, MD: Rowman & Littlefield Publishers, Inc, 2019.

Katz-Hyman, Martha B. "Curatorial Basics 101." *Proceedings of the 2007 Conference and Annual Meeting, El Rancho de las Golondrinas, Santa Fe, New Mexico*, edited by Carol Kennis Lopez, Vol. XXX, 160-63. North Bloomfield, OH: The Association for Living History, Farm and Agricultural Museums, 2008.

———. "Furnishing for Diversity." *Proceedings of the 2022 Conference and Annual Meeting, Tacoma, Washington*, edited by Carol Kennis Lopez, Vol. XLV, 76-82. Rochdale, MA: The Association for Living History, Farm and Agricultural Museums, 2023.

———. "Furnishing Slave Quarters and Free Black Homes: Adding a Powerful Tool to Interpreting African American Life." In *Interpreting African American History and Culture at Museums and Historic Sites*, edited by Max van Balgooy, 105-14. AASLH Interpreting History Series. Lanham, MD: Rowman & Littlefield Publishers, Inc., 2015.

Kazal, Russell A. "Migration History in Five Stories (and a Basement): The Lower East Side Tenement Museum." *Journal of American Ethnic History* 34, no. 4 (Summer 2015): 77.

Keim, Laura C. "Why Do Furnishings Matter? The Power of Furnishings in Historic House Museums." In *Reimagining Historic House Museums*, edited by Kenneth C. Turino and Max A. van Balgooy, 207-16. Lanham, MD: Rowman & Littlefield Publishers, Inc, 2019.

Keogh, Carolyn. "Out of One Story, Many: Frameworks for Making Diverse and Contemporary Connections at Olana." *History News* 77, no. 3 (2022): 20-25.

Kertzner, Daniel. *Mastering Civic Engagement: A Challenge to Museums*. Washington, DC: American Association of Museums, 2002.

Kiihne, Robert. "Creating Minds-on Exhibitions in Historic House Museums." In *Reimagining Historic House Museums*, edited by Kenneth C. Turino and Max A. van Balgooy, 207-16. Lanham, MD: Rowman & Littlefield Publishers, Inc., 2019.

Kinsley, Rose, Margaret Middleton, and Porchia Moore. "(Re)Frame: The Case for New Language in the 21st-Century Museum." *Exhibition* 36, no. 1 (Spring 2016): 57-63.

Kipp, Angela. *Managing Previously Unmanaged Collections: A Practical Guide for Museums*. Lanham, MD: Rowman & Littlefield Publishers, Inc., 2016.

Klaus, Peggy. *The Hard Truth about Soft Skills*. New York: Collins Business, 2007.

Kley, Ron. "Terms of Endearment: Nomenclature—How Did It Begin; Where Is It Going?" *History News* 68, no. 4 (Autumn 2013): 24-27.

Klingler, Stacy, and Conny Graft. "In Lieu of Mind Reading: Visitor Studies and Evaluation." In *Small Museum Toolkit 4: Reaching and Responding to the Audience*, edited by Cinnamon Catlin-Legutko and Stacy Klingler, 37-74. Lanham, MD: AltaMira Press, a Division of Rowman & Littlefield Publishers, Inc., 2012.

Kodek, Amanda, and Wendy Luke. "Mentoring Matters: A Call for Backup." *Museum* 87, no. 2 (March/April 2008): 62-69.

Koslow, Jennifer Lisa. *Public History: An Introduction from Theory to Application*. Hoboken, NJ: John Wiley & Sons, Inc., 2021.

Kouwenhoven, John A. "American Studies: Words or Things?" In *Material Culture Studies in America*, compiled and edited by Thomas J. Schlereth, 79-92. Lanham, MD: AltaMira Press, a Division of Rowman & Littlefield Publishers, Inc., 1999.

Kriebel, Rick, and Tom Reitz. "Uncovering Best Practice in Archaeological Collections, Part 2: Archaeology and NAGPRA." *Proceedings of the 2021 Virtual Conference and Annual Meeting*, edited by Donna R. Braden, Vol. XLIV, 203-7. Rochdale, MA: The Association for Living History, Farm and Agricultural Museums, 2022.

Kyvig, David E., and Myron A. Marty. *Nearby History: Exploring the Past Around You*. Lanham, MD: AltaMira Press, a Division of Rowman & Littlefield Publishers, Inc., 2010.

Labode, Madupe, Will Walker, and Robert Weible, eds. "The Whole is Greater: Building the Inclusive Historian's Handbook." *History News* 74, no. 3 (Summer 2019): 4-7.

Langer, Adina, edited by *Storytelling in Museums*. Lanham, MD: Rowman & Littlefield Publishers, Inc., 2022.
Latham, Kiersten F., and Brenda Cowan, eds. *Flourishing in Museums: Toward a Positive Museology*. London and New York: Routledge, 2024.
Lavad, Maren, and Aleah Vinick. "Creating Intergenerational Oral History Opportunities." *History News* 67, no. 3 (Summer 2012): Technical Leaflet #259.
Leftridge, Alan. *Interpretive Writing*. Fort Collins, CO: The National Association for Interpretation, 2006.
Levy, Barbara Abramoff. "Historic House Tours That Succeed: Choosing the Best Tour Approach." In *Interpreting Historic House Museums*, edited by Jessica Foy Donnelly, 192-209. Walnut Creek, CA: AltaMira Press, a Division of Rowman & Littlefield Publishers, Inc., 2002.
Levy, Barbara Abramoff, Sandra McKenzie Lloyd, and Susan Porter Schreiber. *Great Tours! Thematic Tours and Guide Training for Historic Sites*. Walnut Creek, CA: AltaMira Press, a Division of Rowman & Littlefield Publishers, Inc., 2001.
Lewis, Steve. "Authenticity vs. Practicality." *Proceedings of the 1982 Annual Meeting, King's Landing, New Brunswick, Canada*, edited by Wayne Randolph, Vol. 6, 65-66. The Association for Living Historical Farms and Agricultural Museums. Washington, DC: Smithsonian, 1983.
Lewis, William J. *Interpreting for Park Visitors*. Fort Washington, PA: Eastern National Park and Monument Association, 1981.
Lloyd, Kathryn. "From Neighborhood to Nation: The *Under One Roof* Exhibition at The Tenement Museum." *Exhibition* 38, no. 2 (Fall 2019): 71-81.
Lloyd, Sandra Mackenzie. "Creating Memorable Visits: How to Develop and Implement Theme-Based Tours." In *Interpreting Historic House Museums*, edited by Jessica Foy Donnelly, 210-30. Walnut Creek, CA: AltaMira Press, a Division of Rowman & Littlefield Publishers, Inc., 2002.
Lonetree, Amy. *Decolonizing Museums: Representing Native America in National and Tribal Museums*. Chapel Hill: University of North Carolina Press, 2012.
———. "Museums as Sites of Decolonization: Truth Telling in National and Tribal Museums." In *Contesting Knowledge: Museums and Indigenous Perspectives*, edited by Susan Sleeper-Smith, 334. Lincoln: University of Nebraska Press, 2009.
Lubar, Steven, and Kathleen Kendrick. "Artifact and Analysis: Essays," accessed May 29, 2023, https://smithsonianeducation.org/idealabs/ap/essays/looking.htm#:~:text=We%20suggest%20five%20ways%20to%20think%20about%20artifacts,4%20Artifacts%20capture%20moments.%205%20Artifacts%20reflect%20changes.
Lubar, Steven, and W. David Kingery. *History from Things: Essays on Material Culture*. Washington, DC: Smithsonian Institution Press, 1993.
Luke, Wendy. "Do I Really Need a Cover Letter? (Yes, You Do)." In *A Life in Museums: Managing Your Museum Career*, edited by Greg Stevens and Wendy Luke, 55-57. Washington DC: The AAM Press, 2012.

Lyon, Cherstin M., Elizabeth M. Nix, and Rebecca K. Shrum. *Introduction to Public History: Interpreting the Past, Engaging Audiences*. Lanham, MD: Rowman & Littlefield Publishers, Inc., 2017.

MacArthur, Matthew. "Get Real! The Role of Objects in the Digital Age." In *Letting Go? Sharing Historical Authority in a User-Generated World*, edited by Bill Adair, Benjamin Filene, and Laura Koloski, 56–67. Philadelphia, PA: The Pew Center for Arts & Heritage, 2011.

Mah, Donna M. "Threads in the Fabric of Legacy: The Stories in the Exhibit, 'Chinese Medicine in America: Converging Ideas, People, and Practices.'" In *Storytelling in Museums*, edited by Adina Langer, 191–203. Lanham, MD: Rowman & Littlefield Publishers, Inc., 2022.

Malaro, Marie C., and Ildiko Pogány DeAngelis. *A Legal Primer on Managing Museum Collections*, 3rd ed. Washington, DC: Smithsonian Books, 2012.

Maloney, Beth, Kate Egner Gruber, Rahul Gupta, and Evelyn Orantes. "The Whole Is Greater: Democratizing Curation with TENACITY." *History News* 75, no. 4 (Autumn 2020): 6–7.

"Managing Creativity in the Exhibit Development Process" (entire issue). *NAME Exhibitionist* 18, no. 1 (Spring 1999).

Marling, Karal Ann. *As Seen on TV: The Visual Culture of Everyday Life in the 1950s*. Cambridge: Harvard University Press, 1994.

Martell, Christopher C., and Kaylene M. Stevens. *Teaching History for Justice: Centering Activism in Students' Study of the Past*. New York: Teachers College Press, 2021.

Martin, Ann Smart, and J. Ritchie Garrison, eds. *American Material Culture: The Shape of the Field*. Knoxville: University of Tennessee Press for the Henry Francis duPont Winterthur Museum, 1997.

"MASS Action [Museum as Site for Social Action] Toolkit," 2017, https://static1.squarespace.com/static/58fa685dff7c50f78be5f2b2/t/59dcdd27e5dd5b5a1b51d9d8/1507646780650/TOOLKIT_10_2017.pdf.

Matelic, Candace Tangorra. "New Roles for Small Museums." In *Small Museum Toolkit 4: Reaching and Responding to the Audience*, edited by Cinnamon Catlin-Legutko and Stacy Klingler, 141–62. Lanham, MD: AltaMira Press, a Division of Rowman and Littlefield Publishers, Inc., 2012.

Mautz, Scott. *Leading from the Middle: A Playbook for Managers to Influence Up, Down, and Across the Organization*. Hoboken, NJ: John Wiley & Sons, Inc., 2021.

Maxwell, John C. *The Ultimate Guide to Developing Leaders: Invest in People Like Your Future Depends on It*. Nashville, TN: HarperCollins Leadership, 2023.

———. *The 360° Leader: Developing Your Influence Anywhere in the Organization*. Nashville, TN: HarperCollins Leadership, 2011.

Mayer, Thompson. "Why Old Places Matter." *History News* 71, no. 3 (Summer 2016): 19–23.

McConaghy, Lorraine, and Judy Bentley. "Charles Mitchell Case Study: Researching and Presenting the Marginalized." *Proceedings of the 2022 Conference and Annual Meeting, Tacoma, Washington*, edited by Carol Kennis

Lopez, Vol. XLV, 35–40. Rochdale, MA: The Association for Living History, Farm and Agricultural Museums, 2023.
McKenna-Cress, Polly, and Janet A. Kamien. *Creating Exhibitions: Collaboration in the Planning, Development and Design of Innovative Experiences.* Hoboken, NJ: John Wiley & Sons, Inc., 2013.
McLean, Kathleen. "Museum Exhibitions and the Dynamics of Dialogue," 1999. Reprinted in *Reinventing the Museum: Historical and Contemporary Perspectives on the Paradigm Shift*, edited by Gail Anderson, 193–211. Lanham, MD: AltaMira Press, a Division of Rowman & Littlefield Publishers, Inc., 2004.
———. *Planning for People in Museum Exhibitions.* Washington, DC: Association of Science-Technology Centers, 1993, reprinted 1996.
Meister, Nicolette B., and Jackie Hoff. "Collections Planning: Best Practices in Collections Stewardship." In *Small Museum Toolkit 6: Stewardship Collections and History Preservation*, edited by Cinnamon Catlin-Legutko and Stacy Klingler, 110–32. Lanham, MD: AltaMira, a Division of Rowman & Littlefield Publishers, Inc., 2012.
Middleton, Margaret. "Queer Museum Narratives and the Family Audience." In *Storytelling in Museums*, edited by Adina Langer, 163–75. Lanham, MD: Rowman & Littlefield Publishers, Inc., 2022.
Miller, Steven, edited by *Museum Collecting Lessons: Acquisition Stories from the Inside.* London and New York: Routledge, 2022.
Miller, Steven. *Museum Collection Ethics.* Lanham, MD: Rowman & Littlefield Publishers, Inc., 2020.
Momaya, Masum. "Ten Principles for an Anti-Racist, Anti-Orientalist, Activist Approach to Collections." In *Active Collections*, edited by Elizabeth Wood, Rainey Tisdale, and Trevor Jones, 13–20. London and New York: Routledge, 2018.
Mooney-Melvin, Patricia. "Professional Historians and the Challenge of Redefinition." In *Public History: Essays from the Field*, edited by James Gardner and Peter S. LaPaglia, 26. Malabar, FL: Krieger Publishing Co., 2006.
Moore, Nicole. "Perceptions of Race and Identity and Their Impact on Slavery's Interpretation." In *Interpreting Slavery at Museums and Historic Sites*, edited by Kristin Gallas and James DeWolf Perry, 101–17. AASLH Interpreting History Series. Lanham, MD: Rowman & Littlefield Publishers, Inc., 2015.
Moore, Porchia, Rosa Paquet, and Aletheia Wittman. *Transforming Inclusion in Museums: The Power of Collaborative Inquiry.* Lanham, MD: Rowman & Littlefield Publishers, Inc., 2022.
Morris, Martha. *Managing People and Projects in Museums: Strategies that Work.* Lanham, MD: Rowman & Littlefield Publishers, Inc., 2017.
Morris, Tee, and Pip Ballantine. *Social Media for Writers: Marketing Strategies for Building Your Audience and Selling Books.* Cincinnati, OH: Writer's Digest Books, 2015.
Moua, Mai. *Culturally Intelligent Leadership: Leading Through Intercultural Interactions.* New York: Business Expert Press, LLC, 2010.

Muchinski, Paul M. "Organizations and Organizational Change." In *Psychology Applied to Work*, 9th ed., 248-84. Summerfield, NC: Hypergraphic Press, Inc., 2009.

Mulready, Cyrus. *Object Studies: Introductions to Material Culture*. Cham, Switzerland: Palgrave MacMillan, 2023.

Murawski, Mike. "A Better Future for Museums." *Museum* 100, no. 6 (November/December 2021): 16-19.

———. *Museums as Agents of Change: A Guide to Becoming a Changemaker*. Lanham, MD: Rowman & Littlefield Publishers, Inc., 2021.

Nilsen Adam P., and Miriam Bader. "The Psychology of Empathy: Compelling Possibilities for Museums." In *Fostering Empathy Through Museums*, edited by Elif M. Gokigdem, 115-29. Lanham, MD: Rowman & Littlefield Publishers, Inc., 2016.

Nosek, Elizabeth. *Interpretative Master Planning: A Framework for Historical Sites*. Lanham, MD: Rowman & Littlefield Publishers, Inc., 2021.

Owen, Jo. *The Leadership Skills Handbook: 100 Essential Skills You Need to Be a Leader*, 5th ed. New York: Kogan Page Ltd., 2021.

Owen, Robin White. "The Virtuous Circle: From Local to Global and Back Again." In *Change Is Required: Preparing for the Post-Pandemic Museum*, edited by Avi Y. Decter, Marsha L. Semmel, and Ken Yellis, 37-41. Lanham, MD: Rowman & Littlefield Publishers, Inc., 2022.

Packer, Jan. "Beyond Learning: Exploring Visitors' Perceptions of Museum Experiences." *Curator* 51, no.1 (January 2008): 33-54.

Paris, Scott, and Melissa J. Mercer. "Finding Self in Objects: Identity, Exploration in Museums." In *Learning Conversations in Museums*, edited by Gaea Leinhardt, Kevin Crowley, and Karen Knutson, 401-23. London and New York: Routledge, 2002.

Patterson, Kerry, Joseph Grenny, Ron McMillan, and Al Switzler. *Crucial Confrontations*. New York: McGraw-Hill, 2005.

Pekarik, Andrew A., Zahava D. Doering, and David A. Karns. "Exploring Satisfying Experiences in Museums." *Curator* 42, no. 2 (April 1999): 152-73.

———. "Strangers, Guests, or Clients? Visitor Experiences in Museums." *Curator: The Museum Journal* 42, no. 2 (April 1999): 74-87.

Peña, Elizabeth. "Leadership at All Levels." In *A Life in Museums*, edited by Greg Stevens and Wendy Luke, 144-46. Washington, DC: The AAM Press, 2012.

Phillips, Colette A. M. *The Includers: The Seven Traits of Culturally Savvy, Anti-Racist Leaders*. Dallas, TX: BenBella Books, Inc., 2024.

Piatt, Margaret. "Engaging Visitors Through Effective Communication." In *Interpreting Historic House Museums*, edited by Jessica Foy Donnelly, 231-50. Walnut Creek, CA: AltaMira Press, a Division of Rowman & Littlefield Publishers, Inc., 2002.

Pickering, Nicola. "The Museum Curator's Guide: The Value of Research in Museums," *Lund Humphries*, August 14, 2020 (blog). https://www.lundhumphries.com/blogs/features/the-museum-curator-s-guide-the-value-of-research-in-museums-by-nicola-pickering.

———. *The Museum Curator's Guide: Understanding, Managing and Presenting Objects*. London, UK: Lund Humphries, 2020.
Pine, E. Joseph II, and James H. Gilmore. *The Experience Economy: Work Is Theatre and Every Business a Stage*. Boston, MA: Harvard Business School Press, 1999.
Potvin, Ron M. "Chasing the White Whale? Flexible Use of Museum Collections." *History News* 69, no. 4 (Autumn 2014): 11-16.
———. "Finding Numen at Historic Sites." In *Reimagining Historic House Museums*, edited by Kenneth C. Turino and Max A. van Balgooy, 125-33. Lanham, MD: Rowman & Littlefield Publishers, Inc, 2019.
Prajapati, Sheetal. "Managing from the Middle." In *A Life in Museums*, edited by Greg Stevens and Wendy Luke, 137-41. Washington, DC: The AAM Press, 2012.
Presnell, Jenny L. *The Information-Literate Historian: A Guide to Research for History Students*, 3rd ed. New York: Oxford University Press, 2019.
Pressman, Heather, and Danielle Schulz. *The Art of Access: A Practical Guide for Museum Accessibility*. Lanham, MD: Rowman & Littlefield Publishers, Inc., 2021.
"Prisons Today: Questions in the Age of Mass Incarceration." *Exhibition*, 36, no. 2 (Fall 2017): 92-98.
Prown, Jules David. "Mind in Matter: An Introduction to Material Culture Theory and Method." *Winterthur Portfolio* 17, no. 1 (Spring 1982): 1-19.
Pustz, Jennifer. "Listening for the Silences: Stories of Enslaved and Free Domestic Workers." In *Reimagining Historic House Museums*, edited by Kenneth C. Turino and Max A. van Balgooy, 161-70. Lanham, MD: Rowman & Littlefield Publishers, Inc., 2019.
Quimby, Ian M. G., ed. *Material Culture and the Study of American Life*. New York: W.W. Norton & Co., Inc. for the Henry Francis duPont Winterthur Museum, 1978.
Radcliffe, Jane, and Ron Kley. "Diving Into 'Stuff': Transforming an Accumulation into a Collection." *Proceedings of the 2016 Conference and Annual Meeting*, edited by Debra A. Reid, Vol. XXIX, 97-104. Ashway, RI: The Association for Living History, Farm and Agricultural Museums, 2017.
Rand, Judy. "Less Is More. And More Is Less." *Exhibition* 36, no. 1 (Spring 2016): 36-41.
———. "The 227-Mile Museum, or Why We Need a Visitors' Bill of Rights." *Visitor Studies: Theory, Research and Practice* 9 (1996): 8-26. Reprinted in part in *Reinventing the Museum: Historical and Contemporary Perspectives on the Paradigm Shift*, edited by Gail Anderson, 158-59. Lanham, MD: AltaMira Press, a Division of Rowman & Littlefield Publishers, Inc., 2004.
———. "Write and Design with the Family in Mind." In *Connecting Kids to History with Museum Exhibitions*, edited by D. Lynn McRainey and John Russick, 257-84. Walnut Creek, CA: Left Coast Press, Inc., 2010.
Rand, Judy, Ann Grimes, Robert Kiihne, and Sarah Watkins. "Families First! Rethinking Exhibits to Engage All Ages." *History News* 64, no. 1 (Winter 2009): Technical Leaflet #245.

Rath Tom, and Barry Conchie. *Strengths-Based Leadership: Great Leaders, Teams, and Why People Follow*. New York: Gallup Press, 2008.

Redmond-Jones, Beth, ed. *Welcoming Museum Visitors with Unapparent Disabilities*. Lanham, MD: Rowman & Littlefield Publishers, Inc., 2024.

Reece, Dwandalynn R., ed. *Musical Crossroads: Stories Behind the Objects of African American Music*. Washington, DC: Smithsonian Institution, National Museum of African American History and Culture, 2023.

Reeve, Johnmarshall. "Psychological Needs." In *Understanding Motivation and Emotion*, 4th ed., 101–29. Hoboken, NJ: John Wiley & Sons, Inc., 2005.

Reid, Debra A. "Making Gender Matter: Interpreting Male and Female Roles in Historic House Museums." In *Interpreting Historic House Museums*, edited by Jessica Foy Donnelly, 81–110. Walnut Creek, CA: AltaMira Press, a Division of Rowman & Littlefield Publishers, Inc., 2002.

"Repatriation, Restitution, and Reparations." *Museum* 102, no. 1 (January/February 2023): 31–33.

Richardson, Heather Cox. "The New Social History: Finding the Time for Social Media and Blogging." *The American Historian*, no. 1 (August 2014): 10–11.

Ritchie, Donald A. *Doing Oral History: A Practical Guide*, 3rd ed. New York: Oxford University Press, 2015.

Rizzo, Mary. "Good Intentions Are Not Enough: Lessons for Inclusive Public History." *History News* 72, no. 2 (Spring 2017): 12–16.

Rogers, Ashley. "Plantations." In *The Inclusive Historian's Handbook*, May 20, 2019, https://inclusivehistorian.com/?s=Plan.

Rose, Julia. *Interpreting Difficult History at Museums and Historic Sites*. AASLH Interpreting History Series. Lanham, MD: Rowman & Littlefield Publishers, Inc., 2016.

———. "Interpreting Difficult Knowledge." *History News* 66, no. 3 (Summer 2011): Technical Leaflet #255.

Rosenberg, Francesca. "Adapting the Tour Planning Template for Adults with Alzheimer's Disease and Other Dementias." In Vatsky, *Interactive Museum Tours: A Guide to In-Person and Virtual Experiences*, 175–83. Lanham, MD: Rowman & Littlefield Publishers, Inc., 2023.

Rosenzweig, Roy, and David Thelen. *The Presence of the Past: Popular Uses of History in American Life*. New York: Columbia University Press, 1998.

Roth, Darlene. "Seven Reasons the Past Never Dies." *History News* 68, no. 3 (Summer 2013): 14–18.

Roth, Stacy F. *Past into Present: Effective Techniques for First-Person Historical Interpretation*. Chapel Hill: The University of North Carolina Press, 1998.

Russell, Nan S. In *The Titleless Leader: How to Get Things Done When You're Not in Charge*. Pompton Plains, NJ: The Career Press, Inc., 2012.

Sanborn, Mark. *You Don't Need a Title to Be a Leader*. New York: Currency Doubleday, 2006.

Schlatter, N. Elizabeth. "A New Spin: Are DJs, Rappers and Bloggers 'Curators'?" *Museum* 89, no. 1 (January/February 2010): 49–55.

Schlereth, Thomas J., compiler and editor. *Material Culture Studies in America*. Lanham, MD: AltaMira Press, a Division of Rowman & Littlefield Publishers, Inc., 1999.

Schrag, Zachary M. *The Princeton Guide to Historical Research*. Princeton, NJ: Princeton University Press, 2021.

Schrage, Michael. "Collaboration and Creativity." *Museum News* 83, no. 2 (March/April 2004): 44-48.

Schwartz, Deborah F. "Are We Serious about Changing the Equation?" In *Change Is Required: Preparing for the Post-Pandemic Museum*, edited by Avi Y. Decter, Marsha Semmel, and Ken Yellis, 223-228. Lanham, MD: Rowman & Littlefield Publishers, Inc., 2022.

Screven, Chandler G. "Motivating Visitors to Read Labels." In *Text in the Exhibition Medium*, edited by Andrée Blais, 97-132. Quebec City: La Société des Musées Québécois and Musée de la Civilisation, 1994.

Seale, William. *Recreating the Historic House Interior*. Nashville, TN: American Association for State and Local History, 1979.

Semmel, Marsha. "The Value of 21st Century Skills." In *A Life in Museums*, edited by Greg Stevens and Wendy Luke, 97-100. Washington, DC: The AAM Press, 2012.

Serrell, Beverly. *Exhibit Labels: An Interpretive Approach*, 2nd ed. Lanham, MD: Rowman & Littlefield Publishers, Inc., 2015.

Serrell, Beverly, and Katherine Whitney. *Exhibit Labels: An Interpretive Approach*, 3rd ed. Lanham, MD: Rowman & Littlefield Publishers, Inc., 2024.

Shannon, Jennifer. "The Construction of Native Voice at the National Museum of the American Indian." In *Contesting Knowledge: Museums and Indigenous Perspectives*, edited by Susan Sleeper-Smith, 218-47. Lincoln: University of Nebraska Press, 2009.

Shapiro, Mary. *The HBR Guide to Leading Teams*. Boston, MA: HBR Press, 2015.

Shellman, Cecile. *Effective Diversity, Equity, Accessibility, Inclusion, and Anti-Racism Practices for Museums, from the Inside Out*. Lanham, MD: Rowman & Littlefield Publishers, Inc., 2022.

Shrum, Rebecca. "Material Culture." *The Inclusive Historian's Handbook*, June 3, 2019, https://inclusivehistorian.com/?s=material+culture.

———. "Selling Mr. Coffee: Design, Gender, and the Branding of a Kitchen Appliance." *Winterthur Portfolio: A Journal of American Material Culture* 46, no. 4 (Winter 2012): 271-98.

Silverman, Lois. "Making Meaning Together." *Journal of Museum Education* 18, no. 3 (Fall 1993): 7-11.

———. "Visitor Meaning-Making in Museums for a New Age." *Curator* 38, no. 3 (1995): 161-70.

Simmons, John E. "Managing Things: Crafting a Collections Policy." *Museum News* 83, no. 1 (January/February 2004): 29-31, 47-48.

———. *Things Great and Small: Collections Management Policies*. Lanham, MD: Rowman & Littlefield Publishers, Inc., 2018.

Simmons, John, and Toni Kiser, eds. *Museum Registration Methods*. American Alliance of Museums, 6th ed. Lanham, MD: Rowman & Littlefield Publishers, Inc., 2020.
Simon, Nina. *The Participatory Museum*. Santa Cruz, CA: Museum 2.0, 2010.
Sims, Dr. Gaila, and Theresa Cramer. "A Monumental Responsibility: Exhibiting and Interpreting the Auction Block in Fredericksburg, Virginia." *Exhibition* 42, no. 2 (Fall 2023): 56–65.
Skramstad, Harold, and Susan Skramstad. "Mission and Vision Again? What's the Big Deal?" In *Small Museum Toolkit 1: Leadership, Mission, and Governance*, edited by Cinnamon Catlin-Legutko and Stacy Klingler, 60–76. Lanham, MD: AltaMira Press, a Division of Rowman & Littlefield Publishers, Inc., 2012.
Sleeper-Smith, Susan, edited by *Contesting Knowledge: Museums and Indigenous Perspectives*. Lincoln: University of Nebraska Press, 2009.
Smith, Clint. *How the Word Is Passed: A Reckoning with the History of Slavery across America*. New York: Little, Brown and Company, 2021.
Smith, Laura Donnelly. "Dropping Off: The Blessings and Curses of Doorstop Donations." *Museum* 90, no. 3 (May/June 2011): 48–53.
Sorin, Gretchen Sullivan. *Driving While Black: African American Travel and the Road to Civil Rights*. New York: Liveright Publishing Co., a Division of W.W. Norton & Co., 2020.
———. "Exhibitions." *The Inclusive Historian's Handbook*, December 20, 2021, https://inclusivehistorian.com/?s=exhibitions.
———. "Why Museums Need to Continue the Discussion about Race in America." *History News* 55, no. 4 (Autumn 2000): 7–11.
Spock, Daniel. "Museum Authority Up for Grabs: The Latest Thing, or Following a Long Trend Line?" *NAME Exhibitionist* 28, no. 2 (Fall 2009): 6–10.
———. "A Practical Guide to Personal Connectivity." *History News* 63, no. 4 (Autumn 2008): 11–17.
Stein, Jill, Marianna Adams, and Jessica Luke. "Thinking Evaluatively: A Practical Guide to Integrating the Visitor Voice." *History News* 62, no. 2 (Spring 2007): Technical Leaflet #238.
Steinhauer, Jason. *History Disrupted*. New York: Palgrave Macmillan, 2022.
Stevens, Greg, and Wendy Luke, eds. *A Life in Museums: Managing Your Museum Career*. Washington, DC: The AAM Press, 2012.
Stone, Vickie. "Question the Database!" In *Active Collections*, edited by Elizabeth Wood, Rainey Tisdale, and Trevor Jones, 117–19. London and New York: Routledge, 2018.
Sugawara, Bethany Watkins. "But They're Not Real! Rethinking the Use of Props in Historic House Museum Displays." *History News* 58, no. 4 (August 2003): 20–23.
Summers, John. *Creating Exhibits That Engage: A Manual for Museums and Historical Organizations*. Lanham, MD: Rowman & Littlefield Publishers, Inc., 2018.
Taylor, Mary Jane, and Beth A. Twiss Houting. "Is It Real? Kids and Collections." In *Connecting Kids to History with Museum Exhibitions*, edited by D.

Lynn McRainey and John Russick, 241-56. Walnut Creek, CA: Left Coast Press, Inc., 2010.

Taylor, Sam, and Beverly Serrell, ed. *Try It! Improving Exhibits Through Formative Evaluation.* Washington, DC: Association of Science-Technology Centers, 1992.

The National Summit on Teaching Slavery. "Engaging Descendant Communities in the Interpretation of Slavery at Museums and Historic Sites." *History News* 74, no. 1 (Winter 2019): 14-21.

———. "Engaging Descendant Communities in the Interpretation of Slavery: A Rubric of Best Practices." *History News* 74, no. 1 (Winter 2019): Technical Leaflet #285.

"The Partisan Divide." *Museum* 102, no. 1 (January/February 2023): 24-29.

Tilden, Freeman. *Interpreting Our Heritage*, 4th ed. expanded and updated. Chapel Hill: The University of North Carolina Press, 1967.

Tisdale, Rainey. "Do History Museums Still Need Objects?" *History News* 66, no. 3 (Summer 2011): 19-24.

———. "Objects or People?" In *Active Collections*, edited by Elizabeth Wood, Rainey Tisdale, and Trevor Jones, 21-33. London and New York: Routledge, 2018.

"Trendswatch: Digital Awakening." *Museum* 100, no. 2 (March-April 2021): 28-32.

Turino, Kenneth C. "Historic House Museums." In *The Inclusive Historian's Handbook*, April 12, 2019. https://inclusivehistorian.com/?s=historic+house +museums.

Turino, Kenneth C., and Max A. van Balgooy, eds. *Reimagining Historic House Museums: New Approaches and Proven Solutions.* Lanham, MD: Rowman & Littlefield Publishers, Inc, 2019.

Turino, Kenneth, and Susan Ferentinos. "Entering the Mainstream, Interpreting GLBT History." *History News* 67, no. 4 (Autumn 2012): 21-25.

"Twenty Questions to Ask an Object." Created in 2014 by the Material Culture Caucus of the American Studies Association, https://view.officeapps.live .com/op/view.aspx?src=https%3A%2F%2Fnetworks.h-net.org%2Fsystem %2Ffiles%2Fcontributed-files%2Fmcc-asa-20-questions-handout-2014 .docx&wdOrigin=BROWSELINK.

"20 Years and Counting: James Pepper Henry's Multifaceted View of NAGPRA." *Museum* 89, no. 6 (November/December 2010): 50-56.

Ulrich, Laurel Thatcher. *A Midwife's Tale: The Life of Martha Ballard, Based on Her Diary, 1785-1812.* New York: Alfred A. Knopf, 1990.

Vagnone, Franklin D., and Deborah E. Ryan. *Anarchist's Guide to Historic House Museums: A Ground-Breaking Manifesto.* London and New York: Routledge, 2015.

van Balgooy, Max A., ed. *Interpreting African American History and Culture at Museums and Historic Sites.* AASLH Interpreting History Series. Lanham, MD: Rowman & Littlefield Publishing Co., 2015.

van Balgooy, Max A. "Turning Points: Ordinary People, Extraordinary Change." *History News* 68, no. 2 (Spring 2013): 7–13.

Van Damme, Marieke, and Dan Yaeger. "How to Make a Podcast." *History News* 71, no. 4 (Autumn 2016): Technical Leaflet #276.

Van Slyke, Erik J. *Listening to Conflict: Constructive Solutions to Workplace Disputes.* New York: American Management Association, 1999.

Vatsky, Sharon. *Interactive Museum Tours: A Guide to In-Person and Virtual Experiences.* Lanham, MD: Rowman & Littlefield Publishers, Inc., 2023.

Vaughan, James M. "Rethinking the Rembrandt Rule." *Museum* 87, no. 2 (March/April 2008): 33–35.

Vogt, Jay D. "The Kykuit II Summit: The Sustainability of Historic Sites." *History News* 62, no. 4 (Autumn 2007): 17–21.

Walden, Barbara B. "Like a Good Neighbor: Community Advocacy for Small Museums." In *Small Museum Toolkit 4: Reaching and Responding to the Audience*, edited by Cinnamon Catlin-Legutko and Stacy Klingler, 79–97. Lanham, MD: AltaMira Press, a Division of Rowman and Littlefield Publishers, Inc., 2012.

Walhimer, Mark. *Museums 101.* Lanham, MD: Rowman & Littlefield Publishers, Inc., 2015.

Wallace, Margot. *Writing for Museums*, 1st ed. Lanham, MD: Rowman & Littlefield Publishers, Inc., 2014.

———. *Writing for Museums: Communicating and Connecting with All Your Audiences*, 2nd ed. Lanham, MD: Rowman & Littlefield Publishers, Inc., 2022.

Washburn, Wilcomb E. "Manuscripts and Manufacts." *The American Archivist* 27, no. 2 (April 1964): 245–50.

Wei, William. *Becoming Colorado: The Centennial State in 100 Objects.* Denver and Louisville: History Colorado and University Press of Colorado, 2021.

Wilkening, Susie. "Difficult Issues in History Museums: Finding Community, Engaging Audiences." Finding Community: Engaging Diverse Audiences in a Historic House, December 9, 2013 (blog). https://findingcommunityengagingaudiences.blogspot.com/2013/12/difficult-issues-in-history-museums.html.

Wilkening, Susie, and Erica Donnis. "Authenticity? It Means Everything." *History News* 63, no. 4 (Autumn 2008): 18–23.

Wilkening Consulting. "Audiences and Inclusion Primer." February 2, 2021, accessed April 24, 2023, https://www.aam-us.org/2021/02/09/audiences-and-inclusion-primer/.

———. "Beware! The False Consensus Effect: An Annual Survey of Museum-Goers Data Story," 2022, accessed November 1, 2023, https://www.wilkeningconsulting.com/uploads/8/6/3/2/86329422/false_consensus_data_story_-_2022_asmg.pdf.

Wood, Elizabeth, and Kiersten F. Latham. *The Objects of Experience: Transforming Visitor-Object Encounters in Museums.* Walnut Creek, CA: Left Coast Press, Inc., 2016.

Wood, Elizabeth, Rainey Tisdale, and Trevor Jones, eds. *Active Collections*. London and New York: Routledge, 2018.
Woodcock, Mick. "Physical Control for Collections: Keeping It on the Table after Bringing It All to the Table." *Proceedings of the 2013 Conference and Annual Meeting, Hale Farm & Village, Akron, Ohio*, edited by Debra A. Reid, Vol. XXXVI. North Bloomfield, OH: The Association for Living History, Farm and Agricultural Museums, 2014.
Woodcox, Geoff. "Curation as an Act of Healing with Native American Communities." *History News* 78, no. 3 (2024): 28-32.
Yerkovich, Sally. *A Practical Guide to Museum Ethics*. Lanham, MD: Rowman & Littlefield Publishers, Inc., 2016.
Young, David W. "Expanding Interpretation at Historic Sites: When Change Brings Conflict." In *Interpreting African American History and Culture at Museums and Historic Sites*, edited by Max van Balgooy, 37-44. AASLH Interpreting History Series. Lanham, MD: Rowman & Littlefield Publishers, Inc., 2015.

Index

accessibility, 12, 13; in historic house museums, 144-45; offerings for audiences with special needs, 147-48, 171-74, *172*. *See also* DEAI perspectives
accession records. *See* cataloging
acquisitions, 3, 4, 41, 45, 47, 55-58, 60, 61, 63
Acquisitions Committee. *See* Collections/Acquisitions Committee
African Americans, enslaved: historical research for, 85-86, *86*; in exhibitions, 120-21, *121*; in historic house museums, 131-33, 135, 141, 151-53, 234n35; related objects, 25, 33, 35-36, *36*
African Americans, history of: historical research for, 85-86, *86*, 88; in exhibitions, 119-*21*, *121*; in historic house museums, 26, *150*, 150-52, 153, 234n35; related collections, 45-46, 55; related objects, 25, 33, 35-36, *36*. *See also* African Americans, enslaved
American Museum of Natural History (New York City), *10*
artifacts. *See* material culture; objects
artificial intelligence (AI), 59, 82
audiences. *See* museum audiences
audio tours. *See* tours, audio tours
authenticity, 2, 8, 12, 170, 174; in exhibitions, 97; in historical research, 67, 71; in historic house museums, 131, 134, 137, 153

Big Idea. *See* exhibitions; interpretation
Boston Children's Museum (Boston, MA), 121-22
Brooklyn Children's Museum (Brooklyn, NY), 52

cap. *See* UAW cap
cataloging, 13, 58-59, 63, 173. *See also* acquisitions; collections
Chicago History Museum (Chicago, IL), 51
Chinese/Chinese Americans, 122, 153
Codman House, Historic New England (Lincoln, MA), 150-51
collecting, 3, 3-4, 9, 13, 41-64, *52*, *53*, 65, 155; collecting initiatives, xiv, 50, 55; community-based, 50-53, 64, 214n30; contemporary, 41, 46, *53*, 53-55; as a Curator Core Competency, 42; inclusive, 45-46, 50-55, *52*, 63-64; rapid response, 46, *53*, 53-55
collections, xiv, *3*, 3-4, 9, *10*, 13, 16, 29-32, *52*, *53*, 157, 158, 161-63, 169-71, 174, 177, *178*; *Active Collections* (book), 28-29, 44-45; collections database, 27, 58-59; collections fundamentals, 55-63, 215-16n46; Collections

271

(Management) Policy, 46–47, 63; collections plan/planning, 41–43, 45–50, 56, 63–64; collections tiering/ranking, 45, 60–61, 62, 63; developing collections as a Curator Core Competency, 41–42; digitized, 26–28, 33, 160–61; in historic house museums. *See* historic house museums; inclusive collections. *See* collections, *Active Collections*; shaping and developing, 41–64; storage, 41, 44, 45, 160. *See also* acquisitions; collecting; donors and donations; furnishings; material culture; objects; writing, digital content
Collections/Acquisitions Committee, 57, 60, 63
community/community engagement, xiii, 4, *10*, 12, 13, 28, 32, 156, 184; for blogs, 161; community-based collecting, 45, 46, 50–53, 64, 214n30; community co-curators, 9; for exhibitions, *10*, 13, 96–99, 115–23; for historical research, 67, 90, 91; for historic house museums, 129–32, 136–37, 139, 150, 151, 154; for talks and tours, 165, 166
Community of Practice, 17, 18, 40
content creation. *See* interpretation, interpretive manuals; label-writing; talks; tours; writing
Cook's Cabin. *See* Exchange Place
Crane House and Historic YWCA (Montclair, NJ), 151, *152*
cultural intelligence, 189, 198
curator "chats." *See* talks
Curator Core Competencies (CurCom), 1–7, 16, 18, 19, 42, 66, 95, 98, 156, 203n10, 203n12
curators: as a career choice, 15–20, 181; definitions, 2; job description, 19; types, 6–9, *8*

deaccessioning, 41, 45, 59–60, 63. *See also* collecting; collections; repatriation
DEAI (diversity, equity, accessibility, inclusion) perspectives, xiii, xiv, 9, 11–13, 16, 17, 19; in blogs, 162; collecting, 45–46, 50, *52*, *53*, 63–64; in exhibitions, 100, 115–23, 125; in historic house museums, xv, 130, 132, 149, 154; inclusive leadership, 197–99; objects, 28–29, 33; pushback strategies, 91, 132, 133; research, 83–89. *See also* accessibility; diversity; equity; inclusion
digital content. *See* writing, digital content
digitized collections. *See* collections, digitized
Disney Plus (TV streaming service), 178
disposals, 60, 63
diversity, 12. *See also* DEAI (diversity, equity, accessibility, inclusion) perspectives
domestic servants, 131, 151
donors and donations, 3, 4, 6, 21, 31, 41, 44, 55, 56, 61, 63, 165. *See also* acquisitions; collecting; collections
"dumbing down," 98, 114, 136, 158, 160

Eastern State Penitentiary (Philadelphia, PA), 119
emotional intelligence, 185
empathy, xiii, xv, 6, 11, 14, 165; related to collections, 50; related to exhibitions, 115, 116, 119; related to historical research, 93; related to historic house museums, 131, 146; related to leadership, 185, 189, 195, 198
Enslaved African Americans. *See* African Americans, enslaved
environments, immersive/historical, 108, *109*, 119–20, *120*, *142*. *See*

also furnishings; historic house museums

equity, 12. *See also* DEAI (diversity, equity, accessibility, inclusion) perspectives

Erma Hayman House (Boise, ID), 150, *150*

ethical considerations. *See* museum ethics

evaluation (audience), xii, xiii, 12, 91. *See also* exhibitions; historic house museums; interpretation, interpretive framework

Exchange Place Living History Farm (Kingsport, TN), 151-52

Exhibition (journal), 124

exhibitions, xiii, xv, 2, 5, 7, 9, 13, 33, 52, 62, 94-125, *107, 109, 120, 121*; advisory groups, 97, 100, 119, 122; Big Idea, 105-6, 111, 116, 117; bubble diagram, 107, *107*; community/community engagement for. *See* Community/community engagement; design, 106-8; evaluation (audience), 100, 105, 110, 115, 117, 120, 121, 124, 125, 139-40; floor plan, 107-8; historical research for, 65, 68, 100, 111; in historic house museums, 146; images in, 104, 108-10, 117; initial planning, 102-6; interactives, 99, 108, 117, 119; interpretive materials related to, 110; labels. *See* label-writing; writing; media for, 108, 110, 117, 119; objects in, 42, 45, 50, 100, 104, 108, *109*, 110, 111, 117, 119, *120*, 121, *121*, 123; online, 27; and public history. *See* public history; real-life examples, 118-23; refinements to the exhibition process in today's world, 117-18; storytelling (narrative structure), 99-101, 104, 114-15, 119; teamwork and collaboration, 100-102, 117; theatrical performances in, 119; untold stories, 104; visitor-related goals/outcomes, 106, 139-40. *See* museum audiences and exhibitions. *See also* environments, immersive/historical; writing, digital content

First Americans Museums (Oklahoma City, OK), 123

Five Oaks Museum (Portland, Oregon), 51

Fleming, E. McClung, 29-31

Fredericksburg Area Museum (Fredericksburg, VA), 121, *121*

furnishings, ix, xii, 8, 32, 118. *See also* historic house museums; interpretation; objects

Greenfield Village. *See* The Henry Ford

Heart Mountain Interpretive Center (Powell, WY), 118

Henry Ford Museum of American Innovation. *See* The Henry Ford

historical research, ix, xiii, xv, 4-6, 14, 65-93, 77, 81, 86; analyzing sources, 70-71; for audio tours, 170; for blogs, 161-63; for digital content, 158-64; historical research sources, 72-83; historic landscapes as evidence, 67, 83, 84; for interpretation, 65, 66, 68-69; for interviews (with the media), 178, 179; methodology, 69-72, 89-91; museum audiences and history/historical research, 67-69; for objects, 23, 25-27; objects as historical evidence, 65, 67, 82-84; online research, 27, 72-74, 90; oral histories, 67, 81, 81-82, 84, 100, 150, 151; physical structures as historical evidence, 67, 83, 84; primary sources, 75-80, 77, 84, 86, 126; for proposed acquisitions, 55-57; and

Index 273

public history. *See* public history; secondary sources, 74-75, 84, 86; visual documents and media as evidence, 67, 80-81, 84; why historical thinking matters, 92-93. *See also* DEAI perspectives; exhibitions; historic house museums; marginalized groups

historic house museums, xv, 7-8, 8, *81*, 126-54, *133*, *142*, *150*, *152*, 163; accessibility at, 144-45, 147-48; curators at, 7-8; difficult/uncomfortable history, 131-33, 135-36; digital content for, 148; exhibitions in, 146; furnishings, 140-44, 150-52; historical research for, 126, 133, 136, 137, 140, 144, 151-54; Historic House Museums Affinity Community. *See* Historic House Museums Affinity Community (AASLH); installation, 144-45; interactives in 144, 146; labels, 146-47; layout, 144-45; marginalized groups in. *See* marginalized groups; objects for/in, 126, 133-37, 140-44, *142*, 146, 151, 154; ongoing refinements, 149; programs, 145, 147-48; publications, 148; real-life examples, 149-53; signs. *See* historic house museums, labels; social media for, 148; sustainability of, 129-31; theatrical performances with, 147; tours, 145-46; untold stories, 131-33, 136, 150-53; visitor outcomes, 139-40. *See also* African Americans, enslaved; African Americans, history of; DEAI perspectives; furnishings; immigrants, history of; interpretation; Japanese/Japanese Americans; label-writing; Latine/Latinx; LGBTQ+; reproductions; women; writing

Historic House Museums Affinity Community (AASLH), 129
historic houses. *See* historic house museums
Historic New England (Massachusetts), 150-51
historic sites. *See* historic house museums
historic structures. *See* historic house museums
History Colorado (Denver, CO), 51-52, *52*, 122
History Relevance Initiative (AASLH), 9-11, 16, 18-19

immigrants, history of, 131, 150, 153
inclusion, 12, 14. *See also* DEAI (diversity, equity, accessibility, inclusion) perspectives
inclusive history, see DEAI (diversity, equity, accessibility, inclusion) perspectives; marginalized groups
Indigenous people/groups: objects, *10*, 22, 26; collections, 41, 51, 61-62; exhibitions, *10*, 101, 118-23; historic house museums, 131, 150; repatriation, 61-62, 217n62; researching, 76
internet research. *See* historical research, online research
interpretation, xiii, xv, 13, *81*, 126-54, *133*, *142*, *150*, *152*; Big Idea, 138; definition, 127-28; interpretive approach, 140; interpretive framework, 136-40, 148-49; interpretive labels. *See* historic house museums; label-writing; writing; interpretive manuals, 8, 126-27, 148-49, 154; interpretive planning. *See* interpretation, interpretive framework; interpretive signs. *See* historic house museums; label-writing; writing; interpretive staff, 8, 145-46, 148-49, 154;

interpretive techniques, 145-49, 152; interpretive themes, 137-39, 145, 149; interpretive training, xii, 8, 132, 148-49; living history, 128, 145, 151-52; in parks, 128; thematic interpretation, 137-39. *See also* historic house museums; object interpretation
interviews (with the media), xv, 174-79, *178*

Jamestown Settlement (Jamestown, VA), 120-21
Japanese/Japanese Americans, 118
Jewish/Jewish Americans, 45, 119-20
label-writing, x, xiii, 5, 12; for exhibitions, 28, 37, 40, 100, 107, 109-15, 118, 120, 123-25; for historic house museums, 146-47; labels that tell stories (narrative structure), 114-15; tips for writing effective labels, 113-14; visitors' label-reading behaviors, 109-15. *See also* evaluation; writing
labor unions, *front cover*, 37
Latine/Latinx, 50-51, 123
leadership (mid-level), xv, 5, 16, 181-99, *182*; defined, 182-88; inclusive, 197-99; leading across, 5, 191-93, 198-99; leading down, 193-97, 199; leading up, 189-91; leading yourself, 188-89, 191, 195, 198. *See also* mentoring
lectures. *See* talks
Levi and Catharine Coffin State Historic Site (Fountain City, IN), 152-53
Levine Museum of the New South (Charlotte, NC), 123
LGBTQ+: collecting, 51-52, *52*, 54-55; exhibitions, 52, 121-22; historic house museums, 131; researching, 88-89
living history. *See* interpretation; outdoor museums

Main Message. *See* exhibitions, Big Idea; interpretation, Big Idea
Making History Matter statement. *See* Reframing History Initiative
management. *See* leadership
marginalized groups, 9, 13; related to collecting, 45-46, 50-53; related to exhibitions, 115-23; related to historic house museums, 131-33, 137, 149-53, 234n35; related to objects, 25-27; researching, 79, 83-89, 131-33, 137. *See also* African Americans, enslaved; African Americans, history of; Chinese/Chinese Americans; domestic servants; immigrants, history of; Indigenous people/groups; Japanese/Japanese Americans; Latine/Latinx; LGBTQ+; people/communities of color; women
material culture, ix, xiii, xiv, 13, 21-40, 53; definitions, 23; foundations of material culture studies, 24-29; methodologies, 29-32; value of studying, 23. *See also* collections; objects
mentoring, 6, 193-95, 199
Mercer Museum (Doylestown, PA), ix-x
Mining the Museum (exhibition), 228n44
minoritized communities. *See* marginalized groups
mission, 3, 11, 18; related to collecting, 41-49, 54, 60, 63, 212n6; related to digital content, 161-63, 165; related to exhibitions, 96; related to historical research, 66; related to historic house museums, 127, 130, 132, 136, 150, 153; related to leadership, 184, 190, 193
MSU Museum (Lansing, MI), 119

museum audiences, xii, 5, 9, 13-14; and collecting, 45, 50; and collections planning, 48; and digital content, 159-64; and exhibitions, 96-99, 105, 106, 115-25, 227n32; and historical research, 67-69; and historic house museums, 126-31, 133-36, 138-40, 143, 144, 146, 154; and objects, 37-39; offerings for audiences with special needs, 147-48, *172*; programs for, 147-48; talks and tours for, 156-57, 164-74, *172*; writing for the public, 157-64. *See also* label-writing
museum ethics, 42-46, 57-62, 212nn4-5
Museum of the City of New York (New York City), 55
museum visitors. *See* museum audiences

narrative nonfiction, 124-25
National Museum of African American History and Culture (Washington, D.C.), 55
National Museum of American History (Washington, D.C.), 50
National Museum of the American Indian (New York City), 118-19, 123
Native American Graves Protection and Repatriation Act (NAGPRA). *See* repatriation
"new social history," 25
New York Historical Society (New York City), 55

objects, vii, ix, x, *xi*, xiv, xv, 2, 3, *3*, 5-8, *8*, *10*, 12, 13, 21-40, *34*, *36*, *37*, 161; as historical evidence, 65, 67, 82-83; case studies, 32-37; definitions, 22-23; object interpretation, 5-6; 29-37; 156; for talks and tours, 156, 166-69, 170-74; value of studying, 23.

See also collections; exhibitions; historic house museums; material culture; museum audiences
online collections. *See* collections, digitized
online content. *See* writing, digital content
online exhibitions. *See* exhibitions, online
online research. *See* historical research
online tours. *See* tours, virtual
online writing. *See* writing, digital content
oral histories. *See* historical research
Orange County Regional History Center (Orlando, FL), 54-55
organizational culture, 186-88
outdoor museums, xiv, 7-8, *8*, 26, 128. *See also* historic house museums; interpretation, living history

people/communities of color, 51, 131
Phillips House, Historic New England (Salem, MA), 150-51
podcasts, 174, 176, 179
presentations. *See* talks
Primary Message. *See* exhibitions, Big Idea; interpretation, Big Idea
primary source research. *See* historical research
programs. *See* accessibility; historic house museums
props. *See* reproductions
public history: in doing historical research, 66-69, 91; related to exhibitions, 95-99; related to sharing knowledge with the public, 157
pushback strategies. *See* DEAI perspectives

Reframing History Initiative (AASLH), 67-68; "Making History

Matter," 157; "Value of History" Statement, 92-93
Relevant History Experience. *See* History Relevance Initiative
repatriation, 61-63, 217n62. *See also* deaccessions
reproductions, xii, 8, *8*, 126, 140, *142*, 142-44, 153
research. *See* historical research
research sources. *See* historical research

slavery. *See* African Americans, enslaved
social justice. *See* DEAI perspectives
social media, 110, 148, 161-64. *See also* writing, digital content
soft skills, 16, 19, 184, 189
Solomon R. Guggenheim Museum (New York City), 173
storage. *See* collections
storytelling (narrative structure). *See* label-writing; writing, digital content

talks, xiii, xv, 6, 156; onsite 164-69, *172*; virtual, xv, 169-70, 173-74
teamwork and collaboration, xiii, 191, 198. *See also* exhibitions
Tenement Museum (New York City), 153, 173
The Children's Museum of Indianapolis (Indianapolis, IN), 119-20, *120*
The Henry Ford (Dearborn, MI), x-xiv, xi, 8, 21, 34-37, *34, 36, 37, 53*, 61, 62, 65-66, 77, 81, 86, 94-95, 109, 126-27, *142, 172, 178*; accessibility at, 171-74, *172*; collections, 3, 8, *53*, 58, 61, 77, *86*; in Greenfield Village, xii, *8*, 35-36, *36*, 65-66, *81*, 126-27, 138-39, *142*, 143; in Henry Ford Museum of American Innovation, 62, 107, 109, *172, 178*; *The Henry Ford's Innovation Nation* (TV show),

177, *178*; object case studies, *front cover*, 34-*37, 34, 36, 37*
The Jewish Museum (New York City), 45
The Museum of the Chinese in America (New York City), 122
Tilden, Freeman, 127-28
tours, xiii, xv, 6, 13, 156; audio tours, 170-71; at historic house museums, 145-46; onsite, 164-69; virtual, xv, 169-70

UAW Cap - *Front cover*, 36-37, *37*
untold stories, xiv. *See also* historic house museums; marginalized groups

Value of History statement. *See* Reframing History Initiative
Victoria and Albert Museum (London, England), 54
virtual talks. *See* talks, virtual
virtual tours. *See* tours, virtual
visitors. *See* museum audiences
visitor studies. *See* evaluation (audience)

Winterthur Conference, 25, 26
Winterthur Portfolio (journal), 25-26
Winterthur Program in Early American/American Culture, ix, x
women, 25, 26, *150, 152*; in exhibitions, 120-22; in historic house museums, 131, *150, 150-53, 152*; researching, 65, 87-88
writing, vii, xiii, xv, 5, 12, 156-64; for audio tours, 170-71; blogs, 161-63; as a Curator Core Competency, 5, 156-57; digital content, xv, 12, 37-39, 68, 110, 148, 157-64; interpretive manuals, xii, 126-27; printed materials, 158. *See also* interpretation, interpretive manuals; label-writing

Index 277

About the Author

Donna R. Braden retired from The Henry Ford, Dearborn, Michigan, after forty-five years as a curator of domestic life, then of community and public life, and finally as senior curator overseeing the work of the entire curatorial staff. She is adept at all aspects of curatorial practice, including: engaging in scholarly and material culture research; creating formalized, thematic collecting plans and shaping collections; acquiring and proposing new additions to the collections; deaccessioning collections; interpreting objects and social and cultural history through exhibitions; researching and implementing new interpretation at historic house museums; creating digital content and other forms of writing; delivering presentations to different audiences; and leading in all directions from the middle of an organization.

Braden is the author of the book *Spaces That Tell Stories: Recreating Historical Environments* (Rowman & Littlefield, 2019) as well as completing several books for The Henry Ford and numerous journal articles. She has a B.A. in Anthropology with distinction in American Cultural History from the Ohio State University (1975) and two M.A. degrees: from the Winterthur Program in Early American Culture with Certification in Museum Studies at the University of Delaware (1977) and in Liberal Studies at the University of Michigan-Dearborn (2013).

Currently she is an independent museum professional—contributing to the history museum field through curatorial practice, exhibition development, interpretive planning, writing, and mentorship of current and future museum practitioners.

www.ingramcontent.com/pod-product-compliance
Lightning Source LLC
Chambersburg PA
CBHW021937290426
44108CB00012B/873